François-René de Chateaubriand, Orlando Williams Wight

The Martyrs

François-René de Chateaubriand, Orlando Williams Wight

The Martyrs

ISBN/EAN: 9783742867148

Manufactured in Europe, USA, Canada, Australia, Japa

Cover: Foto ©ninafisch / pixelio.de

Manufactured and distributed by brebook publishing software (www.brebook.com)

François-René de Chateaubriand, Orlando Williams Wight

The Martyrs

THE
MARTYRS

BY

M. DE CHATEAUBRIAND.

A Revised Translation.

EDITED BY

O. W. WIGHT, A.M.

———•••———

NEW YORK:
D. & J. SADLIER & CO., 31 BARCLAY STREET.
BOSTON:—128 FEDERAL STREET
MONTREAL, C. E.:—COR. OF NOTRE DAME & ST. FRANCIS XAVIER STS.
1863.

EDITOR'S PREFACE.

M. DE CHATEAUBRIAND left Paris, July 13, 1806, to visit the East. The imperial murder of the Duc d'Enghien, the loss of a favorite sister, and many other things, had saddened him, and he was going, as he tells us in his *post-mortem* Memoirs, "to mingle his tears with those of the Magdalen." Whether he found any such tears with which to mingle his own, we know not; but we do know that he had already conceived the idea of THE MARTYRS, and his probable object in journeying to Greece and the Holy Land was to make himself familiar with scenes that he intended to describe. He left Madame de Chateaubriand at Venice, embarked at Trieste, traversed Greece, made the tour of Asia Minor and Judæa, coasted along the northern shore of Africa, encamped upon the ruins of Carthage, crossed over to Spain, visited the remains of the Alhambra, and there . . . (prefaces must be discreet) . . took an *ex-post-facto* benefit of his imaginary Magdalen tears.

THE MARTYRS, many pages of which had been written under the sky of Greece, or in the midst of the sands of the desert, appeared in 1809. Such a prodigy was not born without tribulations. M. de Chateaubriand, on his return from the East, had found himself in straitened circumstances: he had long been embroiled with the government of the First Consul: sickness of body and discouragement of soul had returned; he had even thought of exiling himself to the United States. His good friend, M. de Fontaine, who stood between him and the terrible Napoleon, denounced such a project as madness. "What!" said he, "would you join Moreau? Do you see no place in the world for yourself but in that English colony, more mercantile, ruder, and more careless of the arts than the mother country herself? Think of your book; you can finish it and publish it only here. Your book, and the renown it will bring, is your country, your future, your refuge. . . Admirable are the descriptions of Rome, the Catacombs, Naples, the battle of the Franks, and the great debate in the Roman senate on the preservation of the altar of Victory. There are, indeed, some anachronisms; but it matters not; the work is full of genius. I am only solicitous about the revision of certain passages on Diocletian, and perhaps Galerius. No petty allusions, when one writes for immortality. This would be the affair of the 'Mercury'[1] again. It is not necessary to set the lion's teeth on edge."

---

[1] Chateaubriand had bought into the "Mercury" after his return from the East. In this journal appeared the famous allusion, by which M. Guizot was so greatly moved: "when in the silence of abject submission," Chateaubriand wrote, "we hear only the chains of the slave and the voice of the informer; when all tremble before the tyrant, and it is as dangerous to incur favor as to merit disgrace, the historian appears to be charged with

The Martyrs, then, after some finishing touches by the hand of the censor, appeared in 1809. In this country one devoutly prays that his adversary may write a presidential letter; in France one prays that his adversary may write a book. All the dogs of imperialism and irreligion yelped in multitudinous, currish chorus at The Martyrs. Let us leave them, one and all, in oblivion. A Chateaubriand, not *the* Chateaubriand, was sacrificed to appease the imperial wrath. Even the fond, saddened, much bewildered parent of The Martyrs, was thoroughly discouraged, and began to believe that, after all, the offspring of his own brain might be a creature of folly.

Criticism, however, is not wholly at fault. There are many things in The Martyrs that are not pleasing to a severe taste. Nevertheless, the book has been, and will be, extensively read. It has triumphed over all obstacles; it has taken its place in the classical literature of France, and comes to us with the verdict of half a century of time in its favor.

We have used the English translation, but have revised it throughout. Nearly one-third of the original was omitted by the translator, and additions were not wanting. We have translated every line omitted, and retrenched every phrase in the translation not warranted by the original. Faithfulness to

---

the vengeance of nations. It is in vain that Nero triumphs. Tacitus has been born in the empire, he grows up near the ashes of Germanicus, and already uncompromising Providence has handed over to an obscure child the glory of the master of the world." Many other things of like spirit appeared in the "Mercury." It is hardly necessary to say that the journal was suppressed, and that Chateaubriand lost his investment in it.

the author we are translating, is a duty that we invariably endeavor to fulfil. Chateaubriand's work is now, for the first time, given to the English reader in its integrity.

This work is of such a nature that we have been obliged to depart from our usual practice of *literal* translation; the highly colored, elevated, harmonious language of the original, the poetic indefiniteness of the style, the metaphors that, thus to speak, float, cloud-like, in the atmosphere of the book, have made it necessary to paraphrase, but we have endeavored to adhere strictly to the thoughts and sentiments of our author.

Other volumes from Chateaubriand will be added, and in its proper place we shall give a lengthy prolegomena, embracing a life of the author, critical and bibliographical notices, etc.

O. W. WIGHT.

SEPTEMBER, 1859.

CONTENTS.

PREFACE TO EDITION OF 1826, ... **xvii**
PREFACE TO FIRST AND SECOND EDITIONS, ... **xix**

THE MARTYRS.

BOOK FIRST.

Invocation. Exposition. Diocletian holds the Reins of the Roman Empire. Under the government of this Prince, the Temples of the true God begin to dispute Homage with the Temples of Idols. Hell prepares to join Battle in a Final Combat to overthrow the Altars of the Son of Man. The Eternal permits the Demons to persecute the Church, in order to try the Faithful; but the Faithful will come out triumphant from the Trial; the Standard of Salvation will be planted on the Throne of the Universe; the World will owe this Victory to two Victims chosen by God. Who are these Victims? Apostrophe to the Muse that is about to make them known. The Family of Homer. Demodocus, the last Descendant of the Homeridæ, Priest of Homer in the Temple of this Poet, on Mount Ithome, in Messenia. Description of Messenia. Demodocus consecrates to the Worship of the Muses his only Daughter, Cymodoce, in order to conceal her from the Pursuit of Hierocles, Pro-consul of Achaia and Favorite of Galerius. Cymodoce goes alone with her Nurse to the Festival of the Lymnæan Diana; she loses her Way, and finds a Young Man asleep by the side of a Fountain. Eudorus conducts Cymodoce back to the house of Demodocus. Demodocus sets out with his Daughter to offer Presents to Eudorus, and to thank the Family of Lasthenes, ... 31

BOOK SECOND.

Arrival of Demodocus and Cymodoce in Arcadia. They meet an old man at the Tomb of Aglaus of Psophis, who conducts them to the Field where the Family of Lasthenes are gathering in their Harvest. Cymodoce recognizes Eudorus. Demodocus discovers that Lasthenes' Family are Christians. Return to the House of Lasthenes. Customs of the Christians. Evening Prayer. Arrival of Cyril, Bishop of Lacedæmon, the Confessor and Martyr, who comes to urge Eudorus to relate his Adventures. The evening Repast. The Family and Strangers take their seats after Supper in the Orchard on the Banks of the Alpheus. Demodocus asks Cymodoce to play the Lyre. Song of Cymodoce. Eudorus sings in his Turn. The two Families retire to Rest. Dream of Cyril. Prayer of the holy Bishop, ... 49

BOOK THIRD.

The Prayer of Cyril ascends to the Throne of the Almighty. Heaven. The Saints and Angels. Tabernacle of the Mother of the Saviour. Sanctuary of the Father and the Son. The Holy Spirit. The Trinity. The Prayer of Cyril is presented to the Most High, who receives it, but declares that the Bishop of Lacedæmon is not the Victim that must ransom the Christians. Eudorus is chosen as the Victim. Reasons for his Choice. The Celestial Forces take up Arms. Canticle of the Saints and Angels, 67

BOOK FOURTH.

Cyril. The Christian Family. Demodocus and Cymodoce meet again on an Island at the confluence of the Ladon and Alpheus, to hear the Son of Lasthenes recount his Adventures. Commencement of the Recital of Eudorus. Origin of the family of Lasthenes. It opposes the Romans at the time of the Invasion of Greece. The eldest of Lasthenes' Family is obliged to repair as a Hostage to Rome. The Family of Lasthenes embraces Christianity. Childhood of Eudorus. He sets out at the age of sixteen for Rome as a Substitute for his Father. The Tempest. Description of the Archipelago. Arrival of Eudorus in Italy. Description of Rome. Eudorus contracts an intimate Friendship with Jerome, Augustine, and Prince Constantine, the son of Constantius. Characters of Jerome, Augustine, and Constantine. Eudorus is presented at Court. Diocletian. Galerius. Court of Diocletian. The Sophist, Hierocles, Proconsul of Achaia and favorite of Galerius. Enmity of Eudorus and Hierocles. Eudorus falls into the irregularities of Youth, and forgets his Religion. Marcellinus, Bishop of Rome. He threatens Eudorus with Excommunication if he does not return to the bosom of the Church. Excommunication hurled against Eudorus. Amphitheatre of Titus. Forebodings, ... 79

BOOK FIFTH.

Continuation of the Recital. The Court goes to pass the Summer at Baiæ Naples. House of Aglaia. Walks of Eudorus, Augustine, and Jerome. Their Conversation at the Tomb of Scipio. Thraseas, the Hermit of Vesuvius. His History. Separation of the three Friends. Eudorus returns to Rome with the Court. The Catacombs. Adventure of the Empress Prisca and her daughter Valeria. Eudorus, banished from the Court, is sent an Exile to the Armies of Constantius. He quits Rome, and journeys through Italy and Gaul. He arrives at Agrippina, on the Banks of the Rhine. He finds the Roman Army ready to carry War into the Country of the Franks. He serves as a Private Soldier among the Cretan Archers, who compose, with the Gauls, the Vanguard of the Army of Constantius, ... 102

BOOK SIXTH.

Continuation of the Story. March of the Roman Army through Batavia. Encounter with the Army of the Franks. The Field of Battle. Order and Enumeration of the Roman Army. Order and Enumeration of the Army of the Franks. Pharamond, Clodion and Merovius. Songs of the Warriors. War Songs of the Franks. Beginning of the Action. Attack of the Gauls upon the Franks. Cavalry Combat. Remarkable Encounter between Vercingetorix, Chief of the Gauls, and Merovius, Son of the King of the Franks. Vercingetorix is vanquished. The Romans give Way. The Christian Legion descends the Hill and renews the Combat. Mêlée. The Franks retreat to their Camp. Eudorus obtains the civic Crown, and is appointed Chief of the Greeks by Constantius. The Combat recommences at Break of Day. Attack on the Camp of the Franks by the Romans. Rising of the Waves. The Romans flee before the Sea. Eudorus, after a long Struggle, falls, pierced with several Wounds. He is succored by a Slave of the Franks, who bears him to a Cavern, . 125

BOOK SEVENTH.

Continuation of the Recital. Eudorus becomes the Slave of Pharamond. History of Zacharius. Clothilde, the wife of Pharamond. Dawn of Christianity in the Country of the Franks. Customs of the Franks. Return of Spring. The Chase. Northern Barbarians. Tomb of Ovid. Eudorus saves the life of Merovius. Merovius promises Liberty to Eudorus. Return of the Hunters to the Camp of Pharamond. The Goddess Hertha. Festival of the Franks. Deliberations with the Romans on the Question of Peace or War. Dispute of Camulogenus and Chloderic. The Franks decide to treat for Peace. Eudorus is freed, and goes to make Proposals of Peace to Constantius. Zacharius conducts Eudorus to the Frontiers of Gaul. Their Adieus, ... 145

BOOK EIGHTH.

Interruption of the Recital. Beginning of the Love of Eudorus and Cymodoce. Satan seeks to profit by this Love to trouble the Church. Hell. Assembly of the Demons. Speech of the Demon of Homicide. Speech of the Demon of False Wisdom. Speech of the Demon of Voluptuousness. Speech of Satan. The Demons spread themselves over the Earth, ... 165

BOOK NINTH.

Resumption of the Recital of Eudorus. Eudorus at the Court of Constantius. He passes into the Island of Britain. He obtains Triumphal Honors. His Return to Gaul. He is appointed Commandant of Armorica. The Gauls. Armorica. Episode of Velleda, . . . 179

BOOK TENTH.

Continuation of the Recital. Conclusion of the Episode of Velleda, 195

BOOK ELEVENTH.

Continuation of the Recital. Repentance of Eudorus. His public Penitence. He quits the Army. He repairs to Egypt to ask permission of Diocletian to return to his Country. The Voyage. Alexandria. The Nile. Egypt. Eudorus obtains his return from Diocletian. The Thebais. Return of Eudorus to his Father's House. Conclusion of the Recital, 211

BOOK TWELFTH.

Invocation to the Holy Spirit. Conspiracy of the Demons against the Church. Diocletian orders the Christians to be numbered. Hierocles sets out for Achaia. The Love of Eudorus and Cymodoce, . . 233

BOOK THIRTEENTH.

Cymodoce Declares to her Father her Intention of embracing the Christian Religion, in order to become the Wife of Eudorus. Irresolution of Demodocus. They learn of the Arrival of Hierocles in Achaia. Astarte attacks Eudorus, and is conquered by the Angel of Holy Love. Demodocus consents to give his Daughter to Eudorus, to escape the Pursuit of Hierocles. Jealousy of Hierocles. Enumeration of the Christians in Arcadia. Hierocles proffers an Accusation against Eudorus to Diocletian. Cymodoce and Demodocus set out for Lacedæmon, . 247

BOOK FOURTEENTH.

Description of Laconia. Arrival of Demodocus at the Residence of Cyril. Instruction of Cymodoce. Astarte sends the Demon of Jealousy to Hierocles. Cymodoce repairs to the Church to be betrothed to Eudorus. Ceremonies of the Primitive Church. A band of Soldiers, by the order of Hierocles, disperses the Believers. Eudorus Rescues Cymodoce, and defends her at the Tomb of Leonidas. He receives Orders to repair to Rome. The two Families resolve to send Cymodoce to Jerusalem, in order to place her under the Protection of the Mother of Constantine. Eudorus and Cymodoce set out in order to embark at Athens, ... 261

BOOK FIFTEENTH.

Athens. Adieus of Cymodoce, Eudorus and Demodocus. Cymodoce embarks with Dorotheus for Joppa. Eudorus embarks at the same time for Ostia. The Mother of the Saviour sends Gabriel to the Angel of the Seas. Eudorus arrives at Rome. He finds the Senate ready to assemble, in order to pronounce upon the Fate of the Christians. He is chosen to plead their Cause. Hierocles arrives at Rome; he is charged by the Sophists with defending their Sect, and accusing the Christians. Symmachus, High Priest of Jupiter, is to address the Senate in behalf of the ancient Gods of the Country, ... 280

BOOK SIXTEENTH.

Harangues of Symmachus, Hierocles, and Eudorus. Diocletian consents to issue the Edict of Persecution, but wishes first to consult the Sibyl of Cumæ, ... 299

BOOK SEVENTEENTH.

Voyage of Cymodoce. She arrives at Joppa. She ascends to Jerusalem. Helena receives her as her Daughter. Holy Week. Response of the Sibyl of Cumæ. Hierocles dispatches a Centurion to reclaim Cymodoce. Diocletian issues the Edict of Persecution, ... 318

BOOK EIGHTEENTH.

Joy of Hell. Galerius, counselled by Hierocles, forces Diocletian to abdicate. Preparation of the Christians for Martyrdom. Constantine, aided by Eudorus, escapes from Rome and flees to Constantius. Eudorus is cast into the Dungeons. Hierocles, Prime Minister of Galerius. General Persecution. The Demon of Tyranny bears to Jerusalem the News of the Persecution. The Centurion sent by Hierocles sets Fire to the Holy Places. Dorotheus saves Cymodoce. Meeting with Jerome in the Grotto of Bethlehem, ... 333

BOOK NINETEENTH.

Return of Demodocus to the Temple of Homer. His Grief. He learns the News of the Persecution. He sets out for Rome, where he supposes Cymodoce to have been taken by the order of Hierocles. Cymodoce is baptized in the Jordan by Jerome. She reaches Ptolemais, and embarks for Greece. A Tempest, raised by the command of God, forces Cymodoce to land in Italy, ... 355

BOOK TWENTIETH.

Cymodoce, arrested by the Satellites of Hierocles, is conducted to Rome. Public Outbreak. Cymodoce, freed from the Hands of Hierocles, is thrown into Prison as a Christian. Disgrace of Hierocles. He receives an Order to depart for Alexandria. Letter of Eudorus to Cymodoce, 373

BOOK TWENTY-FIRST.

Eudorus is released from his Penitence. Complaints of Demodocus. Prison of Cymodoce. Cymodoce receives the Letter of Eudorus. Acts of the Martyrdom of Eudorus. Purgatory, ... 390

BOOK TWENTY-SECOND.

The Destroying Angel smites Galerius and Hierocles. Hierocles goes to find the Judge of the Christians. Return of the Messenger sent to Diocletian. Sadness of Eudorus, Demodocus and Cymodoce. The Repast of Freedom. Temptation, ... 403

BOOK TWENTY-THIRD.

Satan reanimates the Fanaticism of the People. Feast of Bacchus. Explanation of the Letter of Festus. Death of Hierocles. The Angel of Hope descends to Cymodoce. Cymodoce receives the Robe of Martyrdom. Dorotheus takes Cymodoce away from the Prison. Joy of Eudorus and the Confessors. Cymodoce finds her Father. The Angel of Sleep, 414

BOOK TWENTY-FOURTH.

Adieus to the Muse. Illness of Galerius. The Amphitheatre of Vespasian. Eudorus is led to Martyrdom. Michael plunges Satan into the Abyss. Cymodoce escapes from her Father, and goes to the Amphitheatre to find Eudorus. Galerius learns that Constantine has been proclaimed Cæsar. Martyrdom of the two spouses. Triumph of the Christian Religion, 433

PREFACE

TO THE EDITION OF 1826.

Here is a work which I thought, for some time, had failed; not that in my conscience I found it worse than my former works, but the violence of criticism had shaken my faith as an author, and I finally became convinced that I was mistaken. My friends did not console me, because in reality I was not much afflicted, and because I make but little account of my books; but they maintained that the condemnation was not sufficiently justified, and that the public, sooner or later, would render a different verdict. M. de Fontanes, especially, did not hesitate: I was not Racine, but he might be Boileau; and he never ceased telling me: "They will return to it." His conviction in this respect was so profound that it inspired in him the charming stanzas:

"Le Tasse, errant-de ville," etc.,

without fear of compromising his taste and the authority of his judgment.

In fact, the Martyrs have come up alone; they have obtained the honor of four consecutive editions; they have even enjoyed, among people of letters, a particular favor: a kindly reception has been given to a work evincing some pains as to style, a great respect for the language, and a sincere love of antiquity.

As to criticising the foundations of the work, it has been promptly abandoned. The declaration that I had mixed the profane with the sacred, because I had painted two religions that existed together, and each of which had its beliefs, its altars, its priests, its ceremonies, was saying that I should have renounced history, or rather chosen another subject. For whom did the martyrs die? For Jesus Christ. To whom were they sacrificed? To the *gods* of the empire. There were, then, two religions.

The philosophical question, whether under Diocletian the Romans and the Greeks believed in the gods of Homer, and whether public worship had undergone alterations—this question, as a *poet*, would not concern me, but as a *historian* I would have had much to say on it.

There is no longer any question in regard to this matter. The MARTYRS have succeeded, contrary to my first expectation, and I have only had to busy myself with the care of revising the text.

Finally, this work caused my persecutions under Bonaparte to be redoubled: the allusions in the portrait of Galerius, and in the painting of the court of Diocletian, were so striking that they could not escape the imperial police, the more so that the English translator, who had no discretion to preserve, and who was perfectly indifferent whether he compromised me or not, had called attention to them in his preface. My unfortunate cousin Armand de Chateaubriand was shot upon the appearance of the MARTYRS: in vain did I solicit his pardon; the anger that I had excited extended even to my name. Is it not a singular thing, that I am to-day a *doubtful* Christian and a *suspected* royalist?

PREFACE

TO THE FIRST AND SECOND EDITIONS.

I ADVANCED, in a former work, that Christianity appeared to me more favorable than Paganism for the development of characters and the play of passions in the epic. I further said, that the *marvellous* of this religion might contend for the palm of interest with the *marvellous* borrowed from mythology. These opinions, more or less combated, it is my present object to support by an example.

To render the reader an impartial judge in this great literary process, it seemed to me that it was necessary to choose a subject that would include upon the same canvas the predominant features of the two religions; the ethics, the sacrifices, the ceremonies of both systems of worship; a subject wherein the language of Genesis might be blended with that of the "Odyssey;" wherein the *Jupiter* of Homer might be placed by the side of the *Jehovah* of Milton, without giving offence to piety, to taste, or to probability of manners.

Having once conceived the idea, I had no difficulty in finding a historical epoch, where the two religions met in conjunction.

The scene opens toward the close of the third century, at the moment when the persecution of the Christians commenced under Diocletian. Christianity had not yet become the predominating religion of the Roman empire; but its altars arose near the altars of idols.

The characters are taken from the two religions: I have in the first place made the reader acquainted with these characters; the narrative then shows the state of Christianity in the known world at the time of the action; the remainder of the work develops this action, which is connected by the catastrophe with the general massacre of the Christians.

Perhaps I have suffered myself to be dazzled by the subject: it seemed to me fertile. One sees, in fact, at the first glance, that it places at my disposal all antiquity, sacred and profane. Moreover, I have found means, by the narrative and by the course of events, to introduce a picture of the different provinces of the Roman empire; I have conducted the reader into the country of the Franks and Gauls, to the cradle of our ancestors. Greece, Italy, Judea, Egypt, Sparta, Athens, Rome, Naples, Jerusalem, Memphis, the valleys of Arcadia, the desert of the Thebais, are the other points of view, or perspectives of the picture.

The characters are almost all historical. It is known what a monster Galerius was. I have painted Diocletian somewhat better and more dignified than he appears in the authors of his time; in this I have proved my impartiality. I have thrown all the odium of the persecution upon Galerius and Hierocles.

Lactantius says in his own words:

Deinde . . . in Hieroclem, ex vicario præsidem, qui auctor et consiliarius ad faciendam persecutionem fuit.[1]

. . . . . . "Hierocles, who was the instigator and the author of the persecution."

Tillemont, after having spoken of the council in which the death of the Christians was the subject of deliberation, adds:

"Diocletian consented to refer the business to the council, in order to throw the odium of this resolution on those who had advised it. Some officers of justice and of war were summoned to this deliberation, who, whether by their own inclination, or by obsequiousness, supported the opinion of

---

[1] De Mortib. persec., cap. xvi.

Galerius. Hierocles was one of the most ardent in advising the persecution."[1]

According to the testimony of all history, this governor of Alexandria made the church suffer frightful evils. Hierocles was a sophist, and, in massacring the Christians, he published against them a work entitled "Philalethes," or, the "Friend of Truth." Eusebius[2] has refuted a part of it in a treatise which is still left us; it was also in answer to this that Lactantius composed his "Institutions."[3] Pearson[4] thought that Hierocles, the persecutor of the Christians, was the same as the author of the "Commentary" on the golden verses of Pythagoras. Tillemont[5] seems to be of the opinion of the learned bishop of Chester; and Jonsius,[6] who is anxious to discover in the Hierocles of the "Bibliotheca" of Photius, the Hierocles refuted by Eusebius,[7] serves rather to confirm than destroy the opinion of Pearson. Dacier, who, as Boileau observes, always wishes to make a sage of the writer whom he translates,[8] combats the opinion of the learned Pearson; but the reasons of Dacier are weak, and it is probable that Hierocles, the persecutor and author of the "Philalethes," is also the author of the "Commentary."

At first vicar of the prefects, Hierocles became, afterwards, governor of Bithynia. The Menæa,[9] St. Epiphanius,[10] and the acts of the martyrdom of St. Edesius,[11] prove that Hierocles

---

[1] Mem. Eccles., tom. v, p. 20, edit. 4to.; Paris.
[2] EUSEBII CÆSARIENSIS in Hieroclem liber, cum Philostrato editus; Paris, 1608.
[3] LACT., Instit., lib. v, cap. ii.
[4] In his Prolegomena on the works of Hierocles; printed in 1673, book ii, pp. 3-19.
[5] Mem. Eccles., tom. v, 2d edit. 4to.; Paris, 1702.
[6] De Scriptoribus historiæ philosophicæ, lib. iii, cap. xviii; Frankfort, 1659.
[7] To support his opinion, Jonsius is obliged to say that this Eusebius is not he of Cæsarea.
[8] Bolæana.
[9] Menæa Græcorum, p. 177; Vinet, 1525.
[10] EPIPHANII Panarium adversus hæreses, p. 717; Lutetia, 1622.
[11] De Martyr. Palæst., cap. iv; EUSEB.

was also governor of Egypt, where he perpetrated acts of great cruelty.

Fleury, who here follows Lactantius, in speaking of Hierocles, speaks of still another sophist who wrote at the same period against the Christians. Here is the portrait he draws of this unknown sophist:

"At the same time that they were pulling down the church of Nicomedia, there were two authors who published writings against the Christian religion. The one was a philosopher by profession, but his practice was contrary to his doctrine; in public, he commanded moderation, frugality, poverty; but he loved money, pleasure, and expense, and he lived more luxuriously than those dwelling in palaces: all his vices were concealed by a modest exterior and the simplicity of his attire. . . . . He published three books against the Christian religion. He began by stating, that it was the duty of a philosopher to correct the errors of mankind; . . . that he wished to show the light of wisdom to those who had not seen it, and to cure them of that obstinacy which made them suffer so many torments in vain. In order that the motive which excited him might not be doubted, he expatiated on the praises of the princes, extolled their piety and wisdom, who signalized themselves even in the defence of religion, in suppressing an impious and puerile superstition."[1]

The mean cowardice of this sophist, who attacked the Christians while they were under the sword of the executioner, made the Pagans themselves revolt, and he did not receive from the emperors the recompense that he expected.[2]

This character, drawn by Lactantius, proves that I have given to Hierocles only the manners of his times. Hierocles was at once a sophist, a writer, an orator, and a persecutor.

"The other author," says Fleury, "was of the number of the judges, and one of those who had advised the persecution. It is believed that this was Hierocles, who was born in a small

---

[1] Hist. Eccles. liv. viii, tom. ii, page 420, edit. in 8vo.; Paris, 1717.
[2] LACT. Inst., lib. v, cap. iv, page 470.

town in Caria, and who was afterward governor of Alexandria. He wrote two books, which he entitled 'Philalethes,' that is, the Friend of Truth; these he addressed to the Christians themselves, in order to appear not as attacking them, but as giving them salutary advice. He attempted to show contradictions in the holy Scriptures, and appeared so well instructed in them, that he seemed to have been a Christian."[1]

I have not, therefore, calumniated Hierocles. I respect and honor true philosophy. It may even be observed that throughout my work I have not once employed the term philosopher and philosophy in a bad sense. Every man, whose conduct is noble, whose sentiments are elevated and generous, who never stoops to a mean action, and preserves a lawful independence of mind, appears to me respectable, whatever otherwise his opinion may be. But the sophist,[2] of every age and every country, is worthy of contempt, inasmuch, as by abusing what is held in the highest estimation by mankind, he throws an odium upon that which is considered the most sacred among them.

I next come to the anachronisms of my work. The greatest men that the church has produced, appeared nearly all together between the close of the third and commencement of the fourth century. In order to make these illustrious characters pass under the eye of the reader, I have been obliged to violate the rigid rules of chronological exactness; but the greater part of these holy personages are introduced merely for the sake of episode, and act no important part in the story; my object has been to call up illustrious names, and awaken noble recollections. I presume that my readers will not be sorry to meet at Rome St. Jerome and St. Augustine; to see them led astray by the ardor of youth, and falling into faults which they wept over so long, and painted with such pathetic eloquence. After all, between the death of Diocletian, and the birth of St. Jerome, there was only a space of eight and twenty years. In

---

[1] Hist. Ecclesiast. liv. viii, tom. ii, 8vo.
[2] See, however, Mr. Grote's famous chapter on the sophists in his "History of Greece."—ED.

introducing St. Jerome and St. Augustine as speaking and acting together, I have faithfully adhered to the characters given them in history. These two great characters speak and act in the MARTYRS as they spoke and acted a few years afterward, in the same places, and in similar circumstances.

I know not whether I ought to call the introduction of Pharamond and his sons an anachronism. It is evident from Apollinaris Sidonius, and Gregory of Tours; from the "Epitome of the History of the Franks" attributed to Fredegarius, and from the "Antiquities" of Montfauçon, that there were many of the name of Merovius, Clodion, and Pharamond. We have therefore nothing to do, but to consider the kings of the Franks mentioned in my work, not as those generally known under that name, but other kings their ancestors.

I have placed the scene at Rome, and not at Nicomedia, the habitual residence of Diocletian. A modern reader naturally associates the idea of a Roman emperor with that of Rome itself. There are some things which the imagination cannot separate. It is a just observation of Racine, in the preface to his "Andromaque," that one cannot without violence attribute a strange son to the widow of Hector. To those who feel disposed to blame my anachronisms, I must oppose the example of Virgil, Fénelon, and Voltaire ; these will serve at once as my excuse and my authority.

I was advised to add notes to my work ; indeed I know of few books that would be more susceptible of them. In the authors whom I have consulted, I have found many things generally unknown, and by which I have greatly profited. The reader, who is ignorant of the sources whence I have drawn these extraordinary things, may be ready to set them down as the visions of the author : this has already happened to me in the case of "Atala."

I here offer the reader some examples of these extraordinary facts. Opening the Sixth Book of the MARTYRS, he will read as follows :

"France is a wild and savage country, overgrown with forests, that commence below the Rhine," etc.

In these particulars I rest upon the authority of St. Jerome in his "Life of St. Hilarion." I have moreover the maps of Peutinger,[1] and I believe, too, that Ammianus Marcellinus gives the name of France to the country of the Franks.

I have represented the two Decii as falling in the combat with the Franks; this is not the common opinion, but I have followed the "Chronicles of Alexandria."[2]

In another place I have spoken of the port of Nimes. I adopt there for a moment the opinion of those who believe that the *great tower* was a pharos.

With respect to the sarcophagus of Alexander, the reader may consult Quintus Curtius, Strabo, Diodorus Siculus, etc. The color of the eyes of the Franks, the green color with which the Lombards tinged their countenances, are facts taken from the letters and poems of Sidonius.

As for the descriptions of the Roman fêtes, their public prostitutions, the luxury of the amphitheatre exhibitions, the five hundred lions, the saffron water, etc., Cicero, Suetonius, Tacitus, and Florus, may be consulted; the writers of the Augustan history are full of these details.

With regard to the geographical curiosities respecting the Gauls, Greece, Syria, and Egypt, they are collected from Julius Cæsar, Diodorus Siculus, Pliny, Strabo, Pausanias, the anonymous author of Ravenna, Pomponius Mela, the collection of Panegyrists, Libanius in his discourse to Constantine, and in his book entitled "Basilicus," Sidonius Apollinaris, and lastly from of my own works.

As to the manners of the Gauls, the Franks, and other barbarians, besides the authors above cited, I have read with attention the "Chronicle" of Idacius, Priscus, Panites ("Fragments on the embassies"), the first oration of Julien, and his history of the Cæsars, Agathias and Procopius on the arms of the Franks, the "Chronicles" of Gregory of Tours, Salvianus, Orosius, the Venerable Bede, Isidore of Seville, Saxo Grammaticus, the "Edda," the introduction to history of Charles V, the

---

[1] Peutingeriana Tabula Itineraria, in fol.; Vienna, 1753.
[2] Chronicon Paschale, in fol.; Parisiis, 1688.

remarks of Blair upon Ossian, Peloutier's "History of the Celts," with various articles of du Cange, Joinville, and Froissard.

The manners of the primitive Christians, the formula of the acts of the martyrs, the different ceremonies, the description of the churches, are all taken from Eusebius, Socrates, Sozomenus, Lactantius, the Apologists, the "Acts of the Martyrs," the works of the Fathers, Tillemont and Fleury.

If, therefore, the reader should meet with anything to startle him by its novelty, let him not imagine that it is the offspring of my own imagination: I assure him I have no other view than to introduce some curious traits of ancient manners, some remarkable monuments, some unknown facts. Sometimes, too, in describing a person of the epoch of my story, I have selected a particular word or sentiment from the writings of this personage: not that the thought or sentiment was in itself worthy to be cited as a model of beauty and taste, but because it was characteristic of the person and of the age. All this might, no doubt, serve as material for notes and illustrations; but before I enlarged the volumes, it was necessary to know whether my book would be read, and whether the public would not already find it too prolix.

I began the MARTYRS at Rome, in 1802, some months after the publication of my "Génie du Christianisme." Since that period I have not ceased to labor on the work. The extracts that I have made from different authors are so considerable, that with regard to the Franks and Gauls alone, I have collected the materials for two large volumes. I have consulted friends of different taste, and of different literary principles. In fine, not content with all my studies, all my sacrifices, and all my scruples, I undertook a voyage on purpose to inspect with my own eyes the scenes that I wished to describe. Should my work, therefore, have no other merit, it will at least possess the interest of an accurate description of some of the most famous places of antiquity. I commenced my journey from the ruins of Sparta, and after passing through Argos, Corinth, Athens, Constantinople, Jerusalem, and Memphis, I finished my tour at the mouldering fragments of what once was Carthage. The reader therefore may rest assured that the descriptions which he finds in the MARTYRS, are not mere vague and fanciful combinations of imagery, but were faithfully sketched on the spot. Some of these descriptions are entirely new: no modern traveller, with whom I am acquainted, has given a picture of Messenia,[1] of a part of Arcadia, and of the valley of Laconia. Chandler, Spon, Wheeler, le Roy, M. de Choiseul, never visited Sparta. M. Fauvel, and some English tourists, have lately proceeded as far as this celebrated city, but they have not published the result of their labors. The picture of Jerusalem and of the Dead Sea is equally faithful. The Church of the Holy Sepulchre, the way of sorrow, *Via Dolorosa*, are exactly such as I have described. The fruit which my heroine gathers on the borders of the Dead Sea, and of which the existence has been denied, is found in great abundance within the distance of two or three leagues south of Jericho; the tree, which bears it, is a species of citron, and I brought many of these fruits into France.[2]

Such have been my endeavors to render the MARTYRS not entirely unworthy of public attention. Happy should I feel,

---

[1] Cornelli, Pellegrin, la Guilletière, and many other Venetians, have spoken of Lacedæmon, but in the most vague and unsatisfactory manner. M. de Pouqueville, excellent in the descriptions of everything that he saw, appears to have been deceived with regard to Misitra, which is not Sparta. Misitra is built at two leagues distance from the Eurotas, upon the declivities of Mount Taygetus. The ruins of Sparta are found at a village now called Magoula.

[2] This voyage, which was undertaken for the mere purpose of illustrating the MARTYRS, by describing with accuracy the scenes there introduced, has necessarily furnished me with a fund of observations foreign to my subject. I have selected some important facts, relative to the geography of Greece, to the real situation of Sparta, Argos, Mycenæ, Corinth, and Athens; of Pergamus in Mysia, Jerusalem, the Dead Sea, Egypt, and Carthage, whose ruins are much more curious than is generally imagined, and which occupy a considerable portion of my journal. This journal, even with the exception of those descriptions which I have transferred to the MARTYRS, may still, perhaps, possess some interest. I may, perhaps, on some future occasion, publish it under the title of a "Tour from Paris to Jerusalem, and from Jerusalem to Paris," by the way of Greece, Egypt, Barbary, and Spain.

if my work breathed any portion of that poetical inspiration which still animates the ruins of Athens and Jerusalem! It is not through any vain ostentation that I thus speak of my studies and my travels; it is to show the proper distrust I have in my own talents, and the care I have taken, by all means in my power, to supply the deficiency. By these labors, too, I have evinced my respect for the public, and the importance I attach to everything, that in any degree concerns the interests of religion.

It only remains for me now to speak of the style of this work. I shall take no side in a question that has so long been debated; I shall content myself with quoting authorities.

It is asked whether there can be poems in prose—a question which at the bottom can really be only a controversy of words.

Aristotle, whose judgments are laws, says positively that the epic may be written *in prose or in verse!*

And what is remarkable is, that he [1] gives to the Homeric or simple verse, a name that assimilates it to prose, $\varphi\iota\lambda o\mu\epsilon\tau\rho\iota\alpha$, as he says of poetic prose, $\psi\iota\lambda o\iota$ $\lambda\acute{o}\gamma o\iota$.

Dionysius of Halicarnassus, whose authority is equally respected, says:

"It is possible for a discourse in prose to resemble a fine poem or melodious verse; a poem and lyric songs may resemble oratorical prose." [2]

The author quotes the charming verses of Simonides on Danaë, and adds:

"These verses appear quite similar to beautiful prose."

Strabo, in like manner, confounds prose and verse. [4]

The age of Louis XIV, nourished upon antiquity, appears to have adopted the same sentiments in respect to the epic in prose. When the "Télémaque" appeared, there was no difficulty raised about giving it the name of poem. It was known at

---

[1] ARISTOT., de Art. poet., 8vo., page 2; Paris, 1645.
[2] DION. HALIC., tom. ii, p. 21, cap. xxv.
[3] Ibid., p. 60.
[4] STRAB., lib. i, p. 12, fol. 1597.

first by the title of the "Aventures de Télémaque," or, Sequel to the Fourth Book of the "Odyssey." Now the sequel of a poem can only be a poem. Boileau, who, moreover, judges "Télémaque" with a rigor that has not been sanctioned by posterity, compares it to the "Odyssey" and calls Fénelon a poet.

"There is a charm in this book," says he, "and an imitation of the "Odyssey," which I strongly approve. The avidity with which it is read, shows clearly that if Homer were translated in elegant language, it would produce the effect that it ought to make, and that it has always made. . . . . The Mentor of "Télémaque" says very good things, although they are somewhat daring; and, in fine, M. de Cambrai appears to me a much better *poet* than theologian." [1]

Eighteen months after the death of Fénelon, Louis de Sacy, in giving his approval of an edition of the "Télémaque," calls this book *an epic poem, although in prose.*

Ramsay gives it the same name.

The Abbé de Chanterac, that intimate friend of Fénelon, in writing to Cardinal Gabrieli, expressed himself thus:

"Our prelate had formerly composed this work (the "Télémaque"), following the same plan with Homer in his "Iliad" and "Odyssey," or Virgil in his "Eneid." This book may be regarded as a poem; nothing is lacking but the rhythm. The author sought to give it the *charm and harmony of the poetic style.*" [2]

Lastly, let us hear Fénelon himself.

"As to "Télémaque," it is a fabulous narration in the form of a heroic poem, like those of Homer and Virgil." [3]

This is very definite. [4]

---

[1] Lettres de Boileau et de Brossette, tom. i, p. 46.
[2] Histoire de Fénelon, by M. de Beausset, tom. ii, p. 194.
[3] Ibid., p. 196, "Manuscrits de Fénelon."
[4] To these authorities I shall join here that of Blair: this is not beyond appeal, to the French; but it expresses the opinion of foreigners on "Télémaque;" it is of great weight in everything that concerns ancient literature; and, lastly, Dr. Blair is, of all the English critics, the one that approaches nearest our taste and literary judgments.

"In reviewing the epic poets, it were unjust to make no mention of the amiable author of the "Adventures of Telemachus." His work, though

Faydit[1] and Guedeville[2] were the first critics who contested to "Telemaque" the title of poem, against the authority of Aristotle and of their times; the fact is somewhat singular. Since this epoch, Voltaire and la Harpe have declared that there can be no poem in prose; they were wearied and disgusted by the imitations that had been made of "Télémaque." But is this just? Because bad verses are made every day, must we condemn all verse? and are there not epics in verse of mortal weariness?

If the "Télémaque" be not a poem, what is it? A romance? Surely the "Télémaque" differs still more from a romance than a poem, according to the sense in which we at present understand these two words.

This is the state of the question; I leave the decision to the skilful. If it be wished, I will pass condemnation on the style of my work; I will willingly repeat what I have said in the preface of "Atala:" twenty fine lines of Homer, of Virgil or of Racine will always be incomparably superior to the most elegant prose in the world. After this, I entreat the poets to pardon me for having invoked the Daughters of Memory to aid me in chanting the MARTYRS. Plato, cited by Plutarch, says that he borrows numbers from poesy, as a chariot in which to take flight to heaven. I too would gladly mount this chariot; but I fear that the divinity that would inspire me might be one of those muses unknown upon Helicon, who have no wings and who go on foot, as Horace says, *Musa pedestris.*

---

not composed in verse, is justly entitled to be held a poem. The measured poetical prose in which it is written is remarkably harmonious; and gives the style nearly as much elevation as the French language is capable of supporting, even in regular verses."

[1] La Télémacomanie.   [2] Critique générale du Télémaque.

THE MARTYRS.

BOOK FIRST.

SUMMARY.

Invocation. Exposition. Diocletian holds the Reins of the Roman Empire. Under the government of this Prince, the Temples of the true God begin to dispute Homage with the Temples of Idols. Hell prepares to join Battle in a Final Combat to overthrow the Altars of the Son of Man. The Eternal permits the Demons to persecute the Church, in order to try the Faithful; but the Faithful will come out triumphant from the Trial; the Standard of Salvation will be planted on the Throne of the Universe; the World will owe this Victory to two Victims chosen by God. Who are these Victims? Apostrophe to the Muse that is about to make them known. The Family of Homer. Demodocus, the last Descendant of the Homeridæ, Priest of Homer in the Temple of this Poet, on Mount Ithome, in Messenia. Description of Messenia. Demodocus consecrates to the Worship of the Muses his only Daughter, Cymodoce, in order to conceal her from the Pursuit of Hierocles, Pro-consul of Achaia and Favorite of Galerius. Cymodoce goes alone with her Nurse to the Festival of the Lymnæan Diana; she loses her Way, and finds a Young Man asleep by the side of a Fountain. Eudorus conducts Cymodoce back to the house of Demodocus. Demodocus sets out with his Daughter to offer Presents to Eudorus, and to thank the Family of Lasthenes.

I WISH to recount the combats of the Christians, and the victory which the faithful achieved over the spirits of the abyss, through the glorious efforts of two martyr-spouses.

Celestial Muse! thou that inspired the poet of Sorrentum and the blind man of Albion; thou that settest thy solitary throne upon the Thabor; thou that art pleased with austere thoughts, with grave and sublime meditations; I now implore thy aid. Teach me upon the harp of David the songs that I should make heard; above all, give to my eyes a portion of those tears that Jeremiah shed over the miseries of Zion ! I am to speak of the sorrows of the persecuted Church.

And thou Virgin of the Pindus, lively daughter of Greece, descend in turn from the summit of the Helicon . I will not reject the garlands of flowers with which thou coverest the tombs, O smiling divinity of Fable, thou who hast not been able to make even of death and misfortune a serious thing ! Come, Muse of Falsehood, come struggle with the Muse of Truth. Once she was made to suffer cruel ills in thy name ; adorn her triumph to-day by thy defeat, and confess that she was more worthy than thee to rule the lyre.

Nine times had the Church of Jesus Christ seen the spirits of darkness leagued in conspiracy against her ; nine times had this favored vessel, which storms assail in vain, escaped the fury of the tempest. The earth reposed in peace : with skilful hand Diocletian swayed the sceptre of the world. Under the protection of this great prince, the Christians enjoyed a state of tranquillity, to which they had before been strangers. The altars of the true God began to contest the honors offered on the shrine of idolatry ; the number of the faithful increased daily ; and honors, riches, and glory were no longer the exclusive inheritance of the worshippers of Jupiter ; hell, threatened with the loss of its empire, sought to interrupt the course of these heavenly victories. The Eternal, who saw the virtues of his people languish in prosperity, permitted the demons to excite a fresh persecution ; but this last and terrible trial was ultimately to plant the cross on the throne of the universe, and to humble to the dust the temples of pagan superstition.

How did the ancient enemy of the human race avail himself in his projects of the passions of men, above all, of ambition and love ? Deign, O Muse, to instruct me in this ! But first make known to me the innocent virgin and the illustrious penitent so conspicuous in this day of triumph and of woe : the one chosen by heaven from among an idolatrous people ; the other from among the faithful, to be the expiatory victims both for the Christian and the Gentile world.

Demodocus was the last descendant of one of those families

of the Homeridæ, who formerly inhabited the island of Chios, and who laid pretensions to a direct descent from Homer. In his youth his parents had espoused him to Epicharis, the daughter of Cleobulus of Crete, the fairest of the virgin train who led the dance in the flowery vales of Mount Talctum, Mercury's loved haunt. He retired with his spouse to Gortyna, a city founded by the son of Rhadamanthus, and situated on the banks of the Lethæus, not far distant from the plane-tree that sheltered the amours of Jupiter and Europa. Nine times had the moon repaired her waning light, when, as Epicharis went to tend her flocks on Mount Ida, she was seized on a sudden with maternal throes, and brought into the world the tender Cymodoce, within the woods that adorned its sides: it was in this sacred grove that the three sages of Plato once met to discourse on the laws; the augurs, therefore, declared that the daughter of Demodocus would one day become renowned for her wisdom.

Shortly after, Epicharis was lost to the cheering light of day. The view of Lethæus' stream served now but to renew the affliction of Demodocus; his sole consolation was to take the only offspring of their nuptials upon his knee, to gaze on its smiling countenance, and with eyes, that glistened at once with joy and with tears, to trace in each lovely feature the beauties of Epicharis.

It happened at this time, that the inhabitants of Messenia were erecting a temple to Homer, and they invited Demodocus to fill the office of high priest. He accepted their offer with joy; content to abandon that abode, which heaven in its anger had rendered insupportable. After offering a sacrifice to the manes of his spouse, to the Naiads of the streams, to the hospitable nymphs of Ida, and to the guardian divinities of Gortyna, he departed with his daughter, carrying with him his penates, and a small statue of Homer.

Wafted by favoring breezes, his vessel soon descried the promontory of Tænarus, and coasting along the shores of Œtylus, Thalamæ, and Leuctra, he cast anchor under the overshadowing woods of Chœrius. The Messenians, a people tutored by misfortune, received Demodocus as the descendant of a god, and conducted him in triumph to the sanctuary consecrated to his divine ancestor.

The poet was there represented under the figure of a mighty river, from which the lesser streams filled their urns. This temple commanded a view of the city of Epaminondas, and stood in the centre of a grove of aged olives on Mount Ithome, which rose graceful as an azure vase amid the plains of Messenia. The oracle had ordained that its foundation should be laid on the same spot that Aristomenes had chosen to inter the urn of brass, to which were attached the destinies of his country. Here the eye wandered afar over plains adorned with the lofty cypress, interspersed with swelling mountains, and watered by the cooling streams of Amphissa, Pamisus, and of Balyra, where the blind Thamyris dropped his lyre. The rose-laurel, and the favorite shrubs of Juno, bordered the bed of the torrent, and marked the meandering course of each spring and rivulet. Winding along the channels of the exhausted brook, a thousand odoriferous plants seemed to form rivulets of flowers, and supplied by the coolness of their shade the deficiency of the stream. Cities, monuments of the arts, and ruins were blended in sweet confusion on this rural picture: Andania, witness to the tears of Merope; Tricca which gave birth to Æsculapius; Gerenia which preserves the tomb of Machaon; Pheræ, where the wise Ulysses received from Iphitus the bow that proved so fatal to the suitors of Penelope; and Stenyclerus resounding with the songs of Tyrtæus. This beautiful country, formerly under the dominion of the aged Neleus, thus presented from the summit of Ithome and the peristyle of the temple of Homer, a basket of verdure of more than eight hundred stadii in circumference. To the south and west, the sea of Massenia formed a brilliant barrier; to the north and east the chain of Taygetus, the summits of Lycæus, and the mountains of Elis, arrested the view. This horizon, unparalleled upon earth, recalled to mind the warlike life, the pastoral manners, and the festivities of a people, who dated the misfortunes of their history from the commencement of their pleasures.

Fifteen years had rolled away since the dedication of the temple of Homer, and Demodocus had lived in peaceful retirement within its sanctuary. His daughter Cymodoce grew beneath his eye, like a young olive on the margin of a fountain, that thrives under the fostering hand, and is the delight of earth and of heaven. Could Demodocus have espoused her to one who would have treated her with all his own parental affection, and placed her above dependence, his happiness would have been complete; but no son-in-law dared offer himself, for Cymodoce had had the misfortune to inspire with love Hierocles, the proconsul of Achaia, and the favorite of Galerius. Hierocles had demanded Cymodoce in marriage, but the young Messenian had entreated her father not to yield her hand to this impious Roman, whose very look made her shudder. Demodocus yielded without difficulty to the entreaties of his daughter; for he could not risk her happiness with a barbarian suspected of many crimes, and who, by his inhuman treatment, had hurried his first spouse to an early tomb.

This refusal, while it wounded the pride of the proconsul, served only to inflame his passion: he determined upon seizing her person, and resolved to employ for this purpose all the means that his power, assisted by the natural malignity of his heart, could afford him. To defeat the purposes of Hierocles, Demodocus consecrated his daughter to the service of the Muses. He instructed her in all the ceremonials of sacrifice; he taught her to select the heifer that was unspotted, to crop the hair on the forehead of the devoted bull, to cast it amidst the flames, and to sprinkle over it the sacred barley; above all, he taught her the powers of the lyre, whose strains have even the charm to soothe the breast of misfortune. Often when seated with his beloved daughter on a rock that overhung the deep, would they chant together some select beauties from the "Iliad" and the "Odyssey;" the tenderness of Andromache, the wisdom of Penelope, or the modesty of Nausicaa, the woes which are the portion of mortals, Agamemnon sacraficed by his own spouse, Ulysses begging an alms at the gates of his own palace, formed the subject of their song; the lot of that wretched man, who, expiring far from his native land, was denied the happiness of revisiting his paternal hearth, melted them with pity; over you, too, they wept, unhappy youths, you who tended the flocks of your royal fathers, yet whom an occupation so innocent could not save from the wrath of the implacable Achilles!

Familiarized in the learned society of the Muses with all the noble recollections that antiquity inspires, each day Cymodoce unfolded new charms. Demodocus, whom wisdom had taught the full knowledge of the human heart, sought to temper the effects of this divine education, by inspiring her with a taste for simplicity. He was pleased to see her lay aside her lute, to go and fill her urn at the fountain, or cleanse the veils of the temple in the current of the brook. During the confinement of the long winter hours, while she leaned against a column, and plied the distaff by the light of the taper, he would thus address her: "From thy infancy, Cymodoce, it has been my endeavor to enrich thy mind with every virtue, and with every gift of the Muses; for we ought to treat our soul upon its entrance into the body, as a heavenly guest, whose arrival we should welcome with garlands and perfumes. But, O daughter of Epicharis! let us dread that spirit of vanity and ostentation which is the bane of good sense; let us beseech Minerva to grant us Reason for our guide; from her we shall learn that moderation, the sister of Truth, without whose aid our passions will hurry us into every extreme."

Instruction thus conveyed under beautiful imagery at once enlightened and charmed the mind of Cymodoce. Something characteristic of the Muses, to whom she was consecrated, was visible in her countenance, her voice, and her disposition. When her long and graceful eyelids were inclined to the earth, and traced their shadowy outline on the snowy whiteness of her cheeks, you would have mistaken her for Melpomene in her most serious mood; but when these eyes were raised to heaven, you might have believed her the smiling Thalia. Her raven locks resembled the hue of the hyacinth, and her graceful form the palm-tree of Delos. She had one day gone to some distance with her father to gather dittany. To discover the precious plant, they had followed a doe wounded by an archer of Œchalia, and were seen together on the summit of the mountains. A report immediately spread that Nestor and the fair Polycaste, the youngest of his daughters, had been seen on the chase in the woods of Ira.

The festival of the Lymnæan Diana approached, and preparations were made to solemnize the usual rites on the borders of Messenia and Laconia. This pomp, once the fatal cause of deadly contentions between Lacedæmon and Messene, now attracted only a crowd of peaceful spectators. Cymodoce was chosen by the old men to lead the choir of young virgins, whose duty it was to present the votive offerings to the chaste sister of Apollo. In the simplicity of her heart, she rejoiced at the honors she had won, and applauded her success upon no other motives, than that it would redound to her father's praise : if he but heard the encomiums bestowed on his daughter, if he but touched the garland she had merited, he would desire no higher glory, no greater happiness.

Demodocus, detained by a sacrifice that a stranger came to offer at Homer's shrine, could not accompany his daughter. She therefore departed for the festival with no other attendant than Eurymedusa, daughter of Alcimedon of Naxos. The old man felt no uneasiness, as the proconsul of Achaia was then at Rome with Cæsar Galerius. The temple of Diana, from its lofty situation on Taygetus, commanded a view of the gulf of Messenia; it stood in the midst of a grove of pines, on the branches of which the skins of many wild beasts were suspended by the huntsmen, at once as an offering to the goddess, and as a memorial of their success. The walls of this edifice were of that embrowned and sombre hue which the traveller still beholds on the ruins of Rome and Athens. The statue of Diana, elevated on a shrine in the centre of the temple, was the masterpiece of a celebrated sculptor. He had represented the daughter of Latona in a standing posture, with one foot advanced; she was seizing with her right hand the arrow from the quiver suspended at her shoulder, while the doe of Cerynia, with her horns of gold and feet of brass, was crouching for refuge under the bow which the goddess held inclined in her left.

At the moment the moon had reached her zenith, and silvered over the temple with her rays, Cymodoce, at the head of her companions, who were equal in number to the nymphs of the ocean, raised the hymn in honor of the fair virgin. A band of huntsmen chanted, in response to the virgin choir:

"Come, sisters, form the airy dance, raise the tuneful voice, and reëcho the sacred chorus!

"O Diana! sovereign of the woods, deign propitious to receive the vows which thy chosen virgins, thy chaste children, instructed by the oracles of the Sibyls, presume to offer thee. Under a palm-tree in the floating Delos, didst thou first behold the light of day. To soothe the pangs of Latona, seven times did the swans encompass the isle, as they chanted their harmonious lays; as a memorial of this, thy divine brother invented the seven chords of the lyre.

"Come, sisters, form the airy dance, raise the tuneful voice, and reëcho the sacred chorus!

"The river, the fountain, and the shady grove; the forests of the verdant Cragus, the breezy Algidus, and the gloomy Erymanthus, are thy delight. Diana, who bearest the formidable bow; Cynthia, whose head is adorned with the crescent; Hecate, armed with the serpent and the sword; O threefold goddess! let our youths be pure; grant repose to old age; and to the family of Nestor, offspring, riches, and renown.

"Come, sisters, form the airy dance, raise the tuneful voice, and reëcho the sacred chorus!"

The strain is closed: and now the maidens unbind their wreaths of laurel, and suspend them together with the bows of the huntsmen at the altar of Diana. A white stag is immolated to the Queen of Silence; the crowd disperses, and Cymodoce, followed by her attendant, takes the road that conducts to the residence of her father.

The night was all serene. The transparent shadows seemed

to respect the beautiful heaven of Greece, as if fearful to sully its lustre ; it was not darkness, it was only the absence of day. The air was as soft as milk and honey ; one felt it breathe a charm over the senses which language would in vain attempt to describe. The summits of Taygetus, the sea of Messenia, and the opposite promontories of Colonides and Acritas, lay bathed in floods of the most softened light ; an Ionian fleet lowered its sails to enter the port of Corone, as a flock of doves fold their wearied pinions to repose on some friendly coast ; Alcyone, seated on her nest, sweetly warbled forth her sorrows ; the breeze of night, while it bore the murmurs of the distant deep, wafted the perfumes of the breathing flowers to the senses of Cymodoce ; seated in the valley, the shepherd contemplated the moon, amidst her brilliant retinue of stars, and felt his heart rejoice at the sight.

The youthful priestess of the Muses advanced along the mountain in silent admiration of the scenery around her. Her eyes wandered in rapture over these enchanting retreats, where the ancients placed the cradle of Lycurgus near to that of Jupiter ; to teach us that religion and the laws have one common origin, and that to destroy their mutual union is both impious and unnatural. Filled with a religious awe, Cymodoce magnified every motion of the leaf, every whisper of the breeze, into a prodigy ; the distant murmurs of the ocean were the hollow roarings of the lions of Cybele, as she was descending into the woods of Œchalia ; and the moans of the ring-dove, repeated at intervals, were the echoes of Diana's horn as she led the chase on the heights of Thuria.

She advances ; memory awakens ; a thousand soothing recollections crowd on her mind and banish every fearful emotion : she thinks on the ancient traditions of the famed isle, where she first beheld the light of day ; the labyrinth whose winding figure was still preserved in the dances of the Cretan youth ; the ingenious Dædalus, the imprudent Icarus, Idomeneus and his son, and, above all, the sad tale of the two unfortunate sisters, Phædra and Ariadne. Suddenly she perceives that she has wandered from the mountain track, and that she is no longer followed by her nurse; she utters a sudden shriek of terror, which dies unanswered on the breeze; she implores the aid of the deities of the woods and fountains, but they answer not her voice, and she thinks these absent divinities assembled in the valleys of Menelaium, where the Arcadians offer their solemn sacrifices. At a distance, Cymodoce hears the murmurs of a stream, and hastens to place herself under the protection of the Naiad, till the return of Aurora.

A crystal spring, environed by lofty poplars, fell in foaming waves from the height of a rock; above it stood an altar dedicated to the Naiad of the spring, where travellers in passing deposited their offerings. Cymodoce fled to embrace the altar, and supplicate the divinity of the place to calm the anxiety of her father, when she perceived a youth who lay reclined in slumber against the rock. His head rested on his left shoulder, and was partly supported by his lance, over which his arm was negligently thrown; he had just power to hold the leash of his dog, whose ear seemed ready to catch the faintest sound; a ray of the moon darting through the branches of the cypress, shone full on the huntsman's face: a disciple of Apelles would have thus represented the slumbers of Endymion. Indeed, the daughter of Demodocus really imagined that in this youth she beheld the lover of Diana; in a plaintive zephyr she thought she distinguished the sigh of the goddess, and in a glimmering ray of the moon she seemed to catch a glimpse of her snowy vest as she was just retiring into the thicket. Fearing to have disturbed her mysteries, the trembling Cymodoce fell on her knees and exclaimed: "Dread sister of Apollo! spare an imprudent virgin; pierce her not with thine arrows: I am my father's only child, and my mother, who has already felt thy severity, was never proud of my birth."

The ardor with which this was pronounced aroused the dog; he barked and awakened his master. Surprised at the sight of a maiden in this kneeling posture, he rose precipitately.

"What!" said Cymodoce, confused and still on her knees, "are you not the hunter Endymion?"

"And you," said the youth, not less amazed, "are you not an angel?"

"An angel!" replied the daughter of Demodocus.

"Woman," said the stranger, filled with anxiety, "arise, we should prostrate ourselves before God alone."

After a moment of silence, the priestess of the Muses thus addressed the huntsman:

"If you are not a divinity in human form, you are doubtless some stranger, whom the satyrs have, like myself, led astray in the woods. In what port have you left your vessel? Came you from Tyre, so renowned for its merchants and its riches, or from the delightful walls of Corinth, whose hospitable inhabitants have loaded you with rich presents? Are you one of those who traffic on the seas even to the pillars of Hercules? Are you a follower of Mars the cruel god of battle; or are you not rather the son of one of those chiefs who have long swayed the sceptre of empire, and ruled a land abundant in flocks and cherished by the gods?"

The stranger answered:

"There is but one God, master of the universe; and I am but a mortal, full of weakness and misery. My name is Eudorus, the son of Lasthenes. I came from Thalamæ on my return to my father; night surprised me, and I lay myself down to sleep by this fountain. But you, how are you here alone? may heaven guard your virgin honor; we should dread its loss—yes, after the fear of God, it should be the next of importance to us."

The language of this man confounded Cymodoce. She felt in his presence a mingled sensation of love and respect, of confidence and fear. The gravity of his language, and the grace of his person, formed in her eye a most extraordinary contrast. He seemed to belong to a different race of men, more noble and serious than that with which she was acquainted. Thinking it might increase the interest that Eudorus seemed to take in her misfortune, she said to him:

"I am a descendant of Homer, a name immortalized in song."

The stranger contented himself with replying :
"I know a book more valuable than his."

Disconcerted by the brevity of this reply, Cymodoce whispered to herself :
"This young man is a Spartan."

She then told him her story.

"I will conduct you to your father," said the son of Lasthenes, and he led the way before her.

The daughter of Demodocus followed him. She trembled, and one might have heard her very breath, she drew it with such difficulty. To gain some little assurance, she attempted to speak; she hazarded some remarks on the charms of Night, whom she called the spouse of Erebus, and the mother of Love and the Hesperides; but her guide interupted her :

"I see nothing," said he, "but the stars, which declare the glory of the Most High."

These words filled the priestess of the Muses with fresh confusion. She knew not now what to think of this stranger, whom she had at first taken for one of the immortals. Might it not be some impious demon, who traversed the earth during the solitude of night, hated by men, and pursued by the vengeance of the gods? might it not be some pirate, who had prowled from his vessel, to ravish helpless children from their parents? Cymodoce began to feel the most lively apprehensions; which, however, she feared to discover. But she could no longer conceal her astonishment, when she beheld her guide bend compassionately over a slave, whom they found helpless and abandoned by the roadside, call him brother, and throw his mantle over him to cover his nakedness.

"Stranger," said the daughter of Demodocus, "I doubt not but you supposed this slave some divinity, who had descended on earth in the form of a mendicant, to try the hearts of men?"

"No," replied Eudorus, "I believed him to be a man."

Meanwhile a fresh breeze sprung up in the east, and Aurora did not long delay her appearance. From the bosom of the mountains of Laconia, in unclouded and magnificent simplicity, the sun arose, and spread his enlivening rays around. At the same instant, Eurymedusa sprung from a neighboring wood, and ran with open arms to embrace Cymodoce.

"Oh, my child!" she exclaimed, "what grief have I suffered on your account! I have filled the air with my lamentations; I feared lest you had been carried away by Pan. That dangerous god is always wandering in these forests; often is he met reeling in the dance with the intoxicated Silenus, and then nothing can equal his audacity. How could I have appeared without you in the presence of my dear master? Alas! in my younger days, I myself, while sporting on the shores of Naxos, my native land, was on a sudden borne away by a band of those wretches, who traverse in armed vessels the empire of Tethys, and live on the rich fruits of their plunder. They sold me at a port of Crete, at some distance from Gortyna. Your father came to Lebena, to exchange the corn of Theodosia for the tapestry of Miletus. He redeemed me from the hands of the pirates; the price was two bulls that had never yet traced the furrows of Ceres. At night, having proved my fidelity, he placed me at the door of his nuptial chamber. When the cruel fates had closed the eyes of Epicharis, Demodocus gave you into my arms, and bade me perform toward you the offices of a mother. How many anxieties have you caused me! how many the night that I have watched round your cradle, and danced you on my knee! no food was grateful but from my hands, and you wept if I quitted you but for a moment."

As she said this, she folded Cymodoce in her arms, and shed tears of tenderness. Cymodoce, melted by the affectionate caresses of her nurse, wept also.

"My dear mother," said she, embracing her, "this is Eudorus, the son of Lasthenes."

The youth, leaning on his spear, had fondly sympathized in this scene of tenderness, and the natural austerity of his countenance had softened into an approving smile; but suddenly resuming his wonted gravity:

"Daughter of Demodocus," said he, "you have found your

nurse, and the mansion of your father is not far distant. May God have mercy on your soul."

Without waiting a reply from Cymodoce, he departed with the rapidity of an eagle. The priestess of the Muses, instructed in the arts of augury, no longer doubted that this huntsman was one of the immortals. She turned away her head, fearful lest she should see the present divinity, and not survive the sight. She then hastened to climb the heights of Ithome, and passing the fountains of Arsinoe and Clepsydra, reached the temple of Homer. The aged pontiff had wandered the whole night in the woods, and had sent his slaves to Leuctra, Pheræ and Limnæa. The absence of the proconsul of Achaia no longer served to soothe his parental anxiety: Demodocus feared the violence of the crafty Hierocles, even though the wretch was at Rome, and nothing but evils seemed to threaten his absent Cymodoce. When she arrived with her nurse, she found her unhappy father seated on the ground near the hearth, his head enveloped in his robe, and watering the ashes with his tears. At the sudden appearance of his daughter, he was almost ready to expire with joy. Cymodoce threw herself into his arms, and during some moments nothing was heard but broken sobs: such are the sounds that issue from the nest when the mother brings food to her tender offspring. At length suspending his sorrows:

"My dear child," said Demodocus, "what god hath restored thee to thy father? How could I permit thee to go alone to the sacrifice? I was apprehensive of our enemies; I was apprehensive of the partisans of Hierocles, who despise the gods, and deride the sorrows of unhappy fathers. But I would have traversed the seas in search of thee; I would have thrown myself at the feet of Cæsar; I would have said to him: Restore me my Cymodoce, or take away my life." They should have seen thy father recounting his sorrows to the god of day, and searching thee through every land; I would have followed the example of Ceres, when she recovered by entreaties the daughter that Pluto had ravished from her arms. The destiny of that old man, who dies unblessed with offspring, is worthy of pity. The youth approach not his corpse, or approach it with contempt : " This old man," they say, " was a wretch ; the gods extirpated his race, in punishment of his impiety ; he has left no child to bury him."

Cymodoce pressed in her beauteous hands those of her aged sire ; she smoothed his silver beard, and said :

" Oh, dearest father ! thou favored of the immortals whose praises thou delightest to sing ! I lost my way and wandered in the woods : a youth, or rather some god, brought me here to thy arms again."

At these words, Demodocus hastily arose ; he unfolded his daughter from his embraces, and exclaimed :

" How ! has a stranger restored thee to thy father, and hast thou not introduced him to our abode—thou, the priestess of the Muses, and daughter of Homer ? What had become of thy divine ancestor, had he not better exercised the duties of hospitality ? Shall it be said throughout Greece, that Demodocus, his descendant, shut his gate on the stranger or the suppliant ? Could any more grievous calamity befall me ? alas ! none but that of ceasing to be called the father of Cymodoce."

Eurymedusa seeing the rising anger of Demodocus, sought thus to excuse Cymodoce :

" Demodocus, my dear master, do not condemn your daughter unheard. I will tell you all, in the sincerity of my heart. We did not invite the stranger to accompany us, because he was young, and beautiful as one of the immortals ; we were fearful of exciting those suspicions, which are but too apt to rise in the minds of men."

" Eurymedusa," replied Demodocus, " what expressions have escaped your lips ! till now I never thought you deficient in good sense : but I see some god has troubled your reason. Know then that my heart is never open to unjust suspicions ; I detest nothing so much as the man who is always distrusting the sincerity of his brother."

Cymodoce resolved in her turn to make an effort to appease Demodocus.

"Holy pontiff," said she, "calm, I beseech you, the transports of your wrath; anger, like famine, is the mother of desperate counsels. There is yet room to repair my fault. The young man told me his name; perhaps you may not be unacquainted with his ancient family. He is called Eudorus, and is the son of Lasthenes."

These words, uttered with all the softness of persuasion, went to the very heart of Demodocus, and he pressed Cymodoce to his bosom in a tender embrace.

"Dearest daughter," said he, "my cares to instruct thy early years have not been ineffectual. There is no virgin of thy age that thou dost not surpass in solidity of judgment; to the Graces alone you yield in those arts that adorn your sex. But who can equal the Graces, above all the youngest of them, the divine Pasithea? My daughter, you guess rightly; I know the ancient family of Eudorus, the son of Lasthenes. I yield not to any man in a profound knowledge of the genealogy both of gods and men; nay, there was a time when I too would have yielded in verse to none but Orpheus, Linus, Homer, or the aged bard of Ascra: for the men of former times were far superior to those of the present day. Lasthenes is one of the principal inhabitants of Arcadia. He is a descendant of a race of heroes and of gods, for he received his origin from the river Alpheus, and counts among his ancestors the great Philopœmen, and Polybus the favorite of Calliope, the daughter of Saturn and Astræa. He himself has borne away laurels of triumph in the field of Mars; he is cherished by our princes, and has been invested with the highest honors, both in the state and in the army. To-morrow, as soon as Dice, Irene and Eunomia—the lovely Horæ—have unfolded the gates of day, we will mount our car, and proceed to offer presents to Eudorus, whose wisdom and valor fame has already spread abroad."

As he finished these words, Demodocus, followed by his daughter and Eurymedusa, entered the gate of the temple, whose ornaments seemed on every side to vie with each other in splendor and elegance. A ministering slave poured from a golden ewer into a basin of silver, the purifying stream on the hands of the priest. Demodocus takes a vessel, and having purified it in the flame, mixes wine and water therein, and pours the sacred libation on the earth to appease the offended Lares. Cymodoce retires to her apartment, and after enjoying the refreshment of the bath, throws her wearied limbs on a couch adorned with the tapestry of Lydia, and covered with the finest productions of the Egyptian loom; but sleep was a stranger to her eyes; and it was in vain that she besought night to shed around her its softest shadows, and lull her to repose.

Scarce had the dawn empurpled the east, when the voice of Demodocus was heard, as he called the most faithful and active of his slaves. Immediately Evemon, the son of Boetoüs, flung wide the gates that enclosed the car and its apparatus. The wheels, strengthened with rims of brass, are fitted on; the car of ivory is nicely suspended on the flexile springs, and the polished yoke is made ready. Hestioneus of Epirus, skilful in the management of the courser, leads out two strong mules of dazzling whiteness, conducts them bounding to the yoke, and fits on them the harness glittering with gold. The provident Eurymedusa lays in a supply of wine and bread, the strength of man, and places on the car the present destined for the son of Lasthenes. This was a vase of brass, admirably embossed by the art of Vulcan, who had designed the history of Hercules delivering Alcestes, in gratitude for the hospitality he had experienced from his spouse. Ajax had given this cup to Tychius of Hyle, a celebrated armorer, in exchange for a buckler covered with seven bull-hides, which had been borne by the son of Telamon to the siege of Troy. A descendant of Tychius received under his roof the bard of Ilion, and made him a present of this superb relic. Homer, having visited the isle of Samos, was admitted a guest in the house of Creophylus, and at his death left him this vase, and his poems. Afterward, when Lycurgus, king of Sparta, was traversing every land in search of wisdom, he visited the sons of Creophylus; from them he received the vase of Homer, and those immortal productions which the poet had written under the inspiration of Apollo. At the death of Lycurgus the world inherited the songs of the poet, but the vase was restored to the Homeridæ: it came to Demodocus, the last descendant of this sacred race, who now destined it as a present to the son of Lasthenes.

In the meantime, Cymodoce ornaments herself for her journey. The light sandal is bound to her foot, and a comb of gold confines the perfumed tresses of her hair; the Graces could not attire themselves in more simple elegance. Her attendant brings the white veil of the Muses: this brilliant emblem of her office was carefully kept in an odoriferous casket. Over the head of Cymodoce this virginal tissue is thrown, and she goes forth to find her father. The old man was advancing to meet her; he was clothed in a long robe, which, with the girdle of purple fringe that bound it, was valued at a hecatomb. A crown of papyrus adorned his head, and in his hand he bore the branch sacred to Apollo. He mounts the car, and Cymodoce seats herself at his side. Evemon seizes the reins, the lash resounds, and the mules in their rapid course scarce leave the impression of the wheels on the sand.

"O my daughter!" said the pious Demodocus, as the car rolled swiftly along, "may heaven preserve us from the crime of ingratitude! The gates of hell are less hateful to Jove than an unthankful soul. The days of the ungrateful are short, and they are perpetually haunted by the Furies; but a favoring divinity always watches over those who lose not the memory of benefits received. The gods chose Egypt for their birthplace, because the Egyptians were the most grateful of all mankind."

BOOK SECOND.

SUMMARY.

Arrival of Demodocus and Cymodoce in Arcadia. They meet an old man at the Tomb of Aglaus of Psophis, who conducts them to the Field where the Family of Lasthenes are gathering in their Harvest. Cymodoce recognizes Eudorus. Demodocus discovers that Lasthenes' Family are Christians. Return to the House of Lasthenes. Customs of the Christians. Evening Prayer. Arrival of Cyril, Bishop of Lacadæmon, the Confessor and Martyr, who comes to urge Eudorus to relate his Adventures. The evening Repast. The Family and Strangers take their seats after Supper in the Orchard on the Banks of the Alpheus. Demodocus asks Cymodoce to play the Lyre. Song of Cymodoce. Eudorus sings in his Turn. The two Families retire to Rest. Dream of Cyril. Prayer of the holy Bishop.

WHILST the sun was pursuing his course in the heavens, the mules bore the car rapidly along. At the hour when the magistrate, fatigued with the toils of office, quits his tribunal with joy to take his repast, the priest of Homer reaches the confines of Arcadia; and pauses to rest at Phigalia, celebrated for the piety of the Oresthasians. The noble Ancæus, a descendant of Agapenor, who led on the Arcadians to the siege of Troy, receives Demodocus to his hospitable mansion. The sons of Ancæus loosen the mules from the yoke, bathe their dusty sides in the stream, and feed them with tender herbage from the banks of the Neda. Cymodoce is conducted to the bath by Phrygian damsels, strangers, alas! to the sweets of liberty! Demodocus is clothed by his host in a fine tunic and precious mantle; the prince of youth, the eldest of the sons of Ancæus, crowned with a branch of white poplar, sacrifices to Hercules a boar bred in the woods of Erymanthus: the parts of the victim destined for the sacrifice are covered with fat, and consumed with libations on the coals of the altar. The rest of the victim is dressed before the flame, and the most delicious morsels are offered to the travellers. Demodocus receives a portion three times larger than the rest of the guests. An odorous wine, that ten years have mellowed, flows in purple waves into a golden goblet; and the gifts of Ceres, made known to the pious Arcas by Triptolemus, displace the acorns, with which of yore the Pelasgi, the first inhabitants of Arcadia, were nourished.

But the honors of hospitality cannot detain Demodocus, such is the desire that he feels to reach the abode of Lasthenes. Night had now spread around her shadows; they conclude the sacrifice, and offer a last libation to the mother of dreams. The priest of Homer and his daughter are then conducted under the lofty porticos to the place where the slaves had prepared their couches.

Demodocus waits with impatience the return of light.

"My daughter," said he to Cymodoce, whom some unknown power had also deprived of sleep, "woe to those men from whose eyes neither pity nor gratitude can chase the seductions of Morpheus! As it is forbidden to carry weapons into the sanctuary of the gods, so no one shall enter into Elysium with a heart of brass."

No sooner had Aurora shed her first beams on the temple of Jupiter, which crowns the summit of Lycæus, than Demodocus orders them to yoke the mules to the chariot. In vain the generous Ancæus strives to detain his guest; the priest of Homer departs with his daughter. The chariot rolls through the echoing porticos, and takes its course toward the temple of Eurynome, concealed amid the shadows of a grove of cypress; and after passing Mount Elaius, they reach the grotto where Pan found Ceres, who refused her gifts to the swains, but who suffered herself to be softened by the Fates, for once favorable to mortals.

The travellers cross the Alpheus below the confluence of the Gortynius, and descend to the limpid waters of Ladon. Here an ancient tomb meets their sight, that the nymphs of the mountains had embowered with elms: it was erected in honor of that poor and virtuous Arcadian, Aglaus of Psophis, whom the oracle of Delphos declared more happy than the king of Lydia. Two roads part from this tomb; the one extends along the banks of the Alpheus, the other winds along the mountain.

While Evemon was deliberating which road to take, he perceived a man, venerable for his years, seated near the tomb of Aglaus. His robe differed not from that which the philosophers of Greece wore, except that it was white, and of a coarse texture. He seemed to be waiting the approach of the travellers, but appeared neither curious nor officious. The chariot stops; he rises and addresses Demodocus:

"Traveller," said he, "do you inquire the road, or are you come to visit Lasthenes? If you wish to share his hospitality he will impart it with pleasure."

"Stranger," said Demodocus, "when Mercury met the father of Hector on his way to the Grecian camp, the meeting was not more fortunate. Your robe announces a sage, and your words, though few, are intelligent. To tell you the truth, we are in search of the rich Lasthenes, who, for his extensive possessions, has been termed the happy mortal. Without doubt, he inhabits yonder palace, which I perceive on the banks of the Ladon; one might mistake it for a temple of the god of Cyllene?"

"That palace," replied the stranger, "belongs to Hierocles, the proconsul of Achaia. You have reached the enclosure of the host you are seeking; and the roof of thatch which you see on the declivity of the mountain, is the abode of Lasthenes."

As he said this, the stranger threw open the gate, took the bridle of the mules, and led them within the enclosure.

"Sir," said he to Demodocus, "they are busily engaged in the labors of harvest; let your servant conduct the mules to yonder building, and I will point out the field where you may find Lasthenes."

Demodocus and Cymodoce descended from the chariot, and walked forward with the stranger. They followed for some time a path bordered on each side by vines, and beech trees of immense size which adorned the slope of the mountain. They soon perceived a field covered with sheaves of corn, where laborers of both sexes were vying with each other in activity: some were heaping the loaded wains, others were cutting and binding up the ripened ears.

They reached the busy swains. "The Lord be with you," exclaimed the stranger that conducted them. "May God give you a blessing," replied the swains.

To lighten the fatigues of the day a song was chanted, but the air was solemn and impressive. The gleaners followed, and collected the grain that was spread behind with a liberal hand; such were the orders of the master, that the poor might collect their little harvest without molestation. Cymodoce recognized from afar the young man of the forest; he was seated with his mother and his sisters under a verdant shade. The family arose, and advanced toward the strangers.

"Sephora," said the guide of Demodocus, "my dear spouse, let us bless providence, who has given us an opportunity of exercising our hospitality."

"What!" cried the father of Cymodoce, "was this the rich Lasthenes, and I knew him not? How do the gods sport with the discernment of mortals! I took you for a slave, whose place it was to attend to strangers."

Lasthenes bowed. Eudorus, with downcast eyes, held the hand of the youngest of his sisters, and kept respectfully behind his mother.

"My host," said Demodocus, "and you sage spouse of Lasthenes, who resemble the mother of Telemachus, no doubt your son has acquainted you with the kindness he showed my daughter, who had wandered in the woods. Show me the noble Eudorus, that I may embrace him as my son!"

"See, there is Eudorus behind his mother," said Lasthenes. "I know not what he has done for you: he has not mentioned it to us."

Demodocus remained confounded.

"What," thought he within himself, "is this simple swain

the warrior who triumphed over Carausius, who was tribune of the Britannic Legion, and the friend of Prince Constantine!"

Recovering at length from his astonishment, the priest of Homer exclaimed:

"I ought to have known you, Eudorus; you have the mien of a hero: you yield, however, in stature to Lasthenes; for children possess not in these days the vigor of their sires. O you who might be the youngest of my sons! may the gods grant you the desire of your heart! I bring for your acceptance an urn of inestimable value: my slave shall bring it from the chariot, and from my hands shall you receive it. Young and valiant warrior, Meleager had less manly beauty when he charmed the eyes of Atalanta. Happy the parents in such a son, but more happy the maid destined for such a spouse! If the virgin you found a wanderer in the woods had not been consecrated to the Muses" . . .

Cymodoce was troubled at the words of her father; Eudorus felt no less confusion, and hastened to answer:

"With pleasure," said he, "I will accept your offering, if it has not been used in your sacrifices."

The day was not yet finished, and the family invited the two strangers to repose with them on the margin of a fountain. The sisters of Eudorus seated at the feet of their parents, wove garlands of various-colored flowers, for an approaching festival. A little further on stood the implements of the reapers; and under the shadow of a range of sheaves an infant was sweetly slumbering in its cradle.

"My host," said Demodocus to Lasthenes, "you seem to me to lead here the life of the divine Nestor. I do not recollect to have beheld so pleasing a scene, except that imaged on the shield of Achilles. Vulcan there represented a king in the midst of his attendant reapers; this shepherd of men, with pleasure marked on his countenance, stretches out his peaceful sceptre over the rural scene. Nothing is wanting but a sacrifice to Jupiter, under this spreading oak, his favorite tree. What an abundant harvest! what faithful and laborious slaves!"

"These are not my slaves," said Lasthenes, "my religion forbids slavery, and I have given them their liberty."

"Lasthenes," said Demodocus, "I begin to comprehend that fame, the voice of Jupiter, has told me the truth: without doubt, you have embraced that new sect which adores a God unknown to our ancestors."

"Right," replied Lasthenes; "I am a Christian."

The descendant of Homer remained for a time in silent reverie, and he thus resumed the discourse:

"Generous host, pardon this my frankness: I have ever yielded obedience to truth, the daughter of Saturn and the parent of virtue. The gods are just; how am I to reconcile the prosperity that surrounds you with the impieties of which the Christians are accused?"

"Traveller," replied Lasthenes, "the Christians are not guilty of impiety, and your gods are neither just nor unjust—they exist not at all. If my fields and my flocks prosper in the hands of my family, it is because they are simple in heart, and are submissive to the will of him, who is the only true God. Heaven, as you see, has blessed me with a virtuous spouse. I prayed that she might possess humility, chastity, and constancy, and my prayer was heard. God has given me obedient children, who are the crown of the aged. They love their parents, and are happy, because they are attached to their paternal roof. My spouse and I have grown old together. I have not always seen happy days; yet during the thirty years she has shared my couch, she has never revealed the secret cares and anxieties of my bosom. May heaven repay her sevenfold that peace she has bestowed upon me! but no happiness she can enjoy will equal my wishes."

It was thus that the heart of this primitive Christian expanded as he spoke of his spouse.

Cymodoce listened and admired: manners so amiable touched the very soul of the young infidel, and Demodocus himself was obliged to call Homer and all the gods to his assistance that he might not be drawn away by the force of truth.

After some moments, the father of Cymodoce said to Lasthenes:

"Your words breathe all the wisdom of ancient times, and yet I have not met with them in Homer. Your silence has all the dignity of the silence of sages. Your sentiments are elevated and full of majesty; if they have not the grace of Euripides, they possess the solemnity of Plato. In the midst of a pleasing abundance, you enjoy the delights of friendship; nothing around you seems forced; all is contentment, persuasion, and love. May you long enjoy your happiness and your riches!"

"I never considered," replied Lasthenes, "that these riches were exclusively my own: I amass them for my brother Christians, for Gentiles, for travellers, for the unfortunate. God has given me the direction of them; God perhaps may take them away; his holy name be blessed!"

As Lasthenes finished these words, the sun descended toward the summits of Pholoe: his broadened disc appeared for a moment immovable, and suspended on the summit of the mountain, like the shield of some giant hero. The woods of Alpheus and of Ladon, the distant snows of Telphusa and of Lycæus, were covered with roses: the winds were hushed, and the valley of Arcadia reposed in universal tranquillity. The reapers quitted their work, and the family, accompanied by the strangers, returned to their home. Both masters and servants walked promiscuously together, bearing the different instruments of labor. Mules laden with wood, hewn on the neighboring summits, followed; and the oxen slowly dragged the wain that was piled high with the ripened harvest.

On reaching the house, the sound of a bell was heard.

"We are going," said Lasthenes to Demodocus, "to offer our evening prayer: shall we beg permission to quit you for a moment, or would you rather accompany us?"

"May the gods preserve me from despising the Prayers," exclaimed Demodocus, "those lame daughters of Jupiter, who alone can appease the wrath of Ate."

They assembled in a court surrounded with barns and buildings for cattle. A range of beehives diffused an agreeable odor, which came mingled with perfume from the milk of some heifers that had just returned from the pasture. In the middle of the court was a well, the posts of which were clothed with mantling ivy, and crowned on the top by two branching aloes. A walnut-tree, planted by one of the ancestors of Lasthenes, covered the well with its shadow. Lasthenes, with head uncovered, and countenance turned toward the east, placed himself under this domestic tree. The reapers and other swains fell on their knees on the fresh straw around their master. In an audible voice, the father of the family pronounced this prayer, which was repeated by his children and servants:

"Lord, deign to visit this our mansion during the hours of night, and chase hence every deluding dream. We are about to put off the raiment of the day, cover us with the robe of innocence and immortality, which we lost by the disobedience of our first parents. When our bodies shall sleep in the dust, grant, O Lord, that our souls may repose with thee in heaven!"

When the evening devotions were finished, they all arose, and entered the house where the hospitable repast was prepared. A male and female servant approached, bearing vases of brass, filled with water heated by the flame. The man washed the feet of Demodocus, and the woman those of Cymodoce, and anointed them with an odoriferous oil of great value. The eldest son of Lasthenes, who was of the same age with Cymodoce, descended into a cool and subterranean recess, where all things necessary to the sustenance of man were preserved. On oaken planks attached to the walls were placed skins, filled with oil, which rivalled that of Attica in sweetness; vases of honey from Crete, less white indeed than that of Hybla, but of a finer perfume; and amphoræ, full of the wine of Chios, which the labor of years had mellowed into balm. The daughters of Lasthenes filled an urn with this generous liquor, which rejoices the heart, and gives harmony to the social board

The servants, meanwhile, doubtful whether the feast should be spread under the vine or the fig-tree, as on a day of rejoicing, came to consult their master. Lasthenes ordered them to prepare it on a shining box-wood table that stood in the hall, destined for the Agapæ. They washed it with a sponge, and covered it with willow-baskets, filled with unleavened bread, baked in the ashes. They then brought, on simple earthen platters, a frugal repast of roots, birds, and fish from lake Stymphalis, and destined for the family alone; but before the strangers was placed a kid, which had scarcely begun to browse the arbute of Mount Alipherus and the cytisus of the vale of Menelaium.

The guests were just preparing to seat themselves at table, when a servant announced to Lasthenes that an old man, mounted on an ass, in every respect resembling the spouse of the blessèd Mary, was seen advancing under the avenue of cedars. Shortly after, a man of venerable aspect, bearing under his white mantle the habit of a shepherd, approached. He was not naturally bald, but his head had formerly been shorn by the flames, and his brow was deeply marked with the scars of the martyrdom that he had suffered under Valerian. His snowy beard descended to his girdle, and he supported his steps with a staff resembling a shepherd's crook, which had been sent him by the Bishop of Jerusalem: simple presents that passed between the first Fathers of the Church, as emblems of their pastoral functions, and of the pilgrimage of man here below. It was Cyril, Bishop of Lacedæmon; left for dead by the executioners, in one of the persecutions against the Christians, he had since been raised, despite himself, to the priesthood. For a long time he concealed himself, to avoid the episcopal dignity, but his humility was unavailing; God revealed to the faithful his servant's retreat. Lasthenes and his family received him with marks of the profoundest respect. They prostrated themselves before him, kissed his sacred feet, chanted hosannas, and saluted him as the favorite of Heaven.

"By Apollo!" exclaimed Demodocus, waving his filleted branch of laurel, "this is the most venerable of mortals that my eyes have ever beheld! O thou who art full of days, what is the sceptre that thou bearest? Art thou a king? or a pontiff, consecrated to the altars of the gods? Tell me the name of the divinity thou servest, that I may offer victims to his honor."

For some time Cyril regarded Demodocus with surprise, then, with an amiable smile on his countenance, he replied:

"Sir, what you call a sceptre is the crook with which I conduct my flock; for I am no king, but a shepherd. The God who receives my sacrifices was born among shepherds, and was cradled in a manger. If you wish, I will lead you to the knowledge of him; the only victim he demands of you is the offering of your heart."

Cyril then turned toward Lasthenes: "You know," said he, "the cause that brings me hither. The public penance of our Eudorus, of which all are anxious to learn the cause, has filled the brethren with admiration. He has promised to recount me his history, and during the two days that I have come to spend with you, I hope he will satisfy my wishes."

They then took their seats at table. The priest of Homer was placed at the side of the priest of the God of Jacob. The family ranged themselves around the festive board. Demodocus filled the cup by his side, and was on the point of making a libation to the household gods of Lasthenes, when the Bishop of Lacedæmon arrested his hand, and said, with benignity:

"Our religion forbids these idolatrous ceremonies; you would not, I am assured, wish to wound our feelings."

The conversation at table was tranquil, and full of cordiality. Eudorus, during part of the repast, read some instructions selected from the Gospel and the Apostolic Epistles. Cyril, in the most affecting manner, commented on that passage in which St. Paul speaks of the duties of the married state. Cymodoce trembled, and the pearly tears trickled down her virgin cheeks; Eudorus experienced the same emotions: both masters and servants were moved by the subject. The expressive thanks of a grateful heart closed this evening repast of the primitive Christians.

They then left the house, and seated themselves on a stone

seat, at the entrance of the shrubbery: when Lasthenes had to distribute justice to his servants, this seat served him as a tribunal.

The river Alpheus, like a simple swain whom future glory awaits, poured along at the foot of the shrubbery those waves which were soon to be crowned by the palm-trees of Pisa. Descending from the grove of Venus, and passing the tomb of the nurse of Esculapius, the Ladon wound his meandering stream through these smiling meadows, and united his crystal waters with the current of the Alpheus. The deep valleys, watered by these two streams, were adorned with myrtles, alders, and sycamores. An amphitheatre of mountains bounded the circling horizon. These mountains were clothed with thick forests, the retreat of bears, stags, wild asses, and of those monstrous tortoises, from the shell of which was formed the sounding lyre. Shepherds, clothed in the skin of the wild boar, were seen conducting flocks of goats amid the rocks and pines. These agile animals were consecrated to the god of Epidaurus, because their fleeces were loaded with gum which clung to their beard and hair when they browsed the cistus on inaccessible heights.

Everything in this picture was solemn, yet smiling; simple, yet sublime. The moon in her wane appeared in the midst of the heavens, not unlike the semicircular row of lamps with which the early believers illumined the tombs of the martyrs. The family of Lasthenes contemplated in silence this solemn scene, but their minds were not occupied with the vain speculations of Greece. Cyril was secretly humbling himself before that Power who can bid the spring burst from the stony rock, and at whose presence the mountains leap like the timid lamb, or the bounding roe. He admired that wisdom which has been compared to the majestic cedar on the heights of Lebanon, and to the plane-tree on the borders of the stream. Demodocus, who wished to display the talents of his daughter, interrupted these meditations:

"Young pupil of the Muses," said he to Cymodoce, "charm these thy venerable hosts with a song. Gentle condescension makes all the charm of life ; Apollo withdraws his gifts from haughty minds. Show yourself a true descendant of Homer. The poets are the legislators of men and the preceptors of wisdom. When Agamemnon bade adieu to Clytemnestra, and departed for Troy, he left a bard behind him, to keep alive in her heart the maxims of virtue. Unfortunately she forgot both her duty and her innocence ; but it was not till Ægisthus had transported this disciple of the Muses to a desert isle."

Thus spoke Demodocus. Eudorus brought a lyre and presented it to the young Grecian ; she thanked him ; there was a confusion in her words, but they possessed a wonderful sweetness. She arose, and after a varied and graceful prelude upon the lyre, thus in melodious accents began a eulogium on the Muses :

"To you," said she, "man owes all his knowledge; you are the only consolation of his life ; you add harmony to his joys, and sigh in sympathy with his sorrows. Man has received but one gift from heaven, this is celestial poesy, and you bestowed on him the inestimable present. O daughters of Mnemosyne ! you who cherish the forests of Olympus, the vale of Tempe, and the Castalian spring, assist a virgin consecrated at your altars, give energy to her voice, and music to her lyre !"

After this invocation, Cymodoce chanted the origin of the heavens ; Jupiter saved from the fury of his father ; Minerva's birth from the brain of Jove ; Hebe, the daughter of Juno ; Venus waking into existence from the foam of the sea, and the Graces, of whom she was the mother. She sang the birth of man from the fire that Prometheus stole from heaven ; the fatal box of Pandora ; and the reproduction of human kind by Pyrrha and Deucalion. She recounted the metamorphoses of gods and men : the Heliadæ changed into poplars, and the amber of their tears borne along by the current of the Eridanus—Daphne, Baucis, Clytie, Philomela, and Atalanta— the tears of Aurora changed into dew, and the crown of Ariadne transformed into a constellation, were the subjects of her song. She forgot not you, ye fountains and ye streams, who give beauty to the flower, and cooling foliage to the grove. She named with honor the hoary Peneus, Ismenus, and Erymanthus; Menander, that winds with such gracefulness through the plains, the Scamander famed in song, the Spercheus beloved by the poets, the Eurotas cherished by the spouse of Tyndarus, and that stream which the swans of Mæonia have so often charmed with the melody of their notes.

But how could she pass over in silence the heroes whom her own Homer had celebrated in immortal verse? Enkindling with the darling theme, she sang with fresh energy the anger of Achilles, so destructive to the Grecians; Ulysses, Ajax, and Phœnix, in the tent of the friend of Patroclus; Andromache at the Scæan gate, and Priam at the knees of Hector's murderer. She recounted the anxieties of Penelope, the gratitude of Telemachus and Ulysses to Eumæus, the death of the faithful dog, the aged Laertes occupied in his garden, and weeping at the sight of the thirteen pear-trees that he had given his son.

Cymodoce could not chant the verses of her immortal ancestor without devoting some portion of her song to his memory. She represented the poor and virtuous mother of Melesigenes lighting her lamp, and plying her distaff during the hours of night, to gain by her labor some little sustenance for her son. She described Melesigenes as becoming blind, and receiving the name of Homer; how he travelled from city to city, entreating hospitality, and singing his verses under the poplars of Hyla; she recounted his long voyages, the night that he passed on the isle of Chios, and his adventure with the dogs of Glaucus; lastly, she spoke of the funeral games of the king of Eubœa, where Hesiod dared to dispute with Homer the prize of poesy; but she suppressed the judgment of the old men, who bestowed the laurel crown on the author of the "Works and Days," because his lessons were more instructive to mankind.

Cymodoce was silent; her lyre rested on her bosom, and its last sounds died away on the breeze. The priestess of the Muses stood erect, her naked feet pressed the flowery turf, and her black tresses, waved by the zephyrs of the Ladon and the

Alpheus, fell gracefully over the strings of the lyre. Enveloped in this kind of veil, and standing full in the bright beams of the moon, she appeared like some celestial apparition. Demodocus was ravished, and vainly demanded a cup to make a libation to the god of verse. Seeing that the Christians preserved a strict silence, and gave not to Cymodoce the eulogiums she seemed to merit, he at length exclaimed :

"My friends, are these songs disagreeable to you? Yet both gods and men have felt and owned the powers of harmony. Orpheus charmed the inexorable Pluto; the Parcæ, in their seats above, listen to the music of the spheres, as we learn from Pythagoras, who held commerce with the skies. Men of ancient days, and renowned for their wisdom, found music so beautiful that they gave it the name of Law. As for me, a divinity constrains me to declare, that if this priestess of the Muses were not my daughter, I should have mistaken her voice for that of the dove who carried the ambrosia to Jupiter, as he lay concealed in the forests of Crete."

"Our silence," replied Cyril, "is not caused by the songs themselves, but by the subject of these songs. The day, perhaps, may come, when these ingenious fictions of antiquity shall be considered as fictions only, and, as such, shall form the poet's song. Now, they obscure the mind, they keep it, even in this life, in a state of slavery that is disgraceful to reason; and after death, they will destroy the soul. Think not, however, that we are insensible to the charms of music. No, ours is a religion of harmony and love. Justly do you compare your amiable daughter to a dove, but the notes of this dove would be far more touching did the modesty of the subject correspond with the innocence of the voice. Fly, poor forsaken turtle, fly to the mountain where the bridegroom awaits the spouse; wing thy flight to those mystic bowers where the daughters of Jerusalem would lend a pitying ear to thy plaints!"

Cyril then turned to the son of Lasthenes. "Come, my son," said he, "show Demodocus that we do not merit the reproach that he has cast upon us. Sing us some of those fragments of the sacred books which our brethren the Apollinarises have arranged for the lyre, and prove that we are no enemies to the sweets of poetry, or to any innocent delights. God has often rendered our songs efficacious to touch the heart of the infidel."

From the branches of a neighboring willow was suspended a larger and stronger lyre than that of Cymodoce; it was a Hebrew cinnor. The strings had become loosened by the evening dew. Eudorus detached it from the tree, and, after having tuned it, appeared in the midst of the assembly like the youthful David, when he chased with the powers of his harp the evil spirit from the breast of Saul. Cymodoce seated herself by her father. Eudorus raised his eyes to the vault of heaven, spangled with innumerable stars, and began his noble hymn.

He sang the birth of Chaos; the light, made by a word; the earth, producing trees and animals; man, created after the image of God, and animated with the breath of life; Eve, taken from the side of Adam; the mingled sensations of joy and sorrow which the woman felt as she brought forth her first-born; the holocausts of Cain and Abel; the murder of the latter by his brother's hand, and the blood of man for the first time crying to heaven for vengeance.

Passing to the days of Abraham, he sang in softened cadence of the palm-tree, the well, the camel, the wild ass of the desert, the sojourning patriarch seated before his tent, the flocks of Galaad, the valleys of Lebanon, the summits of Hermon, of Horeb, and of Sinai; the rose-trees of Jericho, the cypress of Cades, the palms of Idumæa and Ephraim, of Sichem, Zion, and Solyma; the torrent of Cedron, and the sacred waters of Jordan. He forgot not the judges assembled at the gates of the city; Boaz in the midst of the reapers; Gideon threshing his corn, and receiving at the same time the visit of an angel; the aged Tobias on his way to meet his son, whose faithful dog had announced his approach; and Hagar turning away her head, that she might not witness the death of her beloved Ishmael. But before celebrating Moses amidst the shepherds of Midian, he recounted the history of Joseph discovering himself to his brethren, his tears mingling with those of Benjamin; Jacob presented to Pharaoh, and the patriarch carried after his death to the cave of Mamre, to repose with his fathers.

Here Eudorus again changed the tones of his lyre, and poured forth the canticle of the holy king Hezekiah, and that of the Israelites, when exiles by the rivers of Babylon; the voice of the weeping Ramah was heard, and the sighs of the son of Amos: " Mourn, ye gates of Jerusalem; mourn, O Zion; thy priests and thy little ones are carried away to captivity!"

He sang the numberless vanities of men: the vanity of riches, of knowledge, of glory, of earthly attachments, of transmitting a name to posterity, and, in fine, the vanity of life! He marked the false prosperity of the wicked, and preferred the just dead to the wicked living. He eulogized the honest poor and the virtuous woman.

" She seeketh wool and flax, and worketh willingly with her hands; she riseth while it is yet night, and giveth meat to her household, and a portion to her maidens; she is clothed in beauty: her children rise up and call her blessed; her husband also, and he praiseth her."

" Almighty ruler!" cried the young Christian, elevated by these grand images, " thou alone art the true Sovereign of heaven; at thy voice the sun advances from the east, like a giant, to run his course, or like the spouse from the nuptial chamber; thou callest the thunder, and in trembling haste it answers, 'I am here;' at thy presence the heavens are bowed down; the earth trembles at the breath of thy anger; and the affrighted dead start from their tombs. O God! how great art thou in all thy works! And what is man that thou shouldst be mindful of him and give him a place in thy heart! And yet is he the eternal object of thy inexhaustible goodness. O God! most mighty and most clement, thou uncreated Essence, thou Ancient of Days, glory be to thy power, and everlasting thanksgiving for thy mercies!"

Thus sang the son of Lasthenes. The grottoes of Arcadia

reëchoed this song of Zion, surprised at repeating, instead of the effeminate tones of the flute of Pan, the sonorous chords of the harp of David. Demodocus and his daughter were too much astonished to give utterance to their emotions. The eyes of their mind, accustomed to the twilight of fable, could not sustain the dazzling lustre of truth; they knew not the divine characters that Eudorus had celebrated; but they mistook him for Apollo, and would willingly have consecrated to him a golden tripod, as yet untouched by the flame, in token of their veneration. Cymodoce, especially, remembered the praise of the virtuous woman, and resolved to attempt the song on her own lyre. On the other side, the Christian family sat buried in the most profound meditation; what to the strangers was but an effort of sublime poesy, was to them full of the mysteries of eternal truth. Silence would have reigned much longer in the assembly had it not been interrupted by the applauses of the shepherds. Borne on the breezes of night the songs of Eudorus and Cymodoce had reached their ears; they had descended in crowds from the mountains to listen to the concert; they imagined that the Muses and the Sirens had renewed that contest which Alpheus had of old witnessed on his banks, in which the daughters of Achelous, vanquished by the learned sisters, had been constrained to despoil themselves of their wings.

Night was at her zenith, when the bishop of Lacedæmon solicited his host to retire. Three times he invoked the name of the Lord, and they all bent in adoration; then the Christians, giving each other the kiss of peace, retired in chaste recollection to their couches.

Demodocus was conducted by a servant to his apartment, not far distant from that of Cymodoce. Cyril, after employing some time in meditation on the word of life, threw himself to repose on a couch of reeds. But scarcely had he closed his eyes in slumber when he fell into a dream: the wounds he had formerly received in defence of his religion seemed to open afresh and with ineffable pleasure he felt his blood streaming from them in defence of the faith of Jesus Christ. At the same time he saw a young man, accompanied by a virgin, ascending from earth to the skies; their bodies shone resplendent with rays of light, and with the palm that they held in their hands they beckoned him to follow; but their heads were veiled, and he could not distinguish their countenances. He awoke, filled with a holy agitation; he thought that this mysterious dream foreboded some calamity to the Christians, and throwing himself on his knees, he prayed with abundance of tears. Often during the silence of the night, his voice was heard as he exclaimed: "O my God, if victims are still wanting, take me for the salvation of thy people!"

BOOK THIRD.

SUMMARY.

The Prayer of Cyril ascends to the Throne of the Almighty. Heaven. The Saints and Angels. Tabernacle of the Mother of the Saviour. Sanctuary of the Father and the Son. The Holy Spirit. The Trinity. The Prayer of Cyril is presented to the Most High, who receives it, but declares that the Bishop of Lacedæmon is not the Victim that must ransom the Christians. Eudorus is chosen as the Victim. Reasons for his Choice. The Celestial Forces take up Arms. Canticle of the Saints and Angels.

THE last words of Cyril ascended to the throne of the Most High. The Almighty accepted the sacrifice, but the Bishop of Lacedæmon was not the victim which God in his anger and his mercy had chosen as an expiation for the Christians.

In the centre of the created worlds, amidst innumerable stars that served it as bulwarks, avenues and pathways, floats that immense city of God, the marvels of which cannot be recounted by mortal tongue. The Eternal himself laid its twelve foundations, and encompassed it with that wall of jasper which the well-beloved disciple saw an angel measure with a golden line. Clothed in the glory of the Most High, the invisible Jerusalem appears like a bride adorned for the bridegroom. Away, monuments of earth! ye compare not with the monuments of the Holy City. The richness of material vies in it with the perfection of form. There are suspended galleries of sapphire and diamond, weakly imitated by the art of men in the gardens of Babylon; there rise triumphal arches, formed of brilliant stars; there are linked together porticos of suns, endlessly prolonged through the space of the firmament, like the columns of Palmyra in the sands of the desert. The architecture has life. The city of God is intelligent in itself. Nothing is material in the home of the Spirit · nothing is dead in the abode of the eternal existence. We are deceived by the rude words that the Muse is forced to employ: they clothe with a body that which exists but as a heavenly dream during a blissful slumber.

Delightful gardens are stretched about the radiant Jerusalem. A river flows from the throne of the Almighty, watering the celestial Eden and bearing along in its waves the pure love and the wisdom of God. The mysterious stream separates into numerous channels, which link themselves together, part, rejoin each other and separate again, and fertilize the immortal vine, the lily, like unto the bride, and the flowers that perfume the couch of the bridegroom. The tree of life rises on the hill of adoration; a little further off, the tree of knowledge throws out its deep roots and its spreading branches on every side, bearing, concealed beneath its golden foliage, the secrets of Divinity, the occult laws of Nature, the moral and intellectual realities, and the immutable principles of good and evil. This knowledge, which would intoxicate us, forms the food of the elect; for, in the dominions of sovereign wisdom, the fruit of knowledge no longer produces death. The too illustrious ancestors of the human race came often to shed tears (such as the just alone can shed) beneath the shade of this wonderful tree.

The light that illumines these happy retreats is composed of the rosy tints of the dawn, the fire of noonday and the purple of evening; yet, no star appears on the resplendent horizon, no sun ever rises or sets in the abodes where nothing has a beginning or an end; but an ineffable brightness, descending on every side like a gentle dew, maintains eternal day in this blissful eternity.

Before the portals of the holy city, and in the fields that surround it, are scattered or assembled the choirs of cherubim and seraphim, of angels and archangels, of thrones and dominions: all ministers of the works and the will of the Eternal. To these has been given all power over fire, air, earth and water; to those belongs the direction of the seasons, the winds and the tempests; to ripen the harvests, raise up the budding flower and bow the aged tree to earth. These are they who sigh in the hoary forests, who speak in the waves of the ocean, and who pour down the rivers from the heights of the mountains. Some guard the twenty thousand chariots of war, of Sabaoth and Elohim; others watch over the quivers of the Lord, his unerring thunderbolts, and his terrible coursers that bear war, pestilence, famine and death. A million of these ardent spirits rule the motions of the stars, relieving each other, in turn, in the brilliant command, like the watchful sentinels of a great army. Born of the breath of God, at different epochs, these angels are not of the same age in the generations of eternity.; an infinite number of them were created with man, to sustain his virtues, to guide his passions and to defend him against the attacks of hell.

There are also assembled for all eternity the mortals that practised virtue upon earth; patriarchs, seated beneath golden palm-trees; prophets, with brows illumined with rays of light; apostles, wearing on their hearts, the holy evangel; scholars, holding a pen in their hand; recluses, retired into celestial grottoes; martyrs, clothed in shining robes; virgins, crowned with the roses of Eden; widows, with heads adorned with flowing veils; and all those peaceful women who, clad in simple linen robes, become the comforters of our tears and the servants of our calamities.

Does it belong to weak and wretched man to speak of these supreme felicities? Fleeting and sombre shades, do we know the nature of happiness? When the soul of a faithful Christian forsakes his body, as a skilful pilot quits the fragile bark when ingulfed by the ocean, it begins alone to know true beatitude. The sovereign good of the elect is to know that this good without measure will be without limit; they are perpetually in the delightful condition of a mortal who has just done a virtuous or heroic action, of a sublime genius who gives birth to a great thought, of a man who feels the transports of lawful love or of friendship long tried by misfortune. Thus noble passions are not extinguished but only purified in the hearts of the just: brothers, spouses and friends continue to love each other; and these attachments, which exist and are concentrated in the bosom of the Divinity itself, imbibe something of the grandeur and eternity of God. Sometimes these satisfied souls repose together on the banks of the river of Wisdom and Love. The beauty and omnipotence of the Most High is their perpetual theme.

"O God!" they say, "how infinite is thy greatness! All to which thou hast given birth is comprised within the limits of time; and time, which appears to mortals as a boundless sea, is but an imperceptible drop in the ocean of thy eternity."

Sometimes the elect, the better to glorify the King of kings, survey his marvellous work: the creation, which they contemplate in the different points of the universe, presents to them a ravishing spectacle: such, if we may compare things like these with trifles, are displayed to the eyes of the traveller the magnificent plains of the Indus, the rich vales of Delhi and Cashmere, the banks covered with pearls and perfumed with amber, where the gentle waves break and lose themselves amidst blossoming cinnamon-trees. The tints of the sky, the disposition and grandeur of the spheres, varying according to motion and distance, are to the blessed spirits an inexhaustible source of admiration. They delight in knowing the laws that cause these heavy bodies to revolve with such ease in the fluid ether; they visit that peaceful moon which, during the calmness of night, shone on their prayers or their friendships here below. The humid, trembling star that precedes the steps of morning; that other planet that seems like a diamond in the golden tresses of the sun; that globe of the long year that moves only by the light of four paling torches; that land in mourning, which, exiled far from the light of day, wears a ring like an inconsolable widow; all these wandering torches of the abode of man attract the meditations of the elect. Lastly, these predestined souls fly to those worlds of which our stars are the suns, and listen to the concerts of the celestial Lyra and Cygnus. God, from whom proceeds an uninterrupted creation, suffers no rest to their holy curiosity; either on the most distant shores of space he shatters in pieces an ancient world, or else, followed by the army of angels, he carries order and beauty into the very bosom of chaos.

But the most surprising of all objects offered to the contemplation of the saints is man himself. They interest themselves still in our troubles and our pleasures; they listen to our petitions; they pray for us; they are our patrons and our counsellors; they rejoice sevenfold when a sinner returns to the flock; they tremble with pitying fear when a terrified soul is brought by the angel of death to the feet of the sovereign Judge. But if they see our passions revealed, they know not, however, by what art so many opposing elements are confounded in our breast; God, who permits the blessed to penetrate the laws of the universe, reserves to himself the marvellous secret of the heart of man.

It is in this ecstasy of admiration and love, in these transports of sublime joy, or in these emotions of tender sadness, that the elect repeat the cry of holy! holy! holy! with which the heavens are eternally ravished. The prophet-king directs the divine melody; Asaph, who gives utterance to the sorrows of David, conducts the wind-instruments; and the sons of Korah preside over the lyres, psalteries and harps that vibrate beneath the touch of the angels. The six days of creation, the rest of the Lord, the feasts of the Old and the New Testament, are celebrated in turn in the incorruptible kingdom. Then the sacred domes are crowned with a more radiant aureola; then, from the throne of God, from the very light diffused through the intellectual abodes, escape sounds of such ravishing sweetness that no mortal could hear them and live. Where wilt thou find images, O Muse, whereby to depict these angelic solemnities? Will it be in the pavilions of the princes of the East, when, seated on a throne sparkling with precious stones, the monarch assembles his gorgeous court about him? Or rather, O Muse, wilt thou recall the remembrance of the earthly Jerusalem, when Solomon dedicated to the Lord the sanctuary of the chosen people? The shrill sound of the trumpets shook the heights of Zion, the Levites chanted canticles in chorus; the elders of Israel walked with Solomon before the tables of Moses; the high-priest sacrificed victims without number; the daughters of Judah paced with measured step about the ark of the covenant; their dances, as pious as their hymns, were in praise of the Creator.

The concerts of the heavenly Jerusalem resound most of all in the pure tabernacle, where dwells in the city of God the adorable Mother of the Saviour. Surrounded by a choir of widows, virtuous women, and virgins without stain, Mary is seated upon a throne of purity. To this throne ascend all the sighs of the earth by secret paths; the Comforter of the afflicted hears the cry of our hidden griefs; she bears to the feet of her Son, upon the altar of perfumes, the offerings of our tears, and in order to render the sacrifice more efficacious, mingles with them her own. The guardian spirits of men come unceasingly to implore the Queen of Mercy in behalf of their mortal friends. The gentle seraphs of grace and charity serve her on their knees; about her are again assembled the persons of the manger, Gabriel, Anna, and Joseph; the shepherds of Bethlehem and the wise men of the East. To this spot are also seen hastening those infants who died on their entrance into the world, and who, transformed into infant angels, seem the companions of the cradled Messiah. They wave before their celestial mother censers of gold, which rise and fall with harmonious sound, emitting, in light vapor, the perfumes of love and innocence.

From the tabernacles of Mary we pass to the sanctuary of the Saviour of man, where the Son preserves by his glances the worlds that the Father has created; he is seated at a mystic table; twenty-four old men, clothed in white robes and wearing crowns of gold, are seated on thrones at his side. Near him is his living chariot, the wheels of which dart forth thunders and lightnings. When the Desire of Nations deigns to manifest himself to the elect in a near and perfect vision, the latter fall as dead before his face; but he stretches out his right hand, exclaiming:

"Rise, fear nothing, ye are the blessed of my Father; look at me; I am the First and the Last."

On the other side, the sanctuary of the Word stretches endless through spaces of fire and light. The Father dwells in the recesses of these abysses of life. The principle of all that was, is, and will be; the past, present, and future are blended in him. There are hidden the sources of truths incomprehensible to heaven itself: the liberty of man, and the prescience of God; the being that has power to fall into nullity, and the nullity that has power to be transformed into being; above all, there is accomplished the mystery of the Trinity, far from the eyes of the wondering angels. The Spirit that ascends and descends without ceasing from the Son to the Father, and from the Father to the Son, mingles with them in these impenetrable recesses. A fiery triangle then appears at the entrance of the Holy of Holies! the spheres pause in respect and terror, the hosanna of the angels is suspended, the immortal forces know not what will be the decrees of the Living Unity; they know not whether the thrice-repeated Holy be not about to change the material and divine forms in the earth and sky, or whether recalling to himself the principle of being, he will not force the worlds to return into the bosom of his eternity.

The primitive essences separate; the fiery triangle disappears; the oracle half uncloses and discovers the three Powers. Borne upon a throne of clouds, the Father holds compasses in his hand; a circle is beneath his feet; the Son, armed with a thunderbolt, is seated at his right hand; the Spirit rises at his left like a pillar of light. Jehovah makes a sign; Time, reassured, resumes his course, the confines of chaos recede, and the stars pursue their harmonious paths. The heavens then lend an attentive ear to the voice of the Almighty, about to declare some purpose concerning the universe.

At the instant that the prayer of Cyril reached the eternal throne, the three persons thus revealed themselves to the dazzled eyes of the angels. God desired to crown the virtue of Cyril, but the holy prelate was not the chosen victim designed for the new persecution; he had suffered already in the name of the Saviour, and the justice of the Almighty demanded an entire sacrifice.

At the voice of his martyr, Christ bows before the Arbiter of mankind, making everything tremble in the immensity of space that did not serve as the footstool of the Almighty. He opens his lips, whence exhales the law of clemency, to present to the Ancient of Days the sacrifice of the bishop of Lacedæmon. The tones of his voice are sweeter than the holy oil with which Solomon was anointed, purer than the fountain of Samaria, and more lovely than the blossoming olive-trees swayed by the breezes of spring in the gardens of Nazareth or the valleys of Thabor.

Implored by the Deity of gentleness and peace on behalf of the menaced Church, the mighty and terrible God makes known to the heavens his designs in respect to the faithful. He utters but a word, yet one of those words that fructify nothingness, give birth to the light, or include the destiny of empires.

This word suddenly unveils to the legions of angels, to the choirs of virgins, of saints, of kings, and of martyrs, the secret of wisdom. They see in the word of the sovereign Judge, as in a clear ray of light, the conceptions of the past, the preparations of the present, and the events of the future.

The moment has arrived in which the people, submissive to the laws of the Messiah, are about to taste without alloy the sweets of auspicious laws. Long enough has idolatry raised up her temples by the side of the altars of the Son of Man ; it is time for them to disappear from the world. Already is the new Cyrus born who shall break the last idol of the spirits of darkness, and bring the throne of the Cæsars within the shadow of the holy tabernacles. But the Christians, unconquerable by fire and sword, have grown enervated amid the delights of peace. To try them better, providence suffered them to know riches and honors : they have been unable to resist the persecution of prosperity. Before the world shall have passed from their power, it is necessary that they should be worthy of their glory; they have kindled the flames of the wrath of the Lord, they will not obtain grace in his sight till they are purified. Satan will be unchained on earth, a last trial is about to begin for the faithful: the Christians have fallen; they will be punished. He whose right it is to expiate their crimes by a voluntary sacrifice was long since marked out in the mind of the Eternal.

Such are the first counsels that the inhabitants of the heavenly abodes discover in the word of God. O Divine Word! how long and how feeble is the succession of time and of thought that human words are forced to use to interpret thee! Thou makest thy elect see and comprehend all this in a moment; while I, thy unworthy interpreter, laboriously express in the language of death the mysteries contained in the language of life! With what holy admiration, with what sublime piety, the just receive the knowledge of the sacrifice demanded, and the conditions that render it pleasing to the Most High! This victim, whose right it is to conquer hell by virtue of the sufferings and the merits of Jesus Christ—this victim, who will march at the head of a thousand others—has not been chosen from among kings and princes. Born in an obscure rank, to better imitate the Saviour of the world, this man, beloved of heaven, descends nevertheless from illustrious ancestors. In him religion will triumph over the blood of pagan heroes and idolatrous sages; in him will be honored, by a martyrdom forgotten of history, those, unknown to the world, about to suffer for the law; those humble confessors who, pronouncing in death no name save that of Jesus Christ, leave their own names unknown to mankind. The friend to all the projects of the faithful, the stay of the prince who will overthrow the altars of the false gods, this chosen Christian must have scandalized the church, then bewailed his errors like the first Apostle, to encourage his guilty brethren and lead them to repentance. Already, to give him the virtues he will need in the hour of combat, the Angel of the Lord has led him by the hand to all the nations of the earth, and he has seen the Gospel becoming established on every side. In the course of these journeys, so useful to the designs of God, the demons have tempted the new elect, not yet returned to the paths of heaven. A great and final error, by precipitating him into a grievous calamity, has forced him to quit the shades of death. His repentant tears are beginning to flow ; a recluse, inspired of God, has revealed to him a portion of his destiny. Ere long he will be worthy of the palm of martyrdom prepared for him. Such is the victim whose immolation will disarm the wrath of the Lord, and precipitate Lucifer again into the abyss.

While the saints and angels penetrate the designs announced by the word of the Most High, this same word discovers another miracle of grace to the choirs of blessed women. The heathen will also have their victim, for Christians and idolaters are to be reunited forever at the foot of Calvary. This victim will be snatched from the innocent flock of virgins, to expiate the impurity of pagan manners. The child of the fine arts that seduce weak mortals, she will humble beneath the yoke of the cross the beauty and genius of Greece. She is not immediately demanded by an irrevocable decree ; she will have neither the merit nor the glory of the first sacrifice ; but, the destined spouse of the martyr, and rescued by him from the temples of idols, she will augment the efficacy of the greater sacrifice by multiplying its trials. Yet God will not abandon his servants, without succor, to the rage of Satan : he desires his faithful legions to put on their armor, to sustain and console the persecuted Christian ; to them he confides the exercise of his mercy, reserving to himself that of his justice. Christ will sustain the confessor devoted for the salvation of mankind ; and Mary will take under her protection the timid virgin whose duty it is to heighten the sorrows, the joys and the glory of the martyr.

This doom of the Church, divulged to the elect by a single word of the Almighty, interrupts the concerts and suspends the functions of the angels ; there is silence in heaven for the space of half an hour, as at the terrible moment when John witnessed the breaking of the seventh seal of the mysterious book ·

the divine forces, smitten by the sound of the eternal word, stood still in mute astonishment. Thus, when the thunder begins to roll over numerous battalions, just ready to join battle in a furious combat, the signal is suspended, half in sunlight, half in the increasing shade, the cohorts remain motionless; banners are unfurled by no breath of air, but fall collapsed on the hand that bears them; the lighted matches smoke uselessly by the side of the mute bronze; and the warriors, furrowed by the flashes of lightning, listen in silence to the voice of the storm.

The spirit that keeps guard over the standard of the cross, causes the immobility of the armies of the Lord to cease. All heaven at once lowers its eyes to the earth; Mary, from the height of the firmament, lets fall a first look of love upon the tender victim confided to her care. The palms of the confessors blossom afresh in their hands; the impetuous squadron opens its ranks to make room for the martyr-spouses, between Felicitia and Perpetua, between the illustrious Stephen and the renowned Maccabees. Michael, the conqueror of the old dragon, makes ready his terrible lance; about him his immortal companions cover themselves with their shining cuirasses. The bucklers of diamond and gold, the quivers of the Lord, and the flaming swords are detached from the eternal portals; the chariot of Emmanuel trembles on its axles of thunder and lightning; the cherubim shake their impetuous wings and kindle the fury of their eyes. Christ again descends to the table of the old men, who offer for his benediction two robes newly whitened in the blood of the Lamb; the Almighty Father shuts himself up in the depths of his eternity, and the Holy Spirit suddenly pours forth a flood of such dazzling light that creation seems plunged again into darkness. Then the choirs of saints and angels raise the song of glory:

" Glory to God in heaven!

" Peace on earth to ye who tread the paths of gentleness and virtue. O Lamb of God that takest away the sins of the world! O miracle of purity and humility, that permittest victims sprung from nothingness to imitate thee, to devote themselves for the salvation of sinners! O servants of Christ! who are persecuted by the world, be not troubled because of the prosperity of the wicked: they suffer not, it is true, from weakness that brings them nigh unto death; they seem to be strangers to human tribulations; they wear pride about their neck like a necklace of gold; they intoxicate themselves at sacrilegious tables; they laugh and sleep as though they had done no evil: they die peacefully upon the couch they have ravished from the widow and orphan; but where do they go?

"The fool has said in his heart; 'There is no God!' Let God arise; let his enemies be scattered! He advances: the pillars of the earth are shaken; the depths of the sea and the bowels of the earth are uncovered in the presence of the Lord. A devouring flame proceeds from his mouth; he takes his flight, mounted upon the cherubim; he hurls his fiery arrows on every side. Where are the children of the wicked? Seven generations have passed away since the iniquity of their fathers, yet God comes to visit the children in his wrath; he comes at the appointed time to punish a guilty people; he comes to arouse the wicked in their palaces of cedar and aloes, and to confound the phantom of their speedy felicity.

"Happy is he who, passing in tears into the valleys, seeks God as the source of every blessing! Happy is he whose iniquities are pardoned, and who finds glory in repentance! Happy is he who builds in silence the temple of his good works, like that of Solomon, in which neither the axe nor the hammer was heard while the architect was building the house of the Lord! All ye who eat on earth the bread of tears, repeat the holy chorus to the praise of the Most High:

"Glory to God in heaven!"

BOOK FOURTH.

SUMMARY.

Cyril. The Christian Family. Demodocus and Cymodoce meet again on an Island at the confluence of the Ladon and Alpheus, to hear the Son of Lasthenes recount his Adventures. Commencement of the Recital of Eudorus. Origin of the family of Lasthenes. It opposes the Romans at the time of the Invasion of Greece. The eldest of Lasthenes' Family is obliged to repair as a Hostage to Rome. The Family of Lasthenes embraces Christianity. Childhood of Eudorus. He sets out at the age of sixteen for Rome as a Substitute for his Father. The Tempest. Description of the Archipelago. Arrival of Eudorus in Italy. Description of Rome. Eudorus contracts an intimate Friendship with Jerome, Augustine, and Prince Constantine, the son of Constantius. Characters of Jerome, Augustine, and Constantine. Eudorus is presented at Court. Diocletian. Galerius. Court of Diocletian. The Sophist, Hierocles, Proconsul of Achaia and favorite of Galerius. Enmity of Eudorus and Hierocles. Eudorus falls into the irregularities of Youth, and forgets his Religion. Marcellinus, Bishop of Rome. He threatens Eudorus with Excommunication if he does not return to the bosom of the Church. Excommunication hurled against Eudorus. Amphitheatre of Titus. Forebodings.

CONCEALED in an obscure valley, amidst the woods of Arcadia, Eudorus and Cymodoce knew not that at this moment both the saints and angels had their eyes fixed upon them, and that the Almighty himself was interested in their destiny; thus the shepherds of Canaan were visited by the God of Nachor, in the midst of their flocks, which were grazing at the west of Bethel.

The swallow twittering on the roof had no sooner announced to Lasthenes the return of day, than he hastened to quit his couch. He wrapped himself in a mantle, spun by his industrious spouse, and lined with wool, so grateful to old men, and preceded by two dogs of Laconia, his faithful guard, advanced toward the place where the bishop of Lacedæmon had reposed;

but he perceived the holy prelate kneeling in the open air, and offering his matin devotions to heaven. The dogs of Lasthenes ran toward Cyril, and, bending their heads with a caressing air, seemed to bring him the homage and respect of their master. The two venerable Christians saluted each other with gravity, and, during their walk along the declivity of the mountain, discoursed on topics of ancient wisdom : thus did the Arcadian Evander conduct Anchises to the forests of Pheneus, when Priam, still prosperous, came to seek his sister Hesione at Salamis; or thus did the same Evander, exiled to the banks of the Tiber, receive the son of his former host, when fortune had overwhelmed with calamities the monarch of Ilion.

Shortly after Demodocus joined them; he was followed by Cymodoce, more beautiful than the new-born day, that was then gilding the eastern mountains.

On the side of the hill that overlooked the mansion of Lasthenes there was a grotto, the favorite retreat of the sparrow and the dove : it was here, in imitation of the solitaries of the Thebais, that Eudorus would retire, and pour forth in secret the tears of penitence. Suspended on the walls of the grotto was a crucifix, and at its foot lay some scattered armor, an honorary crown of oak, and other ornaments, the reward of his valor or his skill. Eudorus began to perceive a soft yet troubled emotion stealing over his heart—a feeling he had but too sensibly experienced before. Alarmed at the new dangers that threatened him, he had passed the whole night in supplication to heaven. When Aurora had dispersed the shadows of night, he washed away in the pure stream every trace of his tears, assumed his usual air of cheerfulness, and preparing to quit the grotto, he sought by the simplicity of his attire to diminish the effect of his personal grace and beauty : he bound on his feet buskins formed of the wild goat's skin, concealed his hair-shirt under the hunter's tunic, and bound round his loins the spoils of a white hind: a cruel herdsman had killed with his sling this queen of the woods, as she was drinking with her fawn on the banks of the Achelous. In his left hand he took two ashen javelins; from his right was suspended a chaplet of coral beads, such as the virgin martyrs were wont to wear when going to death : innocent chaplets, ye served then to count the numbers of prayers that artless hearts repeated to the Lord! Armed at once against the beasts of the forests, and the spirits of darkness, Eudorus descended from the summit of the rocks ; he resembled a Christian soldier of the Theban legion, who returns to the camp after the watches of the night. After passing the waters of the torrent, he came and joined the little troop who awaited him at the bottom of the grove. He approached Cyril, pressed the hem of his mantle to his lips, and bent before him to receive his paternal benediction ; then with downcast looks he saluted Demodocus and his daughter. All the roses of the morn were glowing on the cheek of the youthful daughter of Homer. Shortly after, Sephora and her three daughters came modestly from the gynæceum, when the bishop of Lacedæmon thus addressed the son of Lasthenes :

"Eudorus, you are an object of curiosity to all Christian Greece. Who has not heard of your misfortunes, and of your repentance ? I am persuaded that these your guests from Messenia could not hear without interest the recital of your adventures."

"Venerable sage," cried Demodocus, "whose habit announces you to be a shepherd of men, you speak not a word that is not dictated by Minerva. Yes, like Homer, my divine ancestor, whole years could I willingly spend in uttering or in listening to pleasing narratives. Can anything be more agreeable than the words of a man who has travelled much, and who, seated at the table of his host while the rain and the winds are raving without, recounts, sheltered from all danger, the crosses of his life ? Whilst I quaff the cup of Hercules, I love to feel my eyes moistened by sorrow ; that libation is rendered more sacred which is mingled with our tears ; the story of the evils with which Jupiter afflicts the children of men, tempers the wanton revelry of the board, and brings the gods to our remembrance. And you yourself, my dear Eudorus, will find some pleasure in recalling the storms that you endured with courage; the mariner returned to his paternal fields, feels a secret charm, as he contemplates the rudder and the oars suspended peacefully over the hearth during the terrors of winter."

The Ladon and the Alpheus united their streams at the foot of the grove, and formed an island, which seemed the offspring of their watery union. It was planted with those aged trees, which the people of Arcadia regard as their ancestors. There it was that Alcimedon cut the beech wood with which he made such beautiful cups for the shepherds; there too was seen the fountain of Arethusa and the laurel which held Daphne concealed within its bark. They resolved to adjourn to this solitary spot, that Eudorus might meet with no interruption during his recital. The servants of Lasthenes detached from the banks of the Alpheus a long boat, formed from the trunk of a single pine, and the family and strangers floated down with the current of the river. Demodocus, remarking the skill of his conductors, said in a sorrowful tone:

"Arcadians, there was a time when the Atridæ were obliged to lend you vessels to go to the siege of Troy, and when you mistook the oars of Ulysses for the van of Ceres; but now how great the contrast! you trust yourselves with fearless indifference to the terrors of the deep. Alas! the son of Saturn bids mankind feel a charm even in danger itself, and embrace it with strange enthusiasm!"

They soon reached the eastern point of the island, where two half-ruined altars were erected; the one on the banks of the Alpheus, was consecrated to Tempest; the other by the side of the Ladon, was dedicated to Tranquillity. Between these two altars the fountain of Arethusa rose from the earth, and poured her waves into the bosom of the Alpheus, who received her with amorous caresses. The whole party, impatient to hear the recital of Eudorus, stopped at this place, and seated themselves under the towering poplars that were just tinged with the blushes of morning. After imploring the succor of heaven, the young Christian thus commenced his narrative:

"My friends, I must beg leave for a moment to trespass on your patience with an account of my birth, because it is from my birth that I date the origin of my misfortunes. I am descended by my mother's side from that pious woman of Megara, who interred by stealth the bones of Phocion under her own hearth, while she cried with pious emotion, 'Keep inviolate, O sacred hearth, the remains of a good man!'

"My paternal ancestor was Philopœmen. You know that he dared singly to oppose the Romans, when that free nation ravished liberty from Greece. He fell in this noble enterprise. But what are misfortunes, what is death itself, if our name but descend to posterity; and if two thousand years hence its sound should cause one generous heart to throb with emotion?

"Our expiring country, to be consistent in her ingratitude, forced the last of her great men to die by poison. With mournful and impressive pomp, the young Polybius[1] afterward conveyed the remains of Philopœmen from Messene to Megalopolis. One might have said that the urn, surrounded by wreaths of flowers, enclosed the ashes of all Greece. From this time our natal earth, like an exhausted soil, ceased to produce heroes and statesmen. Her immortal name remains, but she resembles that statue of Themistocles which the Athenians of our days have deprived of its head and substituted that of a slave.

"The chief of the Achaians did not long repose peaceably in his tomb: some years after his death, he was accused of having been an enemy to Rome, and a criminal process was entered against him before the proconsul Mummius, the destroyer of Corinth. Polybius, under the protection of Scipio Nasica, succeeded in saving the statues of Philopœmen from destruction; but this sacrilegious information awakened the jealousy of the Romans against the descendants of the last of the Greeks; they required that for the future the eldest sons of our family, as soon as they had attained their sixteenth year,

---

[1] The historian.

should be sent to Rome, to remain as hostages in the hands of the senate.

"Bowed down by misfortune, and forever deprived of their chief, my family abandoned Megalopolis, and fled for concealment, sometimes amidst these mountains, sometimes to another family estate that we possessed at the foot of Taygetus, on the borders of the Messenian gulf. Shortly after, Paul, the sublime apostle of the Gentiles, brought to Corinth the remedy for all misfortune. When the light of Christianity burst forth upon the Roman empire, every place was filled with slaves, or with princes humbled and degraded; the whole world demanded hope and consolation.

"Disposed to wisdom by hard lessons of adversity, by the simplicity of Arcadian manners, my family was the first in Greece to embrace the law of Jesus Christ. Submissive to his divine yoke, I passed the days of my infancy on the banks of Alpheus, and among the woods of Taygetus. Overshadowed by the fostering wing of religion, my soul, like a delicate flower, was hindered from expanding before its time; thus was the happy ignorance of my younger years prolonged, and the innocence of childhood itself seemed to be rendered more innocent.

"The moment of my exile arrived. I was the eldest of my family, and had attained my sixteenth year; we were dwelling at this time on our estates in Messenia. My father, whose place I was about to take, had by a particular favor obtained permission to return to Greece before my departure: he embraced me, and gave me his advice and his blessing. My mother conducted me to the port of Pheræ, and accompanied me to the vessel itself. As the seamen spread their sails and prepared to depart, she raised her hands to heaven and offered her vows for my welfare with all a parent's fervency. Her heart sunk within her at the thought of these stormy seas, and that still more stormy ocean of the world upon which I was embarking, a voyager, young and without experience. Already was the vessel gaining the open sea, yet Sephora still remained to encourage my youth, as the dove encourages her new-fledged offspring to fly, when for the first time it quits the maternal nest. But at last it was necessary to make a final effort; and tearing herself from my embraces, she descended into the skiff that awaited her, fastened to the side of our trireme. For a long time she made signs to me as the boat approached the shore: I wept aloud; and when I could no longer distinguish this tenderest of mothers, my eyes sought to discover the roof under which I had been nurtured, and the lofty trees that surrounded my paternal mansion.

"Our voyage was long; scarcely had we passed the isle of Theganusa, when an impetuous western gale drove us far to the eastern regions, even to the entrance of the Hellespont. After losing sight of every shore, and being tossed for seven long days by the tempest, we had the good fortune to find refuge at the mouth of the Simois, within view of the tomb of Achilles. When the rage of the tempest was appeased, we strove to regain our western course, but the constant breezes that the celestial Aries brings from the shores of Hesperia long repelled our sails: sometimes we were thrown on the coast of Elis, at others driven into the narrow seas between Thrace and Thessaly. We traversed the Grecian Archipelago, where the beauty of the varied shores, the brilliancy of the sky, the softness of the air, and the breezes wafting perfumes, quite ravished the senses, and seemed to vie with the tender and sublime recollections that the scene inspired. Every promontory, as it successively met our view, was marked with a temple or a tomb. We touched at different ports; we admired the numerous cities, some of which bore the name of a favorite flower, such as the rose, the violet, or hyacinth; and which, overflowing with people like fruitful seeds, seemed to spread and blossom in the sunshine on the shore of the sea. Though as yet but a boy, my imagination was lively, and my heart susceptible of tender and lasting impressions. There was on board our vessel a Greek, fond of his country even to enthusiasm, as are all the Greeks. He named to me the places and objects that we passed.

"'The oaks you see yonder,' said he, 'once followed the

magical lyre of Orpheus; that mountain whose shadows extend so far, was once destined for a statue to Alexander; this other mountain is Olympus, and its valley the vale of Tempe; this is Delos, which once floated in the midst of the waters; that is Naxos, where Ariadne was left desolate; Cecrops first landed on yonder shore; Plato taught on the point of that cape; Demosthenes harangued these waves; Phryne was bathing in these waters when she was taken for Venus. And this country of gods, of arts, and beauty,' cried the Athenian, with tears of anguish and resentment, 'this my country is now become a prey to barbarians!'

"His despair redoubled as we crossed the gulf of Megara. In front was Ægina, to the right the Piræus, and to the left Corinth. These cities, once so flourishing, now presented nothing to the eye but heaps of ruins. The sailors themselves seemed touched by this spectacle. They ran in a crowd upon deck, and for a long time gazed in silent reverie upon the melancholy scene; perhaps each one drew from the spectacle a secret consolation, as he reflected how far our personal evils sink into insignificance when compared with those calamities that strike whole nations, and which had thus humbled in the dust the cities now before their eyes, and left them but the skeletons of their former magnificence.

"This lesson seemed above my reason, yet I understood it; but the other young men who surrounded me felt it not; they were quite insensible. Whence arose this difference? From our religion: they were pagans; I was a Christian. Paganism develops the passions too prematurely, and thus retards the progress of reason; Christianity, on the contrary, while it prolongs the infancy of the heart, accelerates the manhood of the mind. From the first dawn of reason, it instils serious thoughts; even in the swaddling clothes it respects the dignity of man; it treats us even in the cradle as serious and sublime beings, since it acknowledges an angel in the babe that the mother fondles at her breast. My young companions had heard nothing but of the metamorphoses of Jupiter, and they drew no instruction from the ruins before their eyes: as for me, I had already been seated with the prophets on the ruins of desolate cities, and had learnt from Babylon what judgment to form of Corinth.

"And here I ought to notice the first temptation that seduced me into the paths of ruin; and, as it generally happens, the evil by which I was ensnared had nothing in appearance but what was innocent and harmless. Whilst we were meditating on the revolutions of empires, we saw a sacred procession advance on a sudden from the midst of the ruins. Thou smiling genius of Greece! what misfortunes can depress thee, what lessons, however severe, can afford thee instruction! This was a deputation of Athenians to the festival at Delos. The festal vessel, covered with flowers and ribbons, was ornamented with statues of the gods; the white sails, tinged with the purple rays of Aurora, swelled to the breath of the zephyrs, and the gilded oars cleft the crystal waves. The votaries bending over the waters poured out perfumes and libations, the virgins executed on the prow of the vessel the dance of the misfortunes of Latona, whilst the youths chanted verses from Pindar and Simonides. My imagination was enchanted by this spectacle, which quickly glided away like a fleecy cloud of the morn, or the chariot of some deity borne along on the wings of the wind. It was thus for the first time that I witnessed a pagan ceremony without horror.

"At length we again discerned the mountains of Peloponnesus, and again I saluted my native land from afar. It was not long before the coast of Italy began to swell above the bosom of the waves. On landing at Brundusium, I felt a variety of unknown emotions. As I set my foot upon that earth, whence those decrees were issued that govern the world, I was struck with an appearance of grandeur to which I had been a stranger. To the elegant edifices of Greece, succeeded monuments of more ponderous magnificence, and marked with the stamp of a different genius. The farther I advanced on the Appian way, the more my surprise increased. This road, paved with large masses of rock, seems formed to resist the passage of the human race; through the mountains of Apulia, along the gulf of Naples, through the country of Anxur, of Alba, and the Roman Campagna, it presents an avenue of more than three hundred miles in length, lined with temples, palaces, and tombs, and terminating at the eternal city, which is worthy to be the metropolis of the Universe. At the sight of so many prodigies I fell into a sort of delirium, which I could neither resist nor comprehend.

"It was in vain that the friends to whose care my father had intrusted me, sought to arouse me from this enchantment. I wandered from the Forum to the Capitol, from the Carinæ to the Campus Martius; I ran from the theatre of Germanicus to the mole of Adrian, and from the circus of Nero, to the Pantheon of Agrippa; but while with a dangerous curiosity I visited every other place, the humble church of the Christians was forgotten.

"I was never weary of beholding the crowded bustle of a people composed of all the nations upon earth, nor of witnessing the military operations of an army, made up of Romans, Gauls, Germans, Greeks, and Africans; all distinguished by the arms and habits of their respective countries. Here an aged Sabine was passing in his sandals of birch-bark, close to the senator in his robes of purple; there the litter of a consul was intercepted by the chariot of a courtesan; the large oxen of Clitumnus were drawing to the Forum wagons laden with provisions; the hunting equipage of a Roman gentleman obstructed the Sacred Way; the priest was hastening to his duties in the temple, and the rhetorician to his school.

How often did I visit the baths adorned with libraries, and the palaces, some already mouldering to decay, and others half demolished to serve for the construction of new edifices. The vast outlines of Roman architecture, that of themselves formed a magnificent horizon; those aqueducts, which like rays verging to a centre, conveyed the waters over triumphal arches to a kingly people; the ceaseless murmur of the fountains; that multitude of statues which resembled a motionless race in the midst of a bustling people; those monuments of every age and every country, the work of kings, of consuls, and of Cæsars; those obelisks conveyed from Egypt, and tombs ravished from Greece; that indescribable beauty in the light, the vapor and the outlines of the mountains; the violence even of the current of the Tiber; the herds of half-savage mares that came to drink in its stream; that Campagna which the citizen of Rome now disdains to cultivate, reserving to himself the right of declaring each year to the enslaved nations what part of the earth shall have the honor of nourishing him; what shall I say, in fine?—everything at Rome bears the mark of dominion and of duration. I have seen the map of the Eternal City traced on the massive marble of the Capitol, that even its image might never be effaced.

"Oh, how well is that religion acquainted with the human heart, which seeks to preserve the peace of the soul, and knows how to set bounds to our curiosity, as well as to the rest of our earthly affections! That vivacity of imagination to whose influence I yielded myself captive, was the first cause of my ruin. When at last I returned to the ordinary course of my occupations, I felt that I had lost my taste for serious things, and I envied the lot of the pagan youth, who could abandon themselves without remorse to all the pleasures of their age.

"The rhetorician, Eumenes, filled at that time the chair of eloquence at Rome, which he has since transported into Gaul. He had studied, in his early years, under the son of the most celebrated disciple of Quintilian, and his school was frequented by all the young men of eminence. I, too, attended the lectures of this celebrated master, nor was it long before I formed an intimacy with the companions of my studies. There were three who became attached to me with warm and sincere friendship. These were Augustine, Jerome, and the Prince Constantine, son of Cæsar Constantius.

"Jerome, the descendant of a noble family of Pannonia, gave early proofs at once of talents the most brilliant, and of passions the most impetuous. His strong imagination did not leave him a moment's repose. The facility with which he passed from an excess of study to that of pleasure, was inconceivable. Irascible, restless, pardoning with difficulty an affront, of a genius wild and sublime, he seemed destined to become an example either of the greatest disorders, or of the severest virtues: to this ardent spirit, no choice was left between Rome and the desert.

"A hamlet in the proconsulate of Carthage was the birthplace of my second friend. Augustine was the most amiable of men. His temper was hasty, like that of Jerome, yet tempered by a natural turn for contemplation, which breathed a charm and sweetness over his whole character: if there was any point in which my young friend lay open to reproach, it was, that he suffered the ardor of his genius to lead him astray; the extreme tenderness of his feelings, also, hurried him sometimes into excess. He had always at hand a multitude of happy expressions, and of profound thoughts, clothed in the most brilliant imagery. Born under an African sun, he found in women, like Jerome, the snare of his virtue, and the source of his errors. But sensible, even to enthusiasm, of the charms of eloquence, there needs, perhaps, but some inspired orator to reclaim him to the true religion: if ever Augustine should enter the bosom of the church, he will become the Plato of the Christians.

"Constantine, son of an illustrious Cæsar, announced all the qualities of a great man. Joined to force of mind, he possessed all those exterior accomplishments so useful to princes, and which bestow an additional grace even upon noble actions; Helen, his mother, had the happiness to be born in the religion of Jesus; and Constantine, after the example of his father, showed a secret inclination toward this divine law. Though blest with an extreme gentleness of disposition, yet those traits burst forth that point out the hero; and there was something mysterious in his character, with which heaven always marks those who are destined to change the face of the world. Happy will he be, if he escapes those dreadful sallies of passion, so terrible in characters habitually moderate ! How much are those princes to be pitied who are so promptly obeyed ! What indulgence ought we not to show them ! When we witness the terrible effects of their anger, let us always have the charity to suppose that this is the first offence, and that God, as a lesson for the government of their passions, allows them not a moment between the thought and the execution of the deed.

"Such were the three friends with whom I passed my days at Rome. Constantine was like myself, a kind of hostage in the hands of Diocletian. This uniformity of situation, still more than that of age, prepossessed the young prince in my favor: nothing can render two minds more susceptible of friendship than a resemblance in their future lot, especially if that lot be unfortunate. Constantine wished to promote my interest, and introduced me to the court.

"When I arrived at Rome, the sovereign power was no longer exclusively in the hands of Diocletian, but was divided as at present; the emperor had associated in the empire Maximianus, under the title of Augustus; and Galerius and Constantinus, under that of Cæsar. Yet, though the world was divided between four chiefs, it acknowledged but one master.

"And here, my friends, I must give you a description of that court, from which you have the happiness to live retired. May you never hear the roaring of its tempests ! May your days glide away in obscurity like the rivers of this vale ! But, alas, a life of obscurity does not always save us from the power of princes. The whirlwind which tears up the rock, bears away also the grain of sand in its rage; the king with his sceptre often strikes off an unknown head. Since nothing can shield us from the terrors that surround the throne, it is wise and useful to know the hand that may send them to afflict us.

"Diocletian, who was formerly called Diocles, first saw the light at Dioclea, a small town of Dalmatia. In his youth he bore arms under Probus, and became a skilful general. Under

Carinus and Numerianus, he held the important office of prefect of the palace, and afterward became the successor of Numerianus, whose death he had avenged.

"As soon as the legions of the East had elevated Diocletian to the empire, he marched against Carinus, the brother of Numerianus, who reigned in the West: he gained the victory over him, and by the submission of his rival, remained sole master of the world.

"Diocletian possesses eminent qualities. His mind is vast, powerful, and enterprising; but his character is too often weak, and but ill corresponds with the vigor of his genius: this defect is discernible in all his actions, and to this source we may trace all the contradictions which mark his conduct. Sometimes he assumes the prince, is full of firmness, wisdom and courage, fearless of death, conscious of the dignity of his situation, and dares exert his authority, and force Galerius to follow on foot the imperial car like the meanest of his soldiers: at other times he sinks into the coward, trembles before this same Galerius, hesitates irresolute between a thousand projects, abandons himself to superstitions the most humiliating, and endeavors to arm himself against the terrors of the tomb, by impiously assuming the titles of God and Eternal. Regular in his habits, patient in enterprise, and with a mind guarded against the illusions of pleasure, yet a skeptic in virtue, and expecting nothing from the gratitude of mankind, perhaps this chief of the empire may one day be seen to strip himself of the purple, and retire in disgust from the society of men, in order to show the world that Diocletian could descend from the throne with the same ease that he first mounted it.

"Whether through weakness, necessity, or prudential motives, Diocletian has condescended to share the sceptre with Maximianus, Constantius and Galerius. By a policy of which he may hereafter repent, he has taken care that these princes should be his inferiors, and that they should merely serve as a foil to his own merit. Constantius was the only one that gave him any umbrage—he was remarkable for his virtues. He sent him to a distance from his court, to the furthest extremities of Gaul; but Galerius he retained near his person. I shall not speak of Maximianus Augustus, a brave but an ignorant and unpolished prince, without influence at court. I shall pass on to Galerius.

"Born in a hut in Dacia, this youthful barbarian cherished, under his herdsman's garb, the most unbounded ambition. It is the misfortune of a state, that when the laws have not fixed the succession to power, every heart is big with vast desires; every person claims the privilege of canvassing for the empire; and as ambition does not always presuppose talent, for one man of genius who elevates himself you have twenty tyrants of inferior abilities who harass the world.

"Galerius seems to carry on his brow the impression or rather the blight of his vices: he is of gigantic stature, and his voice and looks are full of terror. The pale descendants of the Romans, in revenge for the terrors with which this Cæsar inspires them, have given him the surname of Armentarius. Like a man who has been famished half his life, Galerius passes his days at the table, and prolongs even during the darkness of night his base and brutal orgies. In the midst of these scenes of pompous magnificence, he makes every effort to disguise the baseness of his origin under the pretension of his splendor, but the more closely he wraps himself in the folds of the robe of the Cæsars, the more plainly is visible the sagum of the herdsman.

"Added to an insatiable thirst for power, and a spirit of unrelenting cruelty, Galerius is cursed with another disposition no less calculated to disturb the empire: this is his mortal hatred toward the Christians. The mother of this Cæsar, a woman of a gross and superstitious mind, was accustomed in her native hamlet to offer sacrifices to her mountain divinities. Indignant that the disciples of the Gospel refused to share in her idolatry, she inspired her son with the aversion that she felt toward the faithful. Galerius has already incited the weak and barbarous Maximianus to persecute the church; but he has not yet been able to vanquish the sage moderation of the emperor. Diocletian upon the whole is well affected toward us; he knows that at present we compose the most considerable part of his army; he places confidence in our word when once pledged; he has even stationed us round his person: Dorotheus, the first officer of his palace, is a Christian remarkable for his virtues. You will soon see that the empress Prisca, and her daughter the princess Valeria, have secretly embraced the law of Christ. Filled with the most lively gratitude for the confidence that Diocletian has reposed in them, the faithful form around him a barrier that is almost impregnable. Galerius is aware of this, and it inflames his anger the more; this ungrateful wretch envies the power of his master, and sees that the only way to attain his end, will be to destroy the adorers of the true God.

"Such are the two princes, who like the geniuses of good and evil, are destined to spread happiness or desolation over the empire, according as either party shall succeed, and the fate of war determine. But whence comes it that Diocletian, so well versed in the knowledge of mankind, has conferred on such a character the dignity of Cæsar? This is what we cannot explain, except it be by the decrees of that Providence who renders vain the counsels of princes, and confounds the wisdom of nations.

"Happy would it have been for Galerius, if, enclosed in the precincts of a camp, he had been familiarized with the voice of glory and the sounds of war and danger alone! In the midst of arms he would not have fallen a prey to those base courtiers, who, dead to a sense of shame, make it their study to awaken vice and extinguish virtue. He would not have abandoned himself to the counsels of a perfidious favorite, who is perpetually inciting him to evil. This favorite, sirs, belongs to a class of men, with whom I must make you acquainted, because they will necessarily influence either the events of the age, or the lot of the Christians.

"Rome, grown old in depravity, fosters in her bosom a sect of sophists, the chief among whom are Porphyry, Jamblichus, Libanius, and Maximus, whose manners and opinions would be a fit object for laughter if our follies were not too often the origin of our crimes. These disciples of a vain philosophy attack the Christians, boast of a love for retirement, extol their moderation, and yet live at the feet of the great, and entreat them for gold. Some are seriously occupied with building a city, peopled wholly with philosophers, who, submissive to the laws of Plato, will pass their days in tranquillity like friends and brothers; others are deeply buried in those secrets of nature which they suppose to lie hid in Egyptian symbols; some see everything in thought; others seek everything in matter; still others advocate a republic in the bosom of monarchy : they pretend that it is necessary to overturn society in order to remodel it on a new plan; others, in imitation of the faithful, wish to teach a system of morals to the people : they assemble a crowd in the temples, or at the corners of the streets, and there vend from their rostrums a system of virtue which requires the support neither of works nor of morals. Divided on those points which regard the welfare, united in those which aggravate the evils, of mankind; inflated with vanity, persuaded of the sublimity of their own genius, and boldly superior to vulgar doctrines, there is no folly, however contemptible, of which these sophists are not guilty, no system, however monstrous, which they do not bring forward and support. Hierocles marches at their head, and is worthy, in fact, to lead such a battalion.

"You know too well, my friends, that this favorite of Galerius is now governor of Achaia; he is one of those men whom a combination of fortunate events introduces to the councils of the great, and who becomes useful to them by a kind of talent for common affairs, and by a facility but little desirable, of talking on every subject. Hierocles is of Greek extraction, and is suspected of having been a Christian in his youth; but the pride of human learning having corrupted his mind, he has joined himself to the sect of philosophers. No traces of the religion in which he was brought up are now visible, except it be a kind of delirious rage, into which the mere mention of the God he has quitted throws him. He has assumed the hypocritical language, and all the affected manners, of the school of false wisdom. The words, liberty, virtue, science, the progress of intelligence, the good of mankind, are perpetually in his mouth; but this Brutus is a mercenary courtier; this Cato is the slave of passions the most shameful; this apostle of toleration is the most intolerant of men, and this worshipper of humanity the most bloody minded of persecutors. Constantine hates him; Diocletian fears and despises him; but he has gained the intimate confidence of Galerius; the only man that rivals him in the favor of this prince is Publius, prefect of Rome. Hierocles endeavors to poison the mind of the unhappy Cæsar. He presents to the world the hideous spectacle of a pretended sage, who is corrupting, under the name of enlightenment, a man who reigns over mankind.

"Jerome, Augustine, and myself, had met Hierocles at the school of Eumenes. His sententious and positive tone, and his air of importance and pride, rendered him odious to our simplicity and frankness. His very person appeared to repel affection and confidence: his narrow and contracted brow seemed to announce a spirit of obstinacy and of system; his eyes, wild and wandering, resembled those of some wild beast, and his look was at once timid and malignant; his lips are ever half opened by a false and cruel smile; his hair, thinly scattered, and hanging in loose disorder, seems of a different species from that which forms the ornament of youth, and, as it were, the crown of old age. The whole character of the sophist breathes something cynical and disgusting; his ignoble hands seem but ill suited to bear the weapons of a soldier, but well fitted to guide the pen of the atheist, or the steel of the executioner.

"Such is the deformity of man, when left alone with his body, after renouncing his soul.

"An affront which I had received from Hierocles, and which I repelled in such a manner as to cover him with confusion in the eyes of the whole court, excited an implacable hatred toward me in his heart. I had gained the good will of Diocletian, and the friendship of the son of Constantius; this, too, was unpardonable. His self-love was wounded, and his envy excited; and these passions left him not a moment's repose, till an opportunity to ruin me presented itself, and this he was not long in finding.

"Alas, how little was I worthy of envy! Three years, passed at Rome in all the disorders of youth, had sufficed to make me almost entirely forget my religion. I had even fallen into that state of indifference, from which it is so difficult to recover, and which leaves less resource than a life of crime. Yet would the letters of Sephora, and the remonstrances of my father and friends, often trouble my false security.

"Among the men who preserved a faithful attachment to Lasthenes, was Marcellinus, bishop of Rome, and chief of the universal church. He dwelt in the cemetery of the Christians, in a desert place on the other side of the Tiber, where stood the tombs of St. Peter and St. Paul. His dwelling, composed of two cells, was constructed against the chapel wall of the cemetery. A small bell, suspended at the entrance of this peaceful retreat, announced to him the arrival either of the living or the dead. At his door, which he himself opened to travellers, lay the staff and sandals of the bishops who came to him from all parts of the earth, to render an account of the flock of Christ under their charge. Hither came Paphnucius of the Upper Thebais, who by his word chased away the demons; Spiridion, of the isle of Cyprus, who tended his flock and wrought miracles; James of Nisibis, who received the gift of prophecy; Hosius, confessor of Cordova; Archelaus of Carrha, who confounded Manes; John, who spread through Persia the light of the Gospel; Frumentius, who founded the church of Æthiopia; Theophilus, who had returned from his mission to the Indies; and that Christian slave who, in her captivity, converted the whole nation of the Iberians. Marcellinus's chamber of council was a walk embowered with venerable yews, which threw a holy gloom over the cemetery. Under these he walked, surrounded by the bishops, and conferred with them about the necessities of the Church. To crush the heresies of Donatus, of Novatianus, and of Arius; to publish canons, to assemble councils, to build hospitals, to ransom slaves, to succor the poor, to relieve orphans and strangers, to send apostles to barbarous nations: such were the objects of their conference, and of their pastoral solicitude. Often, during the silence of night, would Marcellinus, for the salvation of all, descend alone into the tombs of the holy apostles, and there, prostrate over their relics, pour forth his ardent prayers for mankind, till the first rays of morning called him from his devotions. Then uncovering his venerable head, and placing his simple tiara on the ground, would this sovereign pontiff, unnoticed and unknown, stretch forth his suppliant hands, and call down a blessing upon the city and the world.

"When I passed from the court of Diocletian, to that of the Christians, I could not help being struck with astonishment at one thing. In the midst of this evangelical poverty, I found all that ancient politeness, that cheerfulness tempered with gravity, that flow of language at once simple and dignified, that varied instruction, good taste, and solid judgment, which strongly called to remembrance the best days of Augustus and Mæcenas. It seemed as if this obscure retreat had been destined by heaven to prove the cradle of another Rome, and the last asylum of arts, of letters, and of civilization.

"Marcellinus left no means unemployed to bring me back to God. Sometimes at sunset would he conduct me to the banks of the Tiber, or to the gardens of Sallust. He discoursed with me on religion, and with all the tenderness of a father endeavored to make me feel the danger of my errors. But the illusions of my youth took from me the love of truth. Far from profiting by these salutary walks, I secretly sighed for the plane-trees of Fronto, the portico of Pompey or that of Livia, adorned with ancient pictures: and to my eternal confusion, be it said, I regretted the temples of Isis and Cybele, the feasts of Adonis, the circus, and the theatres, places whence modesty had long since fled at the accents of the muse of Ovid. After having tried the force of admonition in vain, Marcellinus employed measures more severe. 'I shall be compelled,' would he say to me, 'I shall be compelled to separate you from the communion of the faithful, if you thus continue to dishonor the religion of Jesus Christ, by absenting yourself from its mysteries.'

"I refused to listen any longer to his counsels; I laughed at his menaces; my life became an object of public scandal, and at last the pontiff was obliged to launch against me the thunders of the Church.

"Upon hearing it I went to the abode of Marcellinus, and on gaining admission, I saw the pontiff standing at the entrance of the chapel. In his hand he held the terrible volume, an image of that book, whose sevenfold seal the Lamb alone could open. The deacons, the priests, and the bishops were ranged motionless and in silence on the surrounding tombs, like saints just raised from their graves to witness the judgment of the Lord. The eyes of Marcellinus flashed fire. It was no longer the good shepherd, who bears in his bosom the wandering sheep; it was Moses denouncing the sentence of death against the faithless adorers of the golden calf; it was Jesus Christ scourging forth the profaners of the temple. I was about to advance, when an exorcism arrested my progress. At the same moment the bishops stretched forth their hands against me, and turned away their faces; then the pontiff, in a terrible voice, pronounced this sentence:

"'Let him be accursed, who violates by his corrupt manners the purity of the Christian name! Let him be accursed who ceases to approach the altar of the true God! Let him be accursed, who sees with indifference the abomination of idolatry!'

"All the bishops exclaimed:

"'Let him be accursed!'

"Marcellinus then entered the church, and the gates of the sanctuary were shut against me. The crowd of the elect dispersed; they all avoided meeting me: when I spoke, they answered me not; they fled me like a man affected with some contagious distemper. Thus, like Adam, banished from paradise, I found myself solitary in the midst of a land covered with thorns and thistles, and cursed on account of my fall.

"Seized with a kind of delirium, I mounted my chariot in

disorder; I urged my coursers forward at random; I entered Rome, and after driving with inconsiderate fury through many of the streets, I arrived at the amphitheatre of Vespasian. There I arrested my foaming steeds. I descended from my chariot; I approached the fountain where the gladiators who survived the carnage of the circus came to quench their thirst. I too longed to cool my burning lips. They had been celebrating the vigils of the games given by Aglaia,[1] a rich and celebrated Roman lady; but at this moment these abominable places were deserted. That innocent victim of propitiation which my crimes had once again immolated, seemed from the heights of heaven to denounce vengeance on my guilty head. Like another Cain, a reprobate and an outcast, I entered the dark and solitary galleries. No sound was heard save when some affrighted bird fluttered through the lofty arches. After wandering over the various parts of the edifice, I seated myself on one of the front benches. I sought to forget in the view of this pagan edifice, both the denunciation that had been passed against me, and the religion of my fathers. Vain efforts! Even there, an avenging God presented himself to my memory. It suddenly occurred to my recollection, that this very edifice was the work of a nation, which, according to the prediction of Jesus Christ, was to be dispersed through every land. How astonishing is the destiny of the children of Jacob! Israel, captive under Pharaoh, erected the palaces of Egypt. Israel, captive under Vespasian, built this monument of Roman magnificence. It seems destined that this people, even in the midst of their misfortunes, should have a hand in everything that is great.

"Whilst I abandoned myself to these reflections, a roar issued from the subterranean caverns which enclosed the wild beasts; I started, and casting my eyes on the arena, I saw the sand yet stained with the blood of the unfortunate victims of the recent games. My mind became highly agitated: methought that I too was exposed in the midst of this arena, and reduced to the

---

[1] St. Aglaia.

necessity of perishing by the teeth of these beasts, or of denying the God who shed his blood for me. 'Thou art no longer a Christian,' said I to myself, 'but shouldst thou some day become so again, what wouldst thou do in such a case?'

"I arose; rushed out of the edifice; mounted my chariot; and regained my home. All the night long, the terrible question of my conscience still resounded in my ears. Even at this day, this scene will often recur to my memory, as though there was in it some warning from Heaven."

After having uttered these words, Eudorus suddenly ceased to speak. His eyes were fixed, his whole frame was agitated, and he appeared struck with some supernatural vision. The assembly remained hushed in astonishment, and for some minutes nothing was heard but the murmurs of the Ladon and the Alpheus, as they came swelling on the gale. The mother of Eudorus arose in alarm. But the young Christian, returning to himself, hastened to calm her maternal anxiety, and thus resumed his discourse

BOOK FIFTH

SUMMARY.

Continuation of the Recital. The Court goes to pass the Summer at Baiæ. Naples. House of Aglaia. Walks of Eudorus, Augustine, and Jerome. Their Conversation at the Tomb of Scipio. Thrascas, the Hermit of Vesuvius. His History. Separation of the three Friends. Eudorus returns to Rome with the Court. The Catacombs. Adventure of the Empress Prisca and her daughter Valeria. Eudorus, banished from the Court, is sent an Exile to the Armies of Constantius. He quits Rome, and journeys through Italy and Gaul. He arrives at Agrippina, on the Banks of the Rhine. He finds the Roman Army ready to carry War into the Country of the Franks. He serves as a Private Soldier among the Cretan Archers, who compose, with the Gauls, the Vanguard of the Army of Constantius.

"The impression which this fatal day made on my mind, at present so lively and so profound, was then quickly effaced. My young friends who surrounded me, laughed at my terrors and expressions of remorse; they ridiculed the anathemas of an obscure pontiff, without either influence or power.

"The court, which at this time removed to Baiæ, by tearing me from the theatre of my errors, took from me the remembrance of their punishment. I now believed my return to Christianity impossible, and abandoned myself to my pleasures with thoughtless indifference.

"Among the happiest days of my life I must reckon those I spent this summer with Augustine and Jerome in the neighborhood of Naples, if indeed, sirs, any period of our existence can merit that appellation, which is spent in the forgetfulness of God, and amidst the illusions of the passions.

"The court was pompous and brilliant: all the princes, whether friends or children of the Cæsars, were here assembled. Here were Licinius[1] and Severus,[2] companions in arms with Galerius; Daza,[3] the nephew of the same Cæsar, who had lately come from his native forests; and Maxentius,[4] son of Maximianus Augustus. But Constantine preferred our society to that of these princes, who were all envious of his virtues, his valor and his fame; and were either publicly or secretly his enemies.

"The place where we most frequently met, was the palace of Aglaia, at Naples, a Roman lady, whose name I before had occasion to mention. She was of senatorial rank, and daughter of the Proconsul Arsaces. Her riches were immense; seventy stewards superintended her estates, and three times she had given public games at her own expense. The beauty of her person was equalled by the accomplishments of her mind; whoever, in this decline of the state, possessed either elegance of manners, or a taste for literature and the polite arts, was sure to gain admittance into her society. Happy, if in this decline of Roman virtue, she had chosen rather to become a second Cornelia, than to have recalled the memory of those too celebrated women who are sung by Ovid, Propertius, and Tibullus.

"Sebastian[5] and Pacomius,[6] centurions of the guards under Constantine; Genesius,[7] the celebrated actor, who inherited all the talents of Roscius; with Boniface,[8] first comptroller of the palace of Aglaia, and perhaps but too intimate with his mistress, embellished with their wit and their gaiety the feasts of this voluptuous Roman. But Boniface, though a man abandoned to his pleasures, possessed three good qualities: he was liberal, humane, and hospitable. After leaving the

---

[1] Who became Augustus at the death of Severus.
[2] Cæsar, upon the abdication of Diocletian; and Augustus, after the death of Constantius.
[3] Cæsar, upon the abdication of Diocletian.
[4] The tyrant who usurped the purple, and was vanquished by Constantine at the gates of Rome.
[5] The warlike martyr, surnamed the Defender of the Roman Church.
[6] The recluse of the Thebais, who first bore arms under Constantine.
[7] The martyr.   [8] *Idem.*

sumptuous banquet, he would visit the public places of the city, relieve the poor, and succor the traveller and the stranger. Aglaia herself, in the midst of her disorders, testified great respect for the faithful, and reverence for the relics of the martyrs. Genesius, who was a professed enemy to the Christians, rallied her on this weakness.

"'Well,' she would say, 'I own I have my superstitions. I believe there is virtue in the ashes of a Christian who dies for his God, and I wish Boniface to go and procure relics for me.'

"'Illustrious patron,' would Boniface reply with a smile, 'your wish shall be gratified. I will go in search of the relics you request; but if my own relics should come to you under the name of a martyr's, be sure to receive them.'

"The greater part of our nights was spent in this dangerous and seductive company: in the meantime I resided with Augustine and Jerome at the villa of Constantine, which stood on the declivity of mount Pausilypum. As soon as Aurora shed her first rays, I regularly took my walk under the portico which extended along the sea-shore. Arising from behind Vesuvius, the sun gladdened with his softened rays the mountains of Salernum, the azure of the deep studded with the white sails of the busy fishermen, the isles of Capreæ, of Ænaria, and Prochyta,[1] Cape Misenum, and Baiæ, with all its enchantments.

"The flowers and the fruits, moist with dew, are less sweet and refreshing than the landscape of Naples, when first it emerges from the shadows of night. I was always surprised when I reached the portico to find myself by the sea-side, for the waves in this place fell with such softness on the shore, that they resembled the murmurs of the fountain. In ecstasy before this picture, I would lean against a column, and, free from all thought, desire, or aim, would pass whole hours in inhaling the delicious air. The charm was so powerful, that it seemed to me that this divine air transformed my

---

[1] Ischia and Procida.

own substance, and that with inexpressible pleasure I was borne upward toward heaven like a pure spirit. But, great God! how far was I from being this celestial intelligence, freed from the chains of the passions! How strongly did my grosser part weigh me down to the dust; how melancholy the reflection, that I should be so sensible to the charms of creation, and yet think so little of their Creator! Whilst, free in appearance, I seemed to swim through the fields of light, many a Christian, fettered to the floor of his gloomy dungeon, was truly quitting these scenes of mortality, and mounting to enjoy the radiance of the eternal sun.

"But, alas! insensible to the charms of virtue, we yielded ourselves captives to the seductions of pleasure; the enchantress beckoned, and we heedlessly followed her steps; her path was strewed with flowers, and she conducted us to those groves of myrtle, and those happy plains where Virgil has placed the Elysium of the blessed. Thus our days advanced lightly along, but anguish and remorse followed close behind. Some climates, perhaps, by their luxurious softness, are naturally dangerous to virtue. Is not this the moral intended to be conveyed by that ingenious fable, which describes Parthenope as being built over the tomb of a siren? The plains bathed in softened light, the balmy temperature of the air, the varied and fantastic outlines of the surrounding mountains, the gentle windings of the rivers and valleys, are so many seductions around Naples which lull the senses, and throw a kind of languor over the whole mind. The half-naked Neapolitan, contented to feel himself exist, and blessing the influence of a sky so propitious, refuses all further labor, the moment he has gained the obolus for the day's support. He passes one-half of his life basking inactive in the rays of the sun, the other in being drawn in his chariot and shouting for joy; at night he throws himself upon the steps of some temple, and sleeps, regardless of futurity, at the foot of the statues of his gods.

"Can you believe, my friends, that we were senseless enough to envy the lot of these men, and to think that the happiest of lives which glided away without forecast, and was regardless of the morrow! This was often the subject of our conversations, when, to avoid the burning heat of noon, we retired to a part of the palace that was excavated beneath the sea. Here, stretched on couches of ivory, we heard the murmurs of the waves about our heads. If at any time a storm surprised us in this retreat, the slaves lighted the lamps, filled with precious spikenard of Arabia. A band of Neapolitan damsels was then called in, bearing roses of Pæstum in vases of Nola. To drown the roar of the waves that dashed above us, they raised the choral strain and wove around us the graceful dance; they forcibly reminded me of the manners of Greece, and seemed to realize the fictions of our poets: they were like Nereids sporting in the grotto of Neptune.

"When the sun retired behind the tomb of the nurse of Æneas, leaving a part of the bay of Naples in the shadows of mount Pausilypum, the three friends would separate. Jerome, incited by his love of curious research, would retire to visit the spot where Pliny fell a victim to the same spirit of curiosity: he would wander amidst the ruins of Herculaneum, and endeavor to trace the cause of those sounds that issued from the caverns of Solfatara. Augustine, with a Virgil in his hand, would wander over the scenes sung by the immortal poet: Lake Avernus, the Sibyl's Cave, Acheron, the Styx, and Elysium; above all, he delighted to seat himself at the foot of the tomb of him who sung so sweetly and so feelingly the woes of the unhappy Dido, and there read over the mournful story of her misfortunes.

"Inspired with a noble ardor for instruction, the Prince Constantine would invite me to follow him to those monuments which are consecrated by the memorials of history. We set out in a boat, and made the tour of the bay of Baiæ; we discovered the ruins of Cicero's villa, the place where Agrippina was shipwrecked, the smooth beach on which she was saved, the palace where her brutal son awaited the success of the scheme he had laid to assassinate her; and a little further on, the building in which she laid bare to her murderers the bosom that bore the unnatural Nero. We then sailed to the island of Capreæ,[1] and visited those subterraneous recesses which once bore witness to the infamous pleasures of Tiberius. 'Alas,' cried Constantine, 'how melancholy the thought, to be master of the universe, and to be forced, by remorse for one's crimes, to fly as an exile to these solitary rocks!'

"Sentiments so generous in the heir of Constantius, and perhaps of the Roman empire, redoubled my affection for this protector and companion of my youth. I let no opportunity pass of awakening ambitious sentiments in his mind; for the ambition of Constantine seemed to me to be the hope of the world.

"A voluptuous bath awaited us on our return from these rambles. Aglaia had prepared for us a delicious repast in the midst of her gardens. This evening banquet was laid out on a terrace bordering on the sea, and surrounded with orange-trees in full bloom. The moon lent us her softened light; in unclouded majesty she appeared in the midst of the stars, like a queen surrounded by her court; overpowered by her superior splendor, the flames which issued from the summit of Vesuvius grew pale beneath her ray, which painted with azure the red smoke of the volcano, and formed on its bosom a rainbow of the night. This beautiful phenomenon, the clear disc of the peaceful luminary, and the shores of Sorrentum, of Pompeii and Herculaneum, reflected their shadows on the waves, while the song of the Neapolitan fisherman came mellowed from the peaceful deep.

"We then filled our goblets with some exquisite wine, that had been found in the cellars of Horace, and drank to the three sisters of Love, the daughters of Power and of Beauty. With our brows crowned with verdant evergreens, intermingled with the short-lived rose, we excited each other to the enjoyment of life by the consideration of its shortness.

"'We must quit this earth, this beloved mansion, this adored mistress. Of all the trees that our hands have planted, the gloomy cypress alone shall accompany to the tomb its master of a day.'

---

[1] Capri.

"We then chanted on the lyre the objects of our criminal passion 'Hence with your sacred fillets, with the virgin ornaments, and the virgin song; I wish to sing of Venus, with all her heavenly gifts, and all her wanton wiles! Let others traverse the deep; let them amass the treasures of Hermus or Ganges, or toil for vain honors in the fields of war; I seek no other renown than to live a slave to the charms of beauty. How great the pleasures of a rural life,—the cultivated field, the enamelled meadow, the banks of the cooling stream! Far retired in some woodland retreat, let me wear out my days in inglorious obscurity. What pleasure to meet Delia in the plain, and place on her tender bosom the new-born lamb! If, during the night, the winds howl round my humble cot, and the rain descend in torrents on its roof' . . . .

"But why, my friends, should I continue to depict to you the disorders of three senseless young men? Ah! let me speak rather of the disgust attached to a life so void of real happiness. Think not that we were happy in the midst of these deceitful pleasures. An inquietude, which I have no words to define, incessantly tormented us. That love cannot be complete which meets not with an equal return; for the soul wishes to find its happiness in that which it loves. Of this kind were our attachments; in vain we expected to find constancy and truth; we met with nothing but deceit, tears, jealousies, and indifference. Betraying or betrayed, our affections were ever varying. Sometimes the want of a certain grace, either of body or of mind, hindered our attachment from being durable. And when we thought we had found the visionary object of perfection, a little acquaintance convinced us of our mistake; defects which our partiality hindered us from seeing before, now filled us with disgust, and we regretted the loss of our first victim. A state of mind thus wavering and unsettled, produced a confusion of ideas that troubled the pleasures of the moment, and called up a train of recollections that poisoned our enjoyments. Thus, in the midst of our felicity, we were miserable; because we had abandoned those virtuous thoughts which are the true food of the soul, and had lost all relish for that celestial beauty which alone can fill the immensity of our desires.

"But we soon experienced the goodness of Providence. A sudden ray of divine grace shone through the thick darkness that hung upon our souls, and the Almighty permitted that the first thought of our religion should spring from the excess of our pleasures—so inexplicable are the ways of heaven!

"One day, in our rambles round the environs of Baiæ, we found ourselves near Liternum.[1] Suddenly the tomb of Scipio Africanus met our view: we approached it with reverence.* As it stood close to the sea, a tempest had swept away the statue that once surmounted it. This inscription was still visible on the cover of the sarcophagus:

"'UNGRATEFUL LAND OF MY NATIVITY,
THOU SHALT NOT POSSESS MY BONES.'

"When we called to mind the virtues and the exile of the conqueror of Hannibal, our eyes were filled with tears. The very rudeness of his monument, which formed such a contrast with those superb mausoleums erected in every part of Italy to characters long since forgotten, served to redouble our curiosity. We durst not presume to repose upon the tomb, but seated ourselves in religious silence at its base, as if we had been at the foot of an altar. After some moments spent in solemn contemplation, Jerome thus broke silence:

"'My friends,' said he, 'the ashes of the most illustrious of Romans impress me with the most lively sentiments of our own nothingness, and the inutility of a life whose very pleasures begin to disgust. I feel a void in my heart which I know not how to explain. For a long time past a strong desire to travel has possessed me: twenty times a day am I ready to bid you adieu, and to commence my wanderings over the earth. From what source, then, proceeds this restlessness of mind; whence but from those wavering opinions, and those feverish desires that cannot satisfy the soul? Does not the whole life

---
[1] Patria.

of Scipio condemn our conduct? Do you not shed tears of admiration, do you not feel that there is a happiness very different from that which we are seeking, when you see the African hero generously restoring a spouse to her husband, when Cicero paints this great man among the celestial spirits, showing Emilius in a dream that there is a life where virtue meets reward?'

"'Jerome,' replied Augustine, 'in the history of your feelings you have described my own: like you I suffer without knowing the cause of my misery; yet I have not, like you, the need to be in motion; I sigh, on the contrary, for naught but repose, and I would gladly, after the example of Scipio, place my life in the highest regions of tranquillity. A secret languor consumes me; I know not on what side to turn in search of happiness; the more I consider life, the less attachment do I feel for it. Ah! were there but some hidden truth! Did there but exist somewhere an inexhaustible fountain of love, of whose wave we might drink to thirst no more, and in whose stream we might entirely whelm ourselves in delight! Scipio, if thy dream were not the fond offspring of fancy' . . . .

"'With what transport,' exclaimed the enraptured Jerome, 'would I plunge into this sacred stream! Ye banks of Jordan, and thou grotto of Bethlehem, soon shall you behold me in the number of your anchorites! O mountains of Judea, for the future the idea of your deserts and of my repentance shall be inseparable!'

"Jerome uttered these words with a vehemence that surprised us. His bosom heaved with emotion; he resembled the hind that thirsts after the fountain of living waters.

"'O my friends,' said I, 'strange as the thing may appear, I am forced to make the same confession as yourselves. But I unite in myself the two evils that torment you—the desire to travel, and the thirst for repose. In this distracted state of mind, I often turn my eyes toward the religion of my infancy.'

"'My mother, who is a Christian,' replied Augustine, 'has often discoursed to me on the beauty of her religion, in which I would find, she said, the happiness of my life. Alas! yonder seas separate me from this tender parent; perhaps at this moment she is contemplating them from the opposite shore, thinking, meanwhile, of her son.'

"Augustine had hardly uttered these words, when a man clothed in a philosopher's garb, of the school of Epictetus, came out of Scipio's tomb. He seemed mature in years, yet bordering rather on youth than old age. An air of angelic sweetness and vivacity was spread over his countenance; you would have thought that his lips but opened to utter wisdom.

"'Pardon me, sirs,' said he, hastening to relieve us from our surprise; 'I was seated in this monument on your arrival here, and I have unintentionally heard all your discourse. Since I have learned your history, will you allow me to recount my own; it may be useful to you; perhaps you may find it a remedy for the evils you suffer.'

"Without awaiting our reply, the stranger seated himself in the midst of us, and with graceful familiarity, commenced his narration.

"'I am that Christian solitary of Vesuvius, of whom you may perhaps have heard, as I am the only inhabitant of the summit of the mountain. I sometimes come to visit the tomb of this hero; my motive is this: while Scipio resided at Liternum, and amidst its sequestered scenes consoled himself in the consciousness of his own virtue for the injustice of his country, a band of pirates landed on that part of the coast, and attacked the house of the illustrious exile, without knowing the name of its possessor. Already had they scaled the walls, when they were thus accosted by the slaves who put themselves in a posture of defence: "What! will you dare to violate the residence of Scipio!" Filled with respect at so great a name, the pirates threw down their arms, and after begging permission to have a view of the conqueror of Hannibal, they retired full of admiration at the sight.

"'Thraseas, who was my ancestor, and the descendant of a noble family at Sicyon, was at that time among the pirates. He had been carried away by them in his infancy, and forced to serve on board their vessels. Having concealed himself in

Scipio's house, no sooner were the pirates departed, than he threw himself at the feet of his host, and related his story. Africanus, touched at his misfortunes, sent him back to his country; but the parents of Thraseas had died during his captivity, and their fortune had passed into other hands. He therefore returned to his benefactor, who allowed him a small portion of land near his dwelling, and gave him in marriage to the daughter of a poor Roman knight.

" 'I am descended from this family, and therefore you see that I have a lawful reason for honoring the tomb of Scipio.

" 'My youth was wild and dissipated. I attempted everything, and then abandoned all with disgust. I had gained some celebrity by my eloquence, and often would I say to myself: "What is this literary fame, which is disputed during life, uncertain after death, and often the portion of mediocrity and of vice?" I was ambitious, and had attained a post of eminence, yet I often put this question to myself: "Do these honors repay me for the regret I felt in abandoning a life of peaceful retirement; and is my present gain equivalent to my former loss?" In the same manner I reasoned on everything else. Cloyed with the pleasures of my age, I saw nothing better in the future, and my ardent imagination deprived me of the few that I yet possessed. My young friends, it is a great evil for a man to attain prematurely the summit of his desires; and to pass, in a few years, through the illusions of a long life.

" 'One day, while buried in these melancholy reflections, I wandered to a quarter of Rome, but little frequented by the great, but inhabited by a numerous class of poor people. An edifice of a singular construction, but whose appearance inspired solemnity, struck my view. Under the portico there were many persons in a standing attitude, who appeared immovable and plunged in deep meditation.

" 'My curiosity was excited, and I wished to discover to whom this building belonged; at that moment a man passed by me, whom I knew to be of Greek extraction, but who, like myself, had become naturalized at Rome. He was a descendant of Perseus, the last king òf Macedonia. His ancestors, after being dragged at the car of Paulus Emilius, were reduced to the humble condition of scribes in one of the courts at Rome. This man, the sport of the most capricious fortune, had formerly been pointed out to me, under a sorry shed, at the corner of the Sacra Via. I had sometimes conversed with this Perseus. I therefore stopped him, and demanded to what purpose the edifice before us was applied. "This," said he, "is the place where I come to forget the throne of Alexander: I am a Christian." He then ascended the steps of the portico, passed through the midst of the catechumens, and entered the precincts of the temple. I followed him, full of emotion.

"'The same disproportions which were visible on the outside of the edifice, marked its interior; but these defects were well atoned for by the bold style of its vaulted aisles, and the awe-inspiring effect of their shadows. Instead of the blood of victims, and the orgies that defile the altars of the false gods, purity and meditation seemed to keep their vigils within the tabernacles of the Christians. A reverential silence reigned through the assembly, which was only occasionally interrupted by the innocent voice of some infant at its mother's breast.

"'Night approached, and the last gleams of expiring day, that still lingered in the nave and the sanctuary, seemed to vie with the lustre of the lamps. In every recess stood an altar, before which the Christians were still engaged in prayer; the ceremonies were finished, but the mingled odors of the incense and of the perfumed tapers, that had just been extinguished, were still perceptible.

"'A priest, bearing a book and a lamp, came out of a secret recess, and mounted an elevated rostrum. Immediately the whole assembly was in commotion, and every one fell on his knees. After a silent prayer, he recited aloud the sacred litanies, to which the Christians answered in a low voice from every part of the edifice. There was something touching in the uniformity of these responses, thus murmured forth at equal intervals; but the interest of the scene was doubly aug mented when the words of the pastor were considered in relation to the flock.

"'Thou consolation of the afflicted,' said the priest; 'thou succor of the infirm!'

"'And all the persecuted Christians, completing the unfinished meaning, repeated:

"'Pray for us! Pray for us!

"'In this long enumeration of human infirmities, each one found the particular tribulation that afflicted him, and applied to his own personal necessities some one of these supplications to the throne of mercy. I, too, soon found something applicable to my situation. With a distinct voice, the Levite pronounced these words:

"Thou God of goodness, thou repose of the heart, thou calm in the tempest!"

"'He stopped: my eyes were filled with tears; I thought that his looks were fixed upon me, and that the charitable assembly exclaimed:

"Pray for him! Pray for him!"

"'The priest descended from his rostrum, and the assembly retired. Touched to the heart, I hastened to find Marcellinus, the supreme pontiff of that religion, which alone can afford consolation. I recounted to him the errors of my life; he instructed me in the truths of his worship. I became a Christian, and from that moment my sorrows have vanished.'

"Such was the history of this Christian philosopher. It was related with the most amiable and engaging candor, and we were all charmed with the recital. We put many questions to him, which he answered with perfect sincerity. We could never have grown weary of hearing him, for there was a harmony in his voice that filled us with pleasing emotions. An eloquence at once flowery and chastened flowed naturally from his lips, and there was an air of antiquity even in the least things he uttered, that quite ravished our souls. Like the ancients, he was given to repetition; in any other person this would have been a fault, but to his discourse it added a grace that I know not how to describe. You might have taken him for one of those legislators of Greece who formerly gave laws to men, while they chanted on their golden lyres the beauty of virtue, and the omnipotence of the gods.

"His departure broke off this conference, in which three young men, without religion, concluded that religion was the sole remedy for their ills. The tomb of Africanus was doubtless that which first inspired us with this thought: the ashes of a persecuted hero elevates the mind toward heaven. We quitted the shores of Liternum with regret, and as we embraced each other, a secret presentiment filled our bosoms with sadness: it appeared as if we were taking an everlasting farewell. On our return to Naples, its pleasures had no longer the same attractions. Sebastian and Pacomius had gone to join the army; Genesius and Boniface seemed to have lost their wonted gaiety; Aglaia appeared melancholy, and troubled with remorse. The court quitted Baiæ; Jerome and Augustine returned to Rome, and I followed Constantine to his palace on the Tiber. Here I received a letter from Augustine, who told me that at last he had yielded to the tears of his mother, and was on his way to join her at Carthage; that Jerome was preparing for his travels through Gaul, Pannonia, and those deserts inhabited by the Christian solitaries.

"'I know not,' added Augustine toward the close of his letter, 'I know not whether we shall ever meet again. Alas! my friend, such is life; it is full of brief joys and long sorrows, of intimacies formed but to be broken! By some strange fatality, our friendships are seldom formed at the moment when they might be lasting: we meet with the friend with whom we fondly hope to pass our days; but at that instant fate has fixed his destination far from us: we find the kindred heart we have so long been seeking; but we find it on the very eve of the day when it is to cease beating forever! During life, a thousand accidents separate friend from friend; and then comes the long separation of death, which in a moment destroys all our projects. Do you recollect what we said one day, as we stood contemplating the gulf of Naples? We compared life to a seaport, where men of every tongue, and of every country, are either hastening to depart, or returning home from their voyage. All is bustle and commotion, while the shores resound with their varied cries: some with tears of joy, are springing to the arms of long absent friends; others, as they sorrowfully retire, are bidding an eternal adieu; for we quit the port of life to return no more! Therefore, my dear Eudorus, let us not give way to complaint; let us support with fortitude a separation which a few years would necessarily have produced."

As Eudorus was about to continue his recital, the servants of Lasthenes brought the morning repast. It consisted of the most simple aliments—new wheat, roasted on the embers, various fruits, and new-made cheese, which still bore the mark of the press. The hearts of the audience were variously affected. Without testifying any exterior marks of his feelings, Cyril admired this youth, whose prayer, like that of the royal prophet, had been heard from the bottom of the abyss:

"Lord have mercy upon me, according to the multitude of thy great mercies."

Demodocus scarcely comprehended anything of this recital; he found here neither Polyphemus nor Circe; there were no enchantments to surprise, no shipwrecks to terrify; in this harmony, so new to his ear, he recognized scarcely any of the sounds of Homer's lyre. Not so Cymodoce: she comprehended the narration with wonderful facility! But she could not account for the sadness that came over her mind, when she heard Eudorus say that he had loved much, and yet repented of it as a failing. Reclining her head on her father's bosom, she said to him in a low voice:

"My dear father, I weep as if I were a Christian!"

The repast being finished, Demodocus thus began:

"Son of Lasthenes, your recital has charmed me, though I am unable to comprehend all the wisdom contained in it. This language of Christianity seems a species of poetry and reason intermingled, in which Minerva never instructed me

Proceed and finish your history: and if any of us should be unable to restrain our tears at the affecting narration, let it not interrupt you, for we have had examples of this before. When a son of Apollo chanted the woes of Troy at the table of Alcinous, there was a stranger present, who enveloped his head in his mantle and wept. Excuse, therefore, the tears of my Cymodoce: Jupiter has placed the heart of youth under the dominion of pity. We old men, who are weighed down by the burden of Saturn, have peace and justice for our portion, but are deprived of that exquisite sensibility, and that delicacy of sentiment, which forms the ornament of youthful minds. The gods have made old age like those hereditary sceptres, which passed of old from father to son; they are hallowed by the majesty of ages, but are no longer covered with flowers and foliage as when first severed from the maternal trunk."

Eudorus then resumed his discourse:

"Being thus deprived of my friends, Rome offered nothing to my view but one vast solitude. At the court, too, all was disorder: Maximianus had been obliged to hasten from Milan to Pannonia, which was menaced with invasion by the Goths and the Carpi; the Franks had made themselves masters of Batavia, which was defended by Constantius; in Africa, the Quinquagenti, a new race of barbarians, had appeared in arms; it was even reported that Diocletian himself intended to pass into Egypt, where the revolt of the tyrant Achilleus demanded his presence; in fine, Galerius himself was hastening his departure to oppose the progress of Narses. The war in Parthia, above all, filled the aged emperor with apprehensions; it brought strongly to his mind the wretched fate of Valerian. Galerius, taking advantage of the necessities of the empire, and of the need that was felt for his services, and swayed, as usual, by the suggestions of Hierocles, sought to gain an absolute dominion over Diocletian's mind; he no longer hesitated publicly to announce his jealousy against Constantius, whose merit and high birth filled him with disquieting apprehensions. Constantine was naturally included in this jealousy; and I, being the friend of the young prince, and a person particularly obnoxious to Hierocles, felt its effects; upon me, as the weaker of the two, fell the whole weight of Galerius's vengeance.

"One day, while Constantine was present at the deliberations of the senate, I went to visit the fountain of Egeria. Night surprised me: to regain the Appian way, I directed my course toward the tomb of Cecilia Metella, which was a masterpiece of grandeur and elegance. Whilst crossing the deserted plain, I suddenly perceived the figures of a number of persons gliding through the shades of the evening, who stopped at a particular spot, and then in an instant disappeared. Excited by curiosity, I advanced, and entered boldly into a cavern that yawned before me, and into which these phantoms seemed to descend. I saw long subterranean galleries extending before me, which were but feebly illumined by a few lamps suspended at distant intervals. Along the walls of these funereal vaults stood a triple row of coffins, ranged one above the other. The lamps spread around a melancholy light, and rather increased than diminished the horrors of the scene; for the trembling rays, as they quivered along the sides of these caverns, gave a kind of frightful motion to objects eternally immovable. In vain I listened for some sound toward which I might guide my steps; all was silence: I could distinguish nothing but the strong pulsations of my heart. I wished to retrace my steps, but it was too late: I took a wrong turn, and instead of regaining the entrance of the labyrinth, I penetrated still further into its winding recesses. New avenues, crossing each other in every direction, augmented my perplexity at every step I took. Every effort to find the right direction carried me further from it; sometimes I advanced slowly, then again I quickened my pace: the echoes of my own footsteps alarmed me, and I thought some one was advancing rapidly to overtake me.

"After wandering a long time in a state of violent agitation, my strength began to fail, and I seated myself in a place where many of the passages met. To add to my apprehensions, the expiring lamps shed a feebler ry, and threatened to leave me in total darkness. Suddenly, a burst of celestial music issued from the depth of these sepulchral dungeons, that resembled a choir of distant angels: at fitful intervals these divine sounds swelled on the air in loud music, and then died away in murmurs; and, as they stole through the lengthened windings of this subterranean recess, acquired a more mellow and softened cadence. I arose, and advancing to the spot whence this magical concert issued, I discovered an illuminated hall. On a tomb decked with flowers, Marcellinus was celebrating the Christian mysteries: a choir of young damsels, arrayed in white, were singing around the altar, and a numerous assembly was witnessing the sacrifice. I perceived that I was in the Catacombs![1] A mingled sensation of shame, repentance, and rapture, filled my soul. But judge of my astonishment when I saw the empress and her daughter, accompanied by Dorotheus and Sebastian, on their knees in the midst of the crowd. Never did a more miraculous spectacle strike the eye of mortal; never was God more worthily adored, or was manifested more openly his greatness. Oh, the power of that religion which could induce the spouse of a Roman emperor to steal like an adulteress from the imperial couch to visit the rendezvous of the unfortunate, to seek Jesus Christ at the altar of an obscure martyr, in the midst of tombs, and among men the objects of contempt and proscription! Whilst I abandoned myself to these reflections, a deacon approached the pontiff, and whispered in his ear. In a moment, upon a signal given, the chanting ceased, the lamps were extinguished, and the heavenly vision disappeared. Borne along amidst this holy crowd, I found myself at the entrance of the Catacombs.

"This adventure gave quite a new turn to my destiny. Though entirely undeserving of reproach, I was accused on every side. It is thus that God treats the wicked; he does not immediately punish their transgressions, but, in order to render the chastisement more sensible, he allows even some reasonable

---

[1] The Catacombs of Saint Sebastian.

action of theirs to be misinterpreted, and then abandons them to the injustice of mankind.

"I knew not that the Empress Prisca and her daughter Valeria were Christians: my impiety had hindered the faithful from communicating to me this important conquest. Apprehending the fury of Galerius, the two princesses durst not appear openly at the church; but, accompanied by the virtuous Dorotheus, they came at night to pray in these catacombs. Chance had conducted me to this sanctuary of the dead: the priests who discovered me, naturally imagined that a wretch, who had been excluded from the sacred places, could have descended into these caverns with no other intention than to discover the important secret which it was the interest of the church to conceal; and they had extinguished the lamps in order to hide the empress from my view.

"Galerius, who suspected the empress of a secret inclination to this new religion, had placed spies over her conduct. The commission was intrusted to Hierocles, whose emissaries had followed the princesses to the catacombs; and there awaiting their return, had seen me come out among the number. No sooner was this report carried to the sophist, than he ran to inform Galerius, and Galerius flew to Diocletian.

"'Well,' cried he, 'you who would never believe what was passing under your eyes, see now the effects of your incredulity: the empress and your daughter Valeria are Christians! This very night have they been surprised in a cavern which this impious sect defiles with its execrable mysteries. And who, think you, guided them thither? Who, but this Greek, the descendant of a race that have ever been rebels to the Roman people; this traitor, who, the better to mask his projects, professes openly to have abandoned the religion of those seditious wretches, whose agent he is in secret; this serpent, that unceasingly poisons the mind of Prince Constantine. Know, that a deep-laid plot is formed against you by the Christians, in which they are even now endeavoring to implicate your whole family. Give instant orders to seize Eudorus, and by force of tortures wring from him an avowal of these crimes, and the names of his accomplices.'

"To say the truth, appearances were against me, and I stood condemned by all parties. Among the Christians I passed for a traitor and an apostate. Hierocles, perceiving their error, declared openly that I had denounced the empress. The pagans on their side regarded me as the chief of my religion, and the corrupter of the imperial family. As I passed along the halls of the palace, the courtiers smiled with an air of contempt, and I remarked that the vilest were the most severe; the very people pursued me through the streets with menaces and insults. At last my situation became so dangerous, that without the friendship of Constantine, I seriously believe my life would have been attempted. But this generous prince did not abandon me under my misfortunes; he openly declared himself my friend; he made a point of appearing with me in public; he courageously defended my cause before Augustus, and publicly declared that I was a victim to the jealousy of a sophist, who was attached to Galerius.

"This affair occupied all the attention of Rome and the court; it appeared of the highest importance to hear the name of the empress implicated with that of the Christians. The decision of the emperor was expected with impatience; but it was not the character of Diocletian to form a violent resolution. The aged emperor had recourse to a measure that admirably depicts his political genius. He maintained in a public declaration, that the reports which had been circulated through Rome, were grounded on falsehood; that the princesses had not been from the palace on the night that it was pretended they had been seen at the catacombs; that Prisca and Valeria, so far from being Christians, had actually sacrificed to the gods of the empire; that, in fine, he would severely punish the authors of these falsehoods, and that he forbade the further mention of a story that was as ridiculous as it was scandalous.

"But as it was necessary, according to the custom of courts, that one should suffer for all, I received orders to quit Rome, and join the army under Constantius, which lay encamped on the banks of the Rhine.

"I therefore prepared to pass into Gaul, content to embrace the career of arms and to abandon a state of life incompatible with my character. Yet such is the force of habit, and the secret charm that binds us to places of celebrity, that I could not quit Rome without regret. After receiving Constantine's last embrace, I commenced my journey at midnight. I traversed the lonely streets, and passed by the deserted house which I had once inhabited in the company of Augustine and Jerome. In the Forum all was silence and solitude; the numerous monuments of grandeur with which it was covered, the rostrums, the Temple of Peace, those of Jupiter Stator and of Fortune, the triumphal arches of Titus and Severus, were dimly visible through the shades of night, like the ruins of a mighty city, whose inhabitants had long since disappeared. When I was at some distance from Rome, I turned my head to take a last farewell; the Tiber rolling his waves through these mingled monuments was visible by the light of the stars; the summit of the capitol, too, was distinguishable, and, methought, it seemed to bend under the ponderous spoils of a captured world.

"The Cassian way, which lay toward Etruria, was adorned with but few monuments, and I soon passed them. It conducted me through an ancient forest, that led to lake Volsiniensis, and to those dreary mountains, which are always covered with clouds, and infested with banditti. A mountain whose pointed summits shoot into the sky, and a torrent which winds amidst the rocks and roars in many a foaming cascade, form on this side the boundary of Etruria. To the grandeur of the plains of Rome, narrow valleys succeeded, which were overgrown with shrubs, whose pale verdure was intermingled with the lively tints of the olive. I quitted the Apennines to descend into Cisalpine Gaul. The skies lost their soft and delicate blue, and I sought in vain on these mountains for that species of dewy light which envelops the hills of Greece, and of Upper Italy. I perceived at a distance the white summits of the

Alps, and soon began to ascend their vast acclivities. Everything about these mountains that was the work of nature gave me an idea of grandeur and of durability; everything that had been contrived by man appeared feeble and insignificant: on one side, trees that had braved the rage of centuries, torrents that for ages had roared through the rocks, and rocks themselves the conquerors of Hannibal and of time; on the other, bridges formed of wood, huts of clay, and a few sheepfolds scattered along the declivities. Is it, that struck with the view of the eternal masses that surround him, the Alpine herdsman, impressed with the shortness of human existence, has not taken the trouble to erect monuments more durable than himself?

"I descended the Alps through a species of portico, that had been hollowed out of an enormous rock. I crossed that part of the Viennese territory which is inhabited by the Vocontii,[1] and descended into the colony of Lucius.[2] With what respect I visited the episcopal sees of Irenæus and Pothinus, and the waters of the Rhone that had so often been stained by the blood of the martyrs! I sailed up the Arar,[3] a river bordered with delightful hills, but whose course is so slow, that it is difficult to discern the direction of its stream. It has its name from a young Gaul, who in despair for the loss of his brother, precipitated himself into its waves. Thence I reached the territories of the Treveri,[4] whose city is the most remarkable both for grandeur and beauty in the three Gauls; and following the course of the Rhine and Moselle, I soon arrived at Agrippina.[5]

"Constantius received me with every mark of kindness.

"'Eudorus,' said he, 'to-morrow the legions begin their march; we are going to meet the Franks. You must first serve as a simple archer among the Cretans, who are encamped with the advanced guard on the other side of the Rhine. Hasten to join them; distinguish yourself by your conduct and courage: if you show yourself worthy of the friendship of my

---

[1] Dauphiny.
[2] Lyons.
[3] The Saone.
[4] The province of Trèves.
[5] Cologne.

son, it will not be long before I raise you to the first rank in the army.'

"And here, my friends, I must remark the second of those sudden revolutions, that have continually changed the face of my destinies. From the peaceful valleys of Arcadia, I had been transported to the tumultuous court of a Roman emperor; and now from the bosom of luxury, and of polished society, I passed to a hard and perilous life, in the midst of a barbarous people."

BOOK SIXTH.

SUMMARY.

Continuation of the Story. March of the Roman Army through Batavia. Encounter with the Army of the Franks. The Field of Battle. Order and Enumeration of the Roman Army. Order and Enumeration of the Army of the Franks. Pharamond, Clodion and Merovius. Songs of the Warriors. War Songs of the Franks. Beginning of the Action. Attack of the Gauls upon the Franks. Cavalry Combat. Remarkable Encounter between Vercingetorix, Chief of the Gauls, and Merovius, Son of the King of the Franks. Vercingetorix is vanquished. The Romans give Way. The Christian Legion descends the Hill and renews the Combat. Mêlée. The Franks retreat to their Camp. Eudorus obtains the civic Crown, and is appointed Chief of the Greeks by Constantius. The Combat recommences at Break of Day. Attack on the Camp of the Franks by the Romans. Rising of the Waves. The Romans flee before the Sea. Eudorus, after a long Struggle, falls, pierced with several Wounds. He is succored by a Slave of the Franks, who bears him to a Cavern.

"The country of the Franks is wild and uncultivated; it commences beyond the Rhine, and occupies the space contained between Batavia to the west, Scandinavia to the north, Germany to the east, and Gaul to the south. Of all barbarians, the people who inhabit this desert are the most fierce; they feed on the flesh of wild animals; their weapons are always in their hands; and they regard a life of peace as a life of the most grievous servitude. The chilling blasts, and the bleak snows of these mountains form their delight; they brave the terrors of the deep, and laugh at the rage of the tempest; and so well are they acquainted with every rock and shoal, that it would seem as if the depths of the ocean had been laid open to their view. This restless nation is always harassing the frontiers of the empire. It was under the reign of Gordianus, surnamed the Pious, that they first rose in arms against the affrighted Gauls. The two Decii perished in an expedition against them ; and Probus, who merely repulsed them, gained thence the glorious title of Francicus. Joined to their martial spirit, they have sometimes exhibited such greatness of soul, that, in regard to them alone, that law has been relaxed, which forbids the intermingling of royal blood with that of barbarians; in fine, these terrible conquerors had just made themselves masters of the isle of Batavia, and it was to wrest from them their fresh acquisition that Constantius had now assembled his army.

"After some days' march, we entered the marshy soil of Batavia, which is nothing but a thin crust of earth floating on a body of water. This country, intersected by the branches of the Rhine, frequently inundated by the ocean, and overgrown with impenetrable forests of pine and birch, presented at every step insurmountable difficulties.

"Exhausted by the fatigues of the day, I had only a few hours during the night to rest my wearied limbs. During this short repose, imagination would often transport me to former scenes, and make me forget my present situation ; and when the horns at day-break sounded the air of Diana, I was astonished, on awaking, to find myself in the midst of a forest. Yet the warrior could not but feel a secret satisfaction in thus awakening from the perils of night. I never heard without a certain martial joy, the clangors of the matin trumpet, which reëchoed among the rocks, and as they saluted the dawn, the first neighings of the warlike steeds. I loved to behold the camp buried in sleep, a few half-dressed soldiers emerging from the still closed tents, the centurion parading before the piles of arms as he balanced his pike, the sentinel, immovable in his station, who, to resist the solicitations of sleep, held up one of his fingers as if in the attitude of silence; the horseman that was crossing the river, whose waves were just tinged with the first faint gleams of dawn ; the servant of the priest, drawing water for the sacrifice, and the shepherd leaning on his crook, and looking attentively at his flock as they drank at the yet misty stream.

"So great was the interest I took in these scenes of warfare, that I ceased to think with regret on the luxury and dissipation of Naples and Rome; for the scenery around me awakened a new train of ideas. During the long nights of autumn, it was often my lot to be placed as sentinel in the outposts of the army. While gazing at the watch-fires that blazed at regular distances along the Roman lines, and those of the Franks scattered in wild confusion; while with bow half bent I listened to the murmurs of the hostile army, as they rose on my ear, intermingled with the drowsy roar of the distant deep, and the cries of various birds that fluttered through the obscurity of the night, I reflected on the strangeness of my destiny. I was here fighting the battles of barbarians, the tyrants of Greece, against other barbarians from whom I had never received an injury. The love of my country revived with ardor in my bosom, and Arcadia arose to my view arrayed in all her charms. How often during our painful marches, drenched by the rains, and plunging through the marshes of Batavia; how often under the miserable sheds where we were obliged to pass the night; how often around the watch-fires of the camp; how often, I say, with some other young Greeks who were exiles like myself, have I made my dear country the subject of my conversation. We recounted the sports of our infancy, the adventures of our youth, and the history of our respective families. An Athenian extolled the arts and the polish of Athens; a Spartan was loud in his preference of Lacedæmon; a Macedonian thought the phalanx far preferable to the legion, and would not hear of a comparison between Cæsar and Alexander. 'It is to my country that you owe Homer,' cried a soldier of Smyrna, and at the same instant he began to sing the catalogue of the vessels, and the combat of Ajax and Hector: it was thus that the Athenians, when prisoners at Syracuse, repeated of yore the verses of Euripides, as a charm to soothe the sorrows of captivity.

"But when, casting our eyes around us, we saw the gloomy, unvaried horizon of Germany, whose sky was without brilliancy, whose thick and lowering atmosphere seemed to threaten us with its fall, and whose powerless sun gave no variety of tint to the surrounding objects; when again we called to our recollection the brilliant landscapes of Greece, and its high and richly varied horizons,—the perfume of our orange groves, the beauty of our flowers, the downy azure of a sky forever dressed in golden light, so strong was our desire to revisit our native land, that we all were ready to abandon the eagles of Rome. There was but one Greek of our number who blamed this enthusiasm, and exhorted us to fulfil our duties, and submit to our destiny. We all regarded him as a coward; but some time after he fought and died like a hero, and then we learned that he was a Christian.

"The Franks were surprised by Constantius: at first they avoided the combat, but as soon as their warriors were assembled, they boldly presented themselves before us, and offered us battle on the sea-coast. The night was passed in preparations on both sides, and on the morrow, at break of day, the two armies were drawn up in view of each other.

"The Iron Legion and the Thundering Legion were stationed by Constantius in the centre.

"In front of the first rank were stationed the standard-bearers, distinguished by a lion-skin that covered their head and shoulders. They bore the military ensigns of the cohorts, the eagle, the dragon, the wolf, the minotaur; these standards were perfumed, and for want of flowers were adorned with branches of pine.

"The spearsmen, bearing their lances and bucklers, formed the line immediately behind the standard-bearers.

"The princes, armed with swords, occupied the second rank, and the triarii the third. These wielded their javelins in their left hand; their pikes were planted before them, on which their shields were suspended, and bending on their right knee to the ground they awaited the signal for combat.

"The narrow intervals of the lines were filled with the machines of war.

"In the left wing of the legion, the cavalry of the allies displayed their floating banners. Mounted upon coursers speckled like the tiger, and fleet as the mountain eagle, the horsemen of Numidia, of Saguntum, and the enchanting banks of the Bætis, managed their steeds with grace and agility. A light plumed cap shadowed their foreheads, a short mantle of black wool floated from the shoulder, and a sword hung suspended at their side. With head inclined over the necks of their steeds, the reins firmly held in their teeth, and two short javelins in their hands, they rushed upon the enemy. The young Viriatus rode at the head of these fleet cavaliers, and directed the fury of their attack. Germans of gigantic stature were here and there intermingled, and rose like towers above the surrounding squadrons. The heads of these barbarians were enveloped in caps; they wielded in their hands massive clubs of oak, and were mounted on steeds savage and uncaparisoned. After these, some Numidian horsemen, with no other arms than a bow, and no other clothing than the chlamys, shivered under the unknown rigors of a northern sky.

"In that wing of our army which was opposed to the enemy, stood the gallant troop of Roman knights, in proud array; their helmets were of silver, surmounted with the figure of a wolf; their cuirasses glittered with gold, and at their side hung a weighty Iberian sword, suspended by an azure belt. Their saddles were adorned with ivory, and under them was spread a purple cloth; their hands covered with gauntlets, held the silken reins of their sable steeds.

"The Cretan archers, the Roman velites, and the different Gallic corps, were arranged in the front of the army. The latter possess such a natural instinct for war, that in the heat of conflict the common soldier will perform the duties of a general, rally his scattered companions, offer some important instruction, or point out the post which it will be most advantageous to secure. Nothing can equal the impetuosity of their assault: while the German is deliberating, they have crossed the torrent, and gained the mountain summit; you think them at the foot of the citadel, and they have carried the entrenchment, and are mounting the battered wall. In vain the swiftest horsemen strive to outstrip them in the charge; the Gauls laugh at their efforts, spring before their horses, and seem to say: 'As soon may you attempt to seize the driving blast, or the bird in its airy flight!'

"All these barbarians were remarkable for the ruddy hue of their countenance, the lively blue of their eyes, and a look of fierce defiance; they wore large breeches, and a tunic, covered with patches of purple; and a girdle of skin bound to their side their trusty sword. The Gaul never quits this weapon; if I may use the expression, it is wedded to him, as to its lord and master; it accompanies him through life, it follows him to the funeral pile, and descends with him to the tomb. Such was once the practice with the widowed spouses of the Gauls, and such still prevails on the banks of the Indus.

"To sum up the whole: stationed on the brow of a hill, like a thunder-cloud that threatens destruction, a Christian legion, surnamed the Chaste, formed, in the rear of the army, the corps of reserve, and the guard of Cæsar. This legion filled the same post under Constantius, that the Theban had formerly done, e'er it was butchered by the inhuman Maximianus. Victor,[1] an illustrious warrior of Marseilles, led to the fight the soldiers of that religion, which can as nobly wear the helmet of the veteran, as the hair-cloth of the anchorite.

"And now the eye was struck with a universal movement: here the standard-bearers advanced to mark out the extent of the line; there the cavalry swept along with an impetuous career, and the infantry moved forward in long and undulating succession. On every side was heard the neigh of the impatient steed, the clank of the chains, the lumbering roll of the balistæ and catapultæ, the regular pace of the infantry, the voice of the chiefs as they repeated the word of command, and the sound of the pikes as they rose and fell at the order of the tribunes. The Romans formed themselves in battle array at the flourish of the bugle and trumpet; but we Cretans formed our ranks to the sound of the lyre; still faithful, in the midst of barbarians, to the customs of our country.

---

[1] The martyr.

"But all this apparatus of the Romans, when contrasted with the savage simplicity of the hostile army, served only to render the latter more formidable.

"Arrayed in the skins of every animal that is terrible to the eye, the Franks resembled at a distance a herd of savage beasts. A tunic, that scarcely reached the knee, and fitting close to the body, served to heighten the effect of their gigantic stature. The eyes of these barbarians are of a hue that resembles the deep in a storm; their light hair, hanging long and loose on their shoulders, and dyed with a red liquid, appears like fire intermingled with blood. The most part allow their beard to grow on the upper lip only, which gives their countenance all the terror of the wolf, or the mastiff. Some bear in their right hand a long spear, and in their left a buckler, which they whirl round like a rapid wheel; others are armed with a kind of javelin (called angon), with a double barb of iron at its point; but all wear at their girdle the terrible Frankish battle-axe: this instrument has a double edge, the handle is covered with steel, and in the hands of the Frank it has a deadly efficacy; he raises the death-cry, and hurls it at his victim with unerring exactness.

"Faithful to the customs of the ancient Germans, these barbarians were drawn up in the form of a wedge, their usual order of battle. This formidable triangle, which presented nothing to the eye but a forest of spears, and half-naked bodies, advanced with impetuosity, yet in exact order, to penetrate the Roman line. At the point of the triangle, the bravest of the band were stationed; the beards of these were long and bristling, and they wore a ring of iron on the arm: they had sworn not to quit these marks of servitude till after having sacrificed a Roman. Every chieftain in this vast body was surrounded by the warriors of his own family, as the strongest incitement to sustain the shock with firmness, and either to conquer or die with his friends. Each tribe rallied under some peculiar symbol: the more noble among them were distinguished by a cluster of bees, or by the heads of three lances. Pharamond, the aged king of the Sicambri, directed the operations of the whole army, while his grandson, Merovius, commanded immediately under him. The infantry of the Franks was flanked on both sides by their cavalry, which lay opposed to that of the Romans: their helmets were in the shape of yawning mouths, overshadowed by the two wings of a vulture; their corselets were of iron, and their bucklers painted white; they resembled phantoms of the night, or those fantastic shapes which are formed by the clouds during a tempest. Clodion, the son of Pharamond, and father of Merovius, was conspicuous at the head of this formidable body.

In the rear of the enemy, and stretching along the sands, appeared the camp of the enemy, resembling a village of laborers and fishermen; it was filled with women and children, and its only fortification was a line of wagons, and a kind of rampart of thick hides. In a wood, at a short distance from the camp, three tattered sorcerers were driving young colts from a consecrated grove, to discover from their course to which party Tuisto had decreed the victory. The sea on one side, and a range of deep forests on the other, formed the frame of this magnificent picture.

"Emerging from a cloud of gold, the morning sun suddenly appeared, and illumined the woods, the ocean, and the two armies, with his rays. The whole field appeared in a blaze, from the reflection of the helmets and lances. The warlike instruments struck up the air of Julius Cæsar's march to Gaul, and at the sound every heart beat with tumult, every eye sparkled with rage, and every hand grasped the sword with ardor and impatience. With trembling eagerness, the steed paws the ground, tosses his proud head on high, and dashes the white foam around; all his veins are distended, and he lifts his expanded nostril to the breeze to snuff up the sounds of battle. The Romans shouted the song of Probus:

"'When a thousand warlike Franks shall have yielded to our valor, with what ease shall we vanquish the millions of Persia!'

"The Greeks repeated in chorus the Pæan, and the Gauls the hymn of the Druids. The Franks, in answer to these, began their song of death; they applied their lips to the hollow of their bucklers, and raised a loud and melancholy sound, like the bellowing of the ocean when lashed into fury by the tempest; they then raised a shrill cry, and chanted the war-song to the praise of their heroes:

"'Pharamond, Pharamond, we have fought bravely with our swords.

"'Our battle-axe has been hurled at the foe, and the sweat has flowed in torrents from our limbs. The eagles and all the birds of prey have scented the carnage of the fight, and screamed for joy; the raven has swum in the blood of the slain; long have the virgins wept and lamented.

"'Pharamond, Pharamond, we have fought bravely with our swords.

"'Our fathers fell in battle; all the vultures mourned for them, for our fathers filled them with carnage! Let us celebrate those mothers who suckled their infants with blood, and filled the hearts of their sons with valor. 'Pharamond, the song is ended, the hours of life glides swiftly away, but when death comes, we will smile at his terrors!'

"Such was the song with which forty thousand barbarians rent the air. The horsemen beat time to the tune, and at each burden of the song they struck their iron javelins with violence on their sounding bucklers.

"The Franks were now within reach of the arrows of our light troops. The two armies made a general halt, and a profound silence ensued. Cæsar, from the midst of the Christian legion, gave his orders to raise the purple coat of arms, which was the signal for battle; every bow was bent, every pike was extended; and instantly at the word of command, out flew the swords of the cavalry, whose sudden flash far around illuminated the field. 'Victory to the emperor!' was the universal shout that arose from the legions. The barbarians answered with a deep and terrible roar: the thunder that bursts over the summits of the Apennines, the groan that issues from the caverns of Ætna when it vomits its torrents of liquid fire, the deafening roar of the ocean when whirlwinds tear it from its bed, and rocks the marble shores, are less terrific and appalling.

"The Gauls began the combat : they launched their javelins at the Franks, and then rushed upon them, sword in hand. The enemy received them with intrepidity. Three times they returned to the charge, and three times they fell back without making any impression on the vast body that opposed them. The Greeks, not less brave, and more skilful than the Gauls, rained a tempest of arrows on the Sicambri ; after thus harassing both sides of the hostile triangle, we retreated slowly and in good order. As a bull, the lord of the pastures, though proud of his mutilated horn, and the honorable scars of many a victorious conflict, yet unable to chase off the fly that torments him, rages round the plain and pants beneath the ardors of noon ; so the Franks, pierced by our arrows, grew furious with wounds that were without glory and without revenge. Transported with blind rage, they broke short the arrows that transfixed their bosom, rolled themselves on the earth, and struggled in all the agonies of death.

The Roman cavalry made a motion to fall on the barbarians, and Clodion prepared to meet the shock. The long-haired king was mounted on a black and white gelding, that had been raised among a herd of roes and reindeer in the stud of Pharamond. The barbarians pretended that she was of the race of Rinfax, steed of night, with frozen mane, and Skinfax, steed of day, with mane of sunlight. When in winter she bore her master in his bark chariot, without wheels or axles, her feet never sunk into the rime, and lighter than the birch-leaf moved by the wind, she scarcely grazed the surface of the newly-fallen snow.

"A violent combat now ensued between the horse of the two opposing wings.

"Meanwhile this frightful mass of barbarian infantry was continually threatening to overwhelm the legions. The latter suddenly wheeled about, changed their front of battle, and attacked the two sides of the triangle with their pikes. The velites, the Greeks, and the Gauls, bore down upon the other side, and the Franks were besieged like a vast fortress. The conflict grew warm; a whirlwind of dust arose and involved the combatants. The blood flowed like torrents swelled by the winter rains, like the waves of Euripus in the straits of Euboea. The Frank, proud of his wounds, which were more visible on his half-naked body, resembled a spectre that had burst from the tomb, and was stalking amidst the slain. The arms lost their brilliancy, all was dimmed with dust, with sweat, and with carnage. Broken helmets, scattered plumes, bucklers cloven asunder, and cuirasses pierced with many a stroke, strewed the ground in mingled confusion. The heated breath of a hundred thousand combatants, mingled with the fuming breath of the horses, and the vapor of sweat and blood, formed a kind of meteor on the field of battle, which flitted from sword to sword like a vivid flash of lightning through the darkness of the storm. Amidst the mingled sound of cries, shrieks, and menaces, the clash of swords and javelins, the hissing of darts and arrows, and the deeper murmurs of the machines of war, the voice of the commanders could no longer be distinguished.

"Merovius had made a frightful massacre of the Romans. He was seen standing erect on an immense chariot, in the midst of twelve companions at arms, known as his twelve peers, over whom he towered like a giant. Waving above the chariot, appeared the warlike ensign, named the Oriflamme. The chariot itself was hung round with horrid spoils, and drawn by three bulls, whose feet and horns were stained with gore. The inheritor of the sword of Pharamond was of the same age, and possessed all the beauty and fierceness of that Demon of Thrace, who lights his altars with the fires that consume the cottage and the town. The origin of Merovius was said to be strange and mysterious. Merovius passed, among the Franks, for the strange offspring of the secret intercourse of the wife of Clodion with a sea-monster; the light hair of the young Sicambrian, adorned with a crown of lilies, resembled wavy, golden flax, attached by a snow-white fillet to the distaff of a barbarian queen. One would have said that his cheeks had been painted with the vermilion berries that grow amid the snows on the eglantines of the forests of Germany. Around his neck his mother had hung a collar of shells, as the Gauls suspend relics to the branches of the most promising sapling of a sacred forest. Waving a white flag in his hand, Merovius called his fierce Sicambri to the field of honor; with loud cries they expressed at once the ardor of their attachment and their eagerness for the fight: to behold three generations of heroes at their head, the grandsire, the son, and the father, filled them with an ardor and enthusiasm which they could not restrain.

"Merovius, satiated with slaughter, was seen standing in a thoughtful posture, and contemplating, from the height of his chariot, the carnage with which he had strewed the plain. Such is the repose of the Numidian lion after his ravage among the flock: his hunger is appeased, his breast exhales the odor of carnage, his jaws, heavy with flocks of wool, yawn, wearied with the slaughter; at last he sinks down in the midst of the slain lambs; his mane, moist with a dew of blood, falls each side his neck; he crosses his powerful paws, stretches his head upon his claws, and, with half-closed eyes, licks the soft fleeces around him.

"The chief of the Gauls perceived Merovius buried in this haughty and insulting repose. His fury was enkindled, and advancing toward the son of Pharamond, he exclaimed in a tone of irony:

"'Chief of the long hair, this arm shall soon place you on the throne of Hercules, the Gaul. Young hero, you deserve to bear the mark of the steel to the palace of Teutates. I will not leave you to languish in a shameful old age.'

"'And who art thou,' replied Merovius, with a disdainful smile: 'canst thou boast a noble race? Thou Roman slave, fearest thou not the terrors of my lance?'

"'I fear but one thing,' replied the Gaul, trembling with rage: 'it is lest your sky fall on my head.'

"'Retire,' said the proud Sicambrian, 'and give up your ground!'

"'The ground that I shall give up you shall keep eternally,' cried the Gaul.

"At these words, Merovius flew along the beam of the chariot, sprung with his spear over the heads of the bulls, and presented himself before the Gaul, who had hastened to receive him.

"Both armies paused to witness the combat of their two chieftains. The Gaul rushed, sword in hand, upon the young Frank, pressed hard upon him, and aiming a violent blow, wounded him in the shoulder, and forced him to recoil beneath his chariot. Merovius, recovering himself, hurled his lance at the Gaul, and the double-barbed weapon penetrated firmly into his buckler. At the same instant the son of Clodion sprung forward like a leopard, stamped his foot on the javelin, and in its descent to the earth, brought down also the buckler of his enemy. The unfortunate Gaul was thus left defenceless, and exposed to all the fury of his adversary. At this critical moment, Merovius hurled his battle-axe; it whizzed through the air, and fell, deep buried in the forehead of the Gaul, like the axe of the woodman in the crest of the pine. The head of the warrior was cleft in twain; the brains were spilled on either side, and the eyes rolled on the ground. The body remained for a moment balanced erect, stretching out the convulsed hands, and then it fell weltering in gore.

"At this spectacle, the Gauls sent forth a cry of grief. This chief was the last descendant of that Vercingetorix, who had so long held the fortunes of Julius Cæsar in the balance. His death seemed to determine the fate of the contest; the empire of the Gauls must now necessarily pass to the Franks, who, with loud shouts, surrounded Merovius, mounted him on a buckler, placed him on their shoulders, and proclaimed him king, with his fathers as the bravest of the Sicambri. Panic began to spread among the legions. Constantius, who, from the centre of the body of reserve, watched with a careful eye every movement of the troops, perceived the disorder of the cohorts. Turning to the Christian legion, he exclaimed: 'Brave soldiers, the fortune of Rome is in your hands. Let us march against the enemy!'

"Immediately the faithful lowered their eagles before their commander, in token of submission and respect. Victor gave the word of command; the legion was instantly in motion, and descended the hill in silence. Each soldier wore a cross on his buckler, surrounded with the motto:

"'BY THIS SIGN SHALT THOU CONQUER.'

"All the centurions were martyrs, covered with scars of the fire or sword. What influence could the fear of wounds and of death have on such men? O touching fidelity! these warriors were about to shed the remainder of their blood in the cause of those same princes who had nearly drained its very source in hatred to their religion. Neither fear nor joy agitated the bosoms of these Christian heroes, but tranquil valor was marked on their brow. When the legion advanced to the plain, the Franks perceived themselves arrested in the midway of victory. They afterward recounted that they saw at the head of this legion a pillar of fire and cloud, and a rider, clothed in white, armed with a lance and golden buckler. The Romans who fled, returned to the charge; hope revived in every bosom, and the most feeble were aroused to energy; thus, when, after a tempestuous night, the morning sun darts his cheering rays from the east, the laborer feels his heart revive within him, and admires the mild splendor of returning day; the young sparrow twitters joyfully in the ivy of the ancient cabin, while the aged sire takes his seat at the door, listens delighted to the charming sounds around him, and blesses the Almighty.

"At the approach of the soldiers of Christ, the barbarians close their ranks, the Romans rally to the fight. When arrived on the field of battle, the legion halted, and placing one knee on the earth, received from the hands of a minister of peace, the benediction of the God of armies. Constantius himself removed his crown of laurel, and bent in reverence. The holy troop then arose, and without casting their javelins, marched sword in hand against the enemy. The combat was renewed in every quarter. The Christian legion forced a broad passage through the barbarian ranks; Romans, Greeks, and Gauls, all burst through the opening that Victor had made, and rushed to gain the centre of the broken Franks. And now, to the regular attacks of a disciplined army, succeeded single combats, in the manner of the heroes of Ilion. A thousand groups of warriors meet in fierce and terrible contest; they press forward, they rage, they struggle; grief, and despair, and terror, are seen on every side. Daughters of France, in vain you prepare the balm for wounds that no art can heal! Here, pierced by the deadly javelin to the heart, a warrior falls to the earth, while the fond and sacred images of his country and his home float before his expiring view; there, dashed helpless to the earth by the barbarian's club, another thinks on his spouse afar, and the infant that yet hangs at her breast; but he, alas! shall embrace them no more. One regrets his palace, another his cottage; the former his pleasures, the latter his sorrows: for man is attached to life by misery as well as by prosperity. Here, surrounded by his companions, a pagan soldier is dying, hurling forth imprecations against Cæsar and the gods; there, forsaken and abandoned, a Christian soldier expires in placid resignation, pressing a crucifix to his lips, and supplicating heaven for the emperor's welfare. The Sicambri, all wounded in front, and stretched on their backs, wore even in death so ferocious an air, that the most intrepid scarce dared gaze upon them.

"Nor can I ever forget you, ye generous pair, to whose constancy I was a witness on these plains of slaughter. These faithful friends—more faithful than prudent—in order that their destiny in fight might be the same, had bound themselves together by a chain of iron. One had fallen dead beneath the arrow of a Cretan; the other, though struck with a mortal wound, was still alive, and reclining over his brother in arms. 'Warrior,' cried he, in a faint, expiring voice, 'thou hast fallen asleep after the fatigues of the battle. Thine eyes shall open no more at my call; but the chain of our friendship is not broken, it still links me firmly to thy side.'

"As he finished these words, the young Frank fell exhausted, and died embracing the body of his friend. Their beauteous locks intermingled as they fell, like the wavy flames of a double fire expiring on the altar, like the trembling rays of the constellation Gemini, when it sinks into the sea.

'Meanwhile, the rage of the conflict began to subside. The arm that aimed the deadly blow was fatigued, and had spent its force; the yell of battle sunk by degrees into the cry of plaintive anguish, and the groan of sullen despair. Sometimes a number of the wounded, expiring together, left an interval of terrible silence; sometimes the voice of pain assumed fresh vigor, and mounted in long-drawn accents to heaven. Horses were seen wandering without their riders, and trampling at once over the dead and the dying; several abandoned machines of war were blazing in various directions on the field, like the mournful torches of this immense funeral

"Night covered with her veil of darkness this scene of human ferocity. The Franks, vanquished but still redoubtable, retired within their inclosure of chariots. This night, so necessary for our repose, was to us but a night of terrors and alarm, for every instant we dreaded an attack. The barbarians rendered the darkness of night more terrible by their cries, which resembled the howl of savage monsters; they were lamenting the warriors they had lost, and were animating each other to meet death with equal firmness. We neither durst quit our arms, nor light the watch-fires. The Roman soldiers shivered beneath the cold dews of night; they sought their companions amidst the darkness; they called each other by name; they asked each other for bread or water; and bound up their bleeding wounds with fragments of their tattered garments. The sentinels at regular intervals repeated the watch-word of the night.

"All the chiefs of the Cretans had fallen in battle. The

blood of Philopœmen appearing to my companions a favorable augury, they nominated me as their chief. In drawing upon myself the fierceness of the enemy's attack, I had been so fortunate as to save the Iron Legion from inevitable destruction. The confirmation of this choice, accompanied with a crown of oak, and the eulogium of Constantius, was the reward of this hazardous but fortunate enterprise. At the head of these light troops, I approached almost to the verge of the enemy's camp, and waited with impatience for the return of morning; but what a spectacle did the morn present to our view! it surpassed in horror everything that we had yet witnessed.

"The Franks, during the night had cut off the heads of those Romans who had fallen in battle, and planted them on pikes before their camp, with the countenance turned toward us. With the saddles of their horses, and their broken bucklers, they had raised an immense funeral pyre in the midst of their camp. The aged Pharamond, with eyes that glared with a terrible expression, and whose long, white hair waved to the breezes of morning, was seated on the top of the pile. At the foot of it were stationed Clodion and Merovius: in the guise of brands, they held in their hands the blazing hafts of two broken pikes, ready to set fire to the funeral throne of their father, if the Romans should force the intrenchment of their camp.

"We remained mute with sorrow and astonishment: the conquerors themselves seemed conquered by such a display of barbarity intermingled with heroism and magnanimity. Tears flowed from our eyes at the view of the bleeding heads of so many of our companions; those mouths, closed in death and discolored with gore, seemed still uttering the last night's words of friendship. At the thought, our sorrow was changed into thirst for vengeance. We did not await the signal for attack; nothing could resist the impetuosity of the assault; the troops in an instant burst the barrier of the chariots, and rushed precipitately into the defenceless camp. Here we were met by a new species of opponents: the wives of the barbarians, clad in black apparel, sprung upon us with fury, ran headlong upon our weapons, or endeavored to force them from our hands; some caught the flying Sicambrian by the beard, and forced him back to the fight; others, raving like bacchanals, fell furiously upon their husbands and fathers; many strangled their infant children, and threw them to be trampled on by the advancing ranks of the cavalry and infantry. Some, passing a fatal cord around their necks, attached themselves to the horns of the oxen, and were strangled while being drawn by them. One cried out from the midst of her companions: 'Romans, all your presents have not been fatal; if you have brought us the iron that enchains us in servitude, you have also bestowed that which can give us freedom!' and as she said this, she plunged a dagger in her bosom.

"Happily for the people of Pharamond, that heaven, which perhaps preserves them for some illustrious destiny, interposed in their favor, and saved the residue of their warriors from destruction. An impetuous wind arose from the northwest, and dashed the swelling waves over these flat and sandy shores. It was one of those fierce equinoctial blasts so terrible in these climates, and whose violence is so great, that the whole ocean seems torn from its bed. The sea, like a powerful ally of the barbarians, entered the camp of the Franks, and chased thence their Roman invaders. Our men retreated before the overwhelming waves; the Franks assumed fresh courage; they imagined that the sea-monster, the father of their young prince, had come from the caverns of the ocean to their succor. They profited by our disorder, seconded the efforts of the sea, and pressed on us with vigor. An extraordinary scene now struck the eyes of all parties. Here the affrighted oxen were plunging through the waves, and dragging after them the floating chariots, showing nothing but their crooked horns above the waves, and resembling a multitude of rivers bringing their tribute to the ocean; there the Salians, springing into their boats of skin, overpowered our men as they struggled with the tide. Merovius himself, borne along on a large buckler of osier, and surrounded by his chiefs, as by so many attendant

Tritons, pursued us with rage and desperation. The women, filled with furious joy, clapped their hands at the dreadful scene, and blessed the waves that delivered them from their enemies. The ocean raged with increasing violence, and bore along arms, and horses, and soldiers in its course: here the horseman disappeared beneath the waves; there the foot soldier struggled, with his sword only above the water; the very dead bodies seemed reanimated, and were carried along in the mingled sweep of the tide. Separated from the rest of the legions, and surrounded only by a few faithful followers, I combated long against a host of barbarians; but, at length, overpowered by numbers, I fell pierced with wounds, in the midst of my companions, who were stretched dead around me.

"I remained for many hours in a state of insensibility. When I again opened my eyes to the light, I perceived nothing but the slimy strand, that the waves had abandoned, with bodies drowned, and half-buried in the sand; while the sea that had retreated to an amazing distance, faintly formed the blue line of the horizon. I attempted to rise, but felt myself too weak to effect it, and was forced to remain stretched on my back, with my eyes fixed on the firmament. While my soul hung suspended between life and death, I heard a voice pronounce these words in Latin: 'If any one here is still breathing, let him speak.' I made an effort to turn my head, and beheld a Frank, whom I knew from his sagum of birch bark to be a slave. He saw me move, ran toward me, and knowing my country from my dress: 'Young Greek,' said he, 'take courage!' As he said this he knelt down by my side, and leaning over me, examined my wounds. 'I do not think them mortal,' he continued, after a moment of silence. He immediately produced some balm, some simples, and a vessel of pure water. He bathed my wounds, gently closed them, and bound them up with long bandages of reeds. I could only express my gratitude to him by a movement of my head, and the expression that he read in my almost lifeless eye. It now became necessary to remove me from my present comfortless situation, and his embarrassment was extreme. He looked around him with anxiety; he feared, as he afterward informed me, lest some party of the barbarians should discover him. It was near the time of the tide's return ; charity rendered my deliverer ingenious, and he drew from the danger itself the means of my deliverance : he perceived one of the small boats belonging to the Franks that had run ashore. Raising me half up from the sand, and inclining his body, he drew me gently on his shoulders, and bore me with difficulty to the boat : the task was laborious, for he was now advanced in years. The sea soon covered these long flat sands. The slave snatched up a broken pike, and when the tide raised up the boat, guided me along, by means of his broken weapon, with all the skill of an experienced pilot. The waves carried us far up on the shore, and at last we landed in a creek whose sloping banks were covered with wood.

"These places were well known to the Frank. He sprang from the boat, and taking me as before upon his shoulders, carried me to a kind of cavern, in which the barbarians were accustomed to conceal their corn during the time of war. Here he made me a couch of moss, and gave me a little wine to revive me.

"'Poor unfortunate,' said he, addressing me in my native tongue, 'I must quit you, and you will be forced to pass the night here alone. But to-morrow I hope to bring you good news ; endeavor, meanwhile, to taste the sweets of repose.'

"As he said this, he stripped himself of his miserable cloak, spread it over me as a cover, and then retreated into the woods."

BOOK SEVENTH.

SUMMARY.

Continuation of the Recital. Eudorus becomes the Slave of Pharamond. History of Zacharius. Clothilde, the wife of Pharamond. Dawn of Christianity in the Country of the Franks. Customs of the Franks. Return of Spring. The Chase. Northern Barbarians. Tomb of Ovid. Eudorus saves the life of Merovius. Merovius promises Liberty to Eudorus. Return of the Hunters to the Camp of Pharamond. The Goddess Hertha. Festival of the Franks. Deliberations with the Romans on the Question of Peace or War. Dispute of Camulogenus and Chloderic. The Franks decide to treat for Peace. Eudorus is freed, and goes to make Proposals of Peace to Constantius. Zacharius conducts Eudorus to the Frontiers of Gaul. Their Adieus.

"By Hercules!" cried Demodocus, interrupting the recital of Eudorus, "I always loved the children of Æsculapius! They are acquainted with the secrets of nature, and are kind and attentive to the miseries of man. They are found amidst gods, centaurs, heroes, and shepherds. My son, what was the name of this divine barbarian? for, alas! Jupiter seems not to have drawn his lot from the fortunate urn. This master of the clouds has the destinies of all men at his disposal: on one he showers every blessing that can alleviate the heart, on another he pours all the sorrows of adverse fortune. To such necessities was the ruler of Ithaca reduced, that he was happy to repose on a couch of dried leaves, which his own hands had formed. Formerly, when men were less degenerate than the present race, this favorite of the god of Epidaurus would have been the friend and companion of warriors; now, he is a slave amidst an inhospitable nation. But, son of Lasthenes, proceed, tell me the name of your deliverer, for willingly could I honor him, as Nestor once honored Machaon."

Eudorus smiled, and continued his narrative:

"His name among the Franks was Harold. Faithful to his promise, he returned to visit me with the first rays of morning. He was accompanied by a woman, clothed in a long purple robe, whose neck and arms were uncovered, after the manner of the Franks. There was a mixture of barbarism and humanity in her first appearance, which was quite inexplicable: the natural expression of her countenance was wild and savage, but it was softened and corrected by traits of pity and sweetness.

"'Young Greek,' said the slave, 'thank Clothilde, the spouse of my master, Pharamond. She has obtained your pardon from her husband, and has come in person to shield you from the rage of the Franks. When healed of your wounds, I doubt not you will prove an obedient slave, and repay her kindness by your fidelity and gratitude.'

"By this time many of her attendants were in the cave. They formed a hurdle of the branches of trees, and bore me on it to the camp of my master.

"The Franks, despite their valor, and the sudden swell of the sea, had been obliged to yield the victory to the discipline of the legions; and happy to escape an entire defeat, they had retired before the conquerors. I was thrown into a wagon, with the rest of the wounded. Day and night for two successive weeks they moved rapidly forward in a northern direction, and did not stop their flight, till they imagined themselves far beyond the reach of the army of Constantius.

"Till now I had scarcely felt the horrors of my situation; but as soon as I was refreshed by repose, and my wounds began to heal, I cast my eyes around me with horror. I saw myself in the midst of forests, a slave to barbarians, and a prisoner in a hut, which a circle of young trees surrounded as with a rampart. A gross drink formed from wheat, a little barley pounded between two stones, and morsels of meat thrown to me out of mere compassion, were my only nourishment. During half the day I was left on my bed of straw in solitary misery; but I suffered still more from the presence, than from the absence of the barbarians. The odors of the noisome composition with which they anointed their horses, the vapors of the broiled meats, the confined air of the cabin, and the cloud of smoke that unceasingly filled it, almost suffocated me. It was thus that a just providence made me expiate the luxuries of Naples, the perfumes and delights with which my senses were there intoxicated.

"The aged slave, occupied in his own duties, had but a few moments to bestow on me and my sufferings. I never beheld, without astonishment, that unvaried serenity which reigned on his countenance, in the midst of the toilsome occupations with which he was burdened.

"'Eudorus,' said he, one evening, 'your wounds are now nearly healed. To-morrow you must begin to fulfil your new duties. They intend to send you with some other slaves to fetch wood from the forest. Courage, my son and companion, summon up all your virtue. Heaven will support you if you implore its assistance.'

"At these words, the slave departed, and left me plunged in despair. I passed the night in a state of horrible agitation; I formed a thousand projects, and as quickly rejected them. Sometimes I wished to end my days; then again I planned how to effect my escape. But weak and without succor, how could I attempt to fly? How find a way through these trackless forests? There was but one effectual resource against the evils that oppressed me, and that was religion; but, alas! this was the only means of my deliverance, of which I thought not at all. The return of day surprised me in the midst of these agonizing reflections, and I heard a voice without that cried:

"'Roman slave, arise.'

"They gave me for my covering the skin of a boar, a cup of horn to drink from, and a dried fish for my food; I then followed the slaves, who pointed out the way.

"When arrived at the forest, they began to search amidst the snow and withered leaves, for branches of trees that had been broken off by the wind. They formed them into scattered heaps, and bound them together with bands of bark. They made me signs to follow their example, but seeing that I was ignorant of the method, they were contented to place on my shoulders a bundle of dried branches. My haughty brow was thus forced to humble itself under the yoke of servitude; my naked feet were chilled by the snow; my hair was stiffened by the hoar frost, while the keen blast of the northeast congealed the very tears in my eyes. I supported my faltering steps with a branch torn from my burden; and bent double, like an old man, I slowly urged my way through the trees of the forest.

"I was just ready to sink under the pressure of pain, when I suddenly saw the aged slave at a short distance: he was laden with a weight more oppressive than my own, yet he still smiled on me with that air of peaceful serenity which never forsook him. I was filled with an involuntary confusion at the sight.

"'What,' said I within myself, 'shall this man, weighed down by years, smile under a burden triple my own, while I, in the vigor of youth, weep at it?'

"My deliverer came up and accosted me: 'Eudorus,' said he, 'do you not find this first burden oppressive? Trust me, my young companion, habit, and above all resignation, will render the rest much lighter. Only see, even at my age, what a weight I have accustomed myself to carry.'

"'Ah!' I exclaimed, 'charge me with this burden that bows you down. Would that I might expire in delivering you from your pains!'

"'My son,' replied the old man, 'I feel no pain. But why do you desire to die? Come, I wish to reconcile you to life; come and rest with me in yonder sheltered spot; I will light a fire, and we will have some conversation together.'

"We clambered up some irregular mounds, formed, as I soon perceived, by the ruins of a Roman fortification. When we arrived at the summit, I perceived the inclosure of a deserted camp. This place was covered with immense oaks, which flourished on the same spot where former generations of oak had sunk into decay.

"'This,' said the slave, 'is the wood of Teutoburg, and the

camp of Varus. The mound of earth that you perceive in the midst, is the tomb in which Germanicus inclosed the ashes of his massacred legions. It has, however, been since opened by the barbarians; the bones of the Romans have been strewed over the earth; the skulls that are nailed to yonder trees, attest their impotent rage against the dead. A little further you may still distinguish the altars of turf on which the centurions of the first companies were sacrificed, and the tribunal from which Arminius harangued the Germans.'

"At these words, the old man cast his load upon the snow. He drew some branches from it, and kindled a fire; then inviting me to seat myself near him, and warm my hands that were benumbed with cold, he thus recounted his history:

"'My son, do you still lament over your misfortunes? Dare you speak of your sufferings in sight of the camp of Varus? Ought you not rather to draw this salutary lesson from the view: that man is born to affliction, and that it is unavailing to revolt against the evils inseparable from humanity? I offer you in my own person a striking example of what the false wisdom of the age calls the fickleness of fortune. You groan under your servitude; but what will you say, when you behold in me a descendant of Cassius, a slave, and a slave through choice?

"'When my ancestors were banished from Rome for having arisen in defence of liberty, and we were prohibited from carrying their image to the funeral rites, my family sought refuge in Christianity; the only asylum of true independence.

"'I too was happily educated in the precepts of the divine law, and served as a common soldier in the Theban legion, where I bore the name of Zacharius. This Christian legion, having refused to sacrifice to false gods, was butchered by the order of Maximianus, near Agaune in the Alps. Then was seen a memorable instance of that spirit of meekness which the Gospel alone can impart. Four thousand veterans, grown grey in the service of the state, yet animated with all the vigor of youth, and with arms in their hands, submitted like placid lambs to the sword of the executioner. The thought of self-defence never entered into their minds, so strongly were those precepts of their Divine Master engraven on their hearts, which ordain obedience, and forbid revenge! Maurice, who commanded the legion, was the first who fell, and after him the greater part of my comrades perished by the sword. My hands were bound behind me, and I lay amidst a crowd of victims, expecting the fatal blow. I know not for what purpose Providence preserved me, but I was forgotten in this general slaughter. The heaps of bodies that were piled around me, concealed me from the view of the centurions; and Maximianus having accomplished his design, retired with his army.

"'In this situation I lay till the second watch of the night, when hearing no sound but the dashing of the torrent in the neighboring mountains, I raised my head, and was struck with a miracle. The bodies of my slaughtered companions seemed to emit a brilliant light, and to scent the air with an agreeable odor. I adored the God of miracles, who had not chosen to accept the sacrifice of my life, and though unable to give the rites of sepulture to so many saints, yet I sought for the body of the illustrious Maurice. I found it half covered with the snow that had fallen during the night. Animated with supernatural strength, I burst asunder my bands, and with the head of a lance, scooped out a grave for my general. In this I placed the severed head and trunk of Maurice, beseeching this second Maccabæus to obtain a place for his unworthy servant in the armies of heaven. I then quitted this scene of triumph and of tears; I took the road to Gaul, and made my way to Denis, the first bishop of Lutetia.

"'The holy prelate received me with tears of joy, and admitted me among the number of his disciples. When he thought me capable of assisting him in the sacred ministry, he laid his hands upon me, and ordained me a priest of Jesus Christ, saying: "Humble Zacharius, be charitable; this is the only instruction I have to give you." But, alas! I was always destined to lose my friends, and always by the same hand. Maximianus caused Denis, and his companions Rusticus and Eleuthereus, to be beheaded. This was his last exploit in Gaul, for he shortly after resigned the command of this province to Constantius.

"'I had always before my eyes the precept of my holy bishop. I felt myself urged by an irresistible desire to devote myself to the service of the miserable, and often entreated Denis to obtain this favor for me by his intercession with the son of Mary.

"'The Christians of Lutetia buried their bishop in a cave at the foot of the hill on which he had suffered martyrdom. This hill was called the Mount of Mars, and was separated by a marshy ground from the river Sequana. One day, as I was traversing these marshes, I was met by a Christian woman in tears, who exclaimed: "O Zacharius, I am the most unfortunate of women! My spouse has been carried away captive by the Franks, and I am left with three infant children, destitute of the means of subsistence." I was immediately struck with mingled joy and confusion, in the assurance that God had listened to the petition of his generous martyr in my behalf. I endeavored to conceal my joy, and said to the woman: "Take courage; God will have pity on your distress." And without pausing to deliberate, I instantly set out for the colony of Agrippina.

"'I was acquainted with the captive soldier. He was a Christian, and had been for some time my brother in arms. He was a simple man, and one who feared God in prosperity; but a reverse of fortune had easily discouraged him, and it was to be feared that misfortune might make him forsake the faith. At Agrippina I learned that he had fallen into the hands of the chief of the Salians. The Romans had just concluded a truce with the Franks; I passed over to the barbarians, appeared before Pharamond, and offered myself in exchange for the Christian: I had no other means of paying his ransom, for I possessed nothing in the world. As I was strong and vigorous, and the other was a slave of a weak constitution, my proposal was easily accepted. The only condition I made was, that my master should dismiss his prisoner without disclosing the name of his deliverer. My request was complied with, and this poor father of an indigent family was sent back to his native hearth, to maintain his children, and console his spouse.

"'From that time I have remained here a slave. Heaven has not left me without a recompense; for while residing among these people, I have had the happiness to plant here the faith of Jesus Christ. Above all, it is my custom to explore the banks of the rivers, and counteract the effects of a fatal practice among these barbarians : in order to try whether their children will one day become valiant and renowned, they expose them on the waves in their hollow bucklers ; those who pass down the current in safety are preserved, the rest are left to perish. When I am so happy as to save any of these little angels from a premature and watery grave, I baptize them in the name of the Father, of the Son, and of the Holy Ghost, in order that the gates of Heaven may be opened to them.

"'The field of battle also presents to me an abundant harvest. During the darkness of night I prowl like a famished wolf amidst these scenes of carnage. I comfort the dying, who at first mistake me for the despoiler ; I speak to them of a better life, of the repose that the just will find in Abraham's bosom, and endeavor to arouse them to the desire of this happiness. If they are not mortally wounded, I hasten to succor them, and hope by charity to gain over to heaven the poor and the miserable.

"'As yet, my most remarkable conquest to the faith, is the young spouse of my master, the aged Pharamond. Clothilde has opened her heart to Jesus Christ. The natural violence and cruelty of her disposition have become softened into gentleness and compassion. There is scarcely a day but she assists me in recovering the wounded, or relieving the unfortunate. It is to her bounty that you owe your life. When I ran to acquaint her that you had been found still breathing among the dead, she at first thought of keeping you concealed in the cave, in order to preserve you from slavery. But she learned that the Franks were about to retreat into the interior of the country, and nothing now remained but to reveal the secret to Pharamond, and to obtain your pardon; for though the barbarians set a high value on able and vigorous slaves, yet their natural impatience, added to their own contempt of life, generally leads them to sacrifice the wounded.

"'Such, my son, is the history of Zacharius. If he has done aught to serve you, the only recompense that he asks of you is to calm the violence of your sorrows, and as he has been the means of saving your body, to suffer him to save your soul also. Eudorus, you were born under that gentle climate so near to the land of miracles, among those polished people who have civilized mankind; in that Greece whither Paul, that sublime apostle, carried the light of the Gospel: how many advantages do you possess over these sons of the North, whose minds are so gross, and whose manners are so brutalized! Will you be less sensible than they to the charms of the Gospel?'

"These last words of Zacharius entered like a dagger into my heart. The secret of my life sat heavy on my soul, and I durst not raise my eyes to my deliverer. I who had sustained, without emotion, the haughty looks of the masters of the universe, was now humbled before the majesty of an aged Christian priest, a slave among barbarians! Restrained on the one side by the shame of confessing my forgetfulness of religion, and urged on the other by the desire of avowing the whole, my agitation became extreme. Zacharius perceived it. Apprehensive that my wounds had opened anew, he demanded with anxiety the cause of my inquietude. Overcome, at last, by so much goodness, I could no longer conceal my tears, that burst forth in a torrent, and I threw myself at the old man's feet.

"'O my father, the wounds of my body afflict me not, they are now healed; a more deep and mortal wound is the cause of my anguish. You who perform so many sublime actions in the name of your sacred faith—can you behold the little resemblance there is between us, and believe that I am of the same religion as yourself?'

"'O Christ!' cried the saint, raising his hands toward heaven, 'my divine master, shall you have then here another servant besides myself!'

"'I am a Christian,' I replied.

"The man of charity pressed me to his heart, bedewed me with tears, and cried out, amidst sobs of joy:

"'My brother! my dear brother! I have found a brother!'

"'Yes,' I returned, in broken tones of repentant anguish, 'yes, I am a Christian!'

"During this conversation, the night had descended. We arose, resumed our burdens, and returned to the hut of Pharamond. Early the next morning, Zacharius came to call me, and conducted me to the depths of the forest. In the trunk of an aged beech, whence Segovia, the prophetess of the Germans, had formerly delivered her oracles, I saw a small image of Mary, the mother of the Saviour. A branch of ivy, laden with ripe berries, had been newly placed at the feet of the mother and child; it was not yet covered by the falling snow.

"'Last night,' said Zacharius, 'I informed Clothilde that we had another brother amongst us. Filled with joy at the news, she hastened hither in the darkness to adorn our altar, and to offer this branch to Mary in token of gratitude.'

"Zacharius had scarcely uttered these words when we beheld the spouse of Pharamond hastening toward us. She threw herself on her knees, in the snow at the foot of the beech. We placed ourselves at her side, and she pronounced, in a loud tone and a barbarous idiom, the prayer of the Saviour. Thus I beheld the origin of Christianity among the Franks. Celestial religion, who can speak the charms that surround thy cradle! How divine didst thou appear in Bethlehem to the shepherds of Judea! How miraculous didst thou appear to me in the Catacombs, when I saw an illustrious empress humble herself before thee! And who could have contained his tears at beholding thy first origin amidst the woods of Germany, surrounded with no other votaries than a Roman slave, a Greek prisoner, and a barbarian queen!

"For what was I waiting to return to the fold? Former disgusts had begun to convince me of the vanity of pleasures; the history of the hermit of Vesuvius had made a deep impression on my mind; Zacharius had nearly completed the conquest, by gaining my heart; but it was ordained that I should not return to the truth, till after a long series of sufferings, and by experience purchased at too dear a rate.

"Zacharius redoubled his zeal and solicitude for my welfare, and in his voice I seemed to hear the dictates of heaven. To behold the descendant of Brutus and Cassius a sincere adorer of Jesus, was itself a lesson. The stoical murderer of Cæsar, after a short, yet free, powerful, and glorious life, declares that virtue is but an empty name: the charitable disciple of Christ, a slave, oppressed with years, poor and unknown, pronounces nothing to be substantial here below but virtue. You would have thought that this priest had studied only in the school of charity, and yet he had a mind stored with knowledge, and enriched with a taste for the arts and for polite learning. He was well versed in Hebrew, Greek, and Roman antiquities. The view of such a man, tending the flocks of a barbarian master, and thus learnedly conversing of the wise and great of ancient days, had a charm for me that I can never forget. He often spoke concerning the customs of our barbarous masters.

"'My dear Eudorus,' he would say to me, 'should you again revisit your native land, how will your Grecian brethren crowd around you to listen to your narrative, and wonder at the strange manners of these long-haired kings! Your present afflictions will become to you a source of agreeable recollections. You will be considered by your ingenious countrymen as another Herodotus, come from a distant country to enchant them with your marvellous recitals. You may tell them, that even in the forests of Germany there exists a people who pretend to trace their origin from the Trojans (for, enchanted by the beautiful fables of the Hellenes, all men seek to be in some way allied to them); you may tell them that this people, composed of different tribes of Germans, Sicambrians, Bructeri,

Salians, and Catti, have assumed the name of *Franks*, meaning free, and that they have shown themselves not unworthy to bear the appellation.

"'Their government is, however, essentially monarchical. The sovereign power, divided among several kings, is centered in the hand of one in the time of danger. The tribe of the Salians, of which Pharamond is the chief, has almost always the honor to take the lead, because among the barbarians it has always been esteemed the most noble. It owes its fame to that ancient custom, which excludes females from the sovereignty, and intrusts the sceptre to the hands of a warrior alone.

"'The Franks assemble annually in the month of March, to deliberate on the affairs of the nation. They come in complete armor to this assembly. The king seats himself beneath an oak, and presents are brought him, which he receives with complacency. He listens to the complaints of his subjects, or rather his companions, and renders justice with impartiality.

"'Property is held only by yearly tenure. Each family cultivates annually the land assigned by their prince, and after the harvest has been gathered in, it becomes a part of the common possession.

"'The same simplicity marks the rest of their character. You see that we are clothed in the same dress, that we share the same food, inhabit the same cottages of clay, and sleep on the same beds of skin, as our masters.

"'You were yesterday a witness to the marriage of Merovius. A buckler, a battle-axe, an osier canoe, a horse ready caparisoned, and a yoke of oxen, were the only bridal presents of the inheritor of the crown of the Franks. If in the sports of his age, he exceed the rest in leaping over the lance, and the naked sword ; if he show himself brave in war, and just during peace, he may look after death for the honor of a funeral pile, and even for a pyramid of turf to cover his tomb.'

"Such was the description that Zacharius gave me.

"Spring soon returned to clothe with renovated verdure the naked forests of the North. The face of each wood and valley assumed a new appearance: the black points of the rocks first arose above the melting snow, and broke the dull uniformity of winter; next appeared the dark, waving branches of the pine; while all the early trees of spring replaced with festoons of flowers the wintry crystals that had weighed down their branches. With the beautiful days of spring returned the season for combat.

"One part of the Franks resumed their arms, another prepared for their journey to the more northern regions, to chase the bear and the urus. Merovius headed the hunters' band, and I was comprised in the number of the slaves destined to accompany him. I bade adieu to Zacharius, and was for some time constrained to separate from this most virtuous of men.

"We traversed with incredible rapidity the regions which extend from the Sea of Scandia to the shores of the Euxine. These vast forests serve as a passage for a hundred barbarous nations, who pour in successive torrents toward the Roman empire. It seems as if they had heard a voice from the south that summoned them from the east and north. What are their names, their race, and country? Ask Heaven that conducts them; for they are as unknown to men as the inhospitable regions through which they pass. They come; they find everything prepared for them; for the spreading tree is their tent, and the desert their path. Would you know where they last encamped? Yon scattered bones, those pines broken as by the tempest, those forests on fire, and those plains covered with ashes, will declare it. We had the good fortune not to encounter any of these migratory armies, but we met a few wandering families, compared with which the Franks were a disciplined nation. These unfortunates, without shelter, without clothing, often even without food, had naught to console these ills, but a profitless freedom and a few dances of the desert. But when these dances are executed on the banks of a river in the recesses of the forest, when echo repeats for the first time the accents of the human voice, when the bear looks down from the summit of his rock upon the sports of the savage man, one cannot help finding grandeur in the very rudeness of the picture, and being touched by the fate of this child of solitude, born unknown to the world, treading for a moment those valleys through which he will never return, then hiding his grave beneath the moss of the desert, which has not even retained the imprint of his footsteps.

"It happened one day that I had strayed a short distance from the hunters' band; and I was surprised to find myself on the banks of the Ister, and within view of the Euxine Sea. As I wandered along, engaged with the scene before me, I discovered a tomb, over which grew a laurel. I tore aside the shrubs that concealed the inscription; it was in Latin, and I read this first verse from the Elegies of the unfortunate poet:

PARVE (NEC INVIDEO) SINE ME, LIBER, IBIS IN URBEM.*

"I cannot describe to you the feelings of my soul at this discovery of the tomb of Ovid, in the midst of these deserts. How many sorrowful reflections did I make on the miseries of exile—miseries that, alas! were my own; and on the inutility of talent to promote happiness! Rome, which at this day reads with such rapture the writings of this most ingenious of her poets; Rome, without emotion, witnessed for twenty years the tears of the exiled Ovid. The savage inhabitants on Ister's banks, less ungrateful than the people of Ausonia, still think on this Orpheus, who appeared in their forests. They come and dance around the spot where his ashes repose; they have even retained something of his language; in such grateful remembrance do they hold the Roman, who, in order to gain the attention of the Sarmatians to his song, submitted to be called a barbarian!

"The object of the Franks in traversing these vast countries,

---

* "Haste, little book, I envy not thy doom,
   Though thy fond master go not—haste to Rome."

was to visit certain tribes of their nation, that had formerly been transported by Probus to the banks of the Euxine. On our arrival here we found that these tribes had for some months disappeared, and could learn no account of the route they had taken. Merovius, on this intelligence, took the resolution of immediately returning to the camp of Pharamond.

"Providence had ordained that I should recover my liberty at the tomb of Ovid. As we returned near this monument, a she-wolf, that had concealed herself in the thicket, where she had deposited her young, darted upon Merovius. I happened to be near his person, and slew the furious animal. From this moment my young master regarded me with marked attention, and promised to procure my liberty from his father. I became his companion during the rest of the chase, and he made me sleep under his roof. I sometimes spoke to him of the bloody fight in which I had seen his chariot drawn by three untamed bulls; and he would leap for joy at the recollection of his glory. Sometimes I entertained him with a description of the manners and traditions of my country; but nothing in the whole account gave him so much pleasure as the history of the labors of Hercules and of Theseus. When I attempted to make him understand our arts and refinements, he brandished his spear, and exclaimed with impatience, 'Greek, Greek, I am thy master!'

"After an absence of many months, we arrived at the camp of Pharamond. We found the royal hut deserted. The chief of the long hair had been entertaining his guests, and after lavishing in their honor all the riches he possessed, had gone to reside in the cabin of a neighboring chief, who, ruined in turn by the barbarous monarch, had gone with him to reside at the house of another chief. Here at last we found Pharamond, seated at a grand repast, and enjoying the pleasures of this simple hospitality: we soon learned the subject of these festivities.

"In the midst of the sea of the Suevi, lies an island called the Chaste, which is consecrated to the goddess Hertha. Here the statue of this divinity is placed on a car, and always remains covered with a veil. This car, drawn by white heifers, passes at stated periods through the midst of the German territories. All animosities are then suspended, and for a time the forests of the North cease to echo with the clash of arms. This mysterious divinity had just paid her passing visit to these barbarians, and we arrived in the midst of the rejoicings which were made for her appearance. Zacharius had scarcely a moment to press me in his arms, and welcome my return; for all the chiefs were convoked to a solemn banquet, where the question either for war or peace with the Romans was to be determined. I was charged with the office of cup-bearer, and Merovius took his place in the midst of the warriors.

"They were ranged in a semicircle round the hearth, where the viands for the feast were preparing. Each chief, armed as for war, was placed on his seat of turf or hides; before him stood a small separate table, on which part of the victim was served up to him, proportioned to his valor and rank. The warrior most distinguished for his bravery held the first seat: this was Merovius. Freedmen, armed with lances and bucklers, served up the repast, and filled the cups of horn with a beverage brewed from wheat.

"Toward the conclusion of the banquet, they began their deliberations. Belonging to the party of the Franks was a Gaul named Camulogenus, a descendant of that famous hero who defended Lutetia against Labienus, lieutenant of Julius Cæsar. Brought up amidst the forty thousand disciples of the schools of Augustodunum,[1] he had completed a brilliant education under the most celebrated rhetoricians of Marseilles and Burdigalia;[2] but that inconstancy natural to the Gauls, joined to his savage character, had prompted him to join in the revolt of the Bagaudi. These rebellious peasants were subdued by Maximianus, and Camulogenus joined the party of the Franks, who adopted him in consideration of his valor and his riches. The priest, who presided at Pharamond's banquet, having demanded silence, the Gaul arose, and influ-

---

[1] Autun.   [2] Bordeaux.

enced, perhaps, by the tediousness of his long exile, proposed to send deputies to Cæsar. He spoke in high terms of the discipline of the Roman legions, the virtues of Constantius, the charms of peace, and the blessings of society.

"'Let it not surprise us,' answered Chloderic, the chief of a tribe of the Franks, 'to hear a Gaul speak in this manner; he doubtless expects some recompense from his ancient masters. I confess that the vine-stock of a centurion is wielded with more ease than my massive javelin; nor do I deny that it is less perilous to adore Cæsar amidst the splendor of the Capitol, than to despise him in this hut, and on these our couches of skin. I have seen them at Rome even, these insatiate masters of so many palaces, who would willingly have retired to these our forest-huts, to forget the miseries of greatness. Believe me, these proud conquerors of nations are not so formidable as the fears of a Gaul would represent them to be. Conquered by this nation of women, let the Gauls demand peace if they will; as for Chloderic, he feels something in his bosom that would urge him to lay the Capitol in ashes, and efface from the world the very name of Roman.'

"Loud applauses followed this discourse, and the assembly expressed their approbation by striking their lances with violence against their bucklers.

"'Hasten then,' replied the Gaul, with impetuosity, 'hasten to Rome! Why do you stay amid these forests, in inglorious concealment? What, my brave men, do you speak of passing the Tiber, you who have not yet crossed the Rhine! These Gauls, these slaves, conquered, as you say, by a nation of women, were not tranquilly seated at a repast, when they ravaged that city, which you threaten at a distance. Are you ignorant that the sword of a Gaul has alone served as a counterpoise to the empire of the world? Whenever anything great has been undertaken, you will find that my ancestors have always borne a part in the deed. The Gauls were the only people who felt no emotion at the view of the great Alexander. For ten years Cæsar strove to humble them into submission, and had it not been for the unhappy divisions among their own people, Vercingetorix would have triumphed over Cæsar. Places the most famous in the universe, have yielded to the valor of my ancestors. They ravaged Greece, seized Byzantium, encamped on the ruins of Troy, and made themselves masters of the kingdom of Mithridates : more than this, they carried their arms beyond the Taurus, and conquered the Scythians, a nation that till then had been proof against all the arts of man. The destiny of the world seemed involved in that of my ancestors ; they were marked with a mysterious seal, and destined by the gods to greatness. Every nation on earth seems to have heard in its turn that warning voice which announced the arrival of Brennus at Rome, and which whispered to Ceditius in the dead of night : ' Ceditius, hasten to the tribunes, and tell them that to-morrow the Gauls will be at Rome.'

" Camulogenus was about to continue, when he was suddenly interrupted by a burst of loud laughter from Chloderic, who, striking the table with the hilt of his sword, and overturning the vessel of liquor that stood before him, exclaimed :

" ' Brother kings, do you understand a syllable of the long-winded harangue of this prophetess of the Gauls ? Who among you ever heard of this Alexander, and this Mithridates ? Camulogenus, you are well versed in the language of your masters, and seem to have your lessons by heart ; but you may spare yourself the trouble of repeating them before us. We forbid our children to read or write ; we wish them not to learn the arts of servitude : we wish nothing but the sword, battle and blood.'

" The barbarians answered this last sentence of their chief with loud and tumultuous approbation. Stung with this insult, the Gaul answered with a contemptuous sneer :

" ' Since the famous Chloderic has never heard of Alexander, and is no friend to long discourses, let me speak my mind in one word: if the Franks have no other warrior than he to carry fire and sword to the Capitol, my advice is to accept of peace on any terms.'

"'Traitor,' cried the Sicambrian, foaming with rage, 'before many years have elapsed, I hope that your nation will have changed its master. Then, whilst toiling in the fields of the Franks, shall you acknowledge the valor of the long-haired kings.'

"'If I have but thy valor to dread,' replied the sneering Gaul, 'I shall not be solicitous to gather the serpents' eggs at the new moon, in order to ward off the woes that Teutates is preparing for me.'

"At these words, Chlodoric, wild with passion, brandished his lance toward Camulogenus, and exclaimed, in a voice almost choked with passion:

"'Thou shalt not dare even to cast thine eyes thereon.'

"'Thou liest!' returned the Gaul, as he drew his sword, and rushed fiercely on the Frank.

"The other warriors flew to part the two combatants. The priests interposed their authority, and broke off this new feast of the Centaurs and Lapithæ. On the next day, which was the full moon, they decided in calmness what they had discussed in drunkenness, when the heart cannot feign, but is open to the wildest suggestions of the moment.

"It was determined that proposals of peace should be made to the Romans; and as Merovius, faithful to his promise, had already obtained my liberty from his father, it was determined that I should be the person to carry them to Constantius. Zacharius and Clothilde came to announce my deliverance. They conjured me instantly to set out, acquainted as they were with the natural inconstancy of the barbarians. I was obliged to yield to their solicitations, and Zacharius accompanied me to the frontier of the Gauls. The happiness of recovering my liberty was more than counterbalanced by the sorrow with which I parted from my aged friend. In vain I pressed him to follow me; in vain I feelingly described the evils under which he labored. Gathering a wild lily that grew by the road-side, and whose early blossom but just peeped through the snow, he said:

"'This flower is the device of the chief of the Salians, and of his tribe; it flourishes in greater beauty amidst these woods, than on a soil less exposed to the rigors of winter: the snows which surround it, and which it surpasses in whiteness, give a vigor to the beauteous plant, and preserve it longer from decay. It is my hope that this rude season of my life, thus passed in the family of a barbarous master, will render me one day like this lily in the eyes of God: in order to develop all its powers, the soul requires to be buried for a season under the rigors of adversity.'

"As he finished these words, Zacharias made a stop. He pointed toward heaven, where one day we were to meet again without fear of separation, and without allowing me time to throw myself at his feet, he hastily withdrew, after giving me this last instruction. It was thus that Jesus Christ, whose example he imitated, delighted to walk along the banks of Lake Gennesareth, and make the herbs of the field, and the lily of the valley, speak in lessons of wisdom to his disciples "

BOOK EIGHTH.

SUMMARY.

Interruption of the Recital. Beginning of the Love of Eudorus and Cymodoce. Satan seeks to profit by this Love to trouble the Church. Hell. Assembly of the Demons. Speech of the Demon of Homicide. Speech of the Demon of False Wisdom. Speech of the Demon of Voluptuousness. Speech of Satan. The Demons spread themselves over the Earth.

EUDORUS had now prolonged his recital to the ninth hour of the day. The sun darted his fiercest rays on the mountains of Arcadia, and the silent birds had retired for shelter to the embowering shrubs that grew on the banks of the Ladon. Lasthenes again invited the strangers to a repast, and proposed that the remainder of his son's history should be deferred till the next day. They all arose, quitted the island and the two altars, and regained in silence the hospitable mansion.

The rest of the day was spent in an almost uninterrupted silence. The bishop of Lacedæmon appeared most profoundly interested in the narrative. He admired this picture of the church in its first progress through the world. He reflected particularly on the sketch that Eudorus had given of those men whose arts the faithful had most cause to dread, and whose characters threw a gloom on the future. What gave weight to Cyril's presentiments was, that he had lately received intelligence from Rome of an alarming nature; but he wished not, by communicating it, to interrupt the peace of this virtuous family.

Eudorus, on his side, was far from feeling tranquil. His bosom labored with interior tribulations, for he was yet ignorant of the designs of heaven in his regard. He redoubled his prayers and austerities; yet through his tears of penitence, his eyes remarked, despite himself, the beauteous tresses, alabaster hands, enchanting figure, and ingenuous grace, of the daughter of Homer. He beheld her mild and timid looks incessantly fixed upon him; her lovely and intelligent countenance, on which was reflected every sentiment he expressed, and even those to which he had not yet given utterance. What ingenuous modesty tinged her virgin cheeks, when he described the guilty pleasures of Rome and Baiæ! What a mortal paleness overspread them when he painted the field of combat, and spoke of wounds and slavery!

The priestess of the Muses felt, on her side, a confusion of ideas for which she could not account, and an emotion to which she was before a stranger. Her mind and her heart, at the same time, emerged from their double infancy. The ignorance of her mind vanished before the light of Christianity; and the ignorance of her heart before that of the passions. How extraordinary that this virgin should feel, at the same moment, the anxieties of love and the delights of wisdom!

"My father," said she to Demodocus, "what divine stranger is this that hath invited us to his banquet? How is the son of Lasthenes ennobled, both by the virtues of his heart and the valor of his arms! Is not this one of those primeval inhabitants of the world, whom Jupiter transformed into divinities, the friends of mankind? The sport of cruel destinies, how many battles has he fought, how many woes has he endured! O ye chaste and powerful Muses, ye who are my tutelary divinities, where were you when hands so noble were fettered with ignominious chains? Could you not have loosened the bands of this young hero by the magic of your lyres? But thou, the priest of Homer, thou who knowest all things, and possessest the wise circumspection of age, tell me what is this religion of which Eudorus speaks? It is a most engaging religion! It familiarizes the heart with justice, and calms the turbulence of the passions. Its votary is always ready to succor the unfortunate, not with the cold charity of man to man, but with all the tenderness of a neighbor and a brother. Let us hasten to the temples to sacrifice lambs to Ceres, the bearer of the laws, and to Sol, the seer of the future. Clad in sacred garments, and with the cup of libation in our hands, let us surround their altars in solemn pomp; let us knead the sacred cake, and try to discover the unknown genius that protects Eudorus. . . . I perceive a mysterious divinity speaking to my heart. . . . But ought a virgin to penetrate with dangerous curiosity into the secrets of young men, and seek to know their gods ? Should modesty raise her veil to interrogate the oracles ?"

As she finished these words, Cymodoce bedewed her bosom with tears that streamed from her eyes.

It was thus that heaven first united two hearts, that were to add fresh triumphs to the cross. Satan was about to profit by the love of the predestined couple to excite new tempests, and everything was working toward the accomplishment of the decrees of the Eternal. At that very moment, the prince of darkness had finished the review of the temples of the earth. He had visited the sanctuaries of falsehood and imposture, the cave of Trophonius, the grotto of the Sibyl, the tripods of Delphi, the stone of Teutates, the vaults of Isis, of Mitra and Vishnu. Everywhere the sacrifices were suspended, the oracles abandoned, and the illusions of idolatry ready to vanish before the truth of Christ. Satan groaned at the loss of his power, but he resolved at least not to yield the victory without a struggle. He swore, by the eternity of hell, to destroy the worshippers of the true God, forgetting that the gates of the abode of sorrow could not prevail against the beloved of the son of man. The rebellious archangel knew not the designs of the Eternal, about to punish his guilty Church; but he felt that the dominion over the faithful was for a moment accorded him, and that Heaven left him free to accomplish his dark designs. He quitted the earth at once, and descended to his gloomy empire.

As when, in the fiery mountain of Vesuvius, the burning sulphur and bitumen suddenly obscure the sun, convulse the sea, and make Parthenope reel like a drunken Bacchante: the peak of the volcano changes its mobile form, the lava bursts forth, and the stone that had been suspended in the mouth of the crater, falls and rolls rumbling to the depths of the burning entrails that had cast it forth : thus did Satan, ejected by hell, plunge again into the yawning abyss. Swifter than thought, he crossed the space that must one day be destroyed, and traversing the tempestuous remains of chaos, arrived at the frontier of those regions imperishable as the veageance that formed them; accursed regions, the tomb and the cradle of Death, where Time makes no law, and which will stand when the universe shall have passed away like a tent erected for a single night. An involuntary tear moistened the eye of the perverse spirit as he plunged into the kingdoms of night. His fiery lance scarce served to light his way through the thick shadows about him. He followed no road through the darkness ; but, dragged down by the weight of his crimes, fell straight toward hell. He was not yet in sight of the distant glare of those flames that burn without fuel, but never are extingiushed, yet the moans of the reprobates fell upon his ear. He paused and shuddered at the first murmur of eternal sorrow. Hell astonishes even its master. An emotion of remorse and pity thrilled through the heart of the rebellious archangel.

"It is I, then," cried he, "that have dug these prison-vaults, and gathered together all these ills ! Had it not been for me, evil would have been unknown in the works of the Almighty ! Why did he create for me man, that noble, beautiful creature ?"

Satan was about to prolong the repinings of an unavailing repentance, when the flaming mouth of the abyss opened and suddenly recalled him to other thoughts. The phantom of Death leaped forth upon the inexorable portals. She seemed like a dark spot upon the flames of the burning dungeons behind her; the livid rays of the infernal light passed between the hollows of the bones of her skeleton. Her brow was adorned with a sparkling crown, the jewels of which were stolen from the nations and princes of earth. Sometimes she adorns herself with shreds of purple or tatters of sackcloth, the spoils alike of the rich and poor. Now she wings her flight, then she drags herself slowly along; she takes all forms, even that of beauty. We believe her deaf, yet she hears the slightest noise that betrays the presence of life; she appears blind, yet she discovers the smallest insect that creeps upon the earth. With one hand she holds a sickle like a reaper, with the other she hides the only wound that she has yet received, and that the conquering Christ inflicted in her bosom on the summit of Golgotha.

The gates of Hell were opened by Death and closed by Crime. These two monsters, by a kind of horrible love, had been warned of the approach of their father. No sooner had Death perceived from afar the enemy of mankind, than she flew, full of joy, to meet him.

"My father," exclaimed she, "to thee I bow this head that has never humbled itself before any. Dost thou come to satiate the keen hunger of thy daughter? I am weary of the same feasts, and am awaiting from thy bounty some new world to devour."

Seized with horror, Satan turned away his head to avoid the embraces of the skeleton. He repulsed her with his lance, and replied to her in passing:

"Oh, Death! thou shalt be satisfied and avenged; I am about to deliver to thy rage the numerous people of thy only conqueror."

While uttering these words, the chief of devils entered the abode where his victims were weeping forever, and advanced toward the burning regions. The abyss heaved at the sight of its king; the lighted pile sent forth a more brilliant flame · the reprobates, who had thought themselves at the extremity of anguish, felt themselves pierced with a sharper pang; as, in the desert of Sahara, overcome by the heat of a rainless storm, the black African lays himself down on the sands amidst serpents and lions as thirsty as he, and thinks he has attained the last degree of torment, when a troubled sun, appearing surrounded by arid clouds, inspires him with new tortures.

Who can paint the horror of those places where all the tribulations of life are assembled, increased and perpetuated without end? Bound by a hundred diamond clasps to a throne of bronze, the demon of Despair reigned over the empire of sorrows. Satan, accustomed to the infernal clamors, distinguished at each cry the crime and its punishment. He recognized the voice of the first homicide; he heard the sinful Dives vainly demanding a drop of water; and he laughed at the beggar who demanded, in the name of his rags, the kingdom of heaven.

"Fool," said he, "did you think, then, that poverty would stand in lieu of virtue? Did you think that all the kings were in my empire, and that all thy brethren were grouped around my rival? Vile and contemptible creature, thou wert insolent, lying, slothful, envious of the wealth of others, hostile to everything above thee by education, honor or birth; and thou demandest a crown? Burn here with the pitiless opulence that did right indeed to drive thee from its presence, but that, notwithstanding, owed thee food and raiment."

From the midst of their torments, a crowd of wretches cried to Satan:

"We adored thee, O Jupiter, and it is for this, accursed spirit, that thou retainest us in the flames!"

And the proud archangel, with a smile of irony, replied:

"Thou hast preferred me to Christ, partake of my joys and glory!"

The fiery torment is not the most terrible felt by the condemned: they preserve the memory of their divine origin; they bear within themselves the ineffaceable image of the beauty of God, and regret without ceasing the sovereign good that they have lost; this regret is continually excited by the sight of those souls whose abode borders on hell, and who, after having expiated their crimes, take their flight to the celestial regions. To all these evils, the reprobates also join moral afflictions, and the shame of the crimes that they have committed upon earth; the pains of the hypocrite are augmented by the veneration with which his false virtues continue to inspire the world. The illustrious titles bestowed on the renowned dead by a fallen age constitute the torments of these dead in the flames of truth and vengeance. The prayers that a tender friendship offers to heaven for lost souls, afflict these inconsolable souls, at the depth of the abyss. This it is that forces those guilty ones from the sepulchre that come to reveal to earth the chastisements of divine justice, and to say to men: "Pray not for me ; I am condemned."

At the centre of the abyss, in the midst of an ocean of blood and tears, rose a black castle among the rocks, the work of Despair and Death. An eternal tempest roared about its menacing battlements, a barren tree was planted before its gate, and from the turret of its gloomy walls, folded nine times upon itself, floated the standard of Pride, half consumed by lightning. The demons, styled the Parcæ by the heathen, kept watch at the gate of this sombre palace. Satan arrived before his royal domain. The three guards of the palace rose and let fall the knocker with a lugubrious sound upon the brazen door. Three other demons, adored under the name of the Furies, opened the fiery wicket, disclosing a long row of deserted porticos, like those subterranean galleries where the priests of Egypt concealed those monsters which they forced mankind to adore. The domes of the fatal edifice resounded with the sullen roar of a conflagration, and a pale light descended from the flaming roof. At the entrance of the first vestibule, the Eternity of Sorrows was reclining upon a couch of iron ; she was motionless ; even her heart was without pulsation ; an inexhaustible hour-glass was in her hand. She knew and pronounced but the single word—"Never !"

No sooner had the sovereign of the accursed hierarchies entered his impure habitation, than he ordered the four chiefs of the rebel legions to convoke the senate of hell. The demons hastened to obey the commands of their monarch. They filled to overflowing the vast council-hall of Satan ; they placed themselves on the fiery benches of the amphitheatre ; they came in the characters in which they were adored by mortals, with the attributes of a power that was naught but imposture. This one bore the trident, with which he vainly smote the seas, which were obedient only to God ; that, crowned with a halo of false glory, sought to imitate as a lying star the proud giant whom the Eternal sends forth every morning from the place whence arises the dawn. There reasoned the demon of False Wisdom, there roared the demon of War, there smiled the demon of Voluptuousness, whom men call Venus, known in hell by the name of Astarte, with eyes full of soft languor, a voice bearing trouble into the souls of men, and a brilliant girdle about her waist, the most dangerous of all the works of the powers of the abyss. In fine, in this council were seen reunited all the false deities of the nations, Mitra, Baal, Moloch, Anubis, Brahma, Teutates, Odin, Erminsul, and a thousand other phantoms of our passions and caprices.

The daughters of heaven, the passions, were given us with life. So long as they remain pure within our breasts, they are under the keeping of angels; but as soon as they become corrupted, they pass beneath the dominion of demons. Thus, there is lawful love and guilty love, pernicious anger and holy wrath, criminal arrogance and noble pride, brute courage and enlightened valor. Oh, the grandeur of man! Our vices and virtues make the occupation and constitute a part of the power of heaven and hell.

No longer like that star of the morning that brings us light, but in the image of a terrible comet, Lucifer seated himself on his throne in the midst of a nation of spirits. As in a tempest a wave rises above the rest, and menaces the boatmen with its foaming crest; or, as in a burning city a lofty tower overtops the smoking buildings, its summit crowned with flames: so appeared the fallen archangel in the midst of his companions. He raised the sceptre of hell, to which, by a subtle flame, all the evils were attached, and concealing the chagrin that was devouring him, thus addressed the assembly:

"Gods of nations, thrones and passions, generous warriors, invincible soldiery, magnanimous children of this powerful country, the day of glory has arrived; we are about to reap the fruits of our struggles and perseverance. Since I broke the yoke of the tyrant, I have endeavored to render myself worthy of the power that you have confided to me. I have subjected the universe to your sway; even now you hear the wails of the descendants of that man who was to replace you in the abode of the blessed. To save this miserable race, our persecutor was forced to send his son on earth. This Messiah appeared; he dared penetrate into our kingdoms; and had you seconded my audacity, we would have loaded him with irons and retained him in the depths of these abysses, which would have forever terminated the war between us and the eternal. But that favorable occasion was lost, and thus we are obliged again to take up arms. The followers of Christ are multiplying. Too sure of the justice of our rights, we have neglected to defend our altars: let us therefore combine our strength for a last effort, to overthrow this cross that threatens us, and deliberate on the surest means of attaining this victory."

Thus spoke the blasphemer vanquished by Christ in eternal night, the archangel who saw the Saviour break with his cross the gates of hell and deliver the flock of the just of Israel: the frightened demons fled at the sight of the divine light, and Satan himself, overthrown amid the ruins of his empire, had his head crushed beneath the foot of a woman.

When the Father of Evil had finished his discourse, the demon of Homicide arose. A terrible voice, furious gestures, and arms dyed in blood, all announced in this rebellious spirit the crimes with which he was stained, and the violence of the feelings by which he was agitated. He could not endure the thought that a single Christian should escape his fury. Thus, in the ocean that bathes the shores of the New World, when a sea monster is pursuing his prey through the waves, if the glistening object suddenly unfolds his silver wings, and, the bird of a moment, finds safety in the air, the disappointed monster bounds from the waves, and vomiting forth a whirlwind of foam and vapor, terrifies the sailors with his impotent rage.

"What need is there to deliberate?" cried the atrocious angel. "Are other means necessary to destroy the people of Christ than the flames and the executioner? O gods of nations leave to me the care of reëstablishing thy temples! The prince who will ere long reign over the Roman Empire is devoted to my power. I will excite the cruelty of Galerius.

Let an immense and final massacre cause the altars of our enemy to swim in the blood of his adorers. Satan began the victory by destroying the first man ; I will consummate it by exterminating the Christians."

He spoke, and suddenly all the pains of hell made themselves felt in this ferocious spirit ; he shrieked like a criminal beneath the sword of the executioner, like an assassin pierced by the sting of remorse. A burning sweat appeared on his forehead, something resembling blood oozed from his lips ; he writhed in vain under the weight of reprobation.

Then the demon of False Wisdom rose with a gravity that resembled a melancholy madness. The feigned austerity of his voice, the apparent calmness of his mind, deceived the dazzled multitude, as a beauteous flower, supported by a poisonous stem, allures men to their death. He assumed the form of an old man, the chief of one of those schools so common in Athens and Alexandria. His white locks, crowned with an olive-branch, and forehead partly bald, were at first prepossessing, but regarded near by, an abyss of baseness and hypocrisy was visible, with a deadly hatred of true reason. His crime began in heaven with the creation of the worlds, so soon as these worlds had been abandoned to his vain disputes. He blamed the work of the Almighty ; he wished, in his pride, to establish a different order among angels and in the empire of sovereign wisdom ; he was the father of Atheism, an execrable phantom whom Satan himself did not father, and who became enamored with Death as soon as she appeared in hell. But although the demon of fatal doctrines was proud of his enlightenment, he knew, notwithstanding, how pernicious it was to mortals, and triumphed in the evils that it wrought on earth. More criminal than all the rebel angels, he knew his own perversity, and made thereof a title of glory. This False Wisdom, born after Time, spoke in this wise to the assembly of demons:

" Monarchs of hell, as you well know, I have always been opposed to violence. We shall only obtain the victory by reasoning, gentleness, and persuasion. Leave it to me to diffuse among our worshippers, and among the Christians themselves, those principles that dissolve the bonds of society, and undermine the foundations of empires. Already has Hierocles, the favorite minister of Galerius, cast himself into my arms, and the sects are multiplying. I will deliver men over to their own reason; I will send them my son Atheism, the lover of Death, and the enemy of Hope. They will come even to deny the existence of him who created them. You will not need to engage in combats, the issue of which is always uncertain; I can force the Eternal to destroy his work a second time."

The demons tumultuously applauded this speech of the most deeply corrupted spirit of the abyss. The noise of their lamentable joy was prolonged beneath the infernal arches. The reprobates fancied that their tormentors had been inventing new tortures. These souls, no longer guarded on their funeral piles, at once escaped from the flames, and ran to the council, dragging along with them some part of their punishment: one his blazing winding-sheet, another his leaden cope, a third the icicles suspended from his tearful eyes, and a fourth the serpents that were devouring him. These terrible spectators of a terrible senate, took their seats on the flaming benches. Satan, himself terrified at the sight, summoned the guardian spectres of the shades, the vain Chimeras, the frightful Dreams, the Harpies with their foul claws, Fear with his face of amazement, haggard Vengeance, sleepless Remorse, incomprehensible Madness, pallid Grief, and Death.

"Take back these guilty ones to their chains," cried he, " or tremble lest Satan bind you with them !"

Vain menaces! The phantoms mingled with the reprobates, incited by their example to become spectators of the council of the kings. A horrible combat would perhaps have ensued, had not God, who maintains his justice, and who alone is the author of order, even in hell, caused the tumult to cease. He extended his arm, and the shadow of his hand was outlined upon the wall of the accursed chamber. A profound terror took possession both of the lost souls and the rebel spirits. The former returned to their torments; the latter, after the divine hand had been withdrawn, recommenced their deliberations.

The demon of Voluptuousness, essaying to smile on the seat where she was half reclining, with an effort raised her head. The most beautiful of the fallen spirits, after the rebellious archangel, she had preserved part of the charms with which she had been adorned by the Creator; but behind her mild glances, through the charms of her voice and smile, was an indescribable appearance of perfidy and venom. Born for love, the eternal inhabitant of the abode of hatred, she impatiently endured her misfortune; too refined to utter cries of rage, she wept only, and uttered these words with heavy sighs:

"Gods of Olympus, and ye of whom I have less knowledge, divinities of the Brahmin and the Druid, I shall not attempt to hide it from you—hell crushes me beneath its weight! You are not ignorant that I cherish against the Eternal no cause of hate, and that I only followed a beloved angel in his rebellion and his fall. But since I have fallen with you from heaven, I wish at least for a long life among mortals, and I shall not suffer myself to be exiled from earth. Tyre, Heliopolis, Paphos, and Amathus, all call me. My star still sparkles upon Mount Lebanon: there I have enchanted temples, graceful festivals, swans that draw me in the midst of music, flowers, incense, perfumes, fresh turf, voluptuous dances, and smiling sacrifices. And the Christians would snatch from me this slight compensation for celestial joys! would transform my groves of myrtle, that have given so many victims to hell, into the savage cross, to multiply the inhabitants of heaven! No, I will now make known my power. To conquer the disciples of an austere law, neither violence nor wisdom is needed; I will arm against them the tender passions; this girdle assures to you the victory. Ere long my caresses will have softened these austere servants of a chaste God. I will subdue the rigid virgins, and will trouble in the desert those anchorites that think to escape my enchantments. The angel of wisdom applauds himself for having won Hierocles from our enemy; but Hierocles is also faithful to my worship: already have I lighted in his breast a guilty flame; I know how to continue my work, excite rivalries, overturn the world with the greatest ease, and bring men, through delight, to partake of your misery."

In finishing these words, Astarte fell back on her couch. She attempted to smile, but the serpent that she carried concealed beneath her girdle stung her secretly to the heart: the weak demon grew pale, and the experienced chiefs of the infernal bands divined her wound.

The terrible Sanhedrim was divided among these three counsels. Satan imposed silence upon the assembly:

"Companions," said he, "your counsels are worthy of yourselves; but instead of choosing among opinions equally wise, let us follow them all, and thus obtain a brilliant victory. Let us also summon to our aid Idolatry and Pride. For my part, I will awaken Superstition in the heart of Diocletian, and Ambition in the soul of Galerius. Do you, divinities of the nations, second my efforts: go, haste, stir up the zeal of the priests and people. Ascend the heights of Olympus, revive the fables of the poets. Let the woods of Dodona and Daphne repeat new oracles; let the world be divided between fanatics and atheists; let the gentle poisons of voluptuousness kindle ferocious passions; and with all these evils combined, let us stir up against the Christians a terrible persecution."

Thus spoke Lucifer : three times he smote his throne with his sceptre; three times the caverns of the abyss sent back a prolonged groan. Chaos, the sombre and sole neighbor of hell, felt the rebound, half opened, and suffered a ray of light to pass through its bosom into the night of the reprobates. Never had Satan appeared more formidable since the day when, renouncing his allegiance, he declared himself the enemy of the Eternal. The legions arose, quitted the council, passed through the sea of tears and the region of torment, and flew to the gate guarded by Crime and Death. As the unearthly troop passed in the glare of the fiery furnaces, they appeared like those questionable birds with wings seemingly woven by an impure insect, that take flight at the light of a torch in a subterranean grotto.

Under the vestibule of the palace of hell, before the iron bed upon which reposes the Eternity of Sorrows, a lamp is suspended: there burns the primitive fire of the celestial wrath, from which the eternal braziers are lighted. Satan took a spark of this fire. He departed; at the first bound he reached the starry girdle, at the second he arrived at the abode of men. He carried the fatal spark into all the temples, and relighted the extinguished fires upon the altars of idolatry: directly Pallas moved her lance, Bacchus waved his thyrsus, Apollo bent his bow, Love shook his torch, the ancient Penates of Æneas muttered mysterious words, and the gods of Ilion prophesied at the Capitol. The Father of Falsehood placed a lying spirit in each image of the heathen divinities; and regulating the movements of his invisible cohorts, brought the whole army of demons to act in concert against the Church of Christ.

BOOK NINTH.

SUMMARY.

Resumption of the Recital of Eudorus. Eudorus at the Court of Constantius. He passes into the Island of Britain. He obtains Triumphal Honors. His Return to Gaul. He is Appointed Commandant of Armorica. The Gauls. Armorica. Episode of Velleda.

Too faithful to her promises, the demon of Voluptuousness penetrated beneath the gilded tapestry, where reposed the disciple of false wisdom. She awakened in his heart the flame that had been lulled to sleep; she presented to his desires the image of the daughter of Homer; she pierced him with an arrow which had been dipped in the waters that covered the smoking ruins of Gomorrah. Could Hierocles at this moment have known that the priestess of the Muses was the object of another's affection; could he have beheld her eyes fixed in fond attention upon Eudorus, as he prepared to continue the recital of his adventures, what jealousy would have inflamed the soul of this enemy of the Christians! Alas! the fatal effects of this passion are suspended but for a few days. These few short moments of placid joy that the family of Lasthenes were now spending with their guests, were destined by heaven to be their last on earth. Faithful as the morning watch, Lasthenes, his spouse, and his daughter, attended by Cyril, Demodocus, and Cymodoce, were assembled by the first dawning of Aurora. They took their seats at the entrance of the grove, and listened with attention to the repentant warrior, as he thus resumed his narrative:

"I told you, my friends, that Zacharius left me on the frontier of the Gauls. Constantius was then at Lutetia. After a fatiguing journey of many days, I reached the Belgi,[1] who inhabit the banks of the Sequana. The first object that struck me in the marshes of the Parisii, was an octagon tower, consecrated to eight Gaulish divinities. At the south, about two miles from Lutetia, and by the side of the river that encircled it, stood the temple of Hesus; at a still shorter distance, and in a meadow by the same stream, arose a second temple, dedicated to Isis; and on a hill toward the north, the ruins of a third temple, erected in honor of Teutates, were visible. This hill was the mount of Mars, on which Denis received the palm of martyrdom.

"As I approached the Sequana, I perceived its clear transparent stream through the willows that overshaded the margin; the taste of its waters is excellent, and it is seldom observed to increase or diminish. Some gardens planted with fig-trees, which were bound round with straw to preserve them from the frost, were the only ornament of its banks. It was with difficulty I discovered the village I was in search of; it bears the name of Lutetia, which signifies the beautiful stone, or column. At last a shepherd pointed it out to me in the midst of the Sequana, on an island which in its lengthened form resembled a vessel. Two bridges constructed of wood, and defended by two castles, in which the cautious inhabitants paid tribute to Cæsar, joined this miserable hamlet to the two opposite banks of the river.

"I entered the capital of the Parisii by the northern bridge. The interior of the village presented nothing to my view but huts of wood and clay, covered with straw, and warmed by a hearth of most barbarous construction. I saw therein but one single monument; this was an altar erected in honor of Jupiter, by the Nautii. But out of the isle, and on the southern branch of the Sequana, situated on the hill Lucotitius, stood a Roman aqueduct, a circus, an amphitheatre, and the palace of Thermes, inhabited by Constantius.

---

[1] The inhabitants of the Isle of France.

"No sooner was Cæsar apprised of my being at the gates of his palace, than he exclaimed:

"'Hasten and bring in the friend of my son!'

"I threw myself at the prince's feet; he raised me with condescension, honored me with eulogiums in the presence of his whole court, and taking me by the hand, led me into his council-chamber. I gave him an account of all my adventures among the Franks, and delivered my instructions. Constantius appeared overjoyed to hear that this people had at length consented to lay down their arms, and immediately dispatched a centurion to make overtures of peace. I remarked with sorrow that his countenance was unusually pale, and that his weakness had augmented.

"In the palace of this prince I found the most illustrious of the faithful both of Gaul and Italy. The two brothers Donatian and Rogatian, the most amiable of men, here shone conspicuous; with Gervasius and Protasius, the Orestes and Pylades of the Christians; Procula of Marseilles, Justus of Lugdunum; and lastly Ambrose, the son of the prefect of Gaul, a model of learning, of courage and of candor. It is said of him as of Xenophon, that when an infant he was fed by bees: in him the church expected an orator, and a great man.

"I felt a strong desire to learn from the mouth of Constantius, what changes had taken place at the court of Diocletian during my captivity. He summoned me ere long to the gardens of his palace, which descended in the form of an amphitheatre from Mount Lucotitius, to the meadow where stood the temple of Isis on the banks of the Sequana.

"'Eudorus,' said he, 'we are about to march against Carrausius, and deliver Britain from the tyrant, who has usurped the imperial purple. But before we set out for this province, it will be well for you to learn the state of affairs at Rome, in order that you may regulate your conduct according to the circumstances I shall point out. You may remember, perhaps, that when you set out to join me in Gaul, Diocletian was going to restore tranquillity in Egypt, and Galerius to oppose the Persians. This last has come off victorious; since which time, his pride and ambition have known no bounds. He has espoused Valeria, the daughter of Diocletian, and is no longer solicitous to conceal his desire of obtaining the empire, by forcing his father-in-law to abdicate. Diocletian, who begins to feel the weight of old age, and whose mind is weakened by an inveterate disorder, is scarcely any longer able to resist the artifices of this most ungrateful of men. The creatures of Galerius triumph. Your enemy Hierocles stands the highest in favor; he has been raised to the dignity of proconsul of Peloponnesus, your native country. My son is exposed to a thousand dangers. Galerius has twice sought his destruction; once by obliging him to engage with a lion, and at another time by charging him with a dangerous enterprise against the Sarmatæ. Lastly, Galerius has taken Maxentius, the son of Maximianus, into his favor; not that he has any affection for him, but merely because he knows him to be a rival of Constantine. Thus everything seems to announce an approaching revolution. But as long as I breathe, Eudorus, I fear not the jealousy of Galerius. Let but my son escape the vigilance of those that plot his destruction; let him come and join his father, and they shall learn, if they dare attack me, that the love of his people is an impregnable bulwark to a prince.'

"Some days after this conversation, we set out for the isle of Britain, which the ocean separates from the rest of the world. The Picts had attacked the wall of Agricola—immortalized in the writings of Tacitus. On the other side, Carausius, in order to oppose Constantius, had awakened into a flame the dormant factions of Caractacus and Boadicea. Thus we were at the same time plunged into the horrors of civil discord and of a foreign war. Some small portion of courage, natural to the blood from which I sprung, joined to a series of fortunate acts, conducted me step by step to the rank of first tribune in the Britannic legion. I was soon created master of the horse, and it was my lot to lead the army, when the Picts were vanquished under the walls of Petuaria:[1] this is a colony, which

---

[1] Beverly, in the County of York, in England.

the Parisii of Gaul planted on the banks of the Abus.[1] I also led the attack against Carausius on the river Tamesis,[2] which is covered with reeds, and which bathes the marshy village of Londinum.[3] The usurper had here chosen his field of battle, because on this spot the Britons believe themselves invincible. Here, stationed on an ancient tower, a bard poured forth his animating lay, and in the midst of his prophetic songs, made a mysterious allusion to some Christian tombs, that were to render this place illustrious.[4] Carausius was vanquished, and afterward assassinated by his soldiers. To me Constantius resigned all the glory of this success. He sent my letters to the emperor wreathed with laurel. He solicited and obtained a statue and other honors which are now bestowed in the room of a triumph. Soon after we returned into Gaul, and Cæsar, wishing to give me a fresh proof of his powerful friendship, created me governor of the Armorican provinces. I put myself in readiness to set out for this region, where the religion of the Druids still flourished, and whose borders had often been insulted by fleets of barbarians from the North.

"When all things were ready for my journey, Rogatian, Sebastian, Gervasius, Protasius, and all the other Christians of Cæsar's palace, hastened to bid me adieu.

"'Perhaps,' cried they, 'we may meet again at Rome in the midst of trials and persecutions. May our religion one day unite us all in death, like ancient friends and worthy Christians!'

"I spent several months in visiting the Gauls, before repairing to my province. Never did any country present such a diversity of manners and religions, such a mixture of civilization and barbarity. Divided among Greeks, Romans, and Gauls, among Christians and the adorers of Jupiter and Teutates, it offered the most surprising contrasts.

"Long Roman roads stretched through the forests of the Druids. In the colonies planted by the conquerors in the midst of these savage wilds, arose the most beautiful monu-

---

[1] The Humber.   [2] The Thames.   [3] London.   [4] Westminster.

ments of Greek and Roman architecture: superb aqueducts suspended over torrents, amphitheatres, capitols, and temples of the most perfect elegance; whilst not far from these colonies stood the round huts of the Gauls, and their fortresses of stones and rafters, on whose gates were nailed the feet of wolves, the carcasses of owls, and the bones of the dead. At Lugdunum, Narbonne, Marsillia, and Burdigalia the Gallic youth practised with success the art of Demosthenes and of Cicero; but a few paces beyond, in the mountain, nothing was heard but a barbarous jargon resembling the croak of the raven. A Roman castle crowned the summit of a rock; a Christian chapel appeared at the bottom of the valley, and near it stood the altar where the Druids sacrificed human victims. I have seen the legionary soldier in the midst of a desert, yet keeping his watch upon the ramparts of a camp, and the Gaulish senator entangling his Roman toga in the thicket. I have seen the vines of Falernum spreading on the slopes of Augustodunum, the olive of Corinth flourishing in the environs of Marsillia, and the bee of Attica perfuming the breezes of Narbonne.

"But what principally strikes the stranger with admiration in Gaul, and what forms the chief feature of the country, are its forests. Amidst their vast solitudes we find many a Roman camp deserted; and the skeleton of the horseman and his horse are often seen half-buried amidst the grass. The grain which the soldiers had sown here for their own use, forms a species of strange and civilized colony, in the midst of the native and wild plants of Gaul. I could not behold without a certain softened emotion these domestic vegetables, some of which were natives of Greece. They spread along the valleys and the declivities of the hills, according to the habits they had acquired from their respective soils: thus the exile choses for his residence that spot which most forcibly reminds him of his country.

"I still remember meeting a man amid the ruins of one of these Roman camps, who was one of the barbarian herdsmen. Whilst the famished swine that he tended were rooting up the plants that grew under the walls, and thus undermining the works of the masters of the world, he was unconcernedly seated on a fragment of the ruins, pressing under his arm a skin inflated with wind; with this he animated a species of flute whose sounds had a sweetness that pleased his ear. As I beheld with what profound indifference this shepherd trod the camp of the Cæsars, and how far he preferred his rude instrument and his goat-skin sagum to all the noble recollections of the place, I could but think how little is necessary to the enjoyment of life; and that, after all, in so short a time, it is equally indifferent whether we have alarmed the earth by the sound of the trumpet, or charmed the woods by the sighs of the pipe.

"At last I reached the country of the Redones.[1] Armorica presented nothing to my view but vast forlorn tracts of heath, impenetrable woods, and deep and narrow valleys, which were watered by small streams that no navigator ever explored, and which pour their waters into the ocean unnoticed and unknown: a solitary, sad and stormy region enveloped in fogs, echoing with the howling of the winds, and whose rocky shores were lashed by a furious ocean.

"The castle which I commanded, and which was situated at a distance of some miles from the sea, was an ancient Gaulish fortress, which had been enlarged by Julius Cæsar, when he carried war into the territories of the Veneti[2] and the Curiosolitæ.[3] It was built on a rock, with a forest in the background, and was bathed by a lake in front.

"There, separated from the rest of the world, I spent many months in solitude. This retreat was not without its use. I had leisure to descend into myself, and listen without distraction to the voice of my conscience; I probed those wounds, which, since I had quitted Zacharius, I had never had the courage to touch, and I entered with ardor upon the study of my religion. I felt that every day diminished some portion of that painful inquietude, which a commerce with men served only to augment. I was already confident of a victory, which de-

---

[1] The people of Rennes. [2] The inhabitants of Vannes.
[3] The people in the suburbs of Dinan.

manded strength superior to my own. The dangerous indifference, and the criminal habits under which I had so long labored, had left my soul in a weak and powerless condition; I even found in the ancient doubts, and effeminate sentiments that had occupied my mind, a certain insuperable charm; my passions resembled those seductive females who lull reason to sleep, and hold us captive in their caresses.

"An event suddenly interrupted these researches, the result of which was to be of the utmost consequence to myself.

"The soldiers gave me notice, that for some days past a woman had been seen to come out of the woods about nightfall, enter alone into a small skiff, traverse the lake, land on the opposite bank, and then disappear.

"I was not ignorant that the Gauls are accustomed to trust their women with secrets of the greatest importance, and that they often submit to the determination of their wives and daughters, those affairs which they cannot settle among themselves. The inhabitants of Armorica still preserved their primitive manners, and bore the Roman yoke with impatience. Brave, like all the Gauls, even to rashness, they are distinguished for a frankness of character peculiar to themselves, for extremes both in their attachments and their aversions, and for a stubbornness of opinion that nothing can change or overcome.

"One particular circumstance might have reassured me; there were many Christians in Armorica, and the Christians are always faithful subjects; but Clair, the pastor of the church among the Redones, a man distinguished for his virtues, was then at Condivincum,[1] and he alone could have given me the advice I wanted. The least negligence would have been sufficient to ruin me at the court of Diocletian, and compromise Constantius, my patron and protector. I therefore thought it my duty not to despise the report of the soldiers. But as I knew the brutality of these men, I was resolved to take upon myself the care of observing the Gaul.

---

[1] Nantes.

"Toward evening, I took my arms, and wrapping myself up in my cloak, proceeded secretly from the castle, reached the borders of the lake, and stationed myself on the spot pointed out by the soldiers.

"I waited for some time concealed amidst the rocks, without seeing anything appear: suddenly the wind brought a distant sound to my ear, that seemed to arise from the middle of the lake. I listened, and distinguished the accents of a human voice; at the same instant I discovered a skiff suspended on the summit of a wave; it disappeared in the watery abyss, then rose again on the ridge of a billow, and approached the shore. It was guided by a woman: she sung as she struggled against the rage of the tempest, and seemed to sport amidst the billows: one would have said that they were under her dominion, so fearless did she seem of their fury. From time to time, I saw her throw into the lake, in the semblance of a sacrifice, pieces of cloth, locks of wool, cakes of wax, and small lumps of gold and silver.

"She soon reached the bank, and springing to land, fastened her bark to the trunk of a willow. She then-darted into the woods, and guided her steps with a poplar branch which she held in her hand. She passed close by without observing me. Her figure was tall; a black tunic, short, and without sleeves, was her only covering. A sickle of gold hung suspended at her girdle, and her head was encircled with an oaken branch. The whiteness of her arms, the beauty of her complexion, her eyes of blue, her roseate lips, and her long fair hair that floated over her shoulders, announced the daughter of the Gauls, and formed a strange contrast with her fierce and savage deportment. She chanted in a melodious tone a song full of terror; and her bosom as it rose and fell resembled the white foam on the swelling billow.

"I followed her at some distance. She first traversed a wood of chestnuts, that seemed coeval with time itself, and whose tops were almost all decayed. We afterward marched, for above an hour, over a waste, covered with moss and fern. At the end of this desolate spot we came to a wood, in the midst of which was another heath of many miles in circumference. Never had this soil felt the hand of cultivation, and large stones had been scattered over the surface, that it might be rendered inaccessible to the plough and the sickle. At the extremity of this scene of desolation arose one of those isolated rocks which the Gauls term a dolmen, and which marks the tomb of some warrior. The day may come, when the laborer shall stop in the midst of the furrow to contemplate these misshapen pyramids, till amazed at the grandeur of the monument, he shall superstitiously call that the work of invisible and malignant powers, which remains as the memorial of the energy, and the rude magnificence of his forefathers.

"Night was upon us. The maiden stopped at a little distance from this rock, thrice struck her hands together, and in a loud voice pronounced the words:

"'The mistletoe of the new year!'

"At that instant I saw a thousand lights flash through the deep gloom of the wood; each oak, if I may use the expression, brought forth a Gaul; the barbarians rushed in crowds from their retreats: some were completely armed, others bore a branch of oak in the right hand, and a flaming torch in the left. Favored by my disguise, I mingled with the crowd: when the first tumult of the assembly had subsided, and order was restored, they commenced a solemn procession.

"In front marched the Druids, leading two white bulls as victims for the sacrifice; next followed the bards, chanting on a species of guitar the praises of Teutates; and after them came their disciples. They were accompanied by a herald at arms, clothed in white, who wore a cap surmounted by two wings, and carried in his hand a branch of vervain, encircled by two serpents. Three Senanis,[1] representing three Druids, came after the herald: one carried the bread, another a vase filled with water, and the third bore an ivory hand. Last came the Druidess, for such I now discovered to be the character of this

---

[1] Gaulish philosophers who ranked next the Druids.

mysterious female. She held the place of the Arch-Druid, from whom she was descended.

"They advanced toward the oak of thirty years, on which they had discovered the sacred mistletoe. At the foot of the tree they raised an altar of turf. The Senanis lighted the fire, cast therein a part of the bread, and sprinkled over it some drops of wine. One of the Druids, clothed in white, now mounted the oak, and cut off the mistletoe with the golden sickle, that the priestess wore at her girdle. A white cloth, spread under the tree, received the hallowed branch; immediately the victims fell beneath the stroke of the other Druids, and the mistletoe, divided into equal parts, was distributed among the assembly.

"When this ceremony was ended, they returned to the monumental stone, where they planted a naked sword, to indicate the centre of the council: at the foot of the dolmen were placed two stones, supporting a third in a horizontal position. This tribune the Druidess ascended. The rest of the Gauls formed an armed circle around it, while the Senanis and Druids elevated their torches, to give light to the assembly. There was not a heart but felt softened by the scene that reminded them of their ancient liberty. A few warriors, whose silvery locks announced their years, let fall large tears that trickled down upon their bucklers. Resting on their lances, and with heads inclined forward, they all stood in an attitude of deep attention to the words of the Druidess.

"For some time she surveyed these warriors, the representatives of a people who were the first that dared to say to mankind: 'Woe to the vanquished!'—an impious menace, that had now fallen upon their own heads. They read on the countenance of the Druidess the emotions she felt at this example of the vicissitudes of fortune. After indulging for some time in these reflections, she thus commenced her harangue:

"'Faithful children of Teutates, you, who in the midst of the slavery of your country, have preserved the religion and the laws of your fathers, at the sight of you here assembled I cannot restrain my tears. Are you the only remnant of that nation which gave laws to the world? Where are now those flourishing estates of Gaul, that council of women who forced the mighty Hannibal into submission? Where are those Druids who educated in their sacred colleges our numerous youth? Proscribed by tyrants, a few only exist, immured in savage caverns. Velleda, a feeble Druidess, alone remains to perform your sacrifices. O isle of Sayne, thou venerable and sacred isle! of the nine virgins who performed the hallowed rites of thy sanctuary, I, alas, am the only survivor! Ere long, Teutates will have neither priests nor altars. But shall we lose all hope? Forbid it heaven! I come to announce the succors of a powerful ally: nor do I think that it will be necessary to trace the picture of your sufferings to make you fly to arms. Slaves from your birth, you have scarcely passed the age of infancy when the Romans hurry you away. What then becomes of you! I know not. If here you are suffered to attain the years of manhood, it is but to perish on the frontier in defence of your very tyrants, or to delve the furrow that is to nourish them. Condemned to labors the most severe, you hew down our forests, the pride of our ancestors; forced upon exertions the most incredible, you form those immense roads that conduct slavery into the very heart of your country: the road is laid open, and immediately servitude, oppression, and death, enter upon it in triumph. If, in fine, you survive so many outrages, you are conducted to Rome: there, shut up in the walls of an amphitheatre, you are forced to butcher each other, that your agonies may serve for the sport of a ferocious populace. Gauls, there is another way of visiting Rome, and one more worthy of you. Remember that your name implies a traveller. Hasten to the Capitol, as those terrible travellers, your ancestors, did before you. They demand your presence at the amphitheatre of Titus. Go, obey the illustrious spectators who call you. Go, teach the Romans how to die, though not by shedding your blood in their games: long enough have they studied the lesson; it is now time to teach them its practice. The proposal I make has nothing impossible in it. The tribes of Franks who formerly settled in Spain, are now returning into their country; their fleet is within view of your coast; they wait but the signal to come to your assistance. But if heaven do not crown our efforts with success—if the fortune of the Cæsars be still destined to prevail, we have a last resource, and can fly with the Franks to some corner of the world where slavery is still unknown! And whether strangers will grant us a home or not, we shall find earth enough whereon to live, or if that is impossible, whereon to die.'

"My friends, I cannot depict to you the effect of this discourse, pronounced by the light of torches, in the midst of a heath, at the foot of a tomb, with the blood of mangled victims flowing around: it is thus that the spirits of darkness are represented, when the magician at midnight summons them to infernal conference. The imagination of the audience was too much heated to suffer them to listen to the dictates of reason. They resolved, without further deliberation, to form a union with the Franks. Three times did one of the warriors attempt to offer his advice to the contrary, and three times was he forced to silence; at the third time, the herald at arms cut off the corner of his mantle.

"This was but the prelude to a frightful scene. The crowd demanded with loud outcries the sacrifice of a human victim, that they might the better comprehend the will of heaven. It was usual with the Druids to reserve for these sacrifices some malefactor who had been condemned by the laws. The Druidess was obliged to declare, that since there was no victim marked out, religion demanded an old man, as the most agreeable holocaust to Teutates.

"Immediately an iron basin was brought, in which Velleda was to receive the blood of the victim whom it was her office to kill, which was placed on the ground before her. She did not descend from the fatal tribunal, whence she had harangued the people; but seated herself on a triangle of bronze, with her garments in disorder, her hair dishevelled, a poniard in her hand, and a torch blazing at her feet. I know not how this scene might have concluded:

it would have been rash for me singly to have interrupted the sacrifice; instant death must have been the consequence. But heaven, either in its bounty or its anger, put an end to the sacrifice. The stars were verging toward the horizon, and the Gauls feared lest the light should surprise them. They resolved to wait for the offering of their abominable sacrifice, till Dis, the father of the shades, should have darkened the skies with another night. The crowd immediately dispersed over the heath, and the lights were extinguished. Still here and there the wind would kindle the expiring torch, and flash a momentary splendor on the deep gloom of the woods ; and at intervals the voice of the distant bards would swell on the ear, and I could distinguish in the distance the mournful burden of their song.

" 'Teutates must be satisfied with blood ; he has spoken from the Druid oak. The sacred mistletoe has been cut off with the golden sickle, on the sixth day of the moon. Teutates must be satisfied with blood, for he has spoken from the Druid oak.'

" I hastened my return to the castle, and immediately convoked the Gaulish tribes. When they were assembled at the foot of the fortress, I assured them that I knew of their seditious meetings, and the plots they were laying against Cæsar.

" The barbarians were petrified with dread. Environed by Roman soldiers, they believed this moment to be their last. A voice of loud lament was heard, and immediately a number of women rushed into the midst of the assembly. They were Christians, and bore in their arms their infants, that had been just baptized. They fell at my knees, and demanded pardon for their husbands, their children, and their relatives; they held out their new-born infants, and conjured me in the name of innocence to be merciful.

" Could I resist the eloquence of Nature herself? Could I at this moment forget the charity I had experienced from Zacharius ? I bade each weeping mother arise.

" ' My sisters,' said I, ' I grant you the pardon you demand, in the name of Jesus Christ, our common master. You shall be the sureties for your husbands ; I shall feel satisfied when you have promised that they shall remain faithful to Cæsar.'

"The Armoricans shouted for joy, and extolled to the skies this clemency which cost me so little. Before dismissing them, I drew from them a promise that they should renounce these dreadful sacrifices—dreadful, no doubt, since they had been proscribed even by Tiberius and Claudius. I at the same time demanded that they should deliver up the Druidess Velleda, and her father Segenax, the first magistrate of the Redones. On the same evening these hostages were brought, and I gave them an asylum in the castle. I sent out a fleet to encounter that of the Franks, which was forced to retire from the Armorican shores, and all things were restored to their former tranquillity. This adventure was attended with consequences to myself, that it now remains for me to relate."

Here Eudorus suddenly interrupted his narrative. He appeared embarrassed, he cast his eyes on the ground, and then unconsciously raised them on Cymodoce, who blushed as if she had discovered the thoughts of Eudorus. Cyril perceived their confusion, and immediately addressed himself to the spouse of Lasthenes:

"Sephora," said he, "I wish to offer a holy sacrifice for Eudorus, after he shall have finished his history. Will you have the kindness to prepare the altar for me?"

Sephora arose, and her daughters followed her example. The timid Cymodoce durst not remain alone with the old men, and she accompanied them, though not without a sigh of regret.

Demodocus, as he beheld her pass like a graceful roe over the meadow, could not contain his joy, but exclaimed:

"What glory can equal that of a father, who beholds his child increase under his eyes in loveliness and virtue! Jupiter himself loved his son Hercules with the fondest affection: immortal as he was, he felt all the fears and anxieties of man, since he had assumed the heart of a father. My dear Eudorus, you cause the same alarms and the same pleasures to your parents. Continue your history. I must own, I cannot help loving your Christians : like their mother, the Prayers, they follow the footsteps of Injury, to bind up the wounds that she has made. They are bold as lions and gentle as doves; with all this intelligence, and all this goodness of heart, it is a great pity that they know not Jupiter! But, Eudorus, why do I continue to interrupt you, when I feel so strong a desire to hear the rest of your recital? Such, my son, is the nature of old men: when they once enter upon discourse, they are charmed with their own wisdom: a god incites them, whose power they are unable to resist."

Eudorus then resumed his narrative.

BOOK TENTH.

SUMMARY.

Continuation of the Recital. Conclusion of the Episode of Velleda.

"I TOLD you, my friends, that Velleda inhabited the castle with her father. Grief and anxiety at first preyed upon the mind of Segenax, and threw him into a burning fever. I offered him every succor that humanity required, and went every day to visit the tower in which the father and daughter resided. This conduct, so different from that of the other Roman commanders, charmed my two prisoners; the old man recovered fast, and the Druidess, who had at first manifested great dejection of mind, soon appeared more contented. I often met her walking with an air of joy through the courts of the castle, the galleries, the secret passages, and up the stairs that wound to the top of the fortress; she seemed to haunt my steps, and when I thought her attending at the side of her father, she would glide like an apparition before my eyes, and disappear in some obscure corridor.

"This was truly an extraordinary woman. Like the rest of the Gaulish females, there was something in her manner capricious and yet attractive. Her eye was lively and unsteady; and a smile at once disdainful and captivating played around her lips. There was in her character a strange mixture of dignity and of wildness, of innocence and of art. I should have been astonished to find this barbarian well versed in Grecian learning, and in the history of her own country, had I not known that Velleda was a descendant of the Arch-Druid, and that she had been educated by one of the Senanis, for the purpose of being received into the learned order of the Gaulish priesthood. Pride was her ruling passion, and the elevation of her sentiments often bordered upon extravagance.

"The armory of the castle was a large room that admitted the light only through long and narrow apertures that were cut in the massive walls; one night I was here buried in solitary reflections; the stars shone through these openings, and threw a gleam on the lances and eagles that were ranged round the walls. I had not lighted my torch, but was walking backward and forward amidst the darkness.

"Suddenly, at one of the extremities of the gallery, I beheld a pale, glimmering light. It increased by degrees, and at length I perceived Velleda. She held in her hand a Roman lamp, that was suspended by a golden chain. Her blond hair was dressed in the Grecian manner, and was encircled by a crown of vervain, a plant held sacred by the Druids. Her only clothing was a white tunic; the daughter of a king could not display more beauty, nobleness, and grandeur.

"She suspended her lamp on one of the bucklers, and approaching me, said:

"'My father is asleep; be seated, and listen to me.'

"I took down from the wall a trophy of pikes and javelins, formed them into a pile, and on this we seated ourselves, in front of the lamp.

"'Do you know,' said she with earnestness, 'do you know that I am a fairy?'

"I demanded an explanation of this word.

"'The fairies of Gaul,' said she, 'are possessed of a wonderful power; they can arouse the tempest, and again awe it into tranquillity; they can render themselves invisible, and assume the form of different animals.'

"'I am totally unacquainted with any such power,' answered I with gravity. 'How can you reasonably believe yourself possessed of a power that you have never exercised? My religion forbids such superstitions. Storms are obedient to God alone.'

"'I speak not of your God,' she replied with impatience. 'Tell me, did you not last night hear the murmurs of the fountain in the woods, and the sighing of the breeze through the plants that grow round your window? It was I who was sighing in the fountain and the breeze! I had observed that you were fond of the murmuring of winds and waters.'

"I could but pity the lovely maniac: she read these sentiments in my look.

"'I have excited your compassion,' said she. 'You believe that my reason is injured; but know that you are the cause of it. Why have you exerted your influence to save my father? Why have you treated me with so much kindness? I am a virgin—a virgin of the isle of Sayne; whether I break my vows, or preserve them inviolate, I must die. But remember, you are the cause of it—this is what I wished to tell you. Adieu.'

"She arose, took her lamp, and disappeared. Never till this moment, my friends, had I experienced so poignant an affliction; for nothing can be more frightful than to wound the bosom of innocence. I had slept in the midst of dangers, and had contented myself with resolutions of amendment, and with the wish at some future time to return to the fold of Christ. This state of lukewarmness deserved to meet its punishment: I had nourished in my heart the viper brood of my passions, and therefore I deserved to feel the venom of their sting.

"Heaven seemed at this moment to have deprived me of the means of avoiding the danger. Clair, the pastor of this church, was absent; Segenax was too feeble to quit the castle, and it would have been inhuman to separate the daughter from her father. I was therefore obliged to keep the enemy within my walls, and to remain, despite of myself, exposed to his attacks. In vain I discontinued my visits to the old man, in vain I withdrew myself from the sight of Velleda: I found her in every part: for whole days would she loiter about those places where I was necessitated to pass, and there would she avow her passion.

"I felt, it is true, that Velleda could never inspire me with any real affection; she possessed not that secret charm, which points out the object destined to bless us through life : but the daughter of Segenax was young and beautiful ; when she spoke, my reason was confounded, and all my senses thrown into confusion.

"At some distance from the castle, in one of those woods held sacred by the Druids, stood the trunk of a withered tree, which had been stripped of its bark, and was thus rendered a conspicuous object amidst the dark surrounding trees of the forest. This was adored by the barbarians under the name of Irminsul, as a formidable divinity, who in their sports, as well as in their afflictions, invoked the aid of death alone. This species of idol was surrounded by oaks, whose roots had been bedewed with human blood, and whose branches were hung with arms, and other warlike ensigns of the Gauls ; when the wind agitated the branches, these arms struck against each other, and sent forth a hollow and foreboding sound.

"I often went to visit this sanctuary, that awakened so many recollections of the ancient race of the Celts. One evening I had retired to this favorite spot, to indulge in the solemn feelings that the scene inspired, when on a sudden Velleda appeared.

"'You fly me,' said she, 'you seek the solitude of these woods to hide yourself from my presence ; but it is in vain.'

"She then placed herself before me, crossed her arms, and regarded me for some time in an attitude of silence : at last she exclaimed :

"'I have many things to tell you, and wish for a long conversation. I know that my complaints are disagreeable to you, I know that my love meets with no return, yet I feel a satisfaction in declaring it, and making known to you all its violence. Ah, if you loved me, how great would be our felicity! We would find wherein to express ourselves a language worthy of heaven : now words fail me since your soul responds not to mine.'

"At this moment a blast swept through the forest, and the brazen bucklers sent forth a plaintive sound. Velleda was alarmed; she instantly raised her head, gazed on the suspended trophies, and cried in a voice of terror:

"'These groans issue from the arms of my father: they announce some misfortune to me.'

"After a moment of silence, she added:

"'There must be some reason for your indifference. It is unaccountable that so much affection on my part, should meet with no return: such coldness is extraordinary.'

"Here she was silent again. When suddenly, as if awakening from a profound reverie, she exclaimed:

"'At last I have discovered the true cause of all this! You cannot endure me because I have nothing to offer worthy your acceptance.'

"She then approached me in a kind of delirium, and placing her hand upon my heart: 'Warrior,' said she, 'thy heart remains tranquil under the hand of love; but perhaps a throne might cause it to palpitate. Speak; do you wish the empire? A woman of Gaul once promised it to Diocletian; a woman of Gaul now proposes it to you; she was only a prophetess, but I am both a prophetess and a lover. I can do everything for you. You know it: we have often disposed of the purple. I will hasten and secretly arm our warriors. Teutates will be propitious, and by my arts I will force heaven itself to second your wishes. I will summon the Druids from their forests. I myself will march to the combat, and bear the oaken branch in my hand. If fate should still frown on our undertakings, there are yet caverns in Gaul, in whose gloomy recesses I can, like another Eponine, conceal my spouse. But why, unhappy Velleda, do you speak of a spouse, you who are never to meet a return of love!'

"The voice of the young barbarian expired on her lips; the hand she held pressed to my heart fell lifeless at her side; her head inclined upon her bosom, and the ardor of her passion was extinguished by a torrent of tears.

"This conversation filled me with alarm. I began to fear that resistance would be useless. My emotion was extreme when Velleda ceased to speak, and all the rest of the day I felt her burning touch upon my heart. Wishing to make a last effort to save myself, I took a resolution which was designed to prevent the evil, but which only served to aggravate it; for when God intends to punish us, he turns our very wisdom against ourselves, and makes that prudence of no avail which comes too late.

"I told you that at first it was impossible to remove Segenax from the castle, on account of his extreme weakness; but the old man had now very considerably recovered his strength, and the danger grew every day more pressing: I therefore pretended that I had received letters from Cæsar, containing a command to dismiss my prisoners. Velleda wished for an interview before her departure; but this I refused, that we might both be spared the pain of so melancholy a scene: her filial piety would not permit her to abandon her father, and as I foresaw, she followed him from the castle. The very next day she appeared at the gates, but was told that I had set out on a journey: she bowed her head in silence, and returned to the forest. For several days she presented herself in the same way, and received the same answer. In her last visit she remained for a long time leaning against a tree, with her eyes fixed in a steadfast gaze on the walls of the fortress. Through a window of my apartment I beheld her in this situation, and could not restrain my tears at the sight: with slow and lingering step she at length retired, and returned no more.

"I now began to experience some interval of repose, and hoped that Velleda was at last cured of her fatal passion. Wearied of the prison in which I had been so long immured, I at length ventured forth to breathe the pure air. Throwing over my shoulders the skin of a bear, and with a huntsman's spear in my hand, I quitted the castle, and wandered to a hill, from whose heights the British straits were discernible.

"Like Ulysses regretting his native Ithaca, or like the exiled Trojans on the plains of Sicily, I gazed on the vast expanse of the waves, and wept at the view. 'Born at the foot of Mount Taygetus,' said I to myself, 'the melancholy murmur of the deep was the first sound that struck my infant ear. Since that period, how many lands have I seen laved by the same billows that I now contemplate! Who could have persuaded me some years ago that I should hear on the coast of Italy and Batavia, and on the shores of the Bretons and the Gauls, the dash of the same waves that I once beheld sporting on the beautiful sands of Messenia? What shall be the term of my long pilgrimage? Happy would it have been for me, if death had surprised me before these my adventures, and if I had never had these errors and these wanderings to relate!'

"Such were my reflections, when I heard at no great distance the sounds of a voice accompanied by a guitar. These sounds, which rose and fell at intervals, and were at times interrupted by the cries of the curlew and the gull, and by the murmurs of the sea and the forest, had something in them at once rude and enchanting. I looked to the spot whence the notes proceeded, and beheld Velleda seated on the heath. Her attire announced the disorder of her mind. A collar of eglantine berries adorned her bosom, her guitar was fantastically suspended from her neck by a wreath of ivy, and a white veil flowed from her head down upon her feet. In this singular apparel, pale, and her eyes inflamed with weeping, her beauty was still striking. She sat behind some shrubs that were half-stripped of their foliage: thus the poet represents the shade of Dido, gliding through the myrtle grove, like the new moon when she rises amidst fleecy clouds.

"The motion that I made on discovering the daughter of Segenax drew her attention. At sight of me, a troubled joy overspread her countenance, and making me some mysterious sign, she thus spoke:

"'I was certain I should draw you hither; nothing can resist the power of my voice.'

"She then began to sing:

"'Hercules, thou didst deign to visit the verdant Aquitania. Pyrene, who gave her name to the mountains of Iberia; Pyrene, the daughter of king Bebryx, espoused the Grecian hero; for the Greeks have always stolen the hearts of women.'

"Velleda arose, and advanced toward me.

"'I know not,' said she, 'what enchantment draws me toward you. I am always wandering round your castle, but I am unable to enter it, and retire in sorrowful disappointment. But I have prepared my charms: I shall go to seek the mystic plant; I shall offer first an oblation of bread and wine; clothed in white and with naked feet, with my right hand hidden beneath my tunic, will I pluck the plant and convey it in secret to my left hand. Then nothing will be able to resist me. On the moonbeam I will glide through the windows of the castle; I will take the shape of the turtle-dove, and wing my flight to the tower that you inhabit. If I knew what you preferred... I might... but no: I wish to be loved for myself alone. To love me under any borrowed form, would be infidelity to me.'

"At these words, Velleda sent forth cries of despair.

"Again she was silent, and regarded me with fixed attention, as if she wished to discover in my looks the secrets of my mind. At length she exclaimed:

"'Yes, it is so. Some Roman female, more happy than Velleda, is the object of your affections. Have then the daughters of Rome the advantage over us? The cygnet's down is less white than the bosom of the Gaul: the pure azure of the heavens is seen in the lustre of her eye. Our tresses are so beautiful, that your Roman women despoil us of them to adorn their heads; but the foliage is never beautiful except on the summit of the tree where it was born. Do you see my flowing locks? if I would have yielded them, they would be now on the brow of the empress; they are my diadem; I have kept them for you. Do you not know that our fathers, our brothers and spouses think us divine? The voice of falsehood has, perhaps, told you that the women of Gaul are capricious, light, and inconstant: believe not the accusations. Among the children of the Druids, the passions are serious, and their consequences terrible.'

"I pressed the hands of the unfortunate in my own, and addressed her in a tone of tenderness.

"'Velleda,' said I, 'if you love me, there is a way of proving it: return to your father; he has need of your assistance. Abandon yourself no longer to a grief that has troubled your reason, and will destroy my life.'

"I descended the hill, and Velleda followed me. We advanced into the plain by paths that were little frequented, and overgrown with grass.

"'If you did but love me,' said Velleda, 'with what delight should we traverse these plains! With what happiness should we wander in these solitary roads, like the sheep whose locks of wool are clinging to these briers.'

"She paused, looked at her emaciated arms, and said with a smile:

"'And I too have been torn by the thorns of the desert, and leave here each day some part of my spoil.'

"Then returning to her reveries, she continued:

"'On the borders of this rivulet, at the foot of yonder spreading tree, and along yonder fields—where smiles the young harvest, whose completion I shall never witness—should we have carelessly loitered, and admired the glories of the setting sun. How sweet under the thatch of our cabin, to hear the tempest roar without, and wear away the tedious hours in delightful converse. Do you think that in my dreams of felicity I pant for princely treasures, or the pomps of a palace? Alas! my wishes are more modest, my desires more bounded. I never behold the shepherd's humble hut, without thinking that with you this would be sufficient. More happy than the Scythians, whose story the Druids have told me, we should transport our cot from solitude to solitude, and our habitation would be no more earthly than our lives.'

"We reached the entrance of a wood of pines and larches, when the daughter of Segenax stopped, and thus addressed me:

"'My father inhabits these woods; I would not wish you to accompany me to his dwelling, as he might think you had designs upon his daughter. It cannot make any deep impression on your feelings to behold my sorrows; I am young and vigorous; but the tears of an aged parent break the heart. Adieu, I will seek you again near the castle.'

"As she said this, she quitted me in haste, and I soon lost sight of her in the forest.

"This unexpected meeting proved fatal to my good resolutions. So great is the danger of the passions, that even without sharing in them, we breathe in their atmosphere a poison that intoxicates us. Twenty times, while Velleda was expressing for me feelings so mournful and so tender, was I on the point of throwing myself at her feet, surprising her by my conquest and enchanting her by the confession of my defeat. At the moment in which I was ready to succumb, I owed my safety only to the pity with which this unfortunate inspired me. But this pity, which at first preserved me, at last proved my ruin. I no longer felt any fortitude against the allurements of Velleda; I attributed the wanderings of her mind to my own severity, and bitterly lamented my cruelty. I even felt disgusted with my former courage, relapsed into more than my usual weakness, and feeling that I could no longer rely upon my own efforts, I placed all my hopes in the return of Clair.

"Some days had passed, but Velleda did not appear at the castle as she had promised, and I began to fear that some fatal accident had befallen her. Full of anxiety, I left the castle to repair to the abode of Segenax, when I was overtaken by a soldier, who had hastened from the sea-coast to inform me that the fleet of the Franks was within sight of Armorica. I was immediately obliged to quit the object of my pursuit. The sky was lowering, and everything announced an approaching tempest. Knowing that the barbarians generally chose the fury of the storm for the moment of landing, I redoubled my vigilance. I put all the soldiers under arms, and fortified those places that lay most exposed. The whole day was spent in these laborious exertions, and the rage of the tempest increasing at the approach of night, we were filled with fresh apprehensions.

"There was a part of the coast from which, as it lay flat and unprotected, I apprehended the greatest danger. Scarcely a few wild shrubs grew along the barren sands, where stood a long line of Druidical stones, similar to the kind of tomb at whose foot I formerly met Velleda. Lashed by the billows and beaten by the wind and rain, they stood solitary between earth, sea, and sky. Whether these monuments of Druidical science denoted some secrets in astronomy, or some mystery in religion, is still a matter of doubt. Certain it is, that the Gauls never approach these stones without strong expressions of terror. 'There,' say they, 'the wandering flame is seen, and the voice of the phantom is heard.'

"The solitude of this place, and the terrors that it inspired, appeared to me very favorable to the descent of the barbarians. I therefore determined to place a guard on this coast, and resolved to pass the night there in person.

"The slave that I had dispatched with a letter to Velleda, returned without delivering it. He had not found the Druidess; she had quitted her father about the third hour of the day, and he knew not whither she had gone. This intelligence did but augment my alarm. In order to conceal my emotions from the soldiers, I retired some distance from them to a secret part of the coast. I had not long been there, before a sound awakened me from my reverie, and I thought I saw a figure gliding through the gloom. I arose, seized my sword, and rushed toward the spot. What was my surprise, when I seized upon Velleda.

"'What,' said she, in a low voice, 'is it you? You knew, then, that I was here?'

"'I knew it not,' I replied; 'but will you betray the Romans?'

"'Betray them!' she exclaimed, in a tone of indignation. 'Have I not sworn to undertake nothing against you? Follow me, and you shall see what I am doing here.'

"She took me by the hand, and conducted me to the most elevated point of one of the Druidical monuments.

"The sea broke with loud fury upon the beach below, and covered us with the dashing spray. The moon threw at intervals her uncertain light, from amidst the thick clouds that flew across the sky.

"'Listen to what I am about to tell you,' said Velleda:

'on this coast live fishermen who are unknown to you. When half the night has passed, they hear some one knocking at their doors, and calling to them in a low voice. Upon this they run to the shore, without knowing the power that draws them. Here they find boats, in which no one is seen, yet these boats are so heavily laden with the souls of mortals, that they are but just above the edge of the water. In less than an hour, the fishermen accomplish the voyage of a day, and conduct these souls to the isle of the Bretons. They see no one, either on the passage or during the disembarkation, though they hear a voice naming the new comers to the guardian of souls. If there are any women in the boat, the names of their husbands are declared by the voice. You know, cruel man, whether mine can be named.'

"I vainly attempted to combat these superstitions.

"'Be silent,' said she, as though I had been guilty of impiety; 'you shall see ere long the whirlwind of fire that announces the passage of the souls. Do you not hear their cries already?'

"Velleda was silent, and lent an attentive ear.

"After a few moments' silence, she continued:

"'When I shall be no more, promise to give me news of my father. Whenever any one dies, write me letters and cast them on the funeral pile; they will reach me in the *Abode of Memories;* I shall read them with delight; and we shall thus talk together from either side of the tomb.'

"At this moment, a furious wave dashed against the rock, which it shook to its foundations. A gust of wind rent the clouds asunder, and the moon let fall a faint ray of light upon the surface of the waves. Sinister sounds arose on the shore. The gull—the melancholy bird of the rocks—shrieked its plaintive cry, resembling the cry of a drowning man. The frightened sentinel shouted an alarm. Velleda leaped forward, extended her arms, and cried:

"'They are awaiting me.'

"She sprang into the waves. I caught her by the veil. . . .

"O Cyril, how shall I continue this recital? I blush with shame and confusion, but I owe you the full confession of my faults. I submit them, without concealing anything, to the holy tribunal of your age. Alas! after my shipwreck, I take refuge in your charity as in a port of mercy!

"Exhausted by the combats that I had sustained against myself, I could not resist this last proof of the love of Velleda. Such beauty, passion and despair deprived me of my reason in turn: I was vanquished.

"'No,' said I, in the midst of the darkness and tempest, 'I am not strong enough to be a Christian.'

"I fell at the feet of Velleda. . . . Hell gave the signal for this fatal union; the spirits of darkness howled in the abyss, the chaste spouses of the patriarchs turned away their heads, and my protecting angel, veiling his face with his wings, ascended again to heaven.

The daughter of Segenax consented to live, or rather she had not the strength to die. She remained mute, in a sort of stupor. A mingling of fearful torture and of ineffable delight, love, remorse, shame, fear, and above all, astonishment, agitated the heart of Velleda: she could not believe that I was the same Eudorus that had hitherto been so insensible; she knew not but she was deceived by some phantom of the night, and touched my hands and locks to assure herself of the reality of my existence. To me, my happiness resembled despair, and whoever had seen us in the midst of our felicity, would have taken us for two criminals that had just received the fatal sentence.

"At that moment, I felt myself stamped with the seal of divine reprobation. I doubted the possibility of my salvation, and the omnipotence of the mercy of God. A thick darkness, like a vapor, arose in my soul, of which it seemed to me that a legion of rebellious spirits suddenly took possession. I found thoughts within myself to which I had hitherto been a stranger; the language of hell naturally escaped from my lips, and I uttered the blasphemies of those abodes where there will be eternal wailing and tears.

"Weeping and smiling by turn, Velleda, the happiest and most unfortunate of creatures, kept silence. The dawn began to whiten the heavens. The enemy was not to be seen. I returned to the castle, followed by my victim. Twice did the star that marks the last footsteps of day hide our blushes, and twice did the star that brings back the light restore us to shame and remorse.

"On the third day, Velleda mounted my chariot to go in search of Segenax. She had scarce disappeared in the forest, before there arose in the midst of it a column of smoke and flame. At the moment that I beheld this sight, a centurion came to inform me, that those cries, which among the Gauls are signals, were heard resounding from village to village. Thinking that the Franks had made a descent on some part of the coast, I hastened out of the castle with a party of soldiers, and soon perceived the peasants running together from all quarters, to join a large body that was advancing toward me.

"I marched forward at the head of the Romans toward these rustic battalions. When we were within reach of their javelins, I bade my men halt, and advancing alone, with head uncovered, between the two armies, I said:

"'Gauls, what is the cause of your thus assembling? Have the Franks made a descent upon Armorica? Do you come hither to offer me assistance, or do you stand here as enemies of Cæsar?'

"An old man advanced from the ranks. His shoulders trembled under the weight of his cuirass, and his arm could scarcely sustain his useless sword. O astonishment! I saw before me a suit of the same armor I had formerly beheld suspended in the Druid's grove. O confusion! this venerable warrior was Segenax!

"'Gauls,' cried he, 'by these arms of my youth, which I have taken again from the tree of Irminsul, to whom I had consecrated them, I call you to witness that yonder man has dishonored my grey hairs. A Druid followed my daughter, whose reason is disordered; concealed in a thicket, he beheld the crime of yonder Roman. The virgin of Sayne has been violated. Revenge your daughters and your spouses; revenge the Gauls and your gods.'

"He spoke, and with powerless hands hurled his javelin against me. The feeble dart fell ineffectual at my feet: would to heaven it had pierced me to the heart! With loud cries the Gauls rushed upon me, while my own soldiers advanced to my aid. In vain I wished to arrest the combatants. It was no longer a passing tumult, it swelled into the rage of battle, and loud outcries arose from each party. The divinities of the Druids seemed to have issued from their forests, to animate the Gauls to carnage; such was the boldness that these peasants displayed. Indifferent to the danger that threatened my life, my only thought was to save Segenax. I rescued him from the hands of the soldiers, and endeavored to shelter him under the trunk of an oak; but at this moment, a javelin hurled from the midst of the crowd, hissed by me, and penetrated deep into the aged father's bosom; he fell under the tree which his ancestors had planted, like the aged Priam under the laurel which overshadowed his domestic altar.

"At this moment a chariot appeared at the extremity of the plain. Bending over the heads of her coursers, a woman with dishevelled hair excited their ardor, and seemed desirous of adding wings to their speed. Velleda had not found her father in his hut, and on her way had learnt that he had assembled the Gauls to revenge the violated honor of his daughter. The Druidess saw that she was betrayed, and knew the fatal consequences of her crime. She flew to find her father, reached the scene of combat, drove through the ranks, and discovered me mourning over the lifeless body of her aged parent. Transported with grief, Velleda arrested her steeds, and exclaimed from the height of her chariot:

"'Gauls, suspend the conflict; behold in me the cause of your evils: it is I who slew my father. Cease to expose your lives for the guilty daughter of your chieftain. The Roman is innocent. The virgin of Sayne has not been violated; it was through free choice that she broke her vows. May my death restore peace to my country!'

"As she uttered this, she snatched from her brow her crown of vervain, and seized the golden sickle that hung at her girdle, as if about to offer a sacrifice to her gods.

"'I shall never again,' she exclaimed, 'defile these ornaments of a vestal.'

"Immediately she struck the sacred instrument deep into her bosom, and the blood spouted from the wound. As the reaper, fatigued with the labors of the day, stretches himself near the furrow to repose, so sunk Velleda powerless upon the chariot; the weapon dropped from her fainting hand, and her head gently inclined upon her shoulder. She attempted once again to pronounce the name of him whom she loved, but the sound died away upon her lips in indistinct murmurs; I now existed only in the dreams of the daughter of Gaul: a sleep that knew no waking had closed her eyes forever.

BOOK ELEVENTH.

SUMMARY.

Continuation of the Recital. Repentance of Eudorus. His public Penitence. He quits the Army. He repairs to Egypt to ask permission of Diocletian to return to his Country. The Voyage. Alexandria. The Nile. Egypt. Eudorus obtains his return from Diocletian. The Thebais. Return of Eudorus to his Father's House. Conclusion of the Recital.

"PARDON, sirs, the tears that still flow from my eyes. I forgot to tell you that the centurions had detained me amongst them whilst Velleda despoiled herself of life. Heaven decreed, as an addition to my punishment, that I should not again behold the object of my seduction, except to lay her in the tomb.

"O Cyril, I cannot but reckon this the most important period of my existence, since it was the moment of my return to religion. Hitherto the consequences of my errors had affected me alone; but when I found myself the cause of another's woes, my heart revolted against itself. Clair arrived: I hesitated no longer, but threw myself at his feet, and made a full confession of all the iniquities of my past life. He embraced me with transports of joy, and imposed upon me a part of those penitential exercises, which you see me as yet fulfilling, and which I consider as light when compared with the enormity of my offence.

"The fevers of the soul resemble those of the body; to cure them, change of place is necessary most of all. I resolved to quit Armorica, to renounce the world, and go and bewail my errors under the roof of my fathers. I sent a resignation of my authority to Constantius, and entreated his permission to abandon the army and the world. Cæsar employed every art to retain me in my station; he loaded me with fresh honors;

he named me to the prætorship of Gaul, a post of supreme dignity, the authority of which extended over Spain, and the isles of Britain. Perceiving that I remained firm in my resolution, Constantius at length wrote me a letter, in which were these words, expressive of his usual kindness:

" ' I cannot myself grant you the favor you demand, because you are under the jurisdiction of the Roman people. The emperor alone has a right to decide in this case. Go to him, and solicit his permission to retire; and if Augustus should refuse you, return to Cæsar.'

" I yielded up my command of Armorica to the tribune who was to fill my place, and after tenderly embracing the good pastor Clair, I quitted the woods and the vales that Velleda had once inhabited, filled with deep emotion and remorse. I embarked at the port of Nismes; landed at Ostia, and reached Rome—that theatre of my first errors. In vain some young friends solicited me to join in their festivities; my melancholy dashed the joy of the banquet; I affected to smile, but was obliged to detain the cup at my lips, to conceal the tears that streamed from my eyes. I went and prostrated myself before the chief of the Christians, who had cut me off from the communion of the Faithful, and ardently besought him to receive me once again into the fold. Marcellinus admitted me among the number of the penitents; he even gave me reason to hope that my time of probation might be abridged, and that if I persevered in my course of penitence, the house of the Lord might, after five years, be opened to receive me.

" Nothing now remained but to lay my petition at the feet of Diocletian, who was still in Egypt. I was determined not to await his return, but to pass immediately to the East.

" One of those vessels, which the bishops of Alexandria sent in times of scarcity to import corn for the sustenance of the poor, lay at this time at the mole of Marcus Aurelius. This vessel was ready to set sail for Egypt, and I went on board. We weighed anchor, and with favoring breezes, soon left the shores of Italy behind.

" Alas! I had before traversed this sea, when for the first

time I quitted my native Arcadia. I was then young, and full of hope; glory, riches, and honors seemed already within my grasp: I then knew nothing of the world, but in the fond dreams of imagination. 'Now,' said I to myself, 'what a difference! I am returning from the world I so eagerly desired to visit, and what have I gained by my sorrowful pilgrimage?'

"The whole crew of the vessel were Christians, and the solemnities of our religion, when performed on the deck, seemed to augment the majesty of the scene. If these men did not behold Venus arising from the sparkling deep, and borne to heaven by the winged Hours, they made a right use of their reason, and admired His handiwork, who hollowed out the abyss, and who in his good pleasure can clothe the waves with beauty or with terror. It required not the fables of Alcyone and Ceyx to discover a touching analogy between the birds that flitted over the deep and our own destinies. When we beheld the wearied swallows settle to rest themselves on our mast, we were tempted to interrogate them concerning our country. Perhaps these very birds had flown around our dwelling, and suspended their nests to our roof. Demodocus, let me call your attention to this simplicity of the Christians, which renders them like children. The heart adorned with innocence avails the mariner more than the stern adorned with flowers; and the sentiments that flow from the soul that is unsullied, are more agreeable to the sovereign of the seas than the wine that is poured in libation from the cup of gold.

"At night, instead of addressing the stars in vain and guilty invocations, we regarded the firmament with silent admiration, where these stars rejoiced in pouring forth their light to his honor who created them—that beautiful sky and those peaceful abodes which I had forever shut upon Velleda.

"We coasted along close to Utica and Carthage: these scenes recalled the memory of Marius and Cato; but the crimes of the one, and the virtues of the other, presented a glory that was comparatively insignificant when opposed to their misfortunes. I felt an ardent desire to embrace Augustine on these shores. At the view of the hill on which the palace of Dido formerly stood, I could not restrain my tears. A column of smoke that arose near the shore, seemed to announce to me, as it once did to the son of Anchises, that the funeral pile was lighted for the fatal sacrifice. In the destiny of the queen of Carthage, I found that of the priestess of the Gauls. Concealing my face with both hands, I sobbed aloud. Like Æneas, I had caused the death of the woman that loved me, and was now flying over the seas as he did; but a man without glory or prospects from futurity, I was not, like Æneas, the last heir of Ilion and of Hector; unlike him, I could not plead in excuse the orders of the gods, and the destinies of the Roman empire.

"We passed the promontory of Mercury, and the cape where Scipio hailed the fortune of Rome, and wished to land with his army. The favoring breeze carried us close to the smallest of the Syrtes, and we saw the tower that afforded a retreat to the great Hannibal, when he secretly embarked to fly the ingratitude of his country: on whatever shore we touch, we are sure to meet the traces of injustice or misfortune. Thus on the opposite shores of Sicily, methought I still saw the victims of the cruel Verres; that I beheld them from the height of their instruments of torture turning their dying looks ineffectually toward Rome. Ah, the Christian upon the cross shall not sigh for his country in vain!

"Already we had left, to the right, the delicious isle of the Lotophagi, the altars of Philæ, and of Leptis, the birthplace of Severus. Already the mountains of Crete began dimly to appear above the waves on our left, and the breeze bore us rapidly over the gulf of Cyrene. Twelve times had Aurora gilded the east, when on the thirteenth morn we saw nearly level with the waves, a low and desolate shore that formed an almost imperceptible horizon. In the midst of a vast sandy plain, a high column attracted our regard. The mariners immediately recognized the column of Pompey, lately consecrated to Diocletian by Pollio, the prefect of Egypt. We directed our course toward this remarkable object, that so faithfully announces to the voyager that city, which was built by the conqueror of Arbela, to be a tomb for him who was vanquished at Pharsalia. We cast anchor to the west of Pharos, in the magnificent port of Alexandria. Peter,[1] the bishop of this famous city, received me with paternal affection. He offered me an asylum in the buildings inhabited by his clergy ; but being related to the beautiful and pious Æcaterina, I took up my residence in her house.

"Before I joined Diocletian in Upper Egypt, I spent some days at Alexandria, to visit the wonders of the place. What above all things excited my admiration, was the magnificent library. It was under the care of Didymus, the worthy successor of Aristarchus. Here I met with philosophers from every country, and with most of the illustrious characters who adorned the churches of Asia and Africa, Arnobius[2] of Carthage, Athanasius[3] of Alexandria, Eusebius[4] of Cæsarea, Timotheus[5] and Pamphilus, all apologists, doctors or confessors of Jesus Christ. The wretched seducer of Velleda, scarcely durst raise his eyes amidst this society of holy men, who like conquerors sent by heaven to humble rebellious monarchs to the dust, had vanquished and dethroned their tyrant passions.

" One evening I remained almost alone in this depository of the bane and the antidote of the soul. From the height of a marble gallery I beheld Alexandria burnished with the last rays of departing day. I contemplated a city inhabited by a million of souls, and situated between three deserts : the sea, the sandy wastes of Libya, and Necropolis, the city of the dead, but which in extent resembled one destined for the living. My eyes wandered over innumerable monuments, over Pharos, Timonium, the Hippodrome, the palace of the Ptolemies, and the Needles of Cleopatra ; I beheld the two ports covered with ships, and those waves that had once witnessed the magnanimity of the first Cæsar, and the woes of Cornelia. The very form of the city itself was striking ; it resembled a Macedonian cuirass formed on the sands of Libya.

---

[1] The martyr. An apostolic letter from him still remains.
[2] The apologist whose works remain to us.   [3] The patriarch.
[4] The historian.
[5] The martyr, master of Eusebius.

Perhaps this figure was chosen to perpetuate the memory of its founder; perhaps it was to intimate to the traveller, that the arms of the Grecian hero were fruitful; and that the spear of Alexander could bid cities spring up amidst the desert, as the lance of Minerva called forth the olive from the bosom of the earth.

"Pardon, my friends, this image, drawn from a source that is impure. Full of admiration for Alexander, I entered into the interior of the library, and wandered into a hall that I had not before observed. At the extremity of this hall I observed a small monument of crystal, that reflected the beams of the setting sun. I approached it; it was a coffin. As it was transparent, I beheld stretched at the bottom, a king who had died in the flower of his age; his brow was encircled with a diadem of gold, and he was arrayed in all the splendors of royalty. His features, though fixed in death, still preserved traces of that greatness of soul with which they had once been animated; he seemed to be sleeping the slumber of the brave, who have fallen on the field of glory, and pillowed their heads on their swords as they fell.

"A man was seated near this coffin, who seemed deeply engaged in reading. I cast my eye on the volume, and discovered it to be the Septuagint Bible, that had before been pointed out to me. He held it unrolled at this verse of the Maccabees:

"'When Alexander had overthrown Darius, he passed even to the ends of the world; and the earth was silent before him; and after this he knew that he should die. And all his nobles made themselves kings after his death; they divided the diadem, and evils were multiplied on the earth.'

"I had no sooner read this passage, than I cast my eyes upon the coffin; the figure that it inclosed seemed to bear some resemblance to the busts of Alexander. . . . He before whom the earth was silent, reduced to an eternal silence! An obscure Christian seated near the coffin of this most famous of conquerors, and reading in the Bible the history and the destinies of this conqueror! What a vast subject for reflection! 'Ah!' said I to myself, 'if man with all his grandeur be himself so insignificant, what must the memorials be that he leaves behind! This proud Alexandria shall, in its turn, perish like its founder: swallowed up by the three deserts that press upon it, the sands, the sea, and death shall one day reclaim what has been ravished from their empire, and the Arab shall return and pitch his tent over the scene of desolation!'

"On the following day I embarked for Memphis. We soon found ourselves in the midst of the reddish waters of the Nile. Some palm-trees, that seemed planted in the waves, announced our approach to the shore; though the shore itself was still invisible. At length the land that bore them appeared by degrees above the horizon. The summits of the lofty edifices of Canopus now appeared confusedly in the distance; and at length Egypt, all brilliant with a recent inundation, burst upon our view, like a teeming heifer, that had just bathed in the waters of the Nile.

"We entered the river under full sail. The mariners hailed it with shouts of joy, and sipped the sacred waves in the hollow of their hands. A country quite level with the water, lay stretched on both sides. This fertile marsh was scarcely shadowed by a few scattered sycamores and palm-trees, that seemed like the reeds of this mighty stream. Sometimes the desert, like a treacherous foe, was seen stealing upon the verdant plain, and pouring his sandy waves in barren meanders over the bosom of this scene of fertility. Here men have multiplied the obelisk, the column, and the pyramid; a species of isolated architecture that art has invented to supply the place of the mighty oaks which nature has denied to a soil that each returning year visits with renovated youth.

"We now began to discover on our right the winding vales of Libya, and on our left, the lofty crests of the mountains that rise round the Erythræan gulf. As we advanced, this double chain of mountains gradually unfolded, and we discovered the summits of the two great pyramids above the level of the plain that lay expanded before us. Placed at the entrance of the valley of the Nile, they resemble the funeral portals of Egypt, or rather the triumphal arches that death had erected as memorials of the victories he had here obtained. Pharaoh is there with all his host, and their sepulchres are around him.

"At no great distance, and as it were under the shadow of these abodes of death, stands Memphis, surrounded with tombs. Bathed by Lake Acherusia, over which Charon ferried the dead, and bordering upon the plain of tombs, it seemed but a few paces distant from the infernal regions. I made no long stay in this city, that had so far declined from its former grandeur. Anxious in the search of Diocletian, I ascended to Upper Egypt. I visited Thebes, with its hundred gates; Tentyra, still magnificent in ruins, and some of the other four thousand cities that the Nile visits in its course.

"In vain I sought that Egypt, once so renowned for the wisdom of her counsels, and the solemnities of her religion; that Egypt, which had given Cecrops and Inachus to Greece; which was visited by Homer, Lycurgus and Pythagoras; by Jacob, Joseph, and Moses; that Egypt which judged its kings, even after their death; where the son that borrowed, gave the body of the father as a security for the debt; where the father who had slain his son, was obliged during three days to hold the corpse in his embrace; where the coffin was borne around the festive board; where their houses were named inns, and their tombs were called houses. I interrogated the priests, so renowned for their knowledge of the wonders of the sky, and the records of the earth; but I found them to be impostors, who enveloped truth as they did their mummies, in a thousand strange and fantastic foldings, and ranged it among the dead in their gloomy vaults. Fallen into the grossest ignorance, they no longer understand their hieroglyphic language; their fantastic or shameless symbols are as mute to them as they will be to futurity: thus the greater part of their monuments, their obelisks, their sphinxes, and colossal statues, have no longer any association with their history, or their manners. Everything is changed on these shores except the superstition consecrated by the recollections of antiquity; it resembles those monuments of brass, which time cannot entirely efface in a climate so favorable to their preservation: their extremities lie buried in the sand, but their hideous heads are still conspicuous in the midst of surrounding monuments.

"At last I met Diocletian near the great cataracts of the Nile, where he had just concluded a treaty with the people of Nubia. The emperor deigned to speak of the military honors that I had attained, and to testify some regret at the resolution I had taken.

"'However,' said he, 'if you persist in your resolution, you have my permission to return to your country. This favor I accord to your services; you will be the first of your family that ever returned to the roof of his fathers, without leaving a son as a hostage to the Roman nation.'

"Filled with joy at finding myself again at liberty, I resolved to complete the tour of Egypt. There remained another species of antiquities, more accordant with my present state of mind, humbled as it was by penitence, and torn by remorse; and these I resolved to visit. I was now near the borders of that desert which witnessed the flight of the Hebrews, and was consecrated by the miracles of the God of Israel. I resolved to cross it, and take my route through Syria.

"I again embarked on the Nile, and when within two days' journey of Memphis, took a guide to conduct me to the coast of the Red Sea; thence I intended to pass to Arsinoë,[1] and join the Syrian merchants in their journey to Gaza. Some dates, and some skins filled with water, were the only provisions of our journey. My guide preceded me, mounted on a dromedary; I followed on an Arabian horse. After passing the first chain of mountains that bound the eastern banks of the Nile, and losing sight of these fertile plains, we entered a barren waste: nothing could give a more lively image of the transition from life to death.

"Figure to yourselves, my friends, a region of sand,

---

[1] Suez.

ploughed up by the rains of winter, scorched by the fires of summer, of a dull red aspect, and a frightful sterility. Some few thorny cactuses occasionally meet the view in the midst of these boundless sands; but the blast that sweeps over the deserts cannot bend their inflexible branches. fragments of wood, and of petrified bones, lay scattered over the sands, and struck the senses with horror; while heaps of stones, thrown together at intervals, served to mark out the track for the caravan.

"We halted not during the whole day in our march over this plain. We passed another chain of mountains, and discovered a second plain more extensive and more desolate than the former.

"Night came on. The moon shed her silvery light over the waste : nothing was to be seen in the midst of this shadowless solitude, but the immovable shade of the dromedary and the flitting figure of the passing antelope. No sound broke upon the dead silence of the scene, save that of the wild boar as he ground some withered roots, or the chirping of the cricket, which, amid this scene of barrenness, demanded in vain the hearth of the husbandman.

"We resumed our journey before daybreak. The sun arose, shorn of his rays, and resembling a circle of red-hot iron. The heat increased every instant. Toward the third hour of the day, the dromedary began to manifest signs of inquietude; he thrust his nostrils into the sand, and breathed with violence. At intervals the ostrich uttered a doleful cry. The serpent and cameleon hastened to bury themselves in the bosom of the earth. Seeing my guide grow pale as he surveyed the face of the heavens, I demanded the cause of his anxiety.

"'I fear the burning blast of the south,' cried he, 'let us fly for safety!'

"He turned his face to the north, and urged on the dromedary at full speed. I followed him; but the horrible wind that threatened us, was swifter than we.

"Suddenly the whirlwind rushed from the extremity of the

desert. The sand on which we stood seemed to glide from beneath our feet, while it rose in columns from behind, and rolled over our heads. Distracted amidst a labyrinth of hillocks all in motion, and sweeping along in dreadful succession, my guide declared that he no longer knew what direction to take: to put a finishing stroke to our calamities, our water-skins, in the rapidity of our flight, had sprung a leak. Apprehensive of inhaling the inflamed air, we forcibly held our breath, till we were nearly suffocated; our lips were parched with a burning thirst, and the sweat flowed in streams from our fainting bodies. The hurricane redoubled its fury: it laid bare the ancient foundations of the earth, and hurled into the sky the burning entrails of the desert. Buried in clouds of scorching sand, my guide vanished from my sight. Shortly after, his shriek pierced my ear. I flew to the spot whence the cry proceeded: the unfortunate, blasted by the fiery gale, had fallen dead upon the sand, and his dromedary had disappeared.

"In vain I attempted to reanimate my unhappy companion; all my efforts were useless. I seated myself at some distance, holding my horse by the bridle, and hoping now only in Him who changed the fires of Azariah's furnace into a cool breeze and refreshing dew. An acacia that grew on the spot afforded me some shelter. Under this feeble rampart, I waited till the fury of the storm was past. Toward evening, the northern wind resumed its course: the air lost its scorching heat; showers of sand poured from the sky, and at last the stars appeared through the frightful veil that had obscured their lustre—a lustre that, alas! only served to show me the immensity of the desert.

"Every landmark had disappeared, and every path was effaced. The winds had driven the sand into a thousand varied and fantastic landscapes, that on every side presented a new aspect and a new creation. Exhausted with thirst, with hunger, and fatigue, my horse could no longer support his weight; he fell down and breathed his last at my feet. Day returned to aggravate my sufferings. The heat of the sun deprived me of the little strength yet remaining. I attempted to advance a few paces; but soon, incapable of going further, I fell headlong amidst a clump of the shrubs of the desert, and there awaited or rather invoked the coming of death.

"The sun had now climbed the heights of heaven, when suddenly the roaring of a lion was heard, which aroused my languid spirits. I rose with difficulty, and perceived the terrible animal stalking over the sands. The thought immediately struck me, that he might be on his way to some fountain, known to the beasts of these solitudes. I recommended myself to the power that protected Daniel, and returning thanks to heaven, followed my strange conductor at a distance. It was not long before we reached a small valley, at the bottom of which I beheld with rapture a spring of fresh water, environed with verdant moss. Near its margin grew a date-tree, whose bending branches were covered with ripened fruit. This unlooked for succor restored me to life. The lion satisfied his thirst, and then gently retired, as if to yield me his place at this banquet of providence: thus renewing to me those days in the cradle of the world, when the first man, free from stain, saw the beasts of creation sporting about their king, and demanding of him the name they should bear in the desert.

"To the east of this vale of palms arose a high mountain. I directed my course to this kind of Pharos, that seemed to call me to a haven of security, through the immovable floods and solid billows of an ocean of sand. I reached the foot of the mountain, and began to ascend the black and calcined rocks, which closed the horizon on every side. Night descended. Thinking I heard some sound near me, I halted, and plainly distinguished the footsteps of some wild beast, which was wandering in the dark, and broke through the dried shrubs that opposed his progress. I thought that I recognized the lion of the fountain. Suddenly he sent forth a tremendous roar. The echoes of these unknown mountains seemed to awaken for the first time, and returned the roar in savage murmurs. He had paused in front of a cavern whose entrance was closed with a stone. I beheld a light glimmer ing between the crevices of this rock, and my heart beat high with hope and with wonder. I approached and looked in, when, to my astonishment, I really beheld a light shining at the bottom of the cavern.

"'Whoever thou art,' cried I, 'that feedest the savage beasts, have pity on a wretched wanderer.'

"Scarcely had I pronounced these words, when I heard the voice of an old man who was chanting one of the Scripture canticles. I cried in a loud tone:

"'Christian, receive your brother.'

"Scarcely had I uttered these words, when a man approached, broken with age; his snowy beard seemed whitened with all the years of Jacob, and he was clothed in a garment formed of the leaves of the palm.

"'Stranger,' said he, 'you are welcome. You behold a man who is on the point of being reduced to his kindred dust. The hour of my happy departure is arrived: yet still I have a few moments left to dedicate to hospitality. Enter, my brother, the grotto of Paul.'

"Overpowered with veneration, I followed this founder of Christianity in the deserts of the Thebais.

"A palm-tree, which grew in the recess of the grotto, entwined its spreading branches along the rock, and formed a species of vestibule. Near it flowed a spring remarkable for its transparency; out of this fountain issued a small rivulet, that had scarcely escaped from its source before it buried itself in the bosom of the earth. Paul seated himself with me on the margin of the fountain, and the lion that had shown me the Arab's well, came and couched himself at our feet.

"'Stranger,' said the anchorite, with a happy simplicity, 'how do the affairs of the world go on? Do they still build cities? Who is the master that reigns at present? For a hundred and thirteen years have I inhabited this grotto; and for a hundred years I have seen only two men—yourself, and Anthony, the inheritor of my desert; he came yesterday to visit me, and will return to-morrow to bury me.'

"As he said this, Paul went and brought some bread of

the finest kind from the cavity of the rock. He told me that providence supplied him every day with a fresh quantity of this food. He invited me to break the heavenly gift with him. We drank the water of the spring in the hollow of our hands; and after this frugal repast, the holy man inquired what events had conducted me to this inaccessible retreat. After listening to the deplorable history of my life:

"'Eudorus,' said he, 'your faults have been great; but there is no stain that the tears of penitence cannot efface. It is not without some design that providence has made you a witness of the introduction of Christianity into every land. You will also find it here in this solitude, among the lions, beneath the fires of the tropic, as you have encountered it amidst the bears and the glaciers of the pole. Soldier of Jesus Christ, you are destined to fight and to conquer for the faith. O God, whose ways are incomprehensible, it is thou that hast conducted this young confessor to my grotto, that I might unveil futurity to his view; that by perfecting him in the knowledge of his religion, I might complete in him by grace the work that nature has begun! Eudorus, repose here for the rest of the day; to-morrow, at sunrise, we will ascend the mountain to pray, and I will speak to you before I die.'

"After this, the holy man conversed with me for a long time on the beauty of religion, and on the blessings it should one day shed upon mankind. During this discourse the old man presented an extraordinary contrast; simple as a child, when left to nature alone, he seemed to have forgotten everything, or rather to know nothing, of the world, of its grandeurs, its miseries, and its pleasures; but when God descended into his soul, Paul became an inspired genius, filled with experience of the present, and with visions of the future. Thus in his person two opposite characters seemed to unite: still it was doubtful which was the more admirable, Paul the ignorant, or Paul the prophet; since to the simplicity of the former was granted the sublimity of the latter.

"After giving me many instructions full of a wisdom intermingled with sweetness, and a gravity tempered with cheerfulness, Paul invited me to offer with him a sacrifice of praise to the Eternal; he arose, and placing himself under the palm-tree, thus chanted aloud:

"'Blessed be thou, the God of my fathers, who hast had regard to the lowliness of thy servant!

"'O solitude, thou spouse of my bosom, thou art about to lose him for whom thou didst possess unfading charms!

"'The votary of solitude ought to preserve his body in chastity, to have his lips undefiled, and his mind illuminated with divine light.

"'Holy sadness of penitence, come, pierce my soul like a needle of gold, and fill it with celestial sweetness!

"'Tears are the mother of virtue, and sorrow is the foot-stool to heaven.'

"The old man's prayer was scarcely finished, when I fell into a sweet and profound sleep. I reposed on the stony couch that Paul preferred to a bed of roses. The sun was on the point of setting when I again opened my eyes to the light. The hermit said to me:

"'Arise and pray; take your refreshment, and let us go to the mountain.'

"I obeyed him, and we departed together. For more than six hours we ascended the craggy rocks; and at day-break we had reached the most elevated point of Mount Colzim.

"An immense horizon stretched around us. To the east arose the summits of Horeb and Sinai; the desert of Sür, and the Red Sea, lay stretched in boundless expanse below; to the south the mountains of the Thebais formed a mighty chain; the northern prospect was bounded by the barren plains, over which Pharaoh pursued the Hebrews: while to the west, stretching far beyond the sands amidst which I had been lost, lay the fertile valley of Egypt.

"The first rays of Aurora, streaming from the horizon of Arabia Felix, for some time tinged this immense picture with softened light. The zebra, the antelope, and the ostrich ran rapidly over the desert, while the camels of a caravan passed gently in a row, headed by a sagacious ass, that acted as their conductor. The bosom of the Red Sea was chequered with many a whitening sail, that wafted into its ports the silks and the perfumes of the East, or perhaps bore some intelligent voyager to the shores of India. At last the sun arose, and crowned with splendor this frontier of the eastern and western worlds; he poured a blaze of light on the heights of Sinai—a feeble, yet brilliant image of the God that Moses contemplated on the summit of this sacred mount!

"My hoary conductor now broke silence:

"'Confessor of the faith,' said he, 'cast your eyes around you. Behold this eastern clime, where all the religions, and all the revolutions of the earth, have had their origin; behold this Egypt, whence your Greece received her elegant divinities, and India her monstrous and misshapen gods; in these same regions Jesus Christ himself appeared, and the day shall come when a descendant of Ishmael shall reëstablish error beneath the Arab's tent. The first system of morality that was committed to writing, was also the production of this fruitful soil. It is worthy of your attention, that the people of the East, as if in punishment for some great rebellion of their forefathers, have almost always been under the dominion of tyrants; thus, as a kind of miraculous counterpoise, morality and religion have sprung up in the same land that gave birth to slavery and misfortune. Lastly, these same deserts witnessed the march of the armies of Sesostris and Cambyses, of Alexander and Cæsar. Ye too, ye future ages, shall send hither armies equally numerous, and warriors not less celebrated! All the great and daring efforts of the human species have either had their origin here, or have come hither to exhaust their force. A supernatural energy has ever been preserved in these regions wherein the first man received life; something miraculous seems still attached to the cradle of creation and the source of light and knowledge.

"'Without stopping to contemplate those scenes of human grandeur that have long been closed in endless night, or to consider those epochs so renowned in history, but which have passed away like the fleeting vapor, it is to the Christian, above all others, that the East is a land of wonders.

"'You have seen Christianity, aided by morality, penetrate the civilized countries of Italy and Greece; you have seen it introduced by means of charity among the barbarous nations of Gaul and Germany; here, under the influence of an atmosphere that weakens the soul whilst rendering it obstinate, among a people grave by its political institutions, and trifling by its climate, charity and morality would be insufficient. The religion of Jesus Christ can only enter the temples of Isis and Ammon under the veil of penitence. To luxury and effeminacy it must offer examples of the most rigid privation; to the knavery of the priests, and the lying illusions of false divinities, it must oppose real miracles and the oracles of truth: scenes of extraordinary virtue alone can tear away the crowd from the enchantments of the theatre and the circus: when men have been guilty of great crimes, great expiations are necessary, in order that the renown of the latter may efface the celebrity of the former.

"'Such are the reasons for which those missionaries were established, of whom I am the first, and who will be perpetuated in these solitudes. Admire in this the conduct of our divine chief, who knows how to arrange his armies according to the places and the obstacles they have to encounter. Contemplate these two religions, about to struggle here hand to hand until one shall have humbled the other in the dust. The ancient worship of Osiris, whose origin is hidden in the night of time, proudly confident in its traditions, its mysteries, and its pomps, rests securely upon victory. The mighty dragon of Egypt lies basking in the midst of his waves, and exclaims: "The river is mine." He believes that the crocodile shall always receive the incense of mortals, and that the ox, which is slaughtered at the crib, shall never cease to rank as the first of divinities. No, my son, an army shall be formed in these deserts, and shall march to conquest under the banners of truth. From the solitudes of Thebais and of Scetis shall it advance: it is composed of aged saints, who carry no other weapon than their staff to besiege the ministers of error in their very temples. The latter occupy fertile plains, and revel amidst luxury and sensual gratifications; the former inhabit the burning sands of the desert, and patiently endure all the rigors of life. Hell, that foresees the destruction of its power, attempts every means to ensure its victory: the demons of voluptuousness, of riches, and of ambition, seek to corrupt these faithful soldiers of the cross, but heaven comes to the succor of its children, and lavishes miracles in their favor. Who can recount the names of so many illustrious recluses—the Anthonies, the Serapions, the Macariuses, the Pacomiuses? Victory declares in their favor. The Lord gathers about him Egypt, as a shepherd gathers round him his mantle. Where error once dictated the oracles of falsehood, the voice of truth is now heard; wherever the false divinities had instituted a superstitious rite, there Jesus had placed a saint. The grottoes of the Thebais are inhabited, the catacombs of the dead are peopled with the living who are dead to all the passions of the world. The gods, banished from their temples, return to the river and the plough. A burst of triumphant joy resounds from the pyramid of Cheops even to the tomb of Osymandyas. The posterity of Joseph enters into the land of Goshen; and this victory, purchased by the tears of its victors, costs not one tear to the vanquished!'

"Paul for a moment interrupted his discourse, and then again addressed me.

"'Eudorus,' said he, 'never more abandon the ranks of the soldiers of Jesus Christ. If you are not a rebel to the cause of heaven, what a crown awaits you! what enviable glory will be yours! My son, what are you still seeking amongst men? Has the world still charms for you? Do you wish, like the faithless Israelite, to lead the dance round the golden calf? You know not the ruin that awaits this mighty empire, so long the terror and the destroyer of the human race; know then, that the crimes of these masters of the world are hastening the day of vengeance. They have persecuted the faithful followers of Jesus; they have been drunk with the blood of his martyrs.'

"Here Paul again interrupted his discourse. He stretched forth his hands toward Mount Horeb; his eyes sparkled with animation, a flame of glory played around his head, his wrinkled forehead seemed invested with all the gracefulness of youth: like another Elias, he exclaimed in accents of rapture:

"'Whence come those fugitive families that seek an asylum in the cave of the solitary? Who are those people that flock from the four regions of the earth? Do you see yonder terrific horsemen, the impure children of the demons and of the sorcerers of Scythia?[1] The scourge of God conducts them.[2] Their horses vie with the leopard in speed: numberless as the sands of the desert, their captives flock before them. What seek these kings, clad in the skins of wild beasts, their heads covered with rude hats, and their faces tinged with green.[3] Why do these naked savages butcher their prisoners under the walls of the besieged city?[4] Hold! yon monster has drunk the blood of the Roman who fell beneath his hand![5] They all pour from their native deserts: they all march toward this new Babylon. O queen of cities! how art thou fallen! How is the beauty of thy capitol effaced! How are thy plains deserted, and how dreadful is the solitude that reigns around! But, lo! astonishing spectacle! the cross appears elevated above the scene of surrounding desolation! It takes its station upon new-born Rome, and marks each magnificent edifice as it rises from the dust. Paul, thou father of anchorites, exult with joy ere thou diest! Thy children shall inhabit the ruined palaces of the Cæsars; the porticos whence the sentence of exterminating wrath was pronounced against the Christians, shall be converted into religious cloisters;[6] and penitence shall consecrate the spot where crimes once reigned triumphant.'

"Paul's animation was exhausted, and his hands, that all this while had remained spread toward heaven, fell powerless

---

[1] The Huns.
[2] Attila.
[3] The Goths and Lombards.
[4] The Thermæ of Diocletian, now inhabited by the Carthusians.
[4] The Franks and Vandals.
[5] The Saracen.

at his side. Once again he felt as a mortal, and thus assumed the language of one:

"'Eudorus,' said he, 'we must part. I am no more to descend from this mountain. He who is to bury me approaches; he is coming to perform the last rites to this poor body, and to render dust to dust. You will find him at the foot of the mountain; there await his return, and he will point out the path you are to take.'

"I stood fixed in awe and astonishment, till the old man forced me away. Filled with sorrow, and plunged in the most solemn reflections, I withdrew in silence. When out of sight, I heard the voice of the saint as he chanted his last canticle. About to offer himself as a holocaust upon the altar of his God, this aged phoenix hailed with his last efforts of exultation the eternal youth he was about to assume. At the foot of the mountain I met another aged man, who was hastening as fast as the tardiness of age would permit. In his hand he carried the tunic of Athanasius, which Paul had requested, that it might serve him as a shroud. This was the great Anthony, tried by so many conflicts with hell. I wished to speak to him, but he still continued to hasten forward, and only exclaimed:

"'I have seen Elias, I have seen John in the wilderness, I have seen Paul in Paradise!'

"He passed me, and I waited all the rest of the day for his return, but he came not back till the day following. The tears streamed from his eyes.

"'My son,' cried he, as he approached me, 'the seraph is no longer an inhabitant of our earth. I had scarcely left you yesterday, when I beheld the blessed Paul, arrayed in all the dazzling splendors of immortality, and ascending to heaven, surrounded by a choir of angels and prophets. I hastened to the summit of the mountain, and perceived the saint upon his knees; his head was erect, and his hands spread toward heaven. He seemed still in the act of prayer, but he was no more! Two lions, that came from the neighboring rocks, assisted me to hollow out his grave, and this tunic of palm leaves has become my precious inheritance.'

"Such was the account that Anthony gave me of the death of this first of the anchorites. We then resumed our road, and reached the monastery that was already formed under the direction of Anthony, and in whose holy precincts those heroes were to be trained to action, whose conquests Paul had already announced. One of the recluses conducted me to Arsinoë, whence I soon departed with a company of merchants in their way to Ptolemais. In my journey through Asia, I stopped to visit the Holy Land, where I met the pious Helen, the spouse of Constantius, my generous protector, and the mother of Constantine, my illustrious friend. I afterward visited the seven churches founded by the prophet of Patmos; Ephesus the patient, and Smyrna the afflicted; Pergamus full of faith, and Thyatira the charitable; Sardis, ranked among the cities of the dead; Laodicea, counselled to buy robes of white; and Philadelphia, beloved by him who possesses the keys of David. At Byzantium I had the happiness to meet the young prince Constantine, who deigned to press me to his heart, and intrust me with all his mighty projects. At last, my dearest parents, I returned to your fond embraces, after ten years of absence and of misfortune! Would Heaven but grant my prayers, never again would I quit the valleys of Arcadia; happy to pass my days there in penitence and to sleep there after death in the tomb of my fathers."

Here Eudorus closed his narrative; and for some time the old men, who had heard him, remained in silence. Lasthenes was thanking God in secret for being blessed with such a son. To a young man who thus ingenuously avowed his failings, Cyril could speak only in terms of approbation; he even regarded him with mingled feelings of respect and admiration, as a confessor called by heaven to the highest destinies. Demodocus was almost terrified by the strange language and incomprehensible virtues of Eudorus. The three aged men arose with the dignity of monarchs, and entered the friendly abode of Lasthenes. Cyril, after offering the adorable sacrifice for Eudorus, took leave of his guests, and returned to Lacedæmon. Eudorus retired to his grotto, to fulfil the duties of penitence. Demodocus was left with his daughter, who clasped her tenderly in his arms, and said to her with a melancholy foreboding ·

"Daughter of Demodocus, thou perhaps mayest be as unfortunate in turn; for Jupiter has our destiny at his disposal. But imitate Eudorus; for adversity has but augmented this young man's virtues. It is not always the maturity of age that produces the most heroic virtues: the husbandman half severs the green cluster from the vine, and leaves it early to wither; and yet this yields the sweetest wine that the banks of Alpheus, or the hills of Erymanthus, can boast."

BOOK TWELFTH.

SUMMARY.

Invocation to the Holy Spirit. Conspiracy of the Demons against the Church. Diocletian orders the Christians to be numbered. Hierocles sets out for Achaia. The Love of Eudorus and Cymodoce.

O Holy Spirit, who fructifiest the vast abyss by overshadowing it with thy wings, I have need of thy aid. From the summit of the mountain that looks down upon the heights of Aonia, thou regardest the perpetual commotion of the things of earth, this human society in which everything, even to principle, is subject to change, in which evil becomes good and good becomes evil: thou lookest in pity on the dignities that inflate our hearts and the vain honors that corrupt them; thou menacest the power acquired by crime; thou consolest the calamity purchased by virtue; thou seest the different passions of men, their shameful fears, their contemptible hatreds, their interested prayers, their brief joys, their long anxieties; thou penetratest all these woes, O Creative Spirit! Quicken and vivify the recital that I am about to make: happy shall I be if I can soften the horrors of the picture by depicting therein the miracles of thy love!

Placed at the posts designated by their chief, the spirits of darkness breathed discord and horror of the Christian name on every side. In Rome, they provoked the passions of the chiefs and ministers of the empire. Astarte unceasingly presented before the eyes of Hierocles the image of the daughter of Homer. To this seductive phantom, she gave all the charms that are added to beauty by absence and memory. Satan secretly awakened the ambition of Galerius, depicting to him the faithful that were attached to Diocletian as the only prop that sustained the old emperor upon the throne.

The prefect of Achaia, the deluded votary of false wisdom, and the base deserter of the faith of Jesus, confirmed the infuriate Cæsar in his hatred against the adorers of the true God. The mother of Galerius still reserved with all her former bitterness, the affront that the disciples of the cross had offered her, in refusing to assist at her sacrifices, and supplicate the rural divinities for the success of her son. As when a vulture, the savage child of the mountain, has seized in his talons an innocent dove; perched on the rocks around, his fellows exult at the cruel spectacle, and with cries, excite him to devour his prey: thus Galerius, already violent in his rage for the extinction of the Christian name, was still further incited to carnage by his mother and the impious Hierocles. Intoxicated with his success over the Parthians, and bringing in his train all the luxury and corruption of Asia, he formed the most ambitious projects, and wearied Diocletian with his complaints and menaces.

"Why do you delay," he exclaimed, "to punish this odious race, whom your dangerous clemency has suffered to increase throughout the empire? Our temples are deserted, my mother has been insulted, your empress has been seduced. Dare to strike these rebellious subjects; in their riches you will find the resources you so much need, and you will perform an act of justice agreeable to the gods."

Diocletian was a prince blessed with wisdom and moderation; his advanced age inclined him to clemency in favor of his people: thus the aged tree, while its branches relax their vigor, lowers its fruit nearer the ground. But superstition that enervates, and avarice that steels the heart, sullied the noble qualities of Diocletian. He suffered himself to be seduced by the hope of extorting treasures from the Christians. Marcellinus, the bishop of Rome, was ordered to deliver to the temples of the idols all the riches that adorned the shrines of the new faith, and the emperor attended in person the church where the treasures were to be collected. The gates were thrown open, and he saw a numerous crowd of the poor, of orphans, and of the infirm.

"Prince," said the fearless pastor, "behold the treasures of the church; the jewels, the precious vases, and the golden ornaments of Christ!"

The prince felt all the force of this severe yet affecting lesson, and blushed with confusion. Nothing is more terrible than a monarch, when vanquished in magnanimity; incited by a certain sublime instinct, power naturally pretends to virtue, as the youthful enthusiast believes himself born for beauty; and woe to those who dare to point out the qualities or the graces in which it is deficient.

Satan took advantage of this moment of weakness to augment the resentment of Diocletian, by all the terrors of superstition. Sometimes the sacrifices were suddenly suspended, and the priests declared that the presence of the Christians caused the gods to withdraw their protection from the empire; sometimes the livers of the victims appeared without animation, and the entrails were covered with livid spots that foreboded consequences the most alarming; the divinities, reclining on their pedestals in the public squares, turned away their eyes; the gates of the temples closed of their own accord; while confused sounds were heard to issue from the sacred caves; every moment brought to Rome the report of some new prodigy: the Nile withheld the tribute of its fertilizing waters; the thunder rolled, the earth shook, and volcanoes vomited forth flames; famine and pestilence ravaged the provinces of the East; the West was agitated with dangerous seditions and destructive wars: all of which was attributed to the impiety of the Christians.

Within the vast enclosure of Diocletian's palace, in the midst of the gardens of the Thermæ, towered a lofty cypress, that was watered by a fountain. At the foot of this cypress stood an altar consecrated to Romulus. Suddenly a serpent, whose back was marked with blood-red spots, came hissing from beneath it, and twined itself round the trunk of the cypress. Amidst the foliage of the topmost bough, three young sparrows lay concealed in their nest; the serpent reaches and devours them; the mother, witness of the horrid scene, flies around in agitation, and fills the air with her moans, till seized in the fangs of the pitiless monster, she falls a prey to his ravenous fury. Alarmed at the prodigy, Diocletian sent for Tages, the chief of the haruspices. This man, who had been previously instructed by Galerius, and who was naturally a bigot in the cause of idolatry, cried out:

"O prince, this serpent represents the new sect who are meditating the destruction of the two Cæsars, and the chief of the empire! Hasten to deprecate the effects of the divine displeasure, by punishing the enemies of our gods."

It was now that the Almighty took in his hands the balance of gold, in which are weighed the destinies of kings and of empires: the lot of Diocletian was found wanting. At this instant the rejected emperor felt an extraordinary sensation possess his whole mind; it seemed as if his happiness had fled forever, and that the Fates, those false divinities that he worshipped, were more rapidly weaving out the thread of his days. His usual prudence in a great measure forsook him. He no longer regarded the varied characters and passions of men with his accustomed penetration; he became the dupe of his own passions, and gave orders that such officers of his palace as were Christians, should sacrifice to the gods, and that an exact census should be taken of all the faithful throughout the empire.

Galerius was transported with joy. As in the fertile valleys of Imolus the master of the vineyard walks amidst the blooming scene, and already beholds in imagination the floods of wine that shall sparkle on the table of kings, or fill the chalice of the altar; thus Galerius anticipated, in joyful expectation, the torrents of blood that should flow during the persecution of the Christians. The proconsuls, the prefects, and the governors of provinces, quitted the court to execute the orders of Diocletian. Hierocles humbly kissed the hem of the toga of Galerius, and making an effort, as one who was about to be sacrificed in the cause of virtue, at length presumed to cast a look of deep humility upon the Cæsar.

"Son of Jupiter," exclaimed he, "sublime prince, and lover of wisdom, I depart for Achaia. I am proceeding to punish those factious wretches who blaspheme thy title of Eternal. But, O Cæsar, thou who art my patron divinity, permit me frankly to declare my sentiments. It is the duty of a sage, even at the peril of his life, to speak the whole unvarnished truth to his prince. The divine emperor does not yet manifest sufficient firmness in his conduct toward this detestable sect. Dare I speak out without drawing upon myself the weight of your resentment? Should hands weakened by age let go the reins of the government, is not Galerius, the conqueror of the Parthians, worthy to mount the throne of the universe? But, O hero, beware of the enemies that surround you! Dorotheus, the prefect of the palace, is a Christian. From the fatal moment that an Arcadian was introduced at court, the empress herself has favored the impious. Then the young prince Constantine—O grief! O shame!" . . .

Hierocles suddenly interrupted his discourse; his eyes were filled with tears, and he appeared deeply concerned for the perils that awaited the Cæsar. He thus awakened in the bosom of the tyrant his two ruling passions—ambition and cruelty. At the same time, he laid the foundations of his own future greatness, for Hierocles was not a favorite of the emperor, who was an enemy to the sophists, and he knew that he should never obtain from Diocletian the honors that he hoped from Galerius.

He flew to Tarentum, and thence, without delay, embarked for Messenia. He burned to revisit the shores of Greece, where dwelt the daughter of Homer, and where he might at once satisfy his love for Cymodoce, and his hatred against the Christians. But he had the art to conceal these sentiments; and while malignity rankled at his heart, nothing flowed from his lips but wisdom and humanity: thus the surface of the ocean, while it reflects the varied image and beauteous lustre of the sky, conceals the rocks and quicksands that threaten destruction from beneath.

The demons, anxious to hasten the ruin of the Church, sent

a favoring breeze to the proconsul of Achaia. He passed rapidly over the same waves that once bore the great Alcibiades, when all Italy, with mingled wonder and delight, ran to contemplate this most beautiful of the Greeks. The gardens of Alcinous, and the heights of Buthrotum receded from his eyes,—places immortalized by the two masters of the lyre. Leucate, where still breathe the flame of the daughter of Lesbos, Ithaca, bristling with rocks, Zacynthus, crowned with forests, Cephallenia, favorite isle of the dove, each in turn claims the admiration of Hierocles. The Strophades, the unhallowed retreat of Celæno, then next met his view, and he soon hailed the dim summits of Elis. At his command they now steered eastward, and glided by those sandy shores where Nestor offered a hecatomb to Neptune, when Telemachus came to inquire for Ulysses, that man who was equal to the gods in wisdom. After leaving Pylos, Sphacteria, and Mothone to the left, he entered, under full sail, into the gulf of Messenia, quitted the briny deep, and at length arrested his course in the peaceful waters of Pamisus.

While Hierocles, like a threatening cloud, was thus drawing near to the land of heroes and of gods, the angel of holy love descended into the grotto of the son of Lasthenes: thus the supposed son of Ananias presented himself to the youthful Tobias, to conduct him to the daughter of Raguel. When God wishes to inspire the heart of man with those chaste flames that give rise to miracles of virtue, he confides this important task to the most beautiful of the angels of heaven. His name is Uriel; in one hand he holds a golden arrow drawn from the quiver of the Lord, in the other a torch, lighted from the eternal lightnings. His birth was coeval with the universe: he sprung into being with Eve, at the very moment in which the first woman opened her eyes to the new created light. The creative power bestowed upon the ardent cherub, a mingling of the seductive charms of the mother of the human race and the manly beauty of the father of mankind: he has the smile of modesty and the eye of genius. He who is pierced by his divine arrow, or scorched by his celestial torch, embraces with transport the most heroic acts of devotion, the most perilous enterprises, the most painful sacrifices. The heart thus wounded knows all the refinements of feeling; its tenderness increases with tears, and survives satisfied desires. Love is not to it a limited and trifling inclination, but a great and austere passion, the noble end of which is to give life to immortal beings.

The angel of holy love kindled an irresistible flame in the heart of the son of Lasthenes: the repentant Christian felt it burning beneath the sackcloth of penitence, yet the object of his adoration was an infidel! The remembrance of his past errors alarmed Eudorus: he was fearful of falling into the faults of his early youth, and dreamed of flight as the surest means of escaping the perils that threatened him: thus, while the imprudent bark is allured by the tranquillity of the deep to hoist the sail and quit the port, the experienced fisherman, beholding the storm that is imperceptibly gathering in the horizon, plies the oar with vigor, quits the open sea, and seeks the sheltered shore. Now, for the first time, Eudorus felt his bosom glow with the flames of genuine love. The son of Lasthenes was astonished at the timidity of his sentiments, and the gravity of his projects, which formed such a contrast to that bold and giddy attachment, and that levity of thought, by which he was formerly influenced. Could he but convert this idolatrous woman to the faith of Jesus Christ! could he at once throw open to her the portals of heaven, and those of the nuptial chamber! what a happiness for a Christian!

The sun had now plunged into the sea of the Atlantides, and was gilding with his last rays the Fortunate Isles, when Demodocus prepared to quit the Christian family; but Lasthenes represented that the night was full of peril and perplexity. The priest of Homer consented to await under his roof the return of Aurora When Cymodoce returned to her apartment, she revolved in her mind all that she had heard of the history of Eudorus: at the recollection, her cheeks were suffused with the blush of modesty, and her eyes sparkled with a fire till then unknown. Restless and unable to close her eyes in slumber, the priestess of the Muses arose, and left her couch ; desirous of breathing the freshness of the night, she descended into the gardens on the declivity of the mountain.

Suspended amidst the cloudless skies of Arcadia, the moon like her brother planet, was almost a solitary star ; the planets were overpowered by the blaze of her splendor, except some scattered constellations, that glimmered in the vast immensity of space : the firmament of soft blue was studded with stars and resembled a lily surcharged with pearls of dew. The towering heights of Cyllene, the declivities of Pholoe and Telphusa, the forests of Anemos and Phalantus, formed on every side a dim and misty horizon. Nothing interrupted the deep repose of the scene, save the dash of the torrent and the murmur of the rill that flowed from the mountains of Arcadia and, softened by distance, stole sweetly on the ear. In the valley, where the moonbeams shone reflected from his stream Alpheus seemed still to pursue the footsteps of the flying Arethusa ; Zephyrus sighed amidst the reeds of Syrinx, while from among the laurels of Daphne that shaded the banks of the Ladon, Philomela poured her plaintive song.

This beautiful night reminded Cymodoce of that in which she first encountered the youth whom she mistook for Endymion wearied with the chase. At the thought, her heart palpitated with unusual violence. She strongly imaged to her mind the beauty, the courage, and the many noble qualities of the son of Lasthenes ; she remembered that Demodocus, in speaking of Eudorus, had sometimes mentioned the name of spouse. What! to escape Hierocles should she, think you deprive herself forever of the sweets of connubial love ; forever bind her brow with the icy fillets of a vestal! It is true, no mortal had till then dared to oppose his claim to the of the cruel and tyrannic governor of Achaia ; but Eudorus the triumphant, Eudorus, who had been invested with some of the highest dignities of the empire, who was esteemed by Diocletian, adored by the soldiers, and cherished by the prince who was the inheritor of the purple,—was not he the glorious spouse who could defend and protect Cymodoce ? Oh, it was

Jupiter, it was Venus, it was Love, who had conducted this young hero to the borders of Messenia!

Cymodoce advanced involuntarily toward the spot where the son of Lasthenes had finished the history of his adventures. Should a doe of the Pyrenees, who all day long has reposed in the valley under the eye of the herdsman, wander at night from the fold; she seeks the well known pastures, and the herdsman finds her in the morning reposing under the flowery shrubs that she has chosen for her shelter: thus the daughter of Homer approaches with unconscious step the grotto of the Arcadian hunter. Suddenly she perceives something like a shadow fixed motionless at the entrance of the grotto; she imagines that it is Eudorus. She stops; her knees tremble beneath her; she can neither retreat nor advance. It was the son of Lasthenes himself; he was praying, surrounded by the tokens of penitence: the hair-cloth, the ashes, the skull of a martyr, excited his tears, and animated his faith. He heard the footsteps of Cymodoce, and on turning his head, saw her ready to sink on the earth; he flew to her assistance, supported her in his arms, and could scarcely refrain from pressing her to his heart. He was no longer the cold, severe, and rigid Christian, but a man full of indulgence and of tenderness; one who wishes to draw a soul to God, and to gain a spouse whose virtues may endear her to his heart.

As the shepherd places on his bosom the helpless lamb that the briers have wounded, and gently bears it to the fold; thus the son of Lasthenes raised Cymodoce in his arms, and placed her on a bank of moss at the entrance of the grotto.

"Will you pardon me," cried the daughter of Demodocus in a faltering voice, "for thus again intruding upon your mysteries! Some unknown divinity has guided hither my wandering footsteps, on this, as on a former night."

"Cymodoce," replied Eudorus, not less confused than the priestess of the Muses, "the God who has conducted you hither, is my God: it is my God who has sought you out, and who, perhaps, wishes to bestow you upon me."

"But," replied the daughter of Homer, "your religion forbids any attachment between young men and women; it allows not young women to follow the steps of youth: you only began to love when you proved unfaithful to your God."

Cymodoce blushed. "Alas!" cried Eudorus, "my heart knew not love, while it was a rebel to religion! But now I feel that I love, and that my love is sanctioned by heaven."

The balm that is poured on the throbbing wound, the cool fountain that refreshes the fainting traveller, are not half so soothing, or so reviving, as these words that escaped the son of Lasthenes. They glided into the heart of Cymodoce, and made it thrill with joy. Like two poplars, that during the calm of a summer night, stand graceful on the margin of a spring, when no breeze whispers through their foliage; thus these two lovers, that heaven had marked out for each other, remained silent and motionless at the entrance of the grotto. Cymodoce was the first who broke silence.

"Warrior, pardon the importunity of an ignorant Messenian. We can know nothing till instructed by a skillful master, or unless the gods themselves have tutored our minds to wisdom. A young woman, in particular, can know nothing, till she either mingle with her companions in ingenious occupations, or visit the temples and theatres. As for me, I have never quitted my father, the favorite priest of the immortals. Tell me, since love is not unknown in your religion, have you then a Christian Venus? Is her car drawn by doves? Are the raptures and the quarrels, the secrets and the treacheries of love, with that sweet trifling which steals away the hearts of the most wary of men—are all these concealed beneath her girdle, as my divine ancestor has recounted? Is this goddess formidable in her anger; does she render the tongue embarrassed, and spread at once through the veins a burning flame, and a mortal coldness? Does she oblige her votary to prepare a charm for the faithless lover, to draw the enchanted moon from her sphere, or to address the cruel threshold of the door in tones of supplication and despair? You, who are a Christian, know not, perchance, that Love is the son of Venus; that he was suckled by the savage beasts of the woods; that his first bow was of oak, his first arrows of cypress; that he rides the fondling lion, and takes his seat on the back of the centaur, and the shoulders of Hercules; that he is furnished with wings, and wears a bandage over his eyes; and that he is the attendant of Mars and Mercury, of eloquence and valor?"

"Young infidel," answered Eudorus, "my religion favors not these dangerous passions; but she has the power to give an elevation to the sentiments of the soul, which your Venus could never inspire. Cymodoce, what a strange religion is yours! Nothing is more chaste than your soul, or more innocent than your thoughts, and yet to hear you speak of your gods, who would not think that you were but too well skilled in the most dangerous of mysteries? Your father, as a minister in the service of your idols, imagined he was performing an act of piety, when he instructed you in the worship, the effects, and the attributes of the personified passions. The Christian fears to wound love itself by too free a description. Cymodoce, if I have been so happy as to merit your affection; if I am to be the spouse that in the innocence of your heart you have chosen, what I hope to love in you is not so much the accomplished woman, as God himself, who created you after his own image. When the Almighty had formed the first man from the dust of the earth, he placed him in a garden more delicious than the groves of Arcadia. Ere long the man found his solitude too great, and besought the Creator to give him a companion. The Almighty took a divine creature from the side of Adam, and called her woman; she became the spouse of him of whose flesh and blood she partook. Adam was formed for authority and for valor, Eve for submission and gracefulness; greatness of soul, dignity of character, and powers of reason, were the portion of the former; to the latter were given beauty, affection, and invincible charms. Such, Cymodoce, is the model of a Christian spouse. If you consent to imitate it, I will endeavor to gain your heart, and make you my spouse by an alliance of justice, of pity, and of love; I shall rule over you, Cymodoce, because man is made to command; but I shall love you like the clusters of grapes that we find in the burning desert. Like the patriarch of old, we shall be united with a view to leave behind us an offspring that may inherit the blessings of Jacob: thus when the son of Abraham espoused the daughter of Bethuel, such was the excess of joy which filled his heart that he forgot the death of his mother."

At these words Cymodoce shed tears of tenderness mingled with confusion.

"Warrior," said she, "thy words are sweet as honey, and yet like arrows they penetrate to the soul. I see that the Christians can speak the language of the heart: you have expressed what was before in my mind, but which I knew not how to say. Let your religion be mine, since it teaches to love more fervently."

"What!" cried Eudorus, struck with these expressions of love, and of faith, "do you desire to become a Christian? Shall I gain such an angel for heaven, such a companion for my days?"

Cymodoce bent her head, and replied:

"Finish the lesson you began on the virtue of modesty, for then only shall I dare to answer your questions: she fled with Nemesis from our earth, but the Christians have again brought her down from heaven."

By a sudden movement, the son of Lasthenes let fall the crucifix that he wore in his bosom; at the sight of it the young Messenian uttered a cry of surprise, mingled with a sort of terror.

"This is the image of my God," said Eudorus, as he respectfully took up the sacred figure, "the image of that God who descended into the tomb, and arose again crowned with glory and immortality."

"O," said Cymodoce, "then he is like that fair Arabian, lamented by the women of Byblus, and restored to the light of heaven by the will of Jupiter."

"Cymodoce," replied Eudorus, with mild severity, "the day will come when you will acknowledge the impiety and sacrilege of this comparison: instead of the mysteries of shame and of pleasure, you behold here the miracles of modesty and of woe. You see the son of the Almighty nailed to the cross to open heaven to us, and to exalt misfortune, simplicity and innocence to honor upon the earth. How shall I fix the mind of the priestess of the Muses on an object so serious! But, daughter of Demodocus, austere meditations strengthen lawful attachments in the heart of the Christian, and, by rendering him capable of every virtue, render him thus more worthy to be loved."

Cymodoce lent an attentive ear to this discourse, and felt her bosom labor with strange sensations. It seemed as if a bandage had fallen suddenly from her eyes, and that she discovered a distant and divine light. She beheld for the first time wisdom, reason, modesty, and love united in an unknown alliance. That evangelical sadness which tempers all the sentiments of the Christian, that warning voice which breaks from the bosom of pleasure itself, quite astonished and overpowered the daughter of Homer. Eudorus presented the crucifix to her eyes:

"Behold," cried he, "the God of charity, of peace, and of mercy; and yet a persecuted God! O Cymodoce, if you judge me worthy to become your spouse, it is upon this sacred image alone, that I can receive the testimonials of your faith! The altars of your false divinities, the shrine of love, can never witness the votary of Jesus Christ united to the priestess of the Muses."

What a moment for the daughter of Homer! To pass on a sudden from the voluptuous ideas of mythology, and embrace a love sworn upon a crucifix! to bear the hallowed symbol of salvation in those hands, which had carried nothing but the garlands of the Muses, and the fillets of the sacrifice! Drawn by an irresistible impulse, Cymodoce, who had also been wounded by the angel of pure love, no longer hesitated, but promised to be instructed in the faith of him who is master of her heart.

"And to be my spouse!" cried Eudorus, as he pressed the hands of the bashful virgin.

"And to be thy spouse!" repeated the trembling fair one.

Sweet and fervent oath, pronounced in the presence of the God of tears and afflictions.

As they spoke, a chorus of voices was heard on the mountain; they were celebrating the festival of the Lupercalia. They were singing in honor of the god who protects Arcadia; of Pan, the goat-footed, the terror of the nymphs, and the inventor of the shepherd's flute. This song was the signal of Aurora's approach; she arose, and with her first rays illumined the tomb of Epaminondas, and the woods of Pelagus that waved their lofty summits over the plains of Mantinea. Cymodoce hastened to return to her father, and Eudorus went to awaken Lasthenes.

BOOK THIRTEENTH.

SUMMARY.

Cymodoce Declares to her Father her Intention of embracing the Christian Religion, in order to become the Wife of Eudorus. Irresolution of Demodocus. They learn of the Arrival of Hierocles in Achaia. Astarte attacks Eudorus, and is conquered by the Angel of Holy Love. Demodocus consents to give his Daughter to Eudorus, to escape the Pursuit of Hierocles. Jealousy of Hierocles. Enumeration of the Christians in Arcadia. Hierocles proffers an Accusation against Eudorus to Diocletian. Cymodoce and Demodocus set out for Lacedæmon.

The priest of Homer had already risen, and was offering a libation to Aurora, as she emerged from the waves. He saluted her first rays, so cheering to the traveller, and, touching with one hand the earth moist with dew, prepared to quit the abode of Lasthenes. Suddenly, Cymodoce, trembling with fear and with love, presented herself before her father, and threw herself into his arms. The penetrating eye of Demodocus had already discovered the cause of these new emotions, which began to agitate his daughter's bosom: but being ignorant that the son of Lasthenes partook of the same affection, he sought to console Cymodoce.

"My daughter," said he, "what divinity has robbed thee of repose? Thou weepest, thou whose age should know nothing but innocent sports, and whose brow should wear a continual smile! What secret grief preys upon thy bosom? O, my child, let us have recourse to the altars of our guardian divinities, let us fly to the society of the wise, for they alone can restore our minds to their wonted tranquillity. Though the temple of Juno-Lacinia is open on every side, yet the winds cannot disperse the ashes of the sacrifice: so should it be with our hearts: though the passions may gain an entrance, we should never suffer them to disturb the unalterable repose of the sanctuary."

"O my father," answered the young Messenian, "are you then ignorant of our happiness! Eudorus loves thy daughter; he has told me that he wishes to suspend at my door the garlands of Hymen."

"Thou god of ingenious illusions!" exclaimed Demodocus, "hast thou not deceived me? May I believe thee, my daughter? and has not truth ceased to guard thy lips? Yet why should I be astonished to see thee beloved by a hero? Thou mightest have disputed the palm of beauty with the nymphs of Menelaium, and Mercury would have given thee the preference in the contest on Mount Chelydoria. But tell me, how this Arcadian youth informed thee that he was wounded by the son of Venus?"

"This very night," answered Cymodoce, "I went forth to invoke the Muses, that they would banish from my bosom I know not what uneasiness, that troubled my repose. Eudorus, like one of those beautiful shadows that issue from the ivory portals of Elysium, met me in the twilight. He took me by the hand, and said: 'Virgin, it is my wish that your children and your children's children, to the seventh generation, should be seated on the knees of Demodocus.' But he told me all this in the language of the Christians, and much better than I can attempt to repeat it. He showed me the image of his God, who loves those that weep, and blesses the unfortunate. O my father! I was charmed with this God; among all our divinities we have not one so full of sweetness and compassion. I must become acquainted with the religion of the Christians, and practise its precepts, for upon no other terms can the son of Lasthenes receive me as his spouse."

When two contrary winds dispute the empire of the deep, the wearied seamen shift every sail, and labor by every effort to catch the veering breeze; thus Demodocus rejected or admitted alternately the opposite sentiments that agitated his bosom. The reflection, that Cymodoce should deposit the emblems of her vestal office on the altar of Hymen; and that the family of Homer, which was on the point of being extinguished, should flourish anew, filled his heart with joy. In the son of Lasthenes, Demodocus beheld an illustrious and honorable son-in-law, and what is more, a powerful protector against the favorite of Galerius; but then again he reflected with anguish, that his daughter was about to abandon her paternal divinities, to dishonor the worship of her divine ancestors, and to be guilty of perjury against the Muses.

"O my daughter," cried he, as he pressed her tenderly to his heart, "what a subject of joy and of tears art thou to thine aged father! How can I refuse, and yet how consent to thy demands? Thou art about to quit thy father, in pursuit of a God unknown to our ancestors. What! can we have two separate religions! Can we petition heaven for opposite favors! When our hearts are but one heart, can we cease to offer but one and the same sacrifice?"

"O my father," said Cymodoce, interrupting him, "can you think I will ever leave thee? Never shall my prayers be different from thine! Though a Christian, I will take up my abode near thy temple, and continue to recite with thee the verses of my divine ancestor."

The priest of Homer was unable to return an answer; his bosom heaved with convulsive sobs, and he tore himself from the embraces of his daughter. In solitary anguish he wandered round the dwelling of Lasthenes, and went to seek for counsel from the divinities that presided over the mountain: it was thus that heretofore the eagle of the Alps, the noble augur of the destinies of Rome, winged his upward flight through the storm, and sought in the bosom of the lightning, the secret decrees of heaven. At the sight of the summits of Arcadia, each of which was consecrated by the worship of some divinity, the eyes of Demodocus overflowed with tears, and superstition was on the point of making a conquest over his heart. But how could he disappoint Cymodoce by depriving her of the love of Eudorus? how could he render his beloved daughter eternally unhappy? To forward his immutable purposes, the Almighty completed the conquest of Demodocus,

11.*

and rendered his paternal weakness subservient to the glory of his future elect. By his power he ended the uncertainty of the priest of Homer, dissipated his fears, and represented to his mind the union of Cymodoce and Eudorus under the most flattering auspices. Demodocus returned to the abode of Lasthenes, and found his daughter overwhelmed with grief.

"O virgin," he exclaimed, "worthy of every blessing that heaven can bestow, let not Demodocus draw one tear of anguish from those eyes that he cherishes more than the light of day! Take Eudorus for thy spouse; my only remaining prayer is, that thy new God may never tear thee from thy father's embraces."

At the same time, Eudorus also was revealing to Lasthenes the secret of his bosom.

"My son," said the spouse of Sephora, "oh, that Cymodoce were a Christian! Let the kingdom of heaven be her marriage portion, and I will consent that she shall be thine."

Eudorus, urged on by the angel of holy love, flew to find Demodocus. Supposing that he should meet the priest of Homer alone, he was surprised to find the father and daughter in each other's arms. Doubtful whether his lot was decided, he paused in trembling suspense. Demodocus beheld him.

"Here is your spouse!" exclaimed he.

He could say no more: tears of tenderness suspended the old man's utterance. Eudorus fell at the feet of his new father, and embraced the knees of Cymodoce; at this moment, Lasthenes arrived with his spouse and his daughters. The young Christians embraced the priestess of the Muses; they overpowered her with caresses; they fondly called her their sister, the servant of Jesus Christ, and the spouse of their brother.

Cyril was chosen by common consent to sow the first seeds of faith in the heart of the future catechumen. The two families resolved to remove to Sparta, that the holy bishop might pursue his instructions without interruption, and hasten the nuptials of Cymodoce.

But whilst heaven was pursuing its designs, hell was also

accomplishing its menaces. Scarcely had Demodocus and Lasthenes concluded this family alliance, when the news that Hierocles had arrived in the province, filled the inhabitants of Messenia with consternation. You might have seen mothers pressing their daughters in their arms; the public amusements suspended, as in the time of some general calamity; the churches in mourning, and the pagans themselves in alarm: such an effect has the presence of a wicked man!

Preceded by his lictors, the proconsul entered the walls of Messenia. He instantly ordered the decree for a census of the Christians to be published. As when a ravenous wolf prowls around the fold, marks out with fiery eye the tender victim for destruction, and seems already to taste the blood for which he thirsts; thus Hierocles, incited by his hatred toward the faithful, exulted at the thought of the defenceless virgins, the tender children, and the crowd of Christians that should shortly be dragged to the foot of his tribunal.

Led on, meanwhile, by the most dangerous spirit of the abyss, he mounted the summit of Ithome, and eagerly explored the columns of the temple of Homer, which arose from the midst of a grove of olives. But what was his surprise, when he found that the guardian of the sanctuary had gone with his daughter to visit Lasthenes, whose son had met with Cymodoce in the woods of Taygetus! At this unexpected intelligence, Hierocles changed color, while a thousand confused ideas tormented his bosom. Lasthenes was the richest Christian in Greece; he was the father of Eudorus, the most powerful enemy of Hierocles. How did Eudorus gain permission to quit the army of Constantius? What fatality had brought him to these shores again to counteract the designs of the proconsul of Achaia? Had he touched the heart of Cymodoce? . . . Hierocles burned to clear up these doubts and suspicions; and such was the anxiety which preyed upon his bosom, that he resolved not to lose a moment in the attempt.

Not far from the retreat of Lasthenes, and near the ruins of a temple that was erected to the Graces and the Furies by Orestes, rose a magnificent palace. Hierocles had built it after a plan of one of the descendants of Ictinus and Phidias, when he hoped to ravish Cymodoce from her father, and then to conceal his victim in this delightful abode. But he had been suddenly summoned to the court of the emperor, before he had time to execute his dark designs. He now fixed on this spot as his place of residence, and commanded that all the Christians of Arcadia should repair hither, and deliver in their names. He hoped, too, that in the neighborhood of Lasthenes he should have frequent opportunities of beholding Cymodoce, and of discovering what motive had conducted the priestess of the Muses to the abode of the adorers of Christ.

Swifter than lightning, fame had published the news of the arrival of Hierocles from the summits of Apesas, the favored mountain of the natives of Argos, to the promontory of Malea, which beholds the wearied planets repose on its summit. At the same time she recounted the evils with which the Christians were menaced. Demodocus trembled at the terrible details. Should he suffer his daughter to embrace a religion encompassed with so many perils? But could he violate his promise to Eudorus? Could he render Cymodoce unhappy by refusing her the spouse she still so ardently desired?

The bosom of Eudorus, too, was all tumult and agitation; his spiritual enemy had raised this conflict, and armed against him the generosity of his own heart. To convert a soul to God in defiance of every obstacle that the world can oppose, is the highest happiness that a Christian can enjoy; but Eudorus felt not yet a zeal thus ardent, and a courage thus sublime. Fearful lest Cymodoce should receive the yoke of the cross, hell was active in its attempts to weaken the faith of the son of Lasthenes. Satan summoned Astarte, and ordered her to attack the young Christian whom she had so often conquered, and to wrest him from the power of the angel of holy love.

The demon of Voluptuousness instantly arrayed herself in all her charms, and taking an odoriferous torch in her hand, traversed the woods of Arcadia. The zephyrs gently agitated the flame, and wafted its perfumes around. Wherever the phantom trod, a thousand wonders sprung up beneath her footsteps. All nature seemed animated at her presence; the dove cooed afresh, the nightingale breathed a softer and more tender lay, and the stag pursued his bounding mate with redoubled ardor. The seductive spirits that enchanted the forests of the Alpheus, half opened the charmed oaks, and revealed here and there their nymph-like faces. Mysterious voices whispered from the breezy summits of the pine, and adorned with wreaths of flowers, the sylvan divinities danced around the demon of Voluptuousness.

She entered the grotto of Eudorus, and thus whispered in his ear the sentiments of a love that was purely human:

"You may die for your God, if he demand the sacrifice, but why involve Cymodoce in the same ruin with yourself? Behold that bosom on which love sits enthroned, and those eyes whence he darts the lightnings of desire: could you load those graceful limbs with galling fetters? Ah, how much wiser it would be to relax thy savage virtue! Leave to Cymodoce her ingenious fables: do you think that heaven will arm itself in terrors because your spouse, or, if you wish it, your mistress, shall decorate with a few choice flowers the elegant altars of the Muses, and chant the poetic songs of Homer? Have compassion on her youth and beauty. You were not always so severe."

Such were the dangerous inspirations of the spirit of darkness. At the same moment, with a wanton air, and a perfidious smile, she aimed the same arrow at Eudorus that once pierced the wisest of kings. But the son of Lasthenes was under the protection of the angel of holy love. To the allurements of the senses he opposed the allurements of the soul; to the affection of the moment, an eternal affection. With a pure whisper, he turned aside the arrows of the demon of Voluptuousness, and the impotent darts fell powerless upon the haircloth of Eudorus, as upon a buckler of adamant.

Yet still the penitent warrior felt his heart influenced by the false honor of the world; his attachment to Cymodoce was too timid to stand so severe a trial. He feared that Demodocus might have been taken by surprise, and his consent extorted; he was apprehensive of exposing Cymodoce to the dangers that threatened her, and hastened to find the priest of Homer.

"I come," said he, "to absolve you from your oath. To behold Cymodoce a Christian, and to receive her hand at the altar of the true God, would constitute the happiness of my life; but the Christians are about to be numbered. Not that this announces any approaching evils to our people, for the future reposes in the bosom of God; but, perhaps, it may fill your mind with apprehensions and alarm. Let the offering that you consent to make to Jesus Christ be free and unconstrained; your will alone shall decide upon the destiny of Cymodoce, and on the happiness of my life."

"Generous youth," answered the old man, softened even to tears, "some god has inspired your heart with all the magnanimity of men of better days; and when your mother brought you forth amidst the laurels of the sacred grove, it was Jupiter himself who blessed you with a heart so noble. O my son, what do you wish me to do? You know how dear my daughter is to me; can she not become your spouse without embracing the faith of the Christians? We should thus be free from every apprehension; and without exposing Cymodoce to new perils, you could protect her against the impious Hierocles."

"Demodocus," answered Eudorus in a sorrowful tone, "by an effort more than human, I can renounce your daughter's love; but know that a Christian cannot receive a spouse contaminated by the incense of idolatry. What minister of the altar would dare, at the foot of the cross, to hallow an alliance between heaven and hell? Shall my son hear the name of the Son of Man pronounced over his cradle in conjunction with that of Jupiter? Shall it be a matter of hesitation whether my daughter is to copy the example of the spotless Virgin, or that of the wanton queen of love? Demodocus, our laws forbid us to unite with the woman who is a stranger to the religion of the God of Israel: it bids us seek for a spouse who may share our woes in this life, and partake of the blessings that await us in a life to come."

From the adjoining apartment, Cymodoce had heard the confused voices of her father and the son of Lasthenes. Inspired by the angel of pure love, and filled with generous resolutions by the Mother of the Saviour, she flew to the chamber of Demodocus, and throwing herself at the feet of her father, with her hands extended, in a supplicating posture, exclaimed:

"O my father! may the gods preserve me from ever bringing sorrow on thy grey hairs; but Eudorus must be my spouse. In becoming a Christian, I shall not cease to be thy submissive and devoted daughter. Be not apprehensive for the dangers that may await me; love will give me courage to surmount them all."

Struck with the dignity and the fervor of her sentiments, Eudorus raised his hands to heaven, and exclaimed:

"God of my fathers, what have I done to merit so ample a recompense! My whole life has been spent in opposition to thy holy laws, and yet dost thou load me with blessings! Accomplish thy eternal decrees! Draw this innocent angel to thyself! Her own virtues have rendered her worthy of thy acceptance, and not the love with which a frail and sinful Christian has had the happiness to inspire her."

He had no sooner uttered these words, than they heard a quick footstep advancing toward the door. It was a messenger to Demodocus, who had just arrived from the temple of Homer; the sweat bedewed his forehead, and his naked feet and disordered hair were covered with dust; in his left hand he bore a shattered buckler, with which he had dashed his way through the forest. He thus addressed Demodocus:

"Demodocus, Hierocles has appeared before the temple of your ancestor: his mouth is filled with menaces. Proudly confident of the protection of Galerius, he breathes nothing but threats against your Cymodoce. He swears by the iron bed of the Eumenides that your daughter shall share his couch, should black care, the gloomy companion of the Fates, sit on the threshold of your abode for the rest of your days."

A mortal paleness overspread the cheeks of Demodocus, and his trembling knees were scarcely able to support him; but this open denunciation of their enemy fixed his wavering mind. The orders issued against the faithful, threatened the Christian Cymodoce with a distant and uncertain evil; the love of the proconsul, on the contrary, exposed the priestess of the Muses to perils that were near and inevitable. In this pressing danger, the protection of Eudorus seemed an unexpected blessing, and the only refuge that remained for Cymodoce against the violence of Hierocles.

The old man pressed his daughter to his bosom.

"My child," said he, "I will not violate my oath; I will be faithful to the promise I have pledged: take Eudorus for thy spouse; it is he that must now protect thee and be the faithful companion of thy days. Perhaps it may be the will of the gods to exercise thy virtue; but, O Cymodoce! let not thy heart be dejected in the moment of trial. If the Christians, too, have their Muses, these will lend thee their aid; and their songs, so full of wisdom, will fortify thy heart against the attacks of thy enemies."

Lasthenes entered just as Demodocus had finished these words.

Eudorus, pressing his hand on his heart in sign of his gratitude and tenderness, and with his eyes fixed on the earth, pronounced these words, with unwonted energy:

"Demodocus, I receive the inestimable present, which, through my hands, you offer to the Eternal. At the expense of my life I will protect the virgin that you consecrate to Jesus Christ; by you, Lasthenes, by you, my dearest father, I swear that I will be faithful to Cymodoce!"

The priest of Homer accepted the oath, and departed with his daughter. It was his intention to shut up the temple, and then return to Lacedæmon, where the family of Lasthenes would await his arrival at the residence of Cyril.

Demodocus and Cymodoce took the most unfrequented route, in order to avoid meeting their persecutor; but the proconsul had already arrived at his palace on the Alpheus.

These smiling solitudes, the pure crystal of the murmuring Ladon, the bold swell of the surrounding mountains that were clothed with pines, the freshness that breathed from the valleys of Arcadia ; all these pastoral scenes, and the tender recollections that a thousand sweet names awakened, were unable to calm the anxiety that disturbed the mind of Hierocles. His lictors were dispersed on every side to collect the faithful ; they penetrated into those peaceful retreats, where the shepherds of Evander formerly tended their flocks, and led a life surpassed in innocence by none but the first Christians. Mingled crowds of old men, women and children were seen issuing from the depths of the grottoes consecrated to Pan, and other pastoral divinities, and were driven forward by the inhuman soldiers, to the place where the Roman governor had caused his tribunal to be erected. There was in front of the palace an extensive meadow that stretched along the banks of the Ladon, and here, seated in his chair of ivory, Hierocles received the names of those who were destined to swell the fatal list. On a sudden, a murmur spread among the crowd ; the Christians turned their heads, and beheld the powerful family of Lasthenes being led by the soldiers to the foot of the tribunal.

As when a hunter of the Alps, in pursuit of the chamois that bound over the rocks and torrents, beholds on a sudden a savage boar spring from amidst the trembling fawns ; he recoils with affright, and gazes at the terrible monster, whose bristling back and blood-shot eyes announce his destruction : thus Hierocles stood, confounded at the view of Eudorus, whom he immediately recognized in the midst of his family. All his ancient enmity awakened : he did not, it is true, behold Cymodoce, but the beauty of the son of Lasthenes, his manly and warlike air, and the admiration which he inspired, augmented his alarm. Several of the soldiers of the proconsul's guard, who had formerly served under Eudorus, surrounded their former general, and loaded him with benedictions ; some extolled the gentleness of his disposition, his generosity, and all his valor and his glory. These spoke of the battle with the Franks, in which he bore away the civic crown; those recounted his victories over the Bretons. Expressions of praise and admiration resounded on every side: "This is the young warrior, covered with scars, who triumphed over Carausius; this is the master of the horse, who for a time held the dignity of the prefect of Gaul; this is the favorite of Constantius, and the friend of prince Constantine!" The indignant proconsul grew pale at these expressions of admiration: he hastily dismissed the assembly, and shut himself up in his palace.

Hierocles no longer doubted that his rival was beloved by Cymodoce; he judged that love had followed glory. A thousand sinister projects presented themselves to his mind; this moment he was determined to carry off the daughter of Demodocus by force, and confine Eudorus in a dungeon; the next he was apprehensive of the favor that the son of Lasthenes enjoyed at court. He dared not openly attack a man who had merited the honors of a triumph, and been raised to some of the chief dignities of the empire: he well knew the moderation of Diocletian, who was always an enemy to violence. He took therefore a slower but surer means of satisfying the hatred that he had so long nourished against Eudorus; he wrote to Rome that the Christians of Achaia had refused to submit to the census, and that they were on the point of rising in open rebellion, with the young Arcadian at their head, who had been exiled by the emperor to the army of Constantius.

Hierocles hoped thus to banish Eudorus from Greece, and to pursue his infamous designs upon Cymodoce without interruption. Meanwhile, he surrounded his rival with spies and informers, in hopes to penetrate the important secret that disturbed his repose. The son of Lasthenes was not inattentive to the dangers that threatened his brethren. He was no longer the wild youth, unsteady in his attachments, chimerical in his projects, and a dupe to the illusions of a heated imagination: he was a man tried by adversity, capable of actions the most generous and the most sublime; deliberate, serious, industrious ; eloquent in council, brave in the field ; whose passions, while they soared beyond narrow views and interested considerations, were adapted to more noble and more elevated objects. He was well aware of the influence that Hierocles possessed over Galerius, and Galerius over Diocletian. He foresaw that the Sophist who persecuted Cymodoce would let loose the whole torrent of his indignation against the Christians, the moment he knew of the love and the conversion of the priestess of the Muses. At a single glance, Eudorus beheld all the evils that threatened the Church, and sought to avert their fury ; before he set out with his family for Lacedæmon, he dispatched a faithful messenger, to inform Constantine of the truth, and to prevent the dangerous impression that the report of Hierocles might make on the mind of Augustus.

Just as the prefect of Achaia had left his tribunal, Demodocus and his daughter reached the temple of Homer. The fire on their domestic altars was not yet extinguished, and Demodocus caused them to be lighted afresh. A heifer with gilded horns was conducted to the sanctuary, and a silver cup of beautiful workmanship was placed in the hands of the priest. This same cup had been formerly used by Danaus, and the aged Phoroneus, in their sacrifices. Around its sides the skillful artist had represented Ganymede carried forcibly away by the eagle of Jupiter ; the companions of the Phrygian huntsman seemed overwhelmed with sorrow, while his faithful dog made the forests of Ida reëcho with his plaintive howl. The father of Cymodoce filled the cup with pure wine, clothed himself in a long white tunic, and wreathed a branch of olive round his head : he might have been taken for Tiresias, or the blind Amphiaraus ready to descend to hell with his armor, white chariot and coursers. He then poured out the libation at the foot of Homer's statue ; the heifer fell beneath the sacred knife, and Cymodoce suspended her lyre at the altar of her divine ancestor. She then addressed these words to the Swan of Mæonia :

"Author of my race, thy daughter consecrates at thy shrine this melodious lute, which thou didst sometimes deign to attune. Two divinities, Venus and Hymen, oblige me to pass beneath the empire of other laws: how can a maiden resist the shafts of love, and the decrees of Fate? Andromache—for so thou hast recounted—amidst all the magnificence of Ilion, saw nothing but Astyanax, and her Hector. I have yet no son; but I must follow my spouse."

Such were the adieus of the priestess of the Muses, to the bard of Penelope, and of Nausicaa. The eyes of the young virgin were moist with tears; despite the strength of her love, she regretted those heroes and divinities who formed a part of her family; that temple which was at once the sanctuary of her gods and the residence of her father; and where, instead of her mother's milk, she had been nourished with the nectar of the Muses. Everything around her, recalled to her imagination the beautiful fictions of the poet, everything around her was under the immediate influence of Homer: in spite of herself the new Christian felt overpowered by the mighty genius of the father of fiction: thus, when the dove in her airy flights beholds the serpent stretched amidst the flowers, terrified at his rising crest, and forky sting, and fascinated by the lightnings of his piercing eye, she alights upon a neighboring tree, descends from bough to bough, and at length, rendered dizzy by the magic of his glance, falls powerless to the earth.

BOOK FOURTEENTH.

SUMMARY.

Description of Laconia. Arrival of Demodocus at the Residence of Cyril. Instruction of Cymodoce. Astarte sends the Demon of Jealousy to Hierocles. Cymodoce repairs to the Church to be betrothed to Eudorus. Ceremonies of the Primitive Church. A band of Soldiers, by the order of Hierocles, disperses the Believers. Eudorus Rescues Cymodoce, and defends her at the Tomb of Leonidas. He receives Orders to repair to Rome. The two Families resolve to send Cymodoce to Jerusalem, in order to place her under the Protection of the Mother of Constantine. Eudorus and Cymodoce set out in order to embark at Athens.

DEMODOCUS wept as he closed the gates of Homer's temple. He then mounted his chariot with Cymodoce, and again entered the borders of Messenia. He soon reached the statue of Mercury, which stands at the entrance of Hermeum, and penetrated into the defiles of Taygetus. Immense rocks, piled up to the heavens, stretched into vast declivities on either hand, and scarcely afforded vegetation to a few scattered firs on its barren summits, that appeared like tufts of herbage on a pile of ruins. Concealed beneath the stunted broom and the yellow sage that were half consumed by the heat, the importunate cicada trilled her monotonous song beneath the burning rays of noon.

"My daughter," said Demodocus, "it was by this same road that, like myself, Lyciscus escaped with his daughter toward Lacedæmon, and his flight gave birth to the tragical adventure of Aristomenes. How many generations have since rolled away, to bring us in our turn into these solitary places! May the great Jupiter send us some favorable omen, and avert all calamities from thee!"

Scarcely had he uttered these words, when a vulture

swooped from the top of a withered tree, upon a swallow; an eagle that viewed the scene darted from the mountains, and bore off the vulture in his powerful talons; at the same instant, a sudden flash of forked lightning illumined the east, pierced the sovereign of the air, and precipitated to the earth the victor, the vanquished, and the victim. Demodocus, terrified, vainly sought the decrees of fate in these uncertain freaks of chance. The car, meanwhile, passed the summit of Hermeum, and began to descend toward Pillane. The priest of Homer saluted the Eurotas, whose banks he coasted; he touched at the tomb of Ladas, and ere long discovered the statue of Modesty, that marks the spot where Penelope, on the point of following Ulysses, covered her face with her veil to hide her blushes. He left behind him the monument of the Mysian Diana, the sacred wood of Carneus, the seven columns, and the sepulchre of the Courser, and suddenly found himself on the flowery declivities overlooking the temple of Achilles: Sparta and the valley of Laconia lay stretched beneath his view. The lofty heights of Taygetus, partly crowned with forests, and covered with snow, towered far to the west; while a chain of lesser hills formed the eastern horizon, which, lessening as they stretched into distance, terminated in the dim red summits of Menelaium. The valley that lay between these two ranges of mountains was obstructed toward the north, by a confused mass of irregular hills, which, stretching to the south, formed the gentle acclivities on which Sparta is situated. From Sparta to the sea lay a smooth and fertile plain, intersected by vineyards and fields of corn, and shaded by clumps of olives, sycamores and plane-trees. Half concealed amidst blooming laurels, the Eurotas poured his meandering stream through these smiling solitudes, while the swans of Leda embellished his azure tide.

At the view of this magnificent picture, which was mellowed by all the varied tints of the new-born Aurora, the priest of the gods and Cymodoce could not suppress their admiration. Who could tread the ashes of Sparta with indifference, and contemplate without emotion the country of

Lycurgus and Leonidas? Demodocus had not recovered from his astonishment, when the rapid coursers entered Lacedæmon. After passing the forum, the senate-house, and the portico of the Persæ, they reached the theatre, which lay contiguous to the citadel, and ascended to the residence of Cyril, whose situation was near the temple of Venus Armata.

The bishop of Lacedæmon had been already informed of all that had passed in Arcadia; and the family of Lasthenes was here awaiting the arrival of the new spouse. To place Cymodoce beyond the power of Hierocles, and to give Eudorus a lawful right over her person, Cyril proposed that she should be betrothed to the son of Lasthenes as soon as she was declared a neophyte; but the priestess of the Muses could not become the spouse of Eudorus, till she had received the rites of baptism. The old men saluted the amiable stranger with a grave and holy tenderness; while the mother and sisters of Eudorus were lavish in their attentions, and in every little soothing office of affection. Cymodoce felt a charm in the caresses her new mother and sisters, which she had never before experienced. But she saw not Eudorus, who, in this moment of happiness, had redoubled his watchings and austerities. That very evening, Cyril commenced his course of Christian instructions. She received them with ingenuousness and simplicity: the morality and charity of the Gospel charmed her heart. She wept profusely over the mystery of the cross and the sufferings of the Son of Man; the religious honors paid to the Mother of the Saviour filled her bosom with the tenderest emotions; she solicited the aged martyr to repeat again and again the history of the manger, the shepherds, the angels, and the magi; she repeated in a whisper, "Hail, Mary, full of grace!" words that she had learnt by heart. The awful majesty of the God of the Christians filled her with a certain feeling of alarm; she therefore fled to Mary for refuge, whom, as she possessed none upon earth, she took for her mother in heaven. She would often explain to Demodocus some of the lessons she had learnt; and seated on his knees, would describe, in language the most simple and affecting, the happy lives of the patriarchs, the tenderness of Nachor for his daughter Sarah, and the love of young Tobias for the stranger whom he espoused: she mentioned, also, that lamented maiden whom an apostle called forth from the tomb, and restored to her disconsolate parents.

"Do you not think," she would add, "that the God of the Christians, who commands me to love my father, that my days may be prolonged here upon earth, is more worthy of homage than those gods who never speak to me concerning thee?"

Nothing could be more touching than to behold this new kind of missionary, by turn the disciple of one old man and the instructress of another, placed like Grace and Persuasion between two venerable sages, to make a priest of Homer relish the serious instructions of a priest of Israel.

The enemy of the human race trembled with rage on seeing this innocent virgin escape his power, and accused Astarte of the calamity.

"Feeble demon," cried he, "of what use art thou in the abyss? Thou didst not quit heaven but with regret, and now behold thee again vanquished by the angel of holy love!"

"O Satan, calm thy wrath," returned Astarte. "If I have been unable to prevail over the angel that fills my place in the abode of happiness, my very defeat will serve the success of thy designs. I have a son in hell, but I dare not approach him, so much does his fury intimidate me. Thou knowest him: descend to his prison and bring him to earth. I will await his coming at the side of Hierocles; and when this mortal shall be consumed with his flames and my own, thou wilt need only to deliver the Christians to the demon of Homicide."

She spoke, and Satan plunged to the bottom of the gulf of torments. Beyond the stagnant marshes and the lakes of fire and brimstone in the vast regions of hell, lies a dungeon, the abode of the most wretched of the dwellers in hell. Here the demon of Jealousy utters his everlasting howlings. Reclining amidst vipers and hideous reptiles, slumber never approaches his eyes. Inquietude, suspicion, vengeance, despair, and a sort of ferocious love glare from his eyes; his mind is occupied and tormented with chimeras; he starts, fancying that he hears mysterious sounds, and attempts to pursue vain phantoms. To quench his burning thirst, he drinks from a brazen cup a poison composed of his own sweat and tears. His trembling lips breathe forth homicide: in default of the victim that he seeks without ceasing, he plunges a dagger into his own breast, forgetful that he is immortal.

The prince of darkness descended to the retreat of this monster, then paused at the entrance of the cavern.

"Powerful archangel," said he, "I have always distinguished thee among the innumerable spirits of my empire. To-day thou canst prove thy gratitude: it is necessary to kindle in the breast of a mortal the flame that thou once plantedst in the heart of Herod. The Christians must be destroyed; the sceptre of the world must be regained; the enterprise is worthy of thy courage. Come, O my son, and second the vast designs of thy king!"

The demon of Jealousy removed the poisonous cup from his mouth, and, wiping his lips with his tresses of living serpents, replied, with a deep sigh: "O Satan, will the weight of hell never bend thy proud brow? Dost thou wish to expose me again to the fury of those thunderbolts that hurled thee down into the gulf of tears? What canst thou do against the cross? A woman has crushed thy proud head in the dust. I hate the light of heaven. The chaste love of the Christians has destroyed my dominion on earth. Pursue thine own designs, if thou wilt; but leave me to enjoy my rage in peace and come no more to trouble my fury."

He spoke, and with furious grasp seized the serpents that were clinging to his side, and tore them with his sharp teeth.

Trembling with wrath, Satan replied:

"Pusillanimous angel, whence arises this fear? Has repentance, the cowardly virtue of Christians, entered, then, into thy heart? Look about thee: behold thy eternal abode. Banish vain regrets, and learn to oppose a boundless hatred to ills without end. Dare to follow me: I will soon cause the chaste love that terrifies thee to vanish from the world, and will restore to thee thy empire over vanquished man. But do not wait till my arm shall constrain thee to accord that which I deign to demand of thy zeal."

The demon of Jealousy suffered himself to be persuaded by this mingled threat and hope.

Satan, filled with joy, mounted upon a chariot of fire, and placing by his side the monster whom he called his son, instructed him in what he had to do, and named to him the victim of whom he was to take possession. To avoid the importunity of the spirits of darkness, the two chiefs of hell rendered themselves invisible while traversing the abodes of pain. Death alone saw them pass through the portals of the abyss, and greeted them with a horrible smile. They soon reached the earth, and descended into the valley of the Alpheus. A prey to his fatal love, the proconsul of Achaia lay stretched in disordered slumbers. Confident of the secret pains of Hierocles, the demon of Jealousy concealed himself beneath the semblance of an aged augur. He assumed the wrinkled face, trembling voice, bald forehead, and saintly pallor of the ancient diviner. With a long veil upon his head, and the sacred fillets descending upon his shoulders, he approached the bed of the unbeliever like a frightful dream, and touched the breast of Hierocles with the rod that he held in his hand.

"Thou sleepest," cried he, "while thy enemy triumphs! Cymodoce, conducted to Lacedæmon, has embraced the religion of the Christians, and will soon become the bride of the son of Lasthenes. Awake, and seize thy prey; and, to snatch her from thy rival, destroy, if need be, the entire race of Christians!"

While finishing these words, the demon of Jealousy snatched from his head the veil and priestly fillets. He resumed his horrible form, and leaning over Hierocles, clasped him tightly in his arms, and infused into his veins his own impure blood. Filled with terror, the wretched man struggled beneath the weight of the phantom, and awoke with a cry: as a man who has been buried alive, arouses with terror from his lethargy in the field of the dead, and striking his coffin with his brow, sends forth a wail from the bosom of the earth. All the venom of the infernal monster had passed into the soul of the enemy of the believers. He sprang from his bed, his hair bristling with rage, and summoned his guards: he wished to anticipate the orders of Augustus, to arrest the Christians and disperse their assemblies; he spoke of conspiracies, of treason to the empire.

"I must have blood!" he exclaimed. "Every bosom is catching the flame of sedition. . . Let us not consult the entrails of victims: of what avail to us are vows, and prayers, and sacrifices?"

The fool! Ere long his secret agents arrived from Lacedæmon, and confirmed the truth of the dream that had haunted his imagination.

Though resigned to the decrees of Providence, and ardently desirous of the crown of martyrdom, Eudorus yet dreamt not that the storm impended so nearly over his head. He spent his whole time in preparing his soul, and in endeavoring to render himself more worthy both of the high destiny which Paul had predicted, and of the spouse that God had chosen. As when the master of a vineyard returns from a long absence, and finds the favored plant, in which he placed his greatest expectations, weakened and unproductive, he instantly begins to lop off the useless branches, the tree resumes its more than wonted vigor, and the very next season bends beneath the weight of its fruit; thus the son of Lasthenes, abandoned by his God, had languished without culture; but when the father of the family returned to his inheritance, and once more bestowed his cares on his beloved plant, Eudorus was crowned with all the virtues that his infancy had announced.

The time for the accomplishment of a part of his prayers drew near: he was about to receive the pledge of Cymodoce. The new catechumen had merited, by her docility, her purity, and the readiness with which she received and retained instruction, to be admitted two degrees higher in her Christian course. She was to appear at the church for the first time, on one of the festivals consecrated to the mother of the Saviour; after the celebration of the divine mysteries, she was, at the same time, to swear fidelity to her God and to her spouse.

The first Christians generally chose solitude and silence to accomplish the ceremonies of their religion, and the night was fixed in which Cymodoce was to triumph over hell. The whole preceding day she spent in prayer and meditation; and toward evening Sephora and her two daughters began to array the new spouse. She first laid aside the ornaments of the Muses, and deposited on a domestic altar, dedicated to the queen of angels, her sceptre, her veil, and consecrated fillets: her lyre remained suspended in the temple of Homer. It was not without some tears of regret that she parted with these elegant ornaments of her paternal religion. A white tunic, and a crown of lilies, were substituted in the place of those necklaces, and other ornaments of pearl which were not worn by the Christians. The smile of the Muses was replaced by an evangelical purity, which breathed over her whole person charms worthy of heaven.

At the second watch of the night, she came forth in the midst of a blaze of torches, bearing in her hand a lighted taper. She was preceded by Cyril, the priests, the widows, and the deaconesses; while a choir of virgins awaited them at the porch. When she appeared, a shout of admiration burst from the crowd which this ceremony had attracted to the spot. The Pagans exclaimed:

"This is the daughter of Tyndarus, who is crowned with the nuptial wreath, and is about to bless the couch of Menelaus! This is Venus, when she threw her bracelets into the Eurotas, and showed herself to Lycurgus under the features of Minerva!"

The Christians exclaimed:

"This is a second Eve! This is the spouse of the young Tobias, the chaste Susannah, or the noble Esther!"

The name of Esther, given by the unanimous voice of a faithful people, was immediately chosen for the Christian name of Cymodoce.

Not far from Lessa, and near the tombs of the Agidæ, the Christians of Sparta had erected a church. At a distance from the noise and bustle of the crowd, and environed by courts and gardens, it stood separate from every profane monument. After passing a portico decorated with fountains, in which the faithful purified themselves before joining in prayer, were found three gates that led to the basilica. In the recess at the eastern end stood the altar, and behind the altar, the sanctuary. This altar was of massive gold, enriched with precious stones, and erected over the body of a martyr; four curtains of rich tapestry environed it. A dove of ivory, representing the Holy Spirit, was suspended above the altar, and protected the tabernacle beneath its wings. The walls were decorated with pictures, representing various subjects taken from the Scriptures. Near the door of the church, but isolated, arose the baptistery, at the view of which the catechumen sighed with holy impatience.

Cymodoce advanced toward the sacred portico. She was forcibly struck with the surprising contrast that was visible on every side: here stood the daughters of Lacedæmon, whose loose apparel, and every look and motion, bespoke that wantonness and dissipation, which is acquired in the dances at the festivals of Bacchus and Hyacinthus: the rude memorials of Sparta, that knavery, cruelty, and maternal ferocity to which she gave her sanction, were still legible in the eyes of the idolatrous crowd. On the other side were seen the Christian virgins, in chaste attire; those daughters of Helena, who rivalled their mother in the beauty of their persons, but surpassed her by the charms of their modesty. They were going with the rest of the faithful to celebrate the mysteries of a religion, which, while it renders the heart tender and compassionate toward the infant, and charitable toward the slave, inspires a horror of dissimulation and deceit. It seemed as if two distinct peoples composed this kindred race: so much may men be changed by the power of religion!

When they reached the sacred spot, the bishop, holding the Gospel in his hand, mounted the episcopal throne, which fronted the people, and stood at the further end of the sanctuary. Seated on his right and left, the priests filled the semicircle of the altar ; behind them were ranged the deacons in a standing posture. The people filled the body of the church; the men, who sat in different seats from the women, had their heads uncovered ; while the women were veiled.

Whilst the assembly took their seats, the choir chanted a psalm introductory to the festival of the day. After the canticle, the faithful prayed for some time in silence. The bishop then pronounced a prayer, in which all the vows of the faithful were united. The reader then mounted the pulpit, and chose such texts both from the Old and New Testament, as had a reference to the double festival which they were celebrating. What a spectacle for Cymodoce ! How striking the difference between these holy and peaceful ceremonies, and the bloody sacrifices and impure hymns of Pagan worship! Every eye was turned upon the innocent catechumen ; she was seated in the midst of a company of virgins, whom she far outshone in beauty. Overcome with reverence and awe, she scarcely dared to cast one timid glance around the assembly, to search out him who, next to God, held the highest place in her affections.

When the reader had concluded, the bishop mounted the chair of truth. He begun by explaining the gospel of the day; and after speaking of the conversion of idolaters, and of the happiness which a virtuous maiden was about to enjoy in her union with a Christian spouse, under the patronage of the mother of God, he thus concluded his discourse :

"Inhabitants of Lacedæmon, it is time to remind you of your solemn engagements with Sion. Your ancient monarch, Arius, aware that he was descended, like the faithful people, from the stock of Abraham, reclaimed from the pontiff Onias the laws of his sacred ancestor. In the letter wh'ch he addressed to the Jewish people, he says, ' Our flocks, and all our possessions are yours, and from you we claim an equal return of hospitality.' The Maccabees, acknowledging this common origin, sent a friendly deputation to the Spartans. If, when but Gentiles, you were distinguished by the God of Jacob among the people of Javan, Sethim, and Elisa, what ought now to be your gratitude toward heaven, when you are marked with the seal of the elect? Lo, this is the moment to show yourselves worthy of the cradle of your birth, overshadowed by the palms of Idumæa. The illustrious martyrs, Judas, Jonathan, and their brethren, invite you to tread in their footsteps. You are called to-day to the defence of your celestial abode. O beloved flock, which heaven has intrusted to my care, this is perhaps the last time that your shepherd shall assemble you in the fold! and should it be permitted us to meet again, how small the number that would be found at the foot of this altar! Servants of Jesus Christ, ye virtuous spouses, ye spotless virgins, this day you may exult in having quitted the pomps of the world to lead a life of purity. Would feet, entangled in the silken folds of loosely-flowing drapery, be able to mount the scaffold? Would those ornaments of pearl, which surround too delicate a neck, leave room for the executioner's sword? Let us rejoice, my brethren; the time of our deliverance approaches: deliverance, I say, for without doubt, you would not call the dungeon, and the torture with which you are threatened, by the name of slavery. To a persecuted Christian, the prison is not a scene of suffering, but of delight: when the soul is rapt in prayer, the body feels not the weight of the chain: the whole man is ravished, and borne upward toward heaven!"

Cyril descended from the pulpit, and a deacon exclaimed:
"My brethren, let us pray!"

At these words the assembly arose, turned toward the east, and with hands extended toward heaven, prayed for all Christians, for infidels, for the persecuted, the feeble, the sick, the afflicted, and for all those that weep. The deacons then cleared the sacred place of all those who were not permitted to assist at the holy sacrifice; the Gentile, the dæmoniac, and the penitent. The mother of Eudorus, assisted by two widows, came to seek the trembling catechumen, and conduct her to the feet of Cyril. The bishop thus addressed her:

"Who art thou?"

She replied according to the instructions she had received:

"I am Cymodoce, the daughter of Demodocus."

"What is your wish?" said the prelate.

"To quit the darkness of idolatry, and receive the light of the Gospel of Jesus Christ."

"Have you thought seriously on this your resolution?" said the bishop. "Do you fear neither imprisonment nor death? Is your faith in Jesus Christ lively and sincere?"

Cymodoce paused. She did not expect the first part of the question; the sorrows of her aged father rose to her mind; but at the thought that she was hesitating for a moment to share the lot of Eudorus, she instantly decided, and replied in a firm voice:

"I fear neither dungeons nor death; and my faith in Jesus Christ is lively and sincere."

The bishop then imposed his hands upon her, and marked her forehead with the sign of the cross. A tongue of fire appeared in the vaulted roof of the church, and the Holy Spirit descended upon the predestined virgin. A deacon placed a branch of palm in her hand, her virgin companions adorned her with wreaths of flowers, and, preceded by a hundred blazing tapers, she returned to her seat like a martyr, who is just preparing to take her flight to the skies.

The sacrifice began. The bishop saluted the people, and the deacon exclaimed: "Peace be with you!" and immediately the whole assembly saluted each other with the kiss of peace. The attendant priest received the gifts of the faithful, and the whole altar was covered with bread for the sacrifice. Cyril blessed it; the lamps were lighted; clouds of incense arose, and the Christians chanted the loud hosannahs of gratitude and praise; the sacrifice was accomplished. The sacred host was distributed among the faithful, the agape followed the holy communion, and the attention of the whole assembly was called to a solemn and affecting ceremony.

The spouse of Lasthenes announced to Cymodoce that she was now to pledge her fidelity to Eudorus. Cymodoce, agitated, was supported in the arms of the virgins who surrounded her. But where was the bridegroom? Why did he linger behind, and manifest so little impatience? What part of the temple concealed him from the searching eyes of Cymodoce? While no answer was returned, and all was silence and suspense, suddenly the gates of the church were opened, and a plaintive voice was heard without, exclaiming:

"I have sinned before God, and before man At Rome I forgot my religion, and was rejected from the bosom of the Church; in Gaul, I gave a mortal stab to the bosom of innocence: my brethren, pray for me!"

Cymodoce recognized the voice of Eudorus. The descendant of Philopœmen, clad in sackcloth, with his head covered with ashes, lay prostrate on the floor of the porch, and having now accomplished his term of penitence, was making his public confession. The prelate offered up a prayer of mercy for the humbled Christian, which all the faithful repeated. What a new subject of astonishment for Cymodoce! She was a second time conducted to the altar to be betrothed to her spouse, and repeated the words which the bishop recited in a tone of the tenderest emotion. A deacon attended on Eudorus: standing at the gates of the church, which he was not permitted to enter, the penitent pronounced on his part the words that engaged him to Cymodoce. Exchanged from the altar to the vestibule, their mutual vows were carried from the one to the other by the attendant priest: it seemed like the union of innocence and repentance. The daughter of Demodocus consecrated to the queen of angels a distaff full of spotless wool, the symbol of domestic occupations.

During this affecting ceremony, the whole audience were melted into tears, while the virgins of the new Sion chanted this canticle of the spouse:

"As the lily among thorns, so is my well-beloved among the virgins. O my love, behold thou art fair! Thine eyes are like the sparkling fish-pools of Heshbon, thy mouth is a half-open pomegranate, and thy locks resemble the branches of the palm-tree. The tents of cedar, and the pavilions of

Solomon, are less beautiful than my well-beloved. Who is she that cometh forth like the morning; that arises from the desert like a cloud of aromatic spices? O ye daughters of Jerusalem! I conjure you by the roes of the mountains to support me with fruits, and stay me up with flowers; for my soul hath melted at the voice of my well-beloved. Breathe, thou wind of the south, upon the mandrakes, and the flowery vines of Engedi, and shed thy sweetest perfumes around her who is thy soul's delight! My beloved hath wounded my soul. Open to me the doors of cedar; for my locks are moistened with the dews of night. Let myrtle, and cinnamon, and aloes, embalm thy couch; let thy right hand support my head, because I languish with love; place me as a seal upon thy heart, for love is stronger than death."

Scarcely had the Christian virgins concluded their canticle, when other voices, and a different concert, were heard without. Demodocus had assembled a number of his young friends and relations, who in their turn chanted the nuptial song of Eudorus and Cymodoce:

"The star of the evening shines in the west: young men, it is time to quit the festive board. Behold the virgin-bride approaches! O Hymen, smile propitious on the beauteous maid!

"Son of Urania, thou that dwellest on the heights of Helicon, and whose office it is to conduct to the spouse the timid virgin, come, adorn thy brow with the odoriferous wreath! Assume thy veil, bedecked with all the glowing tints of Aurora, and bind the yellow sandals to thy foot of snow! Come, raise thy harmonious voice, step lightly through the dance, and wave in thy hand the nuptial torch!

"Open the gates of the nuptial chamber, and let the virgin approach. Modesty makes her advance with timidity, and she weeps as she quits her paternal mansion. Matrons, calm the anxiety of the trembling virgin, and raise her drooping soul.

"May children, more beautiful than the day, bless your fruitful union! May we behold a young Eudorus suspended at the bosom of Cymodoce, stretching his little hands toward his mother, and smiling sweetly on the warrior his father!"

In this manner did two religions unite to celebrate a union, which seemed happy, at the very moment that it was menaced by the greatest dangers. These songs of joy had scarcely ceased, when the regular march of a body of soldiers, and the sound of arms, was heard without. A confused murmur spread through the assembly, while a band of ruffians, bearing fire and drawn swords in their hands, entered this asylum of peace. The affrighted crowd rushed out at the various doors that led from the church. The narrow passage that extended from the nave to the vestibule resounded with the horrid shrieks of women, children, and old men, half suffocated in the general pressure and confusion: all were dispersed, and the body of the church was left deserted. Cyril, clothed in his pontifical robes, and all serene and unmoved before the Holy of Holies, was arrested at the altar. A centurion, charged with the orders of Hierocles, sought Cymodoce, and, discovering her in the midst of the crowd, flew to the spot, and was about to lay his profane hands upon her. Eudorus, that peaceful lamb, was changed in an instant into a furious lion. He darted upon the centurion, wrested the sword from his hand, broke it asunder, and seizing the daughter of Demodocus in his arms, rushed out with his lovely burden, in hopes to escape amidst the darkness of the night. The centurion, finding himself disarmed, called his soldiers, and pursued the son of Lasthenes. Eudorus redoubled his speed, and was already within reach of the tomb of Leonidas, when the partisans of Hierocles pressed closely upon his footsteps. His exhausted strength disappointed the ardor of his love; he could no longer support his burden, and placed his spouse beneath the sacred monument. Near the tomb stood a trophy, composed of the arms of the warriors of Thermopylæ. Eudorus seized the lance of the king of Lacedæmon, and at that moment the soldiers arrived. When on the point of rushing upon their prey, they imagined that they beheld, by the pale gleam of their torches, the illustrious shade of the mighty Leonidas, who grasped his lance with one hand, and with the other embraced his sepulchre. The eyes of Eudorus sparkled with rage; his long black hair waved in the night-breeze, while the lance which he brandished in his hand flashed back the glare of their torches: less terrible did Leonidas himself appear to the Persians on that fatal night, when, penetrating almost to the tent of Xerxes, he filled the camp of the barbarians with confusion and slaughter. But what could equal the astonishment of many of the soldiers, when in the supposed phantom they recognized their former general.

"Romans," cried Eudorus, "it is my spouse that you seek to tear from my arms; but I will part from her only with my life."

Touched with the voice of their ancient companion in arms, and alarmed at his terrible air and menacing attitude, the soldiers were arrested in their career. As the reaper beholds the ripened ears fall without resistance beneath his sickle, but on reaching the foot of some oak that towers in the midst of the grain, admires the powerful tree which only the axe can fell, or the storm overthrow; thus, after dispersing the mingled crowd, the soldiers stood arrested before the son of Lasthenes. In vain the cowardly centurion commanded them to advance; they seemed fixed to the spot by some invincible spell. Heaven interposed in favor of its servant, and inspired them with this sacred dread. It did still more: the guardian angel of Eudorus was ordained to shield him from the view of the cohort. The thunder rolled through the sky; the guardian spirit, under the form of a warrior clad in glittering arms, stationed himself at the side of Eudorus; the lightnings flashed around, and discovered the radiant spectre to the eyes of the affrighted soldiers; each threw his buckler over his shoulder, and flew for shelter into the surrounding gloom. Eudorus blessed heaven for its protection, and again raised his well beloved in his arms. Cymodoce, overcome with terror, clung closely to the neck of her spouse: not with more grace does the vine encircle the poplar that supports it; not with more ardor does the flame embrace the trunk of the pine that it consumes, nor the sail twine more closely about the mast, while the tempest howls around. Charged with his treasure, the son of Lasthenes was not long in reaching his father's residence; and for a time, at least, placed his virgin spouse in shelter from the outrage of her enemies.

Hierocles, a prey to the demon of Jealousy, had ventured upon this act of violence against the Christians, with the hope of ravishing Cymodoce from Eudorus before she had pronounced the vow that bound her to her spouse: but his partisans arrived too late, and the courage of Eudorus saved the innocent catechumen. The messenger that the son of Lasthenes had dispatched to Constantine, returned to Lacedæmon on the very night of this outrageous attempt upon his spouse. The intelligence he brought was at once consolatory and distressing. Diocletian had again displayed that moderation which ever marked his character. Upon receiving the false report of Hierocles, the emperor ordered a strict watch to be kept upon the ministers of the Christians, and disperse their secret assemblies; but upon hearing a true statement of the case from Constantine, he no longer hesitated to believe that Eudorus was innocent, and that the story of his being at the head of an insurrection was the mere offspring of malice: he therefore contented himself with recalling him to Rome. Constantine added in his letter:

" My friend, hasten to join me, for we shall soon have need of your counsels and assistance. I have sent Dorotheus to Jerusalem, that he may apprise my mother of the dangers that threaten the Christians. He is to touch at Athens on his way. If you choose to embark at the Piræus, you may hear something of importance from the mouth of your old friend."

In effect, the galley of Dorotheus had just reached the port of Phalerum. The two families of Lasthenes and Demodocus deliberated upon the part that it was most advisable to take.

" Cymodoce cannot remain in Greece after my departure,"

said Eudorus, "without being exposed to the violence of Hierocles; she cannot follow me to Rome, since our union has not yet taken place. But a favorable circumstance offers itself: Dorotheus can conduct Cymodoce to Jerusalem. Under the protection of the spouse of Constantius, she may be fully instructed in all the truths of salvation. As soon as the emperor shall grant me permission, I will go to the tomb of Jesus Christ, and reclaim that faith which the daughter of Demodocus has pledged on his altar."

The two families regarded this plan as an inspiration from heaven: thus, should the seaman amidst the darkness of the night, and the howlings of the tempest, hear on a sudden the clarion of that warlike bird who once aroused the village to its matin labors, but now sits solitary on the deck, he feels a mingled sensation of regret for his home, and of hope amid the terrors of the storm; he blesses the cheering sound, which in the midst of the deep can call up images of pastoral life, and which seems to announce the approach to land. Demodocus himself felt a confidence in the project of Eudorus; regardless of the sorrows of separation, he thought of nothing at present but of the best means to secure his beloved daughter: he would willingly have followed her to the extremities of the earth, but his age, and the duties of his sacred office, enchained him to the soil of Greece.

"Well," said Lasthenes, "may God's will be done! Demodocus shall conduct Cymodoce to Athens, and you, my son, shall immediately depart for the same place. You shall both bid each other adieu, and sail from the same port—the one for Rome, the other for Syria. O my children, the time of our trials is of short duration, and passes with the rapidity of a messenger! Remain firm to your faith, and may heaven sanctify your mutual love."

Their departure was fixed for the following day, in the fear of some new outrage of the proconsul. Before he set out from Lacedæmon, Eudorus wrote to Cyril, whom he was not permitted to see in prison. The confessor, accustomed to chains, sent his benediction to the two persecuted spouses from the depth of his dungeon. O ye tender and affectionate pair, at the very moment when you are counting upon long years of happiness here below, the heavenly choir of virgins and martyrs are beginning to celebrate a union that is more durable, and a felicity that shall never end!

BOOK FIFTEENTH.

SUMMARY.

Athens. Adieus of Cymodoce, Eudorus and Demodocus. Cymodoce embarks with Dorotheus for Joppa. Eudorus embarks at the same time for Ostia. The Mother of the Saviour sends Gabriel to the Angel of the Seas. Eudorus arrives at Rome. He finds the Senate ready to assemble, in order to pronounce upon the Fate of the Christians. He is chosen to plead their Cause. Hierocles arrives at Rome; he is charged by the Sophists with defending their Sect, and accusing the Christians. Symmachus, High Priest of Jupiter, is to address the Senate in behalf of the ancient Gods of the Country.

MOUNTED on a courser of Thessaly, and followed by a single attendant, the son of Lasthenes quitted Lacedæmon, and took the road that led over the mountains of Argos. Religion and love inspired his bosom with a thousand generous resolutions. The Almighty, who willed to raise him to the highest degree of glory, conducted him through those scenes of fallen magnificence that inspire a contempt for all sublunary things. Eudorus traversed the barren summits of the mountains, and trod the patrimony of the King of kings. During three days he urged his courser forward, and at last reached Argos, where he tasted a short repose. Though the various parts of this once flourishing city still retained the memorable names of Hercules and Pelops, of Clytemnestra and Iphigenia, yet nothing met the eye but piles of silent and melancholy ruins. He next beheld the solitary gates of Mycenæ, and the long-forgotten tomb of Agamemnon; at Corinth he sought for no other monuments than those which reminded him of the illustrious apostle, with whose powerful eloquence they had once resounded. In traversing the depopulated isthmus, he was reminded of the games sung by Pindar, which participated, in some degree, in the splendor and omnipotence of the gods; at Megara he sought for the hospitable roof of his ancestors, who paid the last honors to the ashes of Phocion. Eleusis was entirely deserted; and nothing was seen in the straits of Salamis but a solitary fisherman's bark, which was fastened to the loose fragments of a ruined mole. But when following the Sacred Way, Eudorus ascended Mount Pœcile, and beheld the plain of Attica stretched beneath his view, he paused, overcome with admiration and surprise; the citadel of Athens, elegantly cut in the form of a pedestal, was crowned with the temple of Minerva and the Propylæa; the city lay extended at its base, and presented to the view the intermingling columns of a thousand other monuments. The heights of Hymettus formed the background of the picture, while a grove of olives encircled the city of Minerva.

Eudorus, following the windings of the Cephisus, which flows through this sacred grove, inquired the way to the gardens of the Academy. Some tombs scattered along the side of the road pointed out the path to this retreat of philosophy. He discovered the monuments of Thrasybulus, Conon and Timotheus; he saluted the sepulchres of these young men who fell in defence of their country during the Peloponnesian war: Pericles, who compared Athens deprived of its youth to the year without its spring, himself reposed in the midst of these flowers that were cut off before their prime.

A statue of Love announced to the son of Lasthenes the entrance to the gardens of Plato. Adrian, in restoring the Academy to its ancient splendor, had only opened an asylum to the dreams of the human mind. Whoever had attained to the rank of a Sophist, seemed to have acquired the privilege of insolence and error. The Cynic, whose foul and tattered mantle scarce served him for a covering, insulted with his staff and his wallet the Platonist enveloped in his long robe of purple; the Stoic, in his mantle of sombre hue, declared war against the Epicurean crowned with flowers. Every place resounded with the mingled murmurs of the schools, which the Athenians called the song of the swans and sirens; and those embowering walks, which a divine genius had immortalized, were become the retreat of impostors, and of the most useless of mankind.

Through all these places did Eudorus wander in search of his ancient friend, the prefect of the palace. As he passed the different groups of Sophists, he was mistaken for a novice who had just entered the schools; and each sect, willing to draw him over to its particular system, made up to him, and proposed lessons of wisdom in the language of folly. Eudorus could not conceal his contempt, and hastened forward to find Dorotheus. This virtuous Christian was walking apart by himself in an alley over-arched with plane-trees, and cooled by the freshness of a neighboring canal; he was surrounded by a company of young men, already renowned for their talents or their birth. Near him stood Gregory Nazianzen, who already discovered a genius for poetry; John, that new Demosthenes, whose premature eloquence had won him the appellation of "the Golden-mouthed;" Basil, and Gregory of Nyssa, his brother: they all manifested a decisive inclination toward that religion which had been professed by Justin the philosopher, and Denis the Areopagite. Julian, on the contrary, the nephew of Constantine, was attached to Lampridius, the declared enemy of the Gospel: capricious habits and convulsive emotions betrayed in the young prince a sort of disorder of mind and heart.

It was not without some difficulty that Dorotheus recognized Eudorus: the countenance of the son of Lasthenes had assumed that masculine beauty, which the profession of arms, and the exercise of the virtues, alone can bestow. They retired to a solitary spot, and Dorotheus thus opened his heart to the friend of Constantine.

"Immediately on receiving your message," said he, "I quitted Rome. The evil is more threatening than perhaps you think: Galerius assumes a loftier and more importunate tone, and sooner or later Diocletian will be obliged to abdicate the purple. It will be his first object to exterminate the Christians, that the emperor may be deprived of his chief support ; this is an old project of Hierocles, whose counsels are now all-powerful with Cæsar. The former repeats without ceasing that the late census, by discovering a frightful multitude of enemies to the gods, has revealed the dangers of the empire; that it will be necessary to have recourse to more severe measures in order to crush a sect that threatens to overturn the altars of the country. You know the motives of my voyage into Syria; you know, too, that I had nearly incurred the displeasure of Diocletian. Eudorus, our afflicted brethren turn their eyes toward you. The glory which you have acquired in arms, and above all your noble repentance, are subjects of discourse and admiration to all the Faithful. The sovereign pontiff awaits you; Constantine calls you. This prince, surrounded by spies, is scarcely able to retain his place at court, and stands in need of a friend like yourself, either to assist him with counsels, or, if it be necessary, to shield his person from danger."

Eudorus in his turn gave Dorotheus an account of the events that had been passing in Greece. Dorotheus undertook with pleasure to conduct to Helena the spouse of the son of Lasthenes. In the port of Phalerum, and at no great distance from the vessel of Dorotheus, lay a Neapolitan galley, which was shortly to return to Italy; in her he engaged his passage. The two travellers fixed their departure for the thirteenth day of the feast of Panathenæa. Punctual to the melancholy moment, Demodocus came, accompanied by the sorrowful Cymodoce; he hastened to conceal his grief within the walls of the citadel, where the most ancient of the Prytanes, his friend and relative, received him with all the rites of hospitality.

The son of Lasthenes had been received by the learned Pistus, bishop of Athens, the same who was afterward so conspicuous in the council of Nicæa—that illustrious assembly, in which presided three prelates who were gifted with miraculous powers, and had raised the dead; forty bishops, either confessors or martyrs, learned priests and philosophers; in fine, some of the greatest characters either for genius or for virtue, that the Church ever produced.

On the eve of this double separation of a father from his daughter, and of one spouse from another, Eudorus sent a message to Cymodoce to acquaint her that everything was ready, and that on the morrow, about sunset, he would meet her under the portico of Minerva's temple, and bid her farewell.

The fatal day arrived; the son of Lasthenes quitted his abode, and after passing the Areopagus, where the God whom Paul had announced was no longer unknown, he ascended the hill to the citadel, and found he was the first on the appointed spot.

Stationed under the portico of the most beautiful temple in the universe, Eudorus surveyed the scenery around, and was struck with a more brilliant spectacle than he had ever before witnessed. Athens met his view arrayed in all its pomp; Mount Hymettus towered to the east, and seemed arrayed in a vesture of gold; Pentelicus stretched toward the north to form a junction with Permetta, and Mount Icarus, diminishing toward the west, discovered the sacred summits of the distant Cythæron; to the south, the sea, the Piræus, the shores of Ægina, the coast of Epidaurus, and the distant citadel of Corinth terminated the magnificent circle of this country of arts, of heroes, and of gods.

Athens, with all its masterpieces of art, lay stretched below: the polished marble of its edifices, unsullied by the hand of time, reflected the glories of the setting sun; his last radiance lingered on the columns of Minerva's temple, glittered on the Persian bucklers suspended on the front of the portico, and seemed to animate the admirable sculpture of Phidias, that adorned the frieze.

What gave an additional interest to this picture, was the excitement that the festival of Panathenæa caused in the city and the surrounding country. Here a band of youthful Canephori were bearing their sacred baskets to the gardens of Venus; there various choirs of youths and virgins intermingled, were chanting the songs of Harmodius and Aristogiton; chariots were rolling toward the Stadium, and citizens hastening in crowds to the Lyceum, to Pœcile, and Ceramicus;

but the greatest press was toward the theatre of Bacchus, which stood near the citadel, and the voice of the actors, who were representing a tragedy of Sophocles, was borne at intervals on the breeze to the ear of Eudorus.

Cymodoce appeared; from the graceful simplicity of her attire, her virgin brow, her eyes of azure, and the modesty that marked her whole deportment, she might have been mistaken by the Greeks for Minerva herself, who had just quitted her temple, and was about to take her flight to Olympus, after receiving the incense of her votaries.

Filled with admiration and love, Eudorus made an effort to conceal his anxiety, that, by his example, he might inspire the daughter of Homer with confidence.

"Cymodoce," said he, "how can I express to you my gratitude and the feelings of my heart? For my sake, you have consented to quit your native land, to traverse the seas, and to dwell beneath a foreign sky, far from your father; far from him whom you have chosen for your spouse. Did I not believe that I was conducting you toward heaven, to taste of eternal felicity, could I demand such proofs of your affection? Can I suppose that a love, merely human, could induce you to make so many painful sacrifices?"

"My will, and my life," replied Cymodoce, in tears, "are equally at your disposal: the happiness of doing anything for you, would amply repay every privation I could suffer. If I loved you as my spouse only, nothing would then be impossible for me; but when your religion teaches me to love you for the sake of heaven, and in obedience to the will of God, what sacrifice would be too great for me to make? I weep not for myself, but for the sorrows of my father, and for the dangers to which you will be exposed."

"O thou fairest of the daughters of the new Sion," answered Eudorus, "fear not any dangers that may threaten me; pray for me; God will grant the prayers of a soul as spotless as thine. O Cymodoce, death itself is not an evil when it meets us strong in virtue. No destiny, however peaceful or obscure, can shelter us from his darts: he will surprise us under the roof of our ancestors, as well as on a foreign shore. Behold yonder flight of storks, that are at this moment rising from the banks of the Ilissus; every year witnesses their departure to the shores of Cyrene; every year beholds them return to the plains of Erechtheus; but how often have they found that mansion desolate, which they left flourishing and happy! How often have they sought in vain for the roof beneath whose shelter they were accustomed to build their nests!"

"Pardon," cried Cymodoce, "pardon the terrors of an inexperienced maiden, brought up under gods who are less severe, and who chide not the tears that are shed by parting lovers."

At these words, Cymodoce stifled her sighs, and covered her face with her veil. Eudorus pressed the hands of his spouse to his heart, and said:

"Cymodoce, the pride and happiness of my life, let not grief make you blaspheme our divine religion. Forget those gods who can offer you no resource against tribulations of the heart. O Cymodoce, my God is the God of tender souls; the friend of those who weep, and the comforter of the afflicted; it is he who listens to the cry of the little songster of the wood, and who tempers the wind to the shorn lamb. Far from wishing to restrain your tears, he blesses them; he will render you an account of them when he visits you in your last hour, since they have been shed for him, and for your spouse."

At these last words, the voice of Eudorus faltered. Cymodoce uncovered her countenance, and beheld the noble face of the warrior drenched in the tears that flowed down his bronzed cheeks. The gravity of this Christian grief, added to the struggle between religion and nature, gave to the son of Lasthenes an incomparable beauty. By an involuntary movement, the daughter of Demodocus was about to fall at the knees of Eudorus, but he caught her in his arms, and pressed her tenderly to his heart; they both remained ravished in sweet and holy ecstasy: thus at the entrance of Laban's tent, stood Rachel and Jacob taking their last sorrowful farewell; the son of Isaac was obliged to tend his flocks during seven long years before he could obtain his spouse.

Just at this moment Demodocus came out of the temple. Forgetting that he had consented to the departure of his daughter, he gave vent to bitter complaints.

"How," cried he, "can you have the barbarity to tear a daughter from the arms of her father? Had Cymodoce but been your spouse, and had you left behind a lovely infant, who might have smiled away my griefs, and toyed with my silver locks! . . . But to be separated far from me—to wander through inhospitable climes, and over tempestuous seas, where barbarous pirates . . . Ah, should my daughter fall into their hands! Should she be forced to serve a cruel master—to prepare his repast and his couch! O that earth may ingulf me in its bosom ere I experience woes like these. Have the Christians a heart harder than the flinty rock? Is their God a divinity without feeling or compassion?"

During this discourse, Cymodoce had thrown herself upon the old man's bosom, and was blending her tears with his. Eudorus listened to these reproaches of Demodocus with a composure unmingled with severity, and participated, without weakness, in all the sorrows of this aged parent.

"My father," said he, "for I must be permitted to call you by this endearing name, since Cymodoce is already my spouse in the eyes of the Eternal, I tear her not by force from your embrace; she is still free to accept or to reject my religion, for the God I serve wishes not to gain the heart by constraint: if the sacrifice be too great, remain together in Greece. May heaven shed its blessings upon you. As for me, I must accomplish my destiny. But if your daughter loves me, Demodocus, if you think that I can render her happy, if you dread the machinations of Hierocles, endeavor to reconcile yourself to a separation, which, I hope, will not be of long continuance, and which will shield Cymodoce from the evils that threaten her. Demodocus, the Supreme Being disposes of us as he pleases, and it is our duty to submit to his holy will."

"O my son," replied Demodocus, "excuse my grief; I feel

that I am unjust, and that you merit not these reproaches: on the contrary, you are seeking to rescue my Cymodoce from the persecution of an impious wretch, and to place her under the protection of a powerful princess; you are about to bestow on her a noble inheritance, and an illustrious name. But how can I remain solitary in Greece ? Oh, that I were at liberty to relinquish the sacred duties that these people have intrusted to my charge ! Oh, that I were again in the vigor of my age, when to study mankind I visited cities, and traversed foreign lands, with what alacrity would I follow Cymodoce ! Alas! shall I no more behold her lead the dance with her virgin companions on the summits of Ithome ? Thou rose of Messenia, I shall seek thee in vain in the precincts of the temple ! Cymodoce, no more shall I hear the sweet accents of thy voice amidst the sacred hymns of the sacrifice; no more shalt thou present me with the sacred barley, or the hallowed knife; thy lyre, suspended at the altar of our divine ancestors, defiled with dust, and with its chords unstrung, will be perpetually before me to remind me of my loss; my tearful eyes will behold the wreaths of flowers that adorned your hair withering at the foot of the statue of Homer. Alas! I had fondly hoped that your hand should close my dying eyes: must I die then without being able to give you my last benediction? The couch on which I breathe forth my expiring sigh will be solitary, for, my daughter, I can never hope to see you again: already does the voice of fate summon me to the grave; at my age one must not count upon length of days: when the seed of the plant is dry and matured, it becomes light, and the least breath carries it away."

As the priest of Homer uttered these words, a loud burst of applause issued from the theatre of Bacchus; the actor, who performed the part of Œdipus, raised his voice, and these words were distinctly heard by Eudorus, Demodocus, and Cymodoce:

"O Theseus, I thus unite your hands to those of my daughter; promise that you will be a father to my dear Antigone !"

"I promise," exclaimed Eudorus, applying the verses of the poet to his own situation.

"Then she shall be thine," cried Demodocus, as he extended his arms toward Eudorus.

Eudorus eagerly embraced him, and the venerable sire pressed his two children to his heart. Thus have I seen a willow decayed by time, in whose half-open bosom grew a tuft of wild flowers, and which, proud of its blooming treasure, seemed to extend its ancient arms to afford them shelter, and to implore the cooling zephyr and the refreshing dew; but ere long a fierce storm overthrows both the willow and the flowers, lovely children of Earth.

The moon appeared in the horizon; her silvery brow was crowned with the golden rays of the sun, as his broadened disc sunk beneath the billows of the deep. This was the moment when the favoring breezes arose and invited the mariner to spread his sail, and quit the port of Attica. The slaves of Demodocus had prepared the chariots, and were awaiting his return at the foot of the citadel. Fate summoned them to depart, and they were compelled to obey her call; they mounted their chariots; the violence of grief had subsided into settled melancholy, and they proceeded in silence. They soon passed the port of the Pyræus, and the tombs of Antiope, Menander, and Euripides; they next directed their course toward the ruined temple of Ceres, and after passing the field of Aristides, arrived at the port of Phalerum. The gale began to freshen, the waves broke in gentle murmurs on the beach, the galleys unfurled their sails, and the shores resounded with the shouts of the mariners as they heaved the ponderous anchor. Dorotheus was awaiting their arrival on the strand, and the boats stood ready to convey them to their respective ships. The chariots stopped on the margin of the flood, and Eudorus, Demodocus, and Cymodoce dismounted. The priest of Homer could no longer support himself; his knees trembled, and he felt his soul die within him. He said to his daughter in a faint voice:

"This port will be as fatal to me as it was to the father of Theseus: I shall never again behold the return of your whitening sails!"

The son of Lasthenes and the young catechumen bent before Demodocus, and entreated his last benediction. With one foot in the sea, and their faces turned toward the shore, they appeared as if offering a sacrifice of expiation according to the rites of antiquity. Demodocus raised his hands toward heaven, and breathed on his children an ardent, though silent benediction; for his heart was full, and he was unable to utter a word. Eudorus encouraged Cymodoce, and placed in her hands a letter to the pious Helena; then embracing her with tenderness and respect, he said:

"My spouse, delay not to become a Christian; think often on Eudorus, and from the lofty towers of the holy city, may the daughter of Jerusalem sometimes cast a look of regret toward the sea that separates us."

"My father," said Cymodoce, in a voice interrupted by broken sobs, "my dearest father, live, I beseech you, for my sake, and I will endeavor to live for yours. O Eudorus, will the happy day ever arrive when I shall see you, when I shall see my father again?"

"Yes," exclaimed Eudorus, like one inspired, "we shall meet again, never more to be separated!"

Cymodoce entered the boat, and the mariners rowed from the strand. Eudorus threw himself into the bark that was to transport him to his vessel; but the slaves of Demodocus were obliged to tear him from this scene of anguish. The fleet quitted the port of Phalerum; the mariners, crowned with flowers, dashed the ocean into foam beneath the stroke of their oars, while they invoked the Nereids, Palæmon, and Thetis, and saluted as they retreated the sacred tomb of Themistocles.

The vessel of Cymodoce took its course toward the East, while that of the son of Lasthenes turned its prow toward Italy.

The divine mother of the Saviour was watching over the life of the innocent pilgrim; she sent Gabriel to the angel of the seas, to command him to breathe none but his gentlest breezes. Directly Gabriel, after having detached from his shoulders his white wings, tipped with gold, plunged from the skies into the waves

At the springs of the ocean, in deep caves, constantly resounding with the sound of billows, dwells the austere angel that watches over the movements of the abyss. To instruct him in his duties, Wisdom took him with her when she walked beneath the sea at the birth of Time. It was he who, by the order of God, opened to the deluge the cataracts of heaven; it is he who, at the end of the world, will a second time roll the waves over the summits of the mountains. Placed at the cradle of the rivers, he directs their course and swells their waves, or bids them decrease; he forces back into the night of the poles, and retains there under chains of ice, the fogs, clouds and tempests; he knows the most hidden rocks, the most lonely straits, the most distant lands, and discovers them in turn to the genius of man; he sees with a single glance both the gloomy regions of the North and the brilliant climes of the tropics; twice a day he raises the sluices of the ocean, and, reestablishing with his hand the equilibrium of the globe, at each equinox brings back the earth beneath the oblique rays of the sun.

Gabriel penetrated into the bosom of the seas: whole nations and unknown continents were sleeping, swallowed up in the gulf of the waves. How many different monsters which mortal eye shall never behold! What a powerful ray of life even in these gloomy depths! Yet how many *débris* and shipwrecks! Gabriel pitied mankind and admired the divine power. Ere long he perceived the angel of the seas, attentive to some great revolution of the waters; seated upon a throne of crystal, he held in his hand a bridle of gold; his green locks fell damp upon his shoulders, and an azure scarf enveloped his divine form. Gabriel saluted him with majesty.

"Formidable spirit," said he, "O my brother! the power that the Eternal has confided to you, proves clearly the high rank that you occupy in the celestial hierarchies! What a new world! what sublime intelligence! How happy you are in knowing these marvellous secrets!"

"Divine messenger," returned the angel of the seas, "whatever may be the cause that brings you hither, I receive with joy a guest like you. To better admire the power of our master, it would have been necessary, like me, to have seen him lay the foundations of this empire; I was present when he divided into two parts the waters of the abyss; I saw him subject the waves to the movements of the stars, and bind the destiny of the ocean to that of the sun and moon; he covers Leviathan with a cuirass of iron, and sends him to sport in these gulfs; he plants forests of coral beneath the waves; he peoples them with fish and birds; he causes smiling isles to spring from the bosom of a furious element; he regulates the course of the winds; he subjects the storm to laws; and, pausing on the shore, he says to the sea, 'Thus far shalt thou go and no farther, and here shall thy proud waves be stayed.' Illustrious servant of Mary, hasten to tell me what sovereign command has caused you to descend into these mobile caves. Is time fulfilled? Must the clouds be gathered together? Must the dikes of the ocean be broken? Abandoning the universe to chaos, shall I mount again with you to the skies?"

"I bring you a message of peace," said Gabriel with a smile; "man is still the object of the condescension of the Eternal; the cross is about to triumph on the earth; Satan is about to return to hell. Mary orders you to conduct to port those two spouses whom you see quitting the shores of Greece. Suffer none but the gentlest breezes to breathe upon the waves!"

"The will of the Star of the seas be done!" said the angel that rules the tempests, bowing with respect. "Would that Satan might soon be confined in the place of his punishment! Often does he trouble my repose, and unchain the storms despite my efforts."

While uttering these words, the powerful spirit chose the gentle, perfumed breezes that caress the coasts of India and the shores of the Pacific; he directed them toward the sails of Eudorus and Cymodoce, and, with the same breath, propelled both galleys toward two opposite ports.

Favored by this benign influence of heaven, Eudorus soon touched the shore of Ostia. He flew to Rome. Constantine embraced him with tenderness, and related to him the misfortunes of the Church and the intrigues of the court.

The senate had been convoked to deliberate upon the destiny of the faithful. At Rome, all was expectation and terror. Although Diocletian had yielded to the violence of Galerius, yet by a last act of justice he had signified that it was his pleasure to grant the Christians a defender in the senate. The most illustrious among the clergy at Rome were occupied at this moment in choosing an orator worthy to plead the cause of the cross. The council, over which Marcellinus presided, was assembled by the glimmer of lamps in the catacombs: seated on the tombs of the martyrs, these Fathers resembled aged warriors, deliberating on the field of battle, or kings wounded in defence of their peoples. Not one of these confessors but bore on his limbs the scars of some glorious persecution: one had lost the use of his hands, another was deprived of the light of heaven; here stood one, whose tongue had been torn out, but whose heart remained to praise the Eternal; there was another, whose body was entirely mutilated by the executioner, and who resembled a victim half consumed by the fires of the sacrifice. These venerable sages could not agree in their choice of a defender: possessed of no other eloquence than that of their virtues, they were all fearful of compromising the destiny of the Faithful. The pontiff of Rome proposed that the question should be referred to the decision of heaven. The holy Gospel was placed upon the sepulchre of a martyr, which served as an altar: the Fathers then knelt in prayer, and entreated God to point out by some verses of Scripture, the defender that would be agreeable in his sight. God, who had inspired this thought, immediately sent down the angel, whose office it was to register his eternal decrees in the book of life. The celestial spirit, enveloped in a cloud, marked in the midst of the Bible the decrees that they required. The Fathers arose; Marcellinus opened the sacred volume, and read aloud these words from Maccabees:

"And he gained his people great honor, and put on his

breastplate as a giant, and girt his warlike armor about him in battles, and protected the camp with his sword."

Marcellinus, surprised, closed the prophetic volume, and again opened it at these words:

"His memory shall be sweet as the music of the feast. He hath been divinely commissioned to lead the people into the way of repentance."

A third time the sovereign pontiff consulted the oracles of Israel, and all the Fathers were struck with this passage from the Canticles:

"I have fasted and covered myself with sackcloth—I have taken a hair-cloth for my garment."

Immediately a voice (but from what person was unknown), pronounced the name of Eudorus. The aged martyrs, suddenly enlightened, burst into loud hosannahs, which were prolonged through the vaulted roofs of the catacombs. They were all filled with astonishment when they considered with what justice all these expressions might be applied to the son of Lasthenes. Each one admired the counsels of the Most High, and acknowledged the wisdom of the choice. The renown of the young orator, his exemplary penitence, the favor he enjoyed at court, the habit he had been in of addressing princes, the dignities with which he had been invested, the friendship with which Constantine honored him,—everything justified the appointment of heaven. They hastened to acquaint Eudorus with the determination of the Fathers. The son of Lasthenes humbled himself in the dust, and sought to avoid an honor so sublime, and a charge so momentous. They showed him a passage of Scripture; he submitted. He immediately retired amidst the tombs of the saints, and prepared himself by watchings, by tears, and by prayers, to plead the most important cause that was ever brought before a human tribunal.

While the whole soul of the Christian champion was occupied with the importance of the mission with which he was invested, Hierocles, supported by all the powers of hell, arrived at Rome. This enemy of God had heard with despair of the ill success that had attended his violent measures at Lacedæmon, of the flight of Cymodoce, and the departure of Eudorus for Italy. The temperate orders which he had received from Diocletian, convinced him that his calumnies had failed of their expected effects at court. He had hoped to ruin his rival; but this rival had been merely summoned to Rome, to be under the vigilant eye of the chief of the empire. He trembled lest the son of Lasthenes should succeed in destroying him in the favor of Diocletian. In order to prevent any sudden disgrace, he resolved to hasten to Galerius, who had been constantly soliciting him to come, and assist him with his counsels. Meanwhile the spirit of darkness thus consoled the apostate:

"Hierocles," whispered he, "you will soon be powerful enough to tear Cymodoce even from the arms of Helena. This imprudent virgin, in changing her religion, has given you a fresh power over her person. If you can induce the princes to persecute the Christians, your rival will easily be included in the general massacre; you may then either vanquish the daughter of Homer by the fear of torments, or claim her as a Christian slave that has escaped from your power."

The sophist, who mistook these infernal suggestions for the inspirations of his own heart, congratulated himself upon the depth of his genius: deluded wretch! he knew not that he was the instrument of Satan's designs against the cross. Full of these thoughts, the proconsul prepared for his departure; he rushed from the mountains of Arcadia, like the torrent of Styx, which falls from the same mountains, and proves fatal to all those who drink of its waters. He hurried to Epirus, embarked at the promontory of Actium, landed at Tarentum, and stopped not till he reached Galerius, who was at this time at Tusculum, profaning the gardens of Cicero.

Cæsar was at this moment surrounded by the sophists of the school, who pretended that they too were persecuted, since their opinions were treated with contempt. They expected that their judgment was to be consulted on the important question that was to be the subject of debate; for they called themselves the natural judges of everything that concerned the religion of mankind. They had entreated Diocletian to allow them the privilege he had granted the Christians, of having an orator in the senate. The emperor, wearied with their importunities, had granted them this demand. The arrival of Hierocles filled them with joy, and they immediately appointed him orator of the philosophic sects. Hierocles accepted an honor which flattered his vanity, and furnished him with an opportunity of accusing the Christians. The pride of perverted reason, and the fury of love, showed him already the faithful overthrown, and Cymodoce in his arms. Galerius, whose mind he had corrupted, and whose projects he seconded, granted him his powerful protection, and gave him permission to express the opinions of the false sages in the Capitol with full liberty. Symmachus, the high priest of Jupiter, was to speak in favor of the ancient gods of his country.

The day which was to decide the lot of half the inhabitants of the empire, the day on which the destiny of human kind was threatened, in the religion of Jesus Christ, this day so desired and so dreaded by angels, by demons, and by men, arrived. From the first dawn of day, the prætorian guards occupied the avenues of the Capitol. An immense crowd filled the Forum, surrounded the temple of Jupiter Stator, and lined the banks of the Tiber as far as the theatre of Marcellus: those who could not find a place below, mounted on the roofs of the neighboring buildings, and on the triumphal arches of Titus and Severus. Diocletian quitted his palace, and advanced along the Sacred Way, as if he were going to triumph over the Marcomani or the Parthi. So much was the emperor altered, that his people scarcely knew him again: for some time past he had been laboring under a languishing disorder, and under the anxieties Galerius had caused him. In vain had the old man been careful to tinge his cheeks; the paleness of the tomb was visible through the flimsy disguise, and the features of death were already conspicuous beneath the half-fallen mask of human greatness.

Galerius, surrounded by all the pomp of Asiatic magnificence, followed the emperor on a car drawn by tigers. The people trembled with terror at the view of the gigantic stature and furious air of this second Titan. Constantine came next, mounted on a light courser; he attracted the gaze and the prayers both of the soldiers and the Christians. The three orators marched after these masters of the world. The high priest of Jupiter, borne along by the college of priests, preceded by the haruspices, and followed by a band of vestal virgins, saluted the crowd, who hailed with joy the interpreter of the religion of Romulus. Hierocles, covered with the mantle of the stoics, was carried along in a litter, and surrounded by Libanius, Iamblichus, Porphyry, and the troop of Sophists: the people, who are naturally enemies to affectation, and the display of false wisdom, loaded him with railleries and contempt. Last in the train came Eudorus, clad in a habit of deep mourning: he walked alone on foot; with solemn air and downcast eyes, he seemed to bear the whole weight of the woes of the Church. The Pagans beheld with astonishment, under this simple attire, the warrior to whose honor triumphal statues had been erected; the faithful bowed with respect before their defender; the aged sires blessed him, and the women pointed him out to their children as he passed along: while upon every altar the priests of Jesus Christ were offering the holy sacrifice for his success.

There was a hall in the Capitol called the Julian hall, which Augustus had formerly decorated with the statue of Victory. Here were found the column of the *milliarium aureum*, the beam pierced with sacred nails, the wolf of bronze, and the armor of Romulus. The walls were hung with the portraits of consuls: the just Publicola, the generous Fabricius; Cincinnatus, who was taken from the plough, and Fabius, who saved his country by the prudence of delay; Paulus Æmilius, Cato, Marcellus, and Cicero, the father of his country. These illustrious citizens seemed still seated in the senate amidst the successors of Tigellinus and Sejanus, as if at one glance to show the extremities of vice and virtue, and to bear witness to the fearful changes that time produces in empires.

It was in this vast hall that the judges of the Christians

were assembled. Diocletian ascended his throne; Galerius seated himself on the right, and Constantine on the left of the emperor; the various officers of the palace, according to their different ranks, took their seats at the foot of the throne. After having saluted the statue of Victory, and in its presence renewed their oaths of fidelity, the senators ranged themselves upon their seats around the hall, and the orators took their places in their midst. The vestibule and the court of the Capitol were filled by the patricians, the soldiers, and the people. God granted permission to the powers of the abyss, and the dwellers in the divine tabernacles, to take part in this memorable deliberation: immediately the angels and the demons spread themselves through the senate, the former to calm, the latter to excite, the passions; those to enlighten the mind, these to blind it.

They began by offering a white bull to Jupiter, the author of good counsels; during this sacrifice, Eudorus covered his head with his mantle, from which he shook off some drops of the lustral water with which it had been defiled. Diocletian gave the signal, and Symmachus arose in the midst of a burst of universal applause: familiarized with all the majesty of Roman eloquence, his words flowed from his lips like the stream of a mighty river that rolls majestically through the plain which it beautifies in its course

BOOK SIXTEENTH.

SUMMARY.

Harangues of Symmachus, Hierocles, and Eudorus. Diocletian consents to issue the Edict of Persecution, but wishes first to consult the Sibyl of Cumæ.

"Diocletian, our most clement emperor, and you, Cæsar Galerius, thrice happy prince, if ever your godlike minds manifested their love for justice, it is on the present important subject, that has this day assembled the august senate at the foot of your sacred tribunal.

"Are we to proscribe the adorers of this new God; or to allow the Christians to worship their divinity in peace? Such is the question that is now proposed to the senate.

"May Jupiter and the other divinities, who are the avengers of suffering humanity, preserve me from being guilty of the blood, or accessory to the woes of my fellow-men! Why should we persecute men who fulfil all the duties of good citizens? The Christians pursue the useful arts; their riches augment the treasure of the state; they serve with courage in our armies; they often assist at our public councils, and offer advice full of wisdom, justice, and prudence. Moreover, it is not by violence that we shall reach the desired end. Experience has proved that the Christians multiply under the sword of the executioner. Do you wish to gain them over to the religion of your country? Call them to the temple of Mercy, and not to the altar of the Eumenides.

"But after declaring what to me appears reasonable, justice demands that I should also state my grounds for the fears with which the Christians inspire me. It is evident that our gods are the objects of their derision, and sometimes of their insults: this is the only crime that can justly be laid to their charge. How many Romans have been already perverted by their audacious reasonings! Ah! we speak of attacking a strange divinity: let us think rather of defending our own! Let the consideration of all that the Christians have done for us, soften our aversion to their worship. Did we feel sufficiently convinced of the power and goodness of our paternal gods, we should no longer fear to see the sect of Christians grow and increase from deserters of our temples.

"It is a truth long since acknowledged, that Rome is indebted for the empire of the world, to her piety toward the gods. She has erected altars to every beneficent genius, to good Fortune, to Filial Love, to Peace, Concord, Justice, Liberty, Victory; and to the god Terminus, who alone, in the assembly of the gods, refused to rise in the presence of Jupiter. Can this divine family be displeasing to the Christians? What mortal shall dare to refuse his homage to divinities so illustrious? Would you ascend higher into antiquity? you will find the very names of our country, together with all its ancient traditions, connected with our religion, and forming a part of our august ceremonials; you will find the memorials of the golden age, that reign of happiness and of innocence, which every nation envies Ausonia. How many tender recollections does the very name of Latium inspire—a name that was given to the plains of Laurentum, because it was the asylum of a persecuted god! Our ancestors, in recompense for their virtues, received from heaven a disposition for hospitality, and Rome became the refuge of all the exiled unfortunates. How many interesting adventures, how many illustrious names are attached to these migrations undertaken in the primitive ages of the world—Diomedes, Philoctetes, Idomeneus, Nestor! When a forest covered the mountain on which stands this Capitol; when cottages occupied the place of these palaces; when our celebrated Tiber bore only the obscure name of Albula, they were not then solicitous to inquire whether the God of an obscure nation of Judæa were preferable to the gods of Rome! To be convinced of the power of Jupiter, we need but consider the feeble origin of this empire. Four insignificant sources have formed the torrent of the Roman people : Alba, that country so cherished by the fond love of the Curiatii; the Latin warriors, who united themselves to the companions of Æneas; the Arcadians of Evander, who transmitted to Cincinnatus a love of flocks, and the blood of the Hellenes, a fruitful germ of eloquence among the rude foster-children of a wolf; lastly, the Sabines, who gave spouses to the companions of Romulus; those Sabines, clothed in the skins of the flocks which they conducted with a lance; living upon milk and honey, and consecrating themselves to Ceres and Hercules, the one the genius, and the other the arm of the husbandman.

"Are those gods who have performed so many wonders; those gods who inspired Numa, Fabricius and Cato; those gods who protect the illustrious ashes of our citizens; those gods in whose immortal assemblage our emperors shine in deified splendor, divinities without virtue, and without power?

"At this moment, Diocletian, methinks I behold the genius of Rome, venerable in years, appearing in the midst of this Capitol, and thus addressing you:

"'Great prince, have regard to the old age which the gods have granted me in consideration of my piety. Free as I am to change, yet will I ever hold fast by the religion of my ancestors. This religion has subjected the universe to my laws. Her sacrifices have driven Hannibal from my walls and the Gauls from the Capitol. What! shall men one day overthrow this statue of Victory, without fearing to call up my buried legions from the plains of Zama! Have I been preserved from the most formidable enemies, only to behold myself dishonored by my children in my old age?'

"It is thus, O mighty emperor! that suppliant Rome addresses you. Behold those republicans, the conquerors of the Volsci and the Samnites, whose images we here revere, arise from their tombs on the Appian Way: they point to this Capitol, which they have filled with the spoils of victory; they come, crowned with oaken branches, to unite their voice to the voice their country. It is not the depravity of our manners or our laws, that bids them burst the iron slumbers of the tomb; it is not the uproar of the proscriptions of Marius, or the tumult of the triumvirate, that has aroused them from their repose; the cause of heaven has summoned them from the grave, and they come to plead its cause in the presence of their children. Romans, seduced by this new religion, how could you exchange our solemn festivities and our graceful rites for a stranger worship?

"Princes, I repeat it, we do not demand the persecution of the Christians. They say, that the God whom they adore is a God of peace and of justice: we do not refuse to admit him into the Pantheon; for, O most pious emperor! we would fain merit the protection of the gods of every religion: but let them not insult the majesty of Jupiter! Diocletian, Galerius, and you, illustrious senators, my voice is for indulgence to the Christians, and protection to the gods of my country!"

As he finished these words, Symmachus again saluted the statue of Victory, and then seated himself in the midst of the senators. The minds of the audience were variously affected: some were charmed with the dignity of this discourse, which reminded them of the days of Hortensius and Cicero; others blamed the moderation of the high priest of Jupiter. Satan's only hope was now in Hierocles, and he sought to destroy the effect of the high priest's eloquence; the angels of light profited by it, on the contrary, to bring back the senate to more humane sentiments. The plumes of the warriors, the togas of the senators, and the robes and sceptres of the augurs and haruspices were all in commotion: a confused murmur spread through the assembly, the equivocal expression of censure or of praise. When the zephyrs breathe over a field of corn interspersed with useless flowers, at first the slender stalks alone are agitated, but, as the breeze increases, both the grain and the flowers wave together in mingled commotion; such was the appearance of the different parties of the senate as they were agitated by various opinions.

The courtiers watched Diocletian and Galerius with curiosity, in order to regulate their sentiments by those of their masters: Cæsar showed tokens of excitement, but the countenance of Augustus remained impassible.

Hierocles arose; he enveloped himself in his robe, and remained for some time silent, with an air of thoughtfulness and severity. Initiated in all the artifices of Athenian eloquence; armed with every species of sophism; pliant, cunning, full of raillery and hypocrisy; affecting a concise and sententious style; with humanity on his lips, but thirsting in secret for the blood of the innocent; despising the lessons of time and of experience; pretending through a thousand ills to conduct mankind to happiness by new systems; a mind that belied itself while applauding its own justice: such was the orator who appeared in the lists to attack all religion, but particularly that of the Christians. Galerius had given free license to the blasphemies of his minister; Satan urged on this enemy of the faithful to evil, and the hope of destroying Eudorus animated the lover of Cymodoce to fresh ardor. The demon of false wisdom, under the figure of a chief of the school, who had just arrived from Alexandria, took his station near Hierocles: the latter, after a few moments' silence, suddenly unfolded his arms, threw his mantle behind him, and placing both his hands upon his breast, bent to the very pavement before Augustus and Cæsar, and pronounced the following discourse:

"Valerius Diocletian, son of Jupiter, eternal emperor, most clement, divine, and sage Augustus, who hast eight times been honored with the consular dignity; Valerius Maximianus Galerius, son of Hercules, adopted of the emperor, eternal and thrice happy Cæsar, the conqueror of the Parthi, the lover of science, and the votary of true philosophy; most venerable and sacred senate, do you then permit me to raise my voice in your presence! Overcome by so distinguished an honor, how shall I find words to express my feelings with sufficient force and elegance? Pardon the feebleness of my eloquence, in consideration of the truth whose cause I defend.

"The earth, in its primitive fecundity, brought forth men. Men, through chance and necessity, assembled in communities for their common convenience. Then began the system of property; acts of violence followed; man was unable to repress them; he invented gods.

"Religion invented, tyrants profited thereby. Interest multiplied errors; the passions intermingled their dreams.

"Man, forgetting the origin of the gods, soon believed in their existence. The common consent of the passions was mistaken for the common consent of mankind. Tyrants, while crushing mankind, took care to erect temples to mercy and to piety, that the unfortunate might also believe that there were gods.

"The priest, at first the deceiver, became the deceived, and grew enamored of his favorite idol; the youth adored the deified charms of his mistress; the wretched worshiped the images of his grief: hence sprung Fanaticism, that most terrible of all the evils that ever afflicted the human race.

"This monster, waving a torch, traversed the three regions of the earth. By the hands of the magi, he set fire to the temples of Memphis and Athens. He kindled the sacred war that subjected Greece to the dominion of Philip. Even in our days, despite the progress of intelligence, we shall shortly behold the universe plunged into an abyss of miseries, by the increase of an impious sect!

"And here, princes, I shall endeavor to depict the fearful evils that fanaticism has brought upon mankind, by unveiling to you the origin and progress of the most horrible and most ridiculous system of religion that the corruption of the human heart has ever engendered.

"O that I were permitted to bury such shameful turpitude in profound oblivion! But I am summoned to the defence of truth: I must save my emperor; I must enlighten the world. I am well aware, that in so doing I expose my life to the resentment of a dangerous faction. But what then? A friend of wisdom should steel his heart against all fear, as well as against all pity, when the happiness of his brethren and the sacred rights of humanity are in question.

"You are not unacquainted with that people, whom its

leprosy and its deserts separated from the rest of men; that odious race which was exterminated by the divine Titus.

"A certain impostor, named Moses, by a succession of crimes and pretended miracles, delivered this people from servitude. He conducted them through the midst of the deserts of Arabia, and promised them, in the name of the God Jehovah, a land that flowed with milk and honey.

"After forty years, the Jews arrived at this land of promise, whose inhabitants they cruelly butchered. This delicious garden was the barren Judæa, an insignificant valley filled with stones, without corn, without trees, without water.

"Secluded within their den, these brigands distinguished themselves by naught but their hatred of the human race: they lived in the midst of adulteries, cruelties, and murders. What could a race like this produce? Here is the prodigy; it was the execrable parent of a race still more execrable—the Christians, who, in their follies and their crimes, have surpassed the Jews, their fathers.

"Deceived by their fanatical priests, the Hebrews, in their impotency and wretchedness, expected a monarch, who was to subject the whole world to their dominion.

"A report was one day spread, that the wife of a wretched mechanic had given birth to this long-promised monarch. A party of the Jews were easily led into a belief of the prodigy.

"The man whom they call their Christ, lived thirty years miserable and unknown. After this period he began to dogmatize, and associated himself with certain fishermen, whom he called his apostles. He wandered from city to city, concealed himself in the desert, and seduced weak women and a credulous populace. His morality, they say, was pure; but did it surpass that of Socrates?

"Shortly after he was arrested for his seditious discourses, and condemned to die upon a cross. A gardener stole away his body; his apostles exclaimed that Jesus had arisen from the dead, and preached their master to the astonished crowd. Superstition spread, and the Christians became a numerous sect.

"A religion that had its origin among the dregs of the populace; that was propagated by slaves, and concealed at first amidst the obscurity of the desert, has by degrees been polluted by every abomination that secrecy, in conjunction with manners the most vile and ferocious, must naturally engender: hence we find, that cruelty and infamy are the principal ingredients in its mysteries.

"Beneath the friendly veil of night the Christians assemble in the midst of graves and sepulchres. The resurrection of dead bodies forms at once the most absurd, and the most innocent part of their conversation. Seated at an abominable feast, after swearing an eternal enmity to gods and men, and renouncing every legitimate pleasure, they drink the blood of a man that has just been sacrificed, and devour the palpitating flesh of a murdered infant: this they call their sacred bread and wine!

"The repast finished, a number of dogs, skilled in the crimes of their masters, are let into the assembly, who overturn and extinguish the torches: then follows a scene too horrible to meet the ear of modesty; suffice it to say, that the more varied the lewdness, and the more numerous the incests, the greater degree of merit do the Christians attach to these abominations.

"What! was it not sufficient to seduce men to the worship of a seditious wretch, who suffered justly by the vilest of punishments? was it not sufficient thus shamefully to attempt to brutalize human reason? must the Christians also make their religion the school of the most depraved manners, and the most unheard-of abominations!

"Is any other proof of what I have advanced needed, than the general conduct of the Christians? Wherever they insinuate themselves they are sure to disturb the repose of society; they entice our soldiers from their allegiance; they carry disunion into families; they seduce credulous virgins; they set the brother at variance against the brother, and the husband against his spouse. Powerful at present, they have temples and riches, yet they refuse to take an oath to the emperors from whom they hold these blessings; they treat the sacred images of Diocletian with insult, and would rather die than sacrifice at his altars. Lastly, have they not left the divine mother of Galerius to offer alone victims for her son to the innocent genii of the mountains? In fine, joining fanaticism with rebellion, they would gladly hurl the statue of Victory from the Capitol, and tear from their sanctuaries your paternal gods!

"Let it not be supposed that I am now defending those gods, who might, in the infancy of society, have appeared necessary to discerning legislators. We no longer feel the necessity of such resources : reason has commenced her reign ; henceforth altars shall be erected to virtue alone. The human species is making daily advances toward perfection : the time will come, when all men shall submit to the dominion of reason, and guide themselves by her light alone. I am no advocate either for Jupiter, Mitra, or Serapis : but if a system of religion is still to be maintained in the empire, the ancient one claims a just preference. This new worship is an evil which must be extirpated with fire and sword : the Christians must be cured of their folly. A little blood forsooth must flow! Doubtless we shall be moved by the fate of the criminals ; but we shall admire, we shall bless the law that strikes the victim for the consolation of the wise and the happiness of society."

Hierocles had scarcely finished his discourse, when Galerius gave the signal for applause. With a flashing eye, and a countenance red with fury, Cæsar seemed ready to pronounce the sentence fatal to the Christians. His courtiers raised their hands to heaven, as if seized with dread and horror ; his guards trembled with rage at the thought that these impious wretches wished to overturn the altar of Victory ; the people repeated to each other with affright, with horror, these nocturnal incests, and this repast of human flesh. The Sophists, who surrounded Hierocles, extolled him to the skies : they called him the intrepid friend of the princes, the true lover of principles, the supporter of virtue, a second Socrates!

Satan animated these prejudices and hatreds: delighted with the words of the proconsul, he flattered himself that he should reach his end more surely by atheism than by idolatry; seconded by all the powers of hell, he increased the noise and tumult, and gave a prodigious impulse to the excitement of the senate. As the top whirls under the whip of the child, as the distaff rises and falls in the fingers of the matron, as the ebony or the ivory revolves beneath the chisel of the turner, thus were the minds of the assembly agitated. Diocletian alone appeared unmoved; his countenance expressed neither anger, hatred, nor love. The Christians, who were intermingled in the assembly, appeared full of dejection and alarm. Constantine in particular was overwhelmed with the deepest grief; from time to time he threw on Eudorus a look of mingled anxiety and tenderness.

The son of Lasthenes arose, seemingly unaffected by the disfavor of Cæsar, the baseness of the courtiers, or the clamors of the crowd. His mourning attire, and his noble countenance, whose effect was heightened by an expression of sadness, drew the attention of the whole assembly. The angels of the Lord, forming an invisible circle about him, covered him with light, and gave him a divine assurance. From the height of heaven, the four evangelists, leaning over his head, secretly dictated to him the expressions he was to utter. "Is this the Christian? What reply can he make?" was whispered through every part of the senate. In vain did each one strive to discover in those features, at once so calm and so animated, an expression of the crimes of which Hierocles had accused the faithful. Thus, when the hunters, imagining that they have surprised a vulture on the banks of a river, suddenly discover a swan sporting gracefully on the stream, they stop to contemplate the favored bird of the Muses, and admire the whiteness of his plumage, the nobleness of his port, and the gracefulness of his motions, and lend their ear to his harmonious songs. The swan of the Alpheus delayed not to make himself heard: Eudorus bent in reverence before Augustus and Cæsar; then, without saluting the statue of Victory, without any extravagance of gesture, without seeking to seduce either the ear or the eye, spoke as follows:

"Augustus, Cæsar, Conscript fathers, Roman people, I, Eudorus, the son of Lasthenes, a native of Megalopolis in Arcadia, and a Christian, salute you in the name of those men who are the victims of an unjust hatred.

"Hierocles began his discourse by apologizing for the feebleness of his eloquence; I, too, must claim the same indulgence from the senate. I am nothing but a soldier, more accustomed to shed my blood in the service of my prince, than to demand in flowery language the massacre of a crowd of old men, women and children.

"I must, in the first place, return my thanks to Symmachus for the moderation that he has shown toward my brethren. The respect that I owe to the chief of the empire, obliges me to be silent respecting the worship of idols. I shall only observe, that Camillus, Scipio, and Paulus Æmilius, were not accounted great, because they adhered to the worship of Jupiter; but because they departed from the morality and the examples of the divinities of Olympus. In our religion, on the contrary, the more nearly we imitate our God, the greater progress do we make toward perfection. We also place obscure mortals in the eternal abodes; but it does not suffice to acquire this glory, to have worn the royal diadem—it is necessary to have practised virtue: to your heaven, we abandon such men as Nero and Domitian.

"How salutary is the influence of religion upon the soul, of whatever description that religion may be! The high priest of Jupiter has spoken of the Christians with mildness, while a man who acknowledges no God, demands our blood in the name of humanity and virtue. What! Hierocles, is it under the robe of a philosopher that you carry the seeds of desolation which you wish to sow throughout the empire? Roman magistrate, do you call down destruction upon several millions of Roman citizens? For you cannot but be aware, Conscript fathers, that the Christians, though but of yesterday, already fill your cities, your colonies, your camps, the palace, the senate, and the Forum: that we leave no place unfrequented but the temples of your gods.

"Princes, our accuser is an apostate, and confesses himself an atheist: he best knows what other title I could add to these. Symmachus is a man of piety, whose age, knowledge, and manners, are equally worthy of respect. In every criminal cause, the characters of the witnesses are taken into consideration: Symmachus excuses us; Hierocles denounces us: which of the two is most worthy of attention? Augustus, Cæsar, Conscript fathers, and Roman people, deign to lend me an attentive ear: I wish to examine each accusation that Hierocles has brought against us, and to defend the religion of Jesus Christ."

At this sacred name, the orator paused; all the Christians bowed with reverence, and the statue of Jupiter trembled on its pedestal. Eudorus resumed his discourse:

"I shall not, like Hierocles, go back to the cradle of the world, in order to come to the question of the moment. I willingly leave to the disciples of his school that vain display of odious principles, of perverted facts, and of puerile declamation. The question now before the senate, neither regards the formation of the world, nor the origin of society: its sole object is to ascertain whether the existence of the Christians is compatible with the safety of the state; whether their religion is offensive to morals or laws; whether it militates in any respect against that submission which is due to the chief of the empire: in a word, whether morality and sound policy find anything to reprehend in the religion of Jesus Christ. Though not immediately to the purpose, I cannot pass, without some notice, the singular opinions of Hierocles respecting the Hebrews.

"The political motives for the establishment of Jerusalem in the centre of a barren region, lay too deep to be discovered by the accuser of the Christians. The legislator of the Israelites wished to form of them a people that could resist the effects of time, and preserve the worship of the true God amidst the universal spread of error and idolatry, and find in their institutions a power which they had not in themselves: he therefore inclosed them among the mountains. Their laws and their religion were adapted to this state of isolation: they had but one temple, one book, and one sacrifice. Four thousand years have rolled away, yet this people still exists the same. Let Hierocles point out elsewhere an example of legislation as miraculous in its effects, and we will then listen to his railleries upon the country of the Hebrews."

A sign of approbation here escaped from Diocletian, which interrupted the son of Lasthenes. Insensible to the oratory of Symmachus, and the declamations of Hierocles, the emperor was struck by this political reasoning presented by the defender of the faithful. Eudorus had touched upon this subject with address, that he might hit the genius of the prince, and conciliate his favor before he spoke of the Christians. The moderate part of the senate, who feared Galerius; Publius, the prefect of Rome, who was devoted to Cæsar, yet an enemy to Hierocles; the courtiers, always attentive to the motions of their master; the Christians, whose fate hung in doubtful suspense, all perceived the favorable sentiments of Diocletian, and loudly applauded the orator. The soldiers, the centurions, and the tribunes, could not suppress their feelings, when they beheld their former general forced to the necessity of defending his life against the accusations of a sophist: this noble race of men are readily affected with generous sentiments. Such powers of reasoning, united to youth and elegance of person, raised no inconsiderable interest among the crowd, whose minds are easily prepossessed. The grief of Constantine was changed into joy, and he encouraged his friend both by his looks and gestures. The angels of heaven, redoubling their zeal about the Christian orator, gave him new grace at each moment, and prolonged the sounds of his voice like harmonious echoes. As when the snow descends in whitening showers from the ethereal vault, the wind are hushed, and the silent fields receive with joy the numerous flakes that protect the tender plants from the rigors of winter: thus, when the son of Lasthenes resumed his discourse, the assembly remained in profound silence, to catch those pure words, which seemed to descend from heaven to prevent the desolation of the earth.

"Princes," said he, "I shall not enter upon the proofs of the Christian religion: a long series of prophecies that have all been verified, of splendid miracles, and of innumerable witnesses, have long since attested the divinity of him whom we term the Saviour. His sublime virtues have been acknowledged throughout the universe; many Roman emperors, though they embraced not the worship of Jesus Christ, have honored him with their homage; famous philosophers have rendered justice to the beauty of his morality, and Hierocles himself has not presumed to contest it.

"It would be more than strange if those who adored a God like this were monsters worthy of the stake. What! is Jesus Christ the model of gentleness, humanity, and purity, and do we think to honor him by mysteries of cruelty and debauchery? In paganism itself do you celebrate the festivals of Diana, by the prostitutions of the festivals of Venus? 'But Christianity,' say they, 'had its origin amongst the lowest class of the people, and hence arises the infamy attached to it.' Thus is our religion reproached for what constitutes her glory and her excellence. She delights to seek out and console those wretched beings whom the more favored of their fellow-men endeavor to avoid and forget; and this you impute to her as a crime! Think you that there are no miseries but those attached to the purple, and that a God of consolation is made only for the great and for kings? Far from being corrupted by the base and brutalized manners of the people, our religion has corrected these manners. Tell me, is there a man more patient under afflictions than the true Christian; more submissive to his superiors, more faithful to his promise; more punctual in the discharge of his duty, or more chaste in all his actions? So far are we removed from barbarity, that we absent ourselves from your public games, in which the blood of our fellow-creatures forms a part of the spectacle. We believe that there is little difference between committing murder and seeing it committed with pleasure. In such horror do we hold a dissolute life, that we avoid your theatres as a school of corrupt morals, and as an occasion of ruin. . . . But in justifying the Christians on this point, I see that I expose them in another. We fly from society, says Hierocles; we hate mankind!

"If such be the case, our punishment is just. Strike off our heads, but first come to take back from our hospitals the poor and infirm whom you have not succored ; call in those Roman women who have abandoned the fruits of their shame. They perhaps believe that their wretched offspring have fallen into those abodes of infamy, which are the only asylum that your gods offer to abandoned infancy. Let them come, and recognize their newborn in the arms of our spouses ! The milk of a Christian mother has not poisoned them ; the mothers according to grace, shall, ere they die, restore them to the mothers according to nature.

"Some of our mysteries, badly understood, and falsely interpreted, have given birth to these calumnies. Princes, were I but permitted to reveal to your eyes these mysteries of innocence and of purity ! Symmachus has represented the genius of Rome as rising to entreat that you would leave her the divinities of her fathers. Yes, princes, the genius of Rome rises, but not to reclaim these impotent gods ; she rises to claim Jesus Christ, who will establish among her children, purity, justice, moderation, innocency of manners, and the reign of every virtue.

"'Give me,' she exclaims, 'this God, who has already corrected the errors of my laws ; this God who will not sanction infanticide, the pollution of the nuptial couch, and the spectacles of human bloodshed ; this God, who covers my bosom with monuments of his beneficence ; this God, who preserves with such care the knowledge of literature and the arts, and who wishes to abolish slavery from the earth. Ah ! if on some future day it should be again my lot to behold the barbarians at my gates, I foresee that this God alone will be able to save me, and bid my languishing old age flourish in immortal youth.'

"It only now remains to repel the last and the most fearful of the accusations of Hierocles, if the loss of his life and his possessions had any terrors to the Christian. We are seditious, says our accuser: we refuse to adore the images of the emperor, and to offer sacrifices to the gods for the father of his country!

"The Christians seditious! Urged by their persecutors to every extremity, and hunted like wild beasts, they have never been heard to utter the slightest murmur; nine times have they been massacred; but humbling themselves under the hand of God, they have left the universe to rise against their tyrants. Let Hierocles but mention one single Christian who has been engaged in a conspiracy against his prince! Ye Christian soldiers, whom I behold amidst this assembly, Sebastian, Pacomius, Victor, tell me where you received your honorable scars with which you are covered? Was it in some popular tumult, or in traitorously besieging the palaces of your emperors? or rather in confronting, for the glory of your princes, the arrow of the Parthian, the sword of the German, and the battleaxe of the Frank. Alas, my noble companions, brethren and friends, I am not concerned for my own lot, though I have at this moment some ties that attach me strongly to life, but it is for your destiny that I feel more intimately concerned! Why have you not chosen a more eloquent defender! I had once the good fortune to merit a civic crown by saving you from the hands of barbarians; shall I now be unable to shield you from the sword of a Roman proconsul!

"To conclude: Diocletian, you will find the Christians respectful subjects, who will always be submissive to you without baseness, because the principle of their obedience is derived from heaven. They are men of truth; their language does not differ from their conduct; they do not receive benefits from a master while cursing him in their hearts. Demand of such men their fortunes, their lives, their children, and they will comply without a murmur, since these belong to you. But endeavor to force them to offer incense to your idols; they will sooner die than yield to the command! Pardon, ye princes, this Christian liberty; man has duties toward heaven which he must also fulfil. If you demand marks of submission incompatible with these sacred duties, Hierocles may call in his executioners: we will render to Cæsar our blood, which is Cæsar's, but to God our soul, which is God's."

Eudorus resumed his seat, and throwing over his shoulder the mantle that had half fallen off, hastened to cover with a modest blush the scars on his bosom.

It were vain to attempt describing the diversity of sentiments that the discourse of Lasthenes excited through the assembly. It was a mixture of admiration, of fear, and of fury: every one burst into expressions of favor or detestation. These admired the beauty of the accused religion; those saw nothing but a reproach upon their manners and their gods. The warriors were moved and deeply interested in favor of Eudorus.

"Of what avail is it," cried they, "to shed our blood for our country, to suffer slavery amidst barbarians, and to triumph over the enemies of our prince, if a sophist be allowed to plot our destruction in the Capitol?"

For the first time in his life Diocletian appeared moved: even in permitting the persecution of the faithful, God availed himself of this Christian eloquence to scatter the first seeds of faith in the Roman senate. The masculine simplicity that marked the eloquence of Eudorus, triumphed at once over the calumnies of Hierocles, and the powerful recollections which Symmachus had associated with the statue of Victory; everything seemed to announce that the emperor was about to pass a sentence favorable to the Christians.

Hierocles sought to conceal his agitation by assuming the appearance of calmness and superiority; but in spite of his efforts, rage and terror were conspicuous on his countenance: thus when a tiger has fallen into the pit which the shepherd of Libya had prepared to ensnare him, at first the ferocious animal beats himself against the sides of his prison, till at length, fatigued, he couches with apparent tranquillity in the midst of the fatal enclosure; but his wildly glaring eyes, and his jaws that foam with gore, manifest the fear and indignation that he feels.

Galerius soon revived the hopes of his minister. This haughty Cæsar, accustomed only to the base flattery of his courtiers, was indignant at the unvarnished language of virtue, and the noble assurance of an honest man. He declared that if the Christians were not punished he would quit the court, and put himself at the head of the legions of the East.

"For these enemies of the gods," cried he, "are preparing to lay sacrilegious hands upon me."

Hierocles, assuming his wonted audacity, observed, that there were other mysteries of which he had omitted to speak; that after all, these rebels to the state had refused to sacrifice to the emperor, and had endeavored to seduce the soldiery by their seditious harangues.

Accustomed to yield to the violence of Galerius, Diocletian was terrified by these menaces. He knew that in proscribing the Christians he deprived himself of his most powerful support against the ambition of Cæsar; but the aged emperor had not sufficient resolution to encounter the hazard of a civil war. Satan succeeded in terrifying, by a prodigy, the superstitious mind of Diocletian. At this moment the shield of Romulus, which was attached to the roof of the Capitol, gave way, and in its fall wounded the son of Lasthenes, and rolling forward, covered the brazen wolf, which was struck by a thunderbolt at the death of Julius Cæsar. Galerius instantly exclaimed:

"You see, O Diocletian, that the father of the Romans is unable to endure the blasphemies of this Christian! Imitate his example; crush the impious, and protect within this Capitol the genius of the empire."

Then it was, that, in spite of an accusing conscience, and his enlightened policy, Diocletian consented to pass an edict against the faithful: but as a last resource against the conviction of his bosom, he wished that the gods should pronounce in their own cause, and bear, in conjunction with Galerius and himself, that weight of condemnation with which posterity would load them.

"If the sibyl of Cumæ," said he, "approve the resolution which you compel me to take, the edict which you demand shall be published. But, while waiting the response of the oracle, it is my will that all the citizens should be left in the enjoyment of their rights and the liberty of their worship."

As he pronounced these words, the emperor hastily quitted the Capitol. Galerius and Hierocles came forth elated with triumph; the one meditating projects of unbounded ambition, the other mingling with his projects schemes of love and vengeance. Constantine, overcome with grief, withdrew in company with Eudorus from the curiosity of the multitude. Hell uttered a cry of joy, and the angels of the Lord, in holy sadness, winged their flight to the feet of the Eternal.

BOOK SEVENTEENTH.

SUMMARY.

Voyage of Cymodoce. She arrives at Joppa. She ascends to Jerusalem. Helena receives her as her Daughter. Holy Week. Response of the Sibyl of Cumæ. Hierocles dispatches a Centurion to reclaim Cymodoce. Diocletian issues the Edict of Persecution.

BORNE away by the breath of the angel of the seas, Cymodoce shed a torrent of tears. Eurymedusa, who accompanied the daughter of Demodocus, filled the ship with her complaints and lamentations.

"O land of Cecrops," she cried, "land favored by the gods and cherished by the Muses, must I bid thee an eternal adieu? Who will give me wings that I may revisit those places that transport my soul with delight? I would direct my flight to the temple of Homer, and bear tidings of Cymodoce to my beloved master. How vain is the wish! We are crossing the azure plains of Amphitrite, where the Nereids pour forth their songs. Is it a thirst after riches that compels us to brave the fury of Neptune? No; riches have charms; but it is a god far more powerful, the god who made Ariadne perish on a desolate shore, far from her paternal habitation, the god who forced Medea to visit the towers of Iolcus and to pursue the footsteps of a flying hero."

The vessel approached the last promontory of Attica. Already Sunium displayed its beautiful temple on the summit of a rock: the pillars of white marble seemed to dance on the surface of the deep, intermingled with the golden light of the stars. Cymodoce was seated at the stern, which was decorated with flowers, between the ivory statues of Castor and Pollux. Had not her eyes been suffused with tears, she might have been taken for the sister of these lovely gods, just ready to disembark with Paris for the island where the daughter of Tyndareus celebrated her nuptials before her departure for Troy. The vessel sped to the left of the white Cyclades, stretching in the distance along the sea like a flock of swans: directing its course southward, it touched at the island of Cyprus. The inhabitants were celebrating the festival of the Amathusian goddess. Soft and silent waves bathed the temple of Dione, built on a promontory in the midst of an ocean that is ever in repose. A choir of young maidens, in light attire, led the mazy dance in a grove of myrtles that encircled this voluptuous edifice ; a band of youths sung in chorus the chants of the eve of the festivities of Venus. The words were wafted to the vessel on the wings of the breathing zephyrs.

" Let him love to-morrow who has never loved ! Let him who has loved, love to-morrow the more !

" O Venus! soul of the universe ! beloved both by gods and men ; from thee all nature derives its existence ! At thy appearance, the winds are hushed, the clouds are dispersed, the spring returns to clothe the earth with flowers, and Ocean smiles. It is Venus who places on the bosom of the maiden the rose dyed in the blood of Adonis ; it is Venus who forces the nymphs to wander with Love, at night, under the eyes of the blushing Diana. O Nymphs, fear Love : he has laid down his weapons, but he is armed without them. The son of Cytheræa was born in the fields, he was nurtured among the flowers. Philomela has sung his power ; let us not yield to Philomela.

" Let him love to-morrow who has never loved ! Let him who has loved, love to-morrow the more !

" O happy isle, everything on thy delicious shores attests the prodigies of Love. Mariners, wearied with perils, cast anchor in our ports, and furl forever your sails. In the groves of Amathusia, you shall engage only in gentle combats ; you shall fear no more pirates, except artful Love, who is preparing for you chains of flowers. Here the Graces weave the thread of mortal existence. Venus once charmed into slumber the Fates in the abodes of Tartarus : immediately Aglaia took away the spindle from Lachesis, and Euphrosyne the thread from Clotho; but Atropos awoke at the moment that Pasithea was about to steal away the fatal shears. Everything yields to the power of Venus and the Graces!

"Let him love to-morrow who has never loved! Let him who has loved, now love the more."

The sailors felt the powerful influence of these seductive strains. Divided by the brazen prow, the waves broke in gentle murmurs on either side; and the canvas was swelled by the breeze that came laden with the perfume of the orange groves, mingled with the incense of the sacrifice.

A dangerous languor overspread the mind of Cymodoce. Docile to the projects of Satan, Astarte, that impure spirit who triumphs in the temples of Amathusia, was secretly attacking the daughter of Homer. Moved by the corrupting strains, she descended to the cabin of the vessel; she dreamed of her spouse; she knew not how to regulate the emotions of her love so as not to offend her new religion. Dorotheus, to whom she unfolded the secret of her heart, exhorted her to have recourse to heaven; and on his knees, joined with her in supplication to the Omnipotent. Immediately the winds increased, and the waves dashed against the sides of the vessel; these are the only sounds that accompany the prayer of love—that turbulent passion which the mariner cherishes in the solitude of ocean, with as much ardor as the shepherd who tends his flocks in the depth of the forest.

Cymodoce and Dorotheus were still troubled by the memories of Amathusia, when the summit of Mount Carmel burst upon their view. By degrees the plain of Palestine emerged from the waves, and stretched its shadowy outline along the shore of the deep: above this plain arose the mountains of Judæa: the vessel cast anchor during the silent hour of midnight at the port of Joppa: more sacred than the vessel of Hiram laden with cedar for the temple, it bore the living temple of Jesus Christ, and innocence more precious than the spicy grove. The Christian voyagers quitted their vessel, reached the shore, and falling prostrate, kissed with transport the land which saw their salvation completed. Dorotheus and the young catechumen joined a company of pilgrims who were to set out at break of day for Jerusalem.

Scarcely had the first dawn whitened the horizon, when the voice of the Arab guide announced the time of departure. Immediately the pilgrims put themselves in readiness; the dromedaries bent their knees to receive their burdens, and the robust asses and fleet mares were prepared which were destined to convey the travellers. Cymodoce, whose beauty drew the eyes of every one upon her, was seated with her nurse on a camel adorned with rich trappings: not with such modesty did Rebecca appear, when she veiled her face before the presence of Isaac; Rachel seemed less beautiful to the eyes of Jacob when she quitted the roof of her fathers, carrying away with her her household gods. Dorotheus and his attendants walked at the side of the daughter of Demodocus, and guided the steps of the camel.

They quitted the walls of Joppa, which lies embosomed in a grove of lentisk and pomegranates, which with their ripened fruits resembled rose-trees in full bloom; and passed along the valley of Sharon, which, like Carmel and Lebanon, is styled in holy Scripture the image of beauty: it was checkered with those flowers which Solomon in all his glory could not equal in splendor. Ere long they penetrated into the mountains of Judæa, through the village which gave birth to the happy criminal to whom Jesus Christ promised heaven on the cross. The pious travellers saluted you, too, ye cradle of Jeremiah, still breathing the melancholy of the prophet of sorrows. They passed the torrent from whose rocky bed the shepherd of Bethlehem gathered the stones with which he slew the Philistine; and crossed a barren waste where nothing was seen but a few wild fig-trees, which were thinly scattered, and which waved their scorched foliage to the burning wind of the south: here the natural verdure of the country began to fail; the sides of the mountains expanded and assumed at once an air of greater grandeur and sterility: by degrees all vegetation faded and died; the very mosses disappeared; a red and vivid tinge succeeded to the paler hue of the rocks. Ascending the summit of a lofty mountain, the pilgrims descried an ancient wall, surmounted by the roofs of some new edifices. The guide exclaimed: "Jerusalem!" and all the travellers stopping, as if by an involuntary impulse, repeated: "Jerusalem! Jerusalem!"

The Christians immediately sprang from their mares and camels. Some fell prostrate on the ground; others sobbed aloud and struck their breasts; some apostrophized the holy city in the most pathetic language; while others gazed with dumb amazement on the desolate Jerusalem. A thousand thoughts burst at once on the mind—thoughts which embraced nothing less than the duration of the world! O Muse of Sion, thou alone canst paint this desert which breathes the divinity of Jehovah, and the grandeur of the prophets!

Between the vale of Jordan and the plains of Idumæa, arose a vast chain of mountains, which stretched from the fertile fields of Galilee to the sands of Yemen. In the midst of these mountains lay a barren vale, enclosed on all sides by yellow, rocky peaks; these peaks opened only to the east, and disclosed the gulf of the Dead Sea and the distant mountains of Arabia. Situated upon a rugged declivity in the centre of this stony wilderness, enclosed by a shattered wall, that still bears the marks of the battering ram, and fortified by falling turrets, appears a vast pile of ruins: some scattered cypress-trees, bushes of aloes and nopals, with some Arabian cabins which resembled whitened sepulchres, overspread these heaps of ruins: —such was the sorrowful Jerusalem.

At the first aspect of this scene of desolation, a feeling of profound weariness overspread the mind. But when, passing from solitude to solitude, the plain seemed still to lengthen in boundless expanse, the traveller felt a secret awe, which far from depressing the soul, elevated its powers, and inspired it with fresh vigor. Extraordinary spectacles continually presented themselves in this land, which had teemed with so many miracles: the burning sun, the impetuous eagle, the humble hyssop, the towering cedar, the barren fig-tree; all the poetry, all the pictures of Scripture were here: every name conveyed a mystery; every cave proclaimed the future; every hill re-echoed the accents of a prophet. God himself had spoken in these regions: the dried-up torrent, the riven rock, and the yawning tomb, attested the prodigy; the desert appeared still mute with terror, as though the voice of the Eternal had awed it into everlasting silence.

The pious Helena had bent her steps to this holy land. She wished to rescue the tomb of Jesus Christ from the profanations of idolatry; she wished to enclose in majestic edifices so many places that were consecrated by words and the sufferings of the Son of God. She assembled Christians from all quarters of the globe to her assistance; they flocked to the shores of Syria: with naked feet, and eyes bathed in tears, they came, singing songs of praise, toward the mountain where man's redemption was completed. To this holy sanctuary Dorotheus conducted the young catechumen, whom he was about to place under the care of the mother of Constantine.

The caravan entered by the gate of the castle, where the tower of the Pisans was afterwards erected, and where subsequently stood the hospice of the brave Knights of the Temple. The rumor was immediately spread that the first prefect of the emperor's household had arrived in the city, accompanied by a young catechumen more beautiful than Mariamne, and seemingly as unfortunate. Helena sent for Dorotheus. She shuddered at the recital of the dangers that menaced the Church. She received the spouse of the defender of the Christians with the nobility of an empress, the affection of a mother, and the zeal of a saint.

"Esther," said she to Cymodoce, "with pleasure I discern in your features those of a young virgin whom I have often beheld in a dream, seated on the right hand of the divine Mary. You have never known a mother; I will be one to you. Thank God, my daughter, for having conducted you to the tomb of Jesus Christ. Here the highest truths of faith are rendered intelligible to the simplest heart, and brought to a level with the meanest capacity."

At these touching words, Cymodoce shed tears of affection and respect. As a young vine which the fury of the storm has torn from the elm which supported it, trails its tender branches on the ground, but no sooner reaches another tree, than it clings more eagerly to the friendly support, and again spreads its delicate foliage to the enlivening sunbeams: thus the daughter of Demodocus, torn from her father, attached herself with ardor to the mother of the friend of Eudorus.

Helena, meanwhile, dispatched messengers to the seven Churches of Asia, to give timely information of the impending persecution; and in the meantime pointed out to Dorotheus and the spouse of Eudorus the immense labors that would be requisite to restore the city of Solomon to its ancient splendor. The grove consecrated to Venus, on the summit of Mount Calvary, was already cut down, and the true cross had been found. A man, whom the presence of this miraculous cross had snatched from the coffin, unfolded the mysteries of a future state in that Jerusalem, so often instructed by the dead in the secrets of the tomb.

At the foot of Mount Sion, on whose brow stood the ruins of the monument of David, arose a hill forever memorable under the name of Calvary. At the foot of this sacred mount, Helena had inclosed the sepulchre of Jesus Christ in a circular basilica, constructed of marble and porphyry. Illuminated by a dome of cedar, placed in the centre of the church, and covered with a catafalque of white marble, the holy tomb is used for an altar on great solemnities. A gloom favorable to meditation reigns in this sanctuary, along its galleries and its chapels. Sacred songs were there heard at all hours of the day and night. None knew whence they proceeded: they inhaled the fragrance of incense, without perceiving the hand by which it was burned; they could discern nothing but the pontiff, pacing with solemn step through the gloomy aisles of the temple, or preparing to celebrate the dread mysteries, in the very place where they were accomplished.

Cymodoce contemplated these Christian wonders in silent admiration. A daughter of Greece, she admired these masterpieces of art, created by the power of faith in the midst of deserts. The gates of the new edifice drew her particular attention. They were of brass, and turned on hinges of silver and gold. A solitary from the banks of Jordan, inspired with the spirit of prophecy, had given the design of these gates to two celebrated sculptors of Laodicea. The artist had represented thereon the holy city as fallen into the hands of infidels, and besieged by Christian heroes, who were distinguished by the cross that glittered on their garments. The dress and the armor of these warriors were foreign, but the Roman soldiers thought they discovered some resemblance to the Franks and Gauls in these heroes yet unborn. Upon their brow was imprinted daring, the spirit of enterprise and adventure, with a nobleness, frankness, and honor, unknown to Ajax or Achilles. Here the camp appeared moved at the sight of a seductive woman, who seemed to implore the assistance of a band of young princes; there the same enchantress bore aloft a hero on the clouds, and transported him into delightful gardens; in another part, an assembly of the spirits of darkness was summoned in the burning halls of hell; the hoarse blast of the trumpet of Tartarus convoked the inhabitants of the eternal shades; hell's deepest caverns were shaken, and the dismal sounds rolled in lengthened echoes from abyss to abyss. With what emotions of tenderness did Cymodoce behold a female expiring under the armor of a warrior! The Christian who had pierced her breast, while tears of anguish streamed from his eyes, filled his helmet with water, and hastened to give eternal life to that beauty whom he had deprived of a momentary existence. In fine, the holy city was seen attacked on all sides by the Christians, and the standard of the cross waved triumphantly over the walls of Jerusalem. Among so many wonders, the divine artist had not forgotten the poet who was to immortalize them in his songs: seated in the midst of the camp, he seemed to listen to the voice of religion, of honor, and of love, and transported with a noble enthusiasm, penned his heavenly lays on a buckler.

Time, ever fleeting, had ushered in the eve of that day

of sorrows, when Jesus Christ expired on the cross. Cymodoce, with a train of chosen virgins, accompanied Helena to the tomb of the Saviour. Night was in the midst of its course : a dead silence reigned in the Holy Sepulchre, though crowded with the faithful. A candlestick with seven branches burned before the altar ; some lamps with their pale rays half illuminated the rest of the edifice ; all the images of the martyrs and angels were veiled : the sacrifice was suspended, and the host deposited in the holy tomb. Helena placed herself in the midst of the crowd : she had laid aside her diadem, thinking it unbecoming to crown her head with diamonds, in the place where the Redeemer was crowned with thorns. The skill of Cymodoce in the art of song was already known to her companions ; and they invited the daughter of Homer to sigh forth the lamentations of Jeremiah. Helena encouraged her with a look. Cymodoce advanced to the foot of the altar : she was clothed in an azure robe, fastened by a silken girdle, and adorned with golden fringe, according to the manner of the Jewish virgins : her hair, her neck, and her arms were loaded with a variety of costly ornaments : such, in the eyes of the Israelites, appeared Michal, the spouse promised to David as a reward for his victory over the Philistines : she resembled the palm-tree of Syria, whose top is adorned with clustering fruits, as with crystals of coral. Cymodoce raised her harmonious voice, and chanted a part of the lamentations of Jeremiah :

" How solitary stands the city once filled with people ! How is the lustre of the gold obscured ! How have the stones of the sanctuary been dispersed ! The mistress of nations is a widow ; the queen of provinces is subject to a tribute. The ways of Sion mourn, her gates are destroyed ; her priests sigh, her virgins are desolate. O race of Judah, thou hast been treated like a vessel of clay ! Jerusalem, Jerusalem ; in a moment thou hast seen the pride of thy towers thrown down, and thine enemies have fixed their tents on the very spot where the just wept over thee, and foretold thy destruction !"

Thus sung Cymodoce, in a pathetic strain, transmitted to the Christians by the religion of the Hebrews. At intervals the brazen trumpets mingled their notes of woe with the lamentations of Jeremiah. What eloquence in these lessons delivered on the ruins of Jerusalem, near that temple, of which not one stone was left on another, and on the eve of persecution! The pensive voice of the young virgin, torn from the arms of her father, and trembling for the safety of her spouse, added a charm to these canticles. The prayers were prolonged till the break of day; when the solemn procession was arranged which was to advance through the "Via Dolorosa."

The true cross, borne by four bishops and martyrs, headed the procession. A numerous body of clergy, in two divisions, in profound silence, and clothed in habits of mourning, followed the sign of the redemption of mankind. Next came a train of virgins and widows; the catechumens who were to be received into the bosom of the Church; and penitents who were to be reconciled to it. The bishop of Jerusalem, with his head uncovered, and a cord round his neck in token of expiation, closed the parade. Helena walked behind him leaning on the spouse of the defender of the Christians: an innumerable body of the faithful, composed of orphans, the blind and the lame, accompanied, full of hope, that cross which cures the infirm and consoles the afflicted.

They advanced by the gates of Bethlehem, and turning to the east, along the pool of Bethsaida, proceeded to the wells of Nephi, in order to visit the pool of Siloam. At the sight of the valley of Jehosaphat, filled with tombs, of that valley where the trumpet of the Angel of Judgment shall assemble the dead, a secret awe took possession of the souls of the faithful. The religious procession passed the foot of Mount Moriah; and crossed the torrent of Cedron, which rolls a red and muddy stream: they left the sepulchres of Jehosaphat and of Absalom on the right, and entered the garden of Olives, where they all joined in prayers, on the very spot which the Son of Man bedewed with his sweat of blood.

At each station a priest explained to the people, the miracle the expression, or the action, which the sacred place had witnessed. The gate of Palms was opened, and the procession re-entered Jerusalem. Passing over some piles of ruins, they came to the palace of the Prætor, which stands near the enclosure of the temple: here begins the road to Calvary. The priest who addressed the multitude was unable to read the Gospel on account of the tears that dimmed his eyes; you could scarcely hear his voice, that thus spoke in broken accents:

"Here, my brethren, stood the prison where he was crowned with thorns! From this ruined portico Pilate showed him to the Jews, saying: 'Behold the man!'"

At these words, the Christians burst into sobs of grief. They advanced toward Calvary; and the priest resumed his pathetic description of the "Via Dolorosa."

"Here stood the residence of Dives; there Jesus Christ sunk under the weight of his cross; a little further on the Son of God said to the women, 'Weep not for me, but for yourselves and your children.'"

They had now gained the summit of Calvary: the sign of man's salvation was again planted on the place where it once had stood: immediately the sun was clothed with darkness, the earth trembled, the veil of the new temple was rent asunder. Immortal testimonies of the passion of the Saviour, you are again renewed around the true cross: they beheld descending from heaven, Mary, the mother of pity, the penitent Magdalen, Peter bewailing his sin, John who never abandoned his master, the dread spirit who presented the bitter cup to the Redeemer of the world, and the angel of death, still terrified at the blow which he had given the Son of the Eternal.

Far different was the day of triumph that succeeded this day of woe! The images of the saints were unveiled, the new fire was blessed before the altar, and the ancient Halleluia of Jacob echoed through the vaults of the Church.

"O sons and daughters of Sion, the King of Heaven, the Lord of Glory, is about to rise from the tomb! Who is that angel clothed in white, and seated at the entrance of the sepulchre? Hasten, ye apostles! Happy are they who have not seen, and have yet believed."

The people repeated in chorus this hymn of praise and thanksgiving.

But nothing could equal the happiness of the catechumens, who on this solemn day were enrolled in the number of the elect. All, clothed in white and crowned with garlands of flowers, received upon their foreheads the sacred water of regeneration, which was to restore them to primeval innocence. Cymodoce contemplated with envy the happiness of these new Christians; but the daughter of Homer was not yet sufficiently instructed in the truths of the faith. The happy moment of her baptism was, however, not far distant: she was to undergo but one more trial before she was to be received into the religion of her spouse.

Whilst, under the protection of Helena, Cymodoce believed herself secure from every danger, the centurion who pursued the flying dove, was already advancing toward Jerusalem. The haruspex who was to consult the sibyl of Cumae, had quitted Rome; he was accompanied by one of the partisans of Hierocles, secretly commissioned in the name of Galerius to win the oracle to his side: as soon as the prophetess should have pronounced the fatal decree, the minister of the proconsul was ordered to embark for Syria, to seize Cymodoce in the holy city, to reclaim this new Virginia at the tribunal of a second Appius, as a Christian slave who had escaped her master.

Pursuing his infernal purposes, the prince of darkness had fled from Rome to Cumæ, in order to induce the sibyl to utter a false oracle, and thus to effect the overthrow of the faithful. He joyfully discovered Lake Avernus, surrounded by a gloomy forest. Through an opening contiguous to this place, the demons often take their flight from the bosom of the shades: from the bottom of this pestiferous abyss, they take delight in spreading among the people a thousand obscure fables touching the vast abodes of night and silence. But these guilty angels betray, despite themselves, the secret of their sorrows: **for** they place on the road to their empire, Remorse, reclining upon an iron bed; Discord, with locks of adders, fastened with bloody bands; vain Dreams, suspended to the branches of an ancient elm; Labor, Sorrows, Terror, Death, and the guilty Joys of the heart.

The Eternal, who saw Satan advancing toward the sibyl's cave, opposed the full accomplishment of the projects of hell.

If God, in the depths of his counsels, permits his Church to be persecuted, he does not allow the demons to be able to attribute to themselves the criminal glory of this; the very chastisements that he inflicts on the Christians are ultimately to crush the pride of the rebellious spirits. He, therefore, sealed the mouth of the false oracle, and compelled the idols to own themselves vanquished, in order to exalt the triumph of the cross.

An angel bearing the mandates of the Most High, immediately descended to that mount where Dœdalus, after he had traversed the heavens, consecrated his pinions to the genius of enlightenment. The celestial messenger entered the temple of the sibyl. At this moment, the haruspex sent by Diocletian was offering his sacrifice. Four bulls fell beneath his knife in honor of Hecate; a black sheep was immolated to Night, the mother of the Eumenides; the fire was lighted on the altars of Pluto; whole victims were cast into the flames, and floods of oil inundated the burning entrails. Chaos, Styx, Phlegethon, the Fates, the Furies, all the infernal divinities, were invoked, and the lives of the Christians devoted to them. Scarcely was the abominable sacrifice completed, when the sibyl, like one distracted, exclaimed:

"It is time to consult the oracle: the god! behold the god!"

Satan suddenly agitated the priestess of the idols, as she spoke at the entrance of the sanctuary. The features of the sibyl were convulsed, her countenance changed color, her hair bristled on her head, her bosom heaved, her stature seemed to increase, and her voice no longer sounded like that of a human being. Seated on the tripod, she still resisted the inspirations of the prince of darkness.

"Potent Apollo!" cried the haruspex, "god of Smintheus and of Delos, thou whom Fate has chosen to unveil the future to mortals, deign to inform me what will be the destiny of the Christians. Ought the pious emperor to exterminate from the earth these sacrilegious enemies of the gods?"

At these words the priestess rose three times with effort; three times a supernatural force reseated her upon the tripod: the hundred gates of the sanctuary flew open to give a passage to the prophetic words. O prodigy! the sibyl remained dumb. In vain, incited by the demon, she endeavored to break silence: she uttered nothing but confused and inarticulate sounds. The angel of the Lord stood unveiled before the eyes of the priestess: with mouth half open, wandering eyes, and bristling hair, she pointed him out to the spectators: they saw not the celestial apparition, but they were seized with terror. Ruled by the spirit of the abyss, and making a final effort, the sibyl endeavored to order the proscription of the Christians, and uttered but these words:

"The just who are upon the earth hinder me from speaking."

Satan, vanquished by this oracle, took flight, full of grief and shame, yet not without hope and without abandoning his projects. What he could not do himself, he could cause to be done by the passions of men. The haruspex intrusted the answer of the gods to a Numidian horseman, swifter than the winds: Diocletian received it, and the council assembled.

"These pretended just," cried Hierocles, "are the Christians. The oracle designates them in derision by the name which they give themselves. Augustus, it is the Christians, then, that impose silence on the voice of heaven! so detestable are these monsters both to gods and men!"

Diocletian, secretly troubled by the old serpent, was struck with the explanation of Hierocles. He no longer saw that this oracle was favorable to the Christians. Superstition stifled wisdom: he feared to favor men devoted to the Furies.

Yet he hesitated still. Then a report was spread in the council, that the Christians had set fire to the palace. Galerius, acting under the advice of Hierocles, had raised this conflagration in order to triumph over the uncertainties of the emperor. Affecting an air of consternation, he exclaimed: "It is indeed time to deliberate, when wretches are about to make you perish in the midst of the flames."

At these words all the assembly, either seduced or deceived, demanded the death of the impious; and the emperor, himself terrified, ordered the publication of the edict of persecution.

BOOK EIGHTEENTH.

SUMMARY.

Joy of Hell. Galerius, counselled by Hierocles, forces Diocletian to abdicate. Preparation of the Christians for Martyrdom. Constantine, aided by Eudorus, escapes from Rome and flees to Constantius. Eudorus is cast into the Dungeons. Hierocles, Prime Minister of Galerius. General Persecution. The Demon of Tyranny bears to Jerusalem the News of the Persecution. The Centurion sent by Hierocles sets Fire to the Holy Places. Dorotheus saves Cymodoce. Meeting with Jerome in the Grotto of Bethlehem.

SINCE the day on which Satan had seen the first woman raise to her lips the fruit of death, he had not experienced such joy. "Hell," exclaimed he, "open your abysses to receive the souls that Christ had wrested from you! Christ is conquered; his empire is destroyed; man belongs to me without redemption."

Thus spoke the prince of darkness: his voice penetrated to the gulf of sorrows. The reprobates thought they heard the fatal sentence anew, and uttered fearful cries in the midst of the flames. All the demons remaining in the depths of eternal night hastened upon the earth. The air was darked with this flight of unearthly spirits. The cherub that directs the course of the sun recoiled in horror, and covered his brow with a bloody cloud; lamentable voices issued from the bosom of the forests; the idols suffered a horrible smile to escape them on the altars of the false gods; the wicked in every part of the globe felt at the same moment a new attraction toward evil, and conceived projects of revolutions.

Hierocles, above all, was carried away with irresistible ardor; he wished to give the finishing touch to his work. While Diocletian continued on the throne, the apostate could not enjoy an absolute authority. The sophist, therefore, seized the favorable moment, and addressing himself to Galerius, whose passions he knew:

"Prince," said he, "do you wish to reign? You have not a moment to lose. Augustus has just deprived himself of the support of the Christians. In exterminating this rebellious race, you will be screened from that odium which often attaches to a severe measure, since the edict is given under the name of the emperor. Diocletian is alarmed at the resolution he has taken: profit by this moment of fear; represent to the old man that it is time for him to taste the sweets of repose, and leave to a younger hero the care of executing the orders upon which depends the safety of the empire. You will name Cæsars of your own choice; you will cause wisdom to rule: the present generation will owe to you its happiness, and future ages shall resound with your virtues."

Galerius approved the zeal of Hierocles: he called the perfidious adviser his worthy friend, his faithful minister. All the favorites of Cæsar applauded the scheme, even Publius, who, the rival of the apostate in favor, sought only the means of destroying him; but, like an experienced courtier, he took care not to oppose a crime which flattered the ambition of Galerius. The prefect of Rome, he undertook to gain over the prætorian bands, and the legions that were stationed in the Campus Martius.

Galerius immediately repaired to the palace of Thermæ. Diocletian was closeted alone in the most retired apartment of his vast residence. At the moment in which the emperor had pronounced the sentence of the Christians, God had pronounced the sentence of the emperor: his reign expired with his justice. Racked with anxiety and remorse, Augustus felt himself abandoned by heaven, and bitter thoughts filled his soul! Suddenly Galerius was announced. Diocletian saluted him by the name of Cæsar.

"What, always Cæsar!" cried the prince with impatience; "am I never to be anything else than Cæsar?"

At the same time he closed the door, and thus addressed the emperor:

"Augustus, no sooner had your edict been posted in Rome, than the Christians had the insolence to tear it down. I foresee that this impious race will cause many ills to your old age; suffer me to chastise the insolence of your enemies, and to ease you of the burden of empire: your age, your long exertions, your failing health, command you to seek repose."

Without appearing surprised, Diocletian replied:

"It is you who plunge my old age into these misfortunes: but for you I should have left the empire in a state of tranquillity. Shall I, after twenty years of glory, retire to languish in obscurity?"

"Well," cried Galerius, in a rage, "if you will not renounce the empire, I must consult for myself. During fifteen years have I combated against barbarians on the savage frontiers, while the other Cæsars have been reigning in peace over fertile provinces: I am weary of the lowest rank."

"Do you recollect," replied the old man, "that you are in my palace? Herdsman ⊦ weak as I am, I can still make you return to your nothingness; but I have had too much experience to be astonished at ingratitude, and am too weary of governing men, to dispute this mournful honor with you. Unfortunate Galerius, do you know what you demand? During the twenty years that I have held the reins of empire, a tranquil sleep has never closed my eyes; I have seen nothing around me but baseness, intrigue, falsehood, and treason; I shall carry nothing from the throne but the emptiness of grandeur, and a profound contempt for the human race!"

"I shall find means," said Galerius, "to shield myself from intrigues, baseness, falsehood, and treason; I will reëstablish the Frumentarii, which you so imprudently abolished; I will give festivals to the crowd; and, master of the world, I will leave, by brilliant exploits, a lasting remembrance of my greatness."

"In so doing," said Diocletian, contemptuously, "you will make the Roman people laugh at your expense!"

"Well," answered the ferocious Cæsar, "if the Roman

people will not laugh, I will make them weep; they must either serve my glory, or die. I will inspire terror to save myself from contempt."

"The means are not so sure as you suppose," returned Diocletian. "If humanity does not stop you, let your own safety affect you: a violent reign cannot be long. I do not pretend to say, that you would be exposed to a sudden downfall, but there is in the principle of things a certain degree of evil which nature cannot pass. We see ere long, from what cause I know not, the elements of this evil disappear. Of all bad princes, Tiberius alone remained for a long time at the helm of state; but Tiberius was violent only in the latter years of his life."

"All this discourse is useless," exclaimed the impatient Cæsar; "it is not lectures, but the empire that I want. You say that sovereign power has no longer any attractions in your eyes; let it therefore pass into the hands of your son-in-law."

"With me," replied Diocletian, "that title can no longer avail you. Have you rendered my daughter happy? Unfaithful to her, and the persecutor of the religion she loves, you are, perhaps, but awaiting my retreat to exile Valeria to some desert shore. And is it thus that you have requited my benefits? But I shall be avenged: I leave you that power which you would fain wrest from me on the verge of the tomb. Not that I yield to your menaces: I obey a voice from heaven, which tells me that the time of my greatness is past. To you I consign this rag of purple, which to me is now but a funeral shroud: with it I make you a present of all the cares of the throne. Govern a world which is mouldering into decay; in which a thousand seeds of death are springing up on every side; cure the corruption of manners; reconcile warring religions; exterminate that spirit of sophistry which preys upon the very vitals of society; drive back to their forests those barbarians, who will sooner or later devour the Roman empire. I take my departure; from my garden at Salona I shall see you become the execration of the universe. You yourself, ungrateful son, shall not die without being the victim of the ingratitude of your son. Reign, then; hasten the end of this empire, whose downfall I have retarded for a few moments. You are of that race of princes who appear upon earth at the epoch of great revolutions, when families and kingdoms are destroyed by the will of the gods."

Thus the fate of the empire was decided in the palace of Diocletian. The Christians, meanwhile, were deliberating together upon the calamities of the Church. Eudorus was the soul of their councils. The edict, published by the sound of trumpets, ordered the sacred books to be burnt, and the churches to be razed to the ground; it denounced the Christians as infamous; it deprived them of the rights of citizenship; it forbade the magistrates to listen to their complaints in case of outrageous treatment, theft, rape, or adultery; it authorized persons of every description to denounce them to justice, delivered up to torture and condemned to death whomsoever refused to sacrifice to the gods.

This sanguinary edict, dictated by Hierocles, gave a free career to the crimes of the disciple of the sages, and threatened the faithful with total destruction. Each one, according to his character, prepared either for combat or for flight.

Those who were fearful of succumbing beneath the tortures, exiled themselves to the country of the barbarians; many withdrew into the forests and deserts; the faithful were seen embracing in the streets, and bidding a tender farewell, congratulating each other on suffering for Jesus Christ. Venerable confessors, who had escaped the former persecutions, mingled in the crowd, to encourage weakness, or moderate the ardor of zeal. Young men, women, and children, thronged round the venerable Christian sires, who reminded them of the examples of former illustrious martyrs: Laurence, of the church of Rome, exposed upon burning coals; Vincent, of Saragossa, conversing with angels in his prison; Eulalius, of Merida; Pelagius, of Antioch, whose mother and sisters were drowned while clasped in each other's embraces; Felicita and Perpetua, who combated in the amphitheatre of Carthage; Theodorus and the seven virgins of Ancyra; the two youthful spouses, buried in separate tombs, who were found reunited in the same coffin. Thus spoke these aged men; while the bishops concealed the sacred books, and the priests secreted the viaticum in boxes with false bottoms: the most secret and solitary of the catacombs were opened, in order to supply the place of the churches of which they were about to be deprived; deacons were named, who were to go in disguise, and succor the martyrs in the depths of mines, in prisons, and under torture; linen and balm were prepared as on the eve of an important combat; debts were paid, and variances reconciled. All these things were done without noise, ostentation, or tumult; the Church prepared to suffer with simplicity: like the daughter of Jephthah, she demanded of her father but a moment to bewail her sacrifice on the mountain.

The Christian soldiers who were scattered through the legions, came to acquaint Eudorus that a fresh conspiracy was on the point of breaking out; that largesses were made to the army in the name of Galerius; that on the morrow the troops were ordered to assemble in the Campus Martius, and that a report prevailed of the abdication of the emperor.

The son of Lasthenes gained certain information: he then hastened to Tibur, the usual residence of Constantine. This prince dwelt, far from the snares of the court, in a little retreat above the cascade of the Anio, near the temples of Vesta and the sibyl. The villas of Horace and Propertius were seen deserted on the banks of the river, in the midst of olive-groves that were now grown wild. The smiling Tibur, which had so often inspired the theme of the Latin muse, offered nothing to the view but monuments of pleasure now in ruins, and tombs of every epoch. In vain one sought on the sides of Lucretilis the memory of that voluptuous poet who confined to a narrow space his far-extended hopes, and consecrated wine and flowers to the genius who reminds us of the shortness of our days.

It was midnight when the sudden arrival of Eudorus was announced to Constantine. The prince arose, embraced his friend, and conducted him to a terrace, which encircled the temple of Vesta, and commanded a view of the falls of the

Anio. The sky was veiled in clouds and obscurity; the wind moaned through the columns of the temple; a mournful voice arose on the air: they imagined they heard at intervals the groans that issued from the sibyl's cave, or the funeral dirge which the Christians chanted for the dead.

"Son of Cæsar," said Eudorus, "they are not only about to massacre the Christians, but Diocletian is about to resign the sceptre to Galerius. To-morrow in the Campus Martius, in the presence of the legions, this great spectacle is to take place. You will not be called to partake of the sovereignty: your crimes are your glory, that of your father, and your inclination for a divine religion. Daza, the herdsman, son of the sister of Galerius, and Severus, the soldier, such are the Cæsars designed for the Roman people. Diocletian wished to nominate you, but you were rejected with insult. Prince! fond hope of the church and of the world, we must yield to the storm! Galerius fears you, and wishes your destruction. To-morrow, as soon as your lot shall be known, you must fly to your father; everything shall be prepared for your departure. You will take care, at every stage, to disable the horses that you leave behind you, in order to prevent pursuit. Await with Constantius the moment for saving the Christians and the empire; and when the time shall have come, those Gauls, who have already approached so near to the Capitol, shall open for you the way."

Constantine remained for a moment in silence; a thousand thoughts arose in his heart. Indignant at the outrages that were intended him; animated with the hope of revenging the blood of the just; touched, perhaps, by the splendors of a throne, which has always temptations for great souls, he could not resolve to fly; his respect and gratitude for Diocletian alone checked his ardor: the news of the abdication of this prince had burst all the bonds that retained the son of Constantius to his sovereign. He wished to arouse the legions upon the Campus Martius; he breathed nothing but war and vengeance: thus, when bound amidst the burning deserts of Arabia, the impatient courser, to gain some relief from the fiery beams of noon, conceals his head beneath his broadened chest, and while his mane falls disordered, casts a sidelong glance of anger at his master; but no sooner are his feet disengaged from their shackles, than he foams, paws the earth, and at the trumpet's sound, seems to say, "Away!"

Eudorus calmed the warlike transports of Constantine.

"The legions have been bought over," said he; "all your steps are watched, and you would attempt an enterprise that would precipitate the empire into incalculable evils. Son of Constantius, you shall reign one day over the world, and men shall owe to you their happiness. But God still withholds your crown in his hands, and wishes to try his Church."

"Well," said the young prince, with touching vivacity, "you shall accompany me into Gaul, and we will march together to Rome, at the head of those soldiers who have so often been witnesses of your valor."

"Prince," answered Eudorus, in a voice of emotion, "our obligations are not the same; you owe yourself to earth for heaven, I owe myself to heaven for earth. It is your duty to depart; mine to remain. The jealousy with which I have inspired Hierocles, has without doubt hastened the destruction of the Christians; my fortune, my counsels, and my life belong to them; I cannot quit the field on which I have challenged the enemy; my spouse and my father also demand my presence in the East. If my brethren, in fine, need examples of fortitude, God will, perhaps, grant me the virtues which I lack."

At this moment a supernatural light illumined, on the banks of the Anio, the tombs of Symphorosa and her seven infant martyrs.

"See," cried Eudorus, showing Constantine the sacred monument; "see with what strength God, in his good pleasure, can inspire women and children! How much more illustrious do these relics appear to me, than the ashes of the illustrious Romans that repose in this spot. Prince, deprive me not of the glory of such a destiny; permit me only on the tomb of those saints to swear a fidelity to you, that shall end only with my life."

At these words the son of Lasthenes inclined respectfully toward that hand which was destined to sway the sceptre of the world; but Constantine threw himself on the neck of Eudorus, and for a long time pressed his noble and magnanimous friend in his arms.

The prince called for his chariot; he mounted it with Eudorus; they rolled through the darkness, along the deserted porticos of the temple of Hercules. The Anio roared with sullen murmurs over the ruins of the palace of Mæcenas. The descendant of Philopœmen and the heir of Cæsar reflected in silence upon the destiny of men and of empires. Here stretched the forest of Albunea, where the kings of Latium consulted the rural divinities; there dwelt the rural people of Mount Soracte and the valleys of Ustica; this was the birthplace of those Sabines who, running with dishevelled hair between the armies of Tatius and Romulus, exclaimed to the former: " You are our sons and our spouses;" and to the latter: " You are our fathers and our brethren." The bard and the minister of Augustus replaced them on these shores to be trod in their turn by a queen descended from the throne of Palmyra. The chariot drove rapidly past the villa of Brutus, and the gardens of Adrian, and stopped at the tomb of the family of Plotia. Eudorus separated from Constantine at the foot of this monument, and returned to Rome by an unfrequented footpath, in order to prepare for the escape of the prince. Scarcely able to conceal his indignation and anxiety, Constantine took the road that led to the palace of Thermæ.

The attack of Galerius had been so abrupt, and the resolution of Diocletian so prompt, that the son of Constantius, whose whole attention had been engaged by the situation of the Christians, had suffered himself to be surprised by his enemy. He well knew that Cæsar had long been endeavoring to force Augustus to abdicate; but, whether deceived or betrayed, he had imagined this catastrophe as yet distant. He wished for an interview with Diocletian, but everything had changed with a reverse of fortune. One of the officers of Galerius refused the young prince admittance, saying to him in a menacing tone:

"The emperor commands you to repair to the camp of the legions."

At the extremity of the Campus Martius, at the foot of the tomb of Octavius, arose a tribunal of turf, surmounted by a column which bore a statue of Jupiter. At this tribunal, Diocletian was to appear next morning at sunrise, to abdicate the purple in the midst of the soldiers under arms. Since the day on which Sylla resigned the dictatorship, never had a greater spectacle met the eyes of the Romans. Fear, hope, and curiosity had brought an immense crowd to the Campus Martius. All the passions interested in the approach of the new reign, awaited the issue of this extraordinary scene. Who were to be the Augustuses? who were to be the Cæsars? The courtiers erected altars by chance to the unknown gods; they were fearful of offending, even in thought, a power which as yet had no existence. They adored the nothing whence servitude was to spring; they wearied themselves in divining what would be the passion of the future prince, that they might tutor themselves to the baseness which would be most in favor under this reign. While the wicked were studying to display their vices, the good were seeking to conceal their virtues. The people alone, with a stupid indifference, came to see foreign soldiers nominate their masters, on the very spot where this free people once gave their suffrage for the election of their magistrates.

Diocletian soon made his appearance at the tribunal. The legions proclaimed silence, and the emperor spoke:

"Soldiers," said he, "my age obliges me to resign the sovereign power to Galerius, and to create new Cæsars."

At these words, every eye was turned toward Constantine, who had just arrived. But suddenly Diocletian proclaimed Daza and Severus Cæsars. The people stood confounded; they demanded of each other who this Daza was, and whether Constantine had changed his name. Galerius arose, and rudely repulsing the son of Constantius, seized Daza by the arm, and presented him to the legions. The emperor divested himself of his purple mantle, and threw it over the shoulders of the young herdsman. At the same time he gave Galerius his poniard, the symbol of absolute power over the lives of citizens.

Diocletian, transformed again into Diocles, descended from his tribunal, mounted his chariot, passed through Rome without uttering a word, without looking at his palace, without turning his head, and taking the road to Salona, his native place, left the universe divided between admiration for the reign that had ended, and terror for the reign that was about to begin.

While the new Augustus and the new Cæsar were receiving the salutations of the soldiers, Eudorus glided through the crowd, and reached Constantine. This prince was still wavering between astonishment, indignation, and grief.

"Son of Constantius," said Eudorus, in a low but impressive tone of voice, "what are you doing? You know your destiny; the tribune of the prætorians has already received the order for your arrest: follow me, or you are lost."

He dragged away the heir of the empire; they passed the gates of Rome, and reached a desert spot, where Constantine afterward built the basilica of the Holy Cross.

Some faithful servants were here awaiting the fugitive prince: bursting into tears, he again sought to persuade Eudorus to flee with him, but the martyr in hope remained inflexible, and entreated the son of Helena to depart. Already they heard the soldiers who were seeking Constantine. Eudorus addressed this prayer to the Eternal:

"Great God, if thou art reserving this prince to reign over thy people, force this second David to fly before Saul, and deign to show him the way through the deserts of Ziklag!"

Immediately the thunder muttered through the serene sky; the lightning struck the ramparts of Rome; an angel traced out a luminous path in the west.

Constantine obeyed the orders of heaven: he embraced his

friend, and sprang on his courser. He fled ; Eudorus cried in parting :

"Remember me, when I shall be no more! Prince, be a protector and a father to Cymodoce!"

Useless prayers! Constantine disappeared. Eudorus, abandoned, without a protector, was left alone charged with the wrath of the emperor, with the hatred of a rival now become first minister, with the destiny of the faithful, and, as it were, with the whole weight of the persecution. On the same evening, denounced as a Christian by a slave of Hierocles, he was thrown into the dungeon.

Satan, Astarte, and the Spirit of False Wisdom, all three uttered a shout of triumph, and delivered the world to the Demon of Homicide.

When this furious angel, quitting the abode of sorrows, saddens the earth with his presence, he takes up his usual residence not far from Carthage, in the ruins of a temple in which human victims were formerly burned in his honor. Hydras, with frightful eyes, dragons like unto those which attacked the whole army of Cato, strange monsters, such as are engendered every year in Africa, the plagues of Egypt, pestiferous breezes, diseases, civil wars, unjust laws that depopulate the earth, tyranny that ravages it, crawl about the feet of the demon of Homicide. He awoke at the cry of Satan ; he took flight from the midst of ruins, leaving after him a long whirlwind of dust ; he crossed the sea, and arrived in Italy. Enveloped in a fiery cloud, he paused near Rome. In one hand he waved a torch, in the other a sword : thus in olden times, he gave the signal for carnage, when the first Herod caused the massacre of the children of Israel.

Ah! if the Muse would but sustain my genius, if she would accord me for a moment the song of the swan or the golden tongue of the poet, how easy would it be for me to repeat in touching language the woes of persecution. I would call to mind my country : in depicting the calamities of the Romans, I should depict the calamities of the French. All hail, thou spouse of Jesus Christ, afflicted yet triumphant Church! And we, too, in our days, have seen thee upon the scaffold and in the catacombs. But it is in vain that thou art tormented, the gates of hell shall never prevail against thee; in thy most severe afflictions, thou always beholdest upon the mountains the feet of him who brings glad tidings of peace; thou hast no need of the light of the sun, for thou dost walk in the light of thy God; in thy presence the dungeon loses its gloom. The beauty of Bashan and of Carmel shall fade, the flowers of Lebanon shall wither and decay; thou alone shalt flourish in immortal youth!

The persecution spread in an instant from the banks of the Tiber to the extremities of the empire. On every side was heard the churches falling under the hands of the soldiers; the magistrates, dispersed through the temples and the halls of justice, forced the multitude to sacrifice; whoever refused to worship the gods, was condemned and delivered to the executioners; the prisons were glutted with victims; the roads were covered with crowds of mutilated men, who were sent to die in the depths of the mines, or in the public works. The rack, the scourge, the hooks of iron, the cross, and the wild beasts tore to pieces infants with their mothers; here women were suspended naked by the feet to stakes, and left to expire in this shameful and cruel torture; there the limbs of a martyr were bound to two trees forcibly bent together, which springing back to their natural position, rent asunder the body of the victim. Each province had its particular punishment: the slow fire in Mesopotamia, the wheel in Pontus, the axe in Arabia, and the melted lead in Cappadocia. Often in the midst of his torments, they allayed the confessor's thirst, and sprinkled water in his face, fearful lest his burning fever should hasten his death. Sometimes, fatigued with burning the faithful separately, whole crowds were precipitated at once into the fire, their bones were reduced to powder, and scattered with their ashes to the winds.

Galerius took delight in viewing these tortures; he was at great expense to procure bears of a prodigious size, and of a ferocity equal to his own. On each of these beasts he bestowed some terrible name. During his repasts, the successor of the wise Diocletian would cause men to be thrown to them to be devoured. The government of this monster of avarice and debauchery, in spreading discontent through the provinces, increased still more the violence of the persecution. The cities were placed under the control of military judges, without knowledge and without education, and ignorant of everything except how to put men to death! Commissaries made the most rigid scrutiny into the goods and possessions of the subjects of the empire; the lands were measured, the vines and trees were numbered, and a register was kept of the flocks and herds. Every citizen was obliged to enter his name in the book of the census, now become a book of proscription. Fearful lest some one should secrete a portion of his possessions from the avarice of the emperor, children were forced by the violence of torture to depose against their fathers, slaves against their masters, and women against their husbands. Often the executioners constrained the unfortunates to accuse themselves, and to lay claim to riches which they did not possess. Neither weakness nor infirmity were any excuse for dispensing with answering the summons of the exactor; misfortune and infirmity themselves were forced to appear; in order to involve the whole nation in these tyrannic laws, years were added to infancy, and retrenched from old age: the death of a man took nothing from the treasures of Galerius, and the emperor divided the spoil with the grave: this man, though struck from the number of the living, was not effaced from the list of the census, and continued to pay for having had the misfortune to exist. The poor, from whom nothing could be exacted, alone seemed sheltered from violence by their misery; but this did not screen them from the derisive pity of the tyrant: Galerius ordered them to be crowded into leaky vessels, and sunk in the depths of the sea, in order to cure them of all their ills.

There was but one species of insult that yet remained unpractised upon the Christians, and this Hierocles would not spare them. In the midst of this noble display of Christian heroism in the cause of the faith of Jesus Christ, the disciple of the sages generously published two books of blasphemies against the God whom he had once adored, and who was also the God of his mother: so cowardly and ferocious was the pride of the infidel! Indefatigable in his hatred and his love, the apostate waited with impatience the moment when the daughter of Homer should come to adorn his triumph. He expressly suspended the punishment of Eudorus, in order that the hope of saving the life of his favored rival might be a temptation to the virgin of Messenia.

"I will employ," said he to himself, with a mingled sensation of shame, despair, and exultation, "I will employ this last method to overcome the resistance of an insolent beauty; I shall see her fall into my arms to purchase the life of Eudorus, consummating then my double vengeance, I will show her my rival in the hands of the executioners, and tell the Christian in dying that his spouse is dishonored."

Intoxicated with his power, Hierocles had no longer any command over his passions. This wretch, who had denied the Eternal, by a deplorable contradiction, believed in the existence of an evil genius, and in all the secrets of the magic art.

There was at Rome a Hebrew who had forsaken the faith of his fathers: he lived among the sepulchres, and the voice of the people accused him of holding a secret commerce with hell. This man usually resided in the vaults of the ruined palace of Nero. Hierocles commissioned one of his confidants to go at midnight and find the infamous Israelite. Instructed in the questions he was to ask, the slave departed, and passing through the rubbish, descended into the depths of the subterranean recesses. He perceived an old man, covered with rags, warming his hands over a fire of human bones.

"Old man," said the slave, trembling with terror, "canst thou transport in a moment, from Jerusalem to Rome, a Christian who has escaped from the power of Hierocles? Take this gold, and speak without fear."

The glitter of the gold, and the name of Jerusalem, drew a ghastly smile from the Israelite.

"My son," said he, " I know thy master; there is nothing that I would not attempt to satisfy him: I will go and interrogate the abyss."

He spoke, and digging in the earth, discovered the blood-stained urn that contained the remains of Nero: moans issued from this urn. The magician poured out on an iron altar the ashes of the first persecutor of the Christians. Thrice he turned toward the east, thrice he struck his hands together, thrice he opened the profaned Bible; he uttered mysterious words, and from the bosom of the shades invoked the demon of tyrants. God permitted hell to reply; the fire that consumed the spoils of the dead went out; the earth trembled; the slave was chilled to the bones with terror, and his hair bristled on his head; a spirit passed before his eyes; he beheld some one whose countenance he did not know, and heard a feeble voice, like the faint whispers of the breeze.

"What," cried the Hebrew, "has detained thee so long? Tell me; canst thou transport from Jerusalem to Rome a Christian who has escaped from her master?"

"I cannot," replied the spirit of darkness: "Mary protects this Christian against my power; but, if you wish, I will convey in an instant into Syria the edict of the persecution, and the commands of Hierocles."

The slave accepted the proposition of hell, and hastened to convey the answer to the impatient Hierocles. Transformed into a rapid messenger, the spirit of darkness flew to Jerusalem, to the house of the centurion who was to claim Cymodoce. He urged him in the name of the minister of Galerius, to execute his mission with alacrity, and delivered the fatal edict to the governor of the city of David: immediately the gates of the holy places were closed, and the soldiers dispersed the faithful. In vain the spouse of Constantius sought to protect the Christians: Constantine an exile, Galerius triumphant, changed in a moment the fortunes of Helena: to sovereigns, prosperity is the mother of submission; the misfortunes of kings absolve subjects from their oath of fidelity.

It was the hour when sleep seals the eyes of mortals; the

birds were reposing in their nests, and the flocks in the valley; labor was suspended ; the housewife scarcely plied the distaff before the dying embers of her humble hearth. Cymodoce, after having offered up her prayers for her spouse and her father, had at length fallen asleep. Demodocus appeared to her in a dream. His beard hung neglected, big tears fell from his eyes, he gently waved his augural sceptre, and deep sighs escaped his breast. Cymodoce thought that she thus addressed him :

"O my father, why have you so long abandoned your daughter ! Where is Eudorus ? Has he come to reclaim the faith which he pledged ? Whence these tears that bedew your cheeks ? Do you not wish to press Cymodoce to your heart ?"

The phantom seemed to reply :

"Fly, my daughter, fly ! The flames encompass you; Hierocles pursues you. The gods whom you have forsaken deliver you to his power. Thy new God will triumph ; but what floods of tears will he cause thy father to shed !"

The apparition vanished, bearing away with it the taper which Cymodoce received at the altar on the day of her union with Eudorus. Cymodoce awakened. The light of a burning building reddened the walls of her apartment and the curtains of her bed. She arose, and beheld the church of the Holy Sepulchre enveloped in flames. Wrapped in volumes of smoke, the blaze mounted even to heaven, and threw a dark red lustre on the ruins of Jerusalem, and the mountains of Judæa.

From the time that the news of the persecution had been spread through Syria, Cymodoce had never once quitted the Princess Helena ; shut up in an oratory with the rest of the Christian virgins, she sighed over the woes of the new Sion. The minister of Hierocles, despairing of meeting the young catechumen, and hindered by the remnant of respect which he still felt for the spouse of a Cæsar, had refrained from violating her asylum, and had set fire to the Holy Sepulchre. The palace of Helena adjoined the sacred edifice ; the centurion hoped thus to force Cymodoce from her inviolable retreat, and waited with his soldiers to seize on her amidst the tumult.

Dorotheus had discovered these designs: he forced his way over the falling walls, amidst the blazing beams that fell on every side of him, and penetrated into the palace of Helena. The galleries were already deserted; only a few distracted women were assembled in an interior court, around one of the altars of the kings of Judah. He discovered Cymodoce, who was seeking in vain for her nurse, whom she was never more to behold. Thy fate, Eurymedusa, remains unknown!

"Let us fly!" cried Dorotheus; "Helena herself could not save you. Your enemies would snatch you from her arms. I know a secret portal, and a subterraneous passage which will conduct us beyond the walls of Jerusalem: Providence will do the rest."

At the extremity of the palace, on the side next to the mountain of Sion, there is a secret door which leads to Calvary: it was through this that Helena stole from the homage of the people when she went to pray at the foot of the cross. Dorotheus, followed by Cymodoce, opened the portal with precaution, and advanced his head to see if there was any one without. All was secure; he took Cymodoce by the hand, and they quitted the palace. Sometimes they stole slowly along the ruins; sometimes they reached a more open spot, and advanced with speed; now they imagined that they heard the sound of advancing footsteps, and hid themselves amidst the ruins; sometimes they were startled by the gleaming armor of some soldier, who was groping his way through the darkness. They heard far behind them the crackling of flames, and the confused clamors of the multitude, while they crossed the desert valley which separates the hill of Calvary from the mountain of Sion.

On one of the sides of this mountain opened an unknown passage, the entrance to which was concealed by clumps of aloes, and roots of wild olive-trees. Dorotheus made his way through these, and penetrated into the subterranean recess: he struck fire from a flint, lighted the branch of a cypress-tree, and by the light of this torch, entered the gloomy vault with Cymodoce. David had formerly bewailed his sin in this place;

on every side were seen, along the walls, verses which had been traced by the hand of the penitent monarch, when he shed his immortal tears. His tomb stood in the midst of the cave, where, engraven on its base, the crook, the harp, and the crown, were still visible. The terror of the present, the recollections of the past, the mountain whose summit had witnessed the sacrifice of Abraham, and whose sides still guarded the tomb of the royal prophet—all agitated the heart of the two Christians: they soon emerged from these mazes, and found themselves in the midst of the mountains that extend along the road to Bethlehem; they traversed the silent plains of Rama, where Rachel refused to be comforted, and came to repose at the cradle of the Messiah.

Bethlehem was entirely deserted: the Christians had been dispersed. Cymodoce and her guide reached the Manger: they were filled with admiration at the view of this grotto, where the King of heaven condescended to be born; where the angels, the shepherds, and the magi, came to adore him, where all the nations upon earth were one day to come and pay their homage. The offerings left in this place by the shepherds of Judæa abundantly fed the two unfortunate wanderers. Cymodoce shed tears of tenderness: the miracles of the cradle of Jesus spoke to her heart.

"It was here, then," said she, "that the divine infant first smiled on his divine mother! O Mary, protect Cymodoce! Like you, she is a fugitive in Bethlehem."

The daughter of Demodocus then thanked the generous Dorotheus, who exposed himself, for her sake, to so many fatigues and perils.

"I am an old Christian," replied he; "I rejoice in tribulations."

Dorotheus then prostrated himself before the Manger.

"Father of mercies!" he exclaimed, "take pity upon us, and remember that thy son offered in this spot his first tears for the salvation of mankind!"

The sun approached the end of his course. Dorotheus quitted the grotto with Cymodoce, in hopes of meeting some shepherd; he perceived a man descending from the mountain of Engedi: a girdle of bulrushes was bound around his loins; his beard and hair fell in disorder; and on his shoulders he bore a basket filled with sand, which he was bearing with difficulty to the entrance of a cave. As soon as he discovered the travellers, he threw down his burden, and casting upon them a look of indignation, exclaimed:

"Delights of Rome, do you come to haunt me even in this desert? Avaunt! Armed with penitence, I discover your snares, and laugh at your efforts."

He spoke, and like the sea-eagle that plunges into the waves, precipitated himself into his grotto. Dorotheus knew from his language that he was a Christian; he advanced, and addressed him through an aperture of the rock:

"We are fugitive Christians: deign to give us hospitality."

"No, no," cried the solitary; "this woman is too beautiful to be merely the daughter of men."

"This woman," replied Dorotheus, "is a catechumen who is fulfilling that probation which Jesus Christ demands of his servants. She is a Greek, and her name is Cymodoce; she is betrothed to Eudorus, the defender of the Christians, whose name may have perhaps reached your ears: I am Dorotheus, the first officer of Diocletian."

The solitary darted forth from his grotto, like a vigorous athlete, who crowns his brow with an olive wreath, and suddenly presents himself at the games of Olympus.

"Spouse of my friend," cried he, "enter into my grotto."

The solitary then told them his name. Cymodoce recognized him as that friend of Eudorus, who had talked with him at the tomb of Scipio. Dorotheus, who had known Jerome at court, contemplated with astonishment this anchorite, worn with vigils and austerities, once known as the gay disciple of Epicurus. He followed him into the interior of the cave: nothing was to be seen but a Bible, a skull, and the scattered leaves of a translation of the Holy Scriptures. The two Christians and the young pilgrim soon explained everything to their mutual satisfaction. A thousand tender recollections, a thousand interesting narratives, melted them into tears : they resembled those streams that, descending from different mountains, mingle their waters in the same valley.

"My errors," said Jerome, "have led me to repentance ; I shall never again quit the precincts of Bethlehem. The cradle of the Saviour shall be my tomb."

The anchorite then asked Dorotheus what he intended to do.

"I am going," replied Dorotheus, "to seek some friends at Joppa. . . ."

"What !" cried Jerome, interrupting him, "do you tell me that you are unfortunate, and yet rely upon finding friends ! A Moabite descended from his native mountains to go to Jericho. It was spring-time ; the air was fresh and the sky serene. The Moabite felt no thirst : he met with fountains of water at every step. He returned to his habitation in the season of storms, amidst the burning heats of summer : thirst consumed the Moabite, and he sought for some drops of that water which he had seen on the mountains : all the torrents were dry."

For some moments Jerome remained silent; he then exclaimed :

"O illustrious destiny ! Eudorus, thou art then chosen as the defender of the Christians ! O my friend, what can I do to serve you ?"

Suddenly the solitary arose, as if struck with a supernatural light.

"Whence these fears ?" cried he. "Woman, dost thou love, and yet canst thou fly ? Perhaps at this moment thy spouse is confessing the faith, and thou art not there to dispute with him the glory of the stake. Thinkest thou, that when united to the army of the martyrs, he will deign to receive thee without thy crown ? A monarch, he can place only a queen at his side ! Do thy duty, hasten to Rome, claim thy spouse, and seize the palm that is to adorn thy nuptial pomp . . . . But what do I say ? thou art not yet numbered among the chosen flock ?"

Once more the solitary was silent; he hesitated, then again exclaimed:

"Thou shalt be a Christian; this hand shall pour on thy forehead the water of salvation. The Jordan is near; come, and receive in its waters the strength that fails thee; thy life is in danger; thou must be sheltered from death. Yes; thou art sufficiently instructed. The best doctrine is that which is learned in the school of persecution: whoever has wept for Jesus Christ, has nothing else to learn."

Thus spoke Jerome, with the authority of a priest and a doctor. The gentle and timid Cymodoce replied:

"Lord, be it done unto me according to thy word. Let me be baptized: I aspire not to the honors of a queen, let me but be as a handmaid at the side of my spouse. If there is anything in this life that I regret, it is that I shall no more visit the flocks on Mount Ithome in company with my father; that I shall not be able to cherish in his old age the author of my days, as he cherished me in my infancy."

Cymodoce wept, and at the same time blushed at what she had uttered. The confused accents of her first religion and her new faith were discernible in her language: thus, in the deep repose of night, two Eolian harps mingle their fugitive melodies; thus the solemn accents of the Doric lyre swell in harmonious concert with the voluptuous cadence of the Ionian lute; thus, when in the savannahs of Florida, two silvery storks clap their sounding pinions in concert, and mingle their sweet murmurs in the air, seated in the edge of the forest, the Indian listens to the pleasing sounds, and fancies that he discerns in the melody the voice of the souls of his fathers.

BOOK NINETEENTH.

SUMMARY.

Return of Demodocus to the Temple of Homer. His Grief. He learns the News of the Persecution. He sets out for Rome, where he supposes Cymodoce to have been taken by the order of Hierocles. Cymodoce is baptized in the Jordan by Jerome. She reaches Ptolemais, and embarks for Greece. A Tempest, raised by the command of God, forces Cymodoce to land in Italy.

Who can ever tell the bitterness of paternal sorrows?

After the fatal separation, the slaves had reconducted Demodocus to the citadel of Athens. He passed the night under the portico of Minerva's temple, that he might discover by the first gleams of day the vessel of Cymodoce. When the star of morning appeared above Mount Hymettus, the tears of the old man streamed in greater abundance.

"O my daughter," cried he, "when wilt thou return from the east, like this star, to rejoice thy father?"

The dawn soon enlightened the solitary waves, where the straining eye sought the sail in vain, though the white wake of the vessel was still visible on the waves. Now emerging from the wave, the sun burnished the surface of the deep. Of the fleecy clouds that were scattered over the azure sky of Attica, some remained motionless, others, tinged with a roseate hue, floated around the star of day, like the scarf of the Hours. This spectacle only augmented the grief of the priest of Homer. He sobbed aloud; this was the first time, since his daughter had come into the world, that he had beheld, at a distance from her, the rising of this luminary. Demodocus refused all the cares of his host, who, as he witnessed this excess of grief, applauded himself for having lived without children and without a spouse : thus the shepherd, in the bosom of a valley, shudders as he listens to the thunder of the distant cannon ; he laments the victims who have fallen on the field of battle, and blesses his rocks and his cabin.

On the following day, Demodocus expressed his desire to quit Athens, and return to Messenia. His grief did not long permit him to follow the road that he had traversed with Cymodoce. At Corinth he took the road to Olympus ; but he could not support the sight of the joy and brilliancy of the festivities they were then celebrating on the banks of the Alpheus. When, after passing the mountains of Elis, he perceived the summits of Ithome, he sunk insensible into the arms of his slaves. They soon restored him to life ; pale and trembling, he reached the temple of Homer. Already the threshold of its gates was strewed with withered leaves ; the grass was growing in its walks ; so quickly are the footsteps of men effaced from the earth ! Demodocus entered the sanctuary of his ancestors ; the lamp was extinguished. The ashes of the last sacrifice that the father of Cymodoce had offered to the gods for his daughter, still lay upon the altar. Demodocus prostrated himself before the image of the poet.

" O thou," cried he, " who art now all my family, thou who hast chanted the woes of Priam, weep now over the ills of the last scion of thy race !"

At this instant one of the chords of Cymodoce's lyre burst with a sound that made the old man start. He raised his head, and beheld the lyre suspended at the altar.

" It is done," cried he ; " my daughter is destined to die ! the Fates give me warning of her destiny, by breaking the chord of her lyre."

At this cry, the slaves ran to the temple, and forced Demodocus, in spite of himself, to retire.

Each day increased his grief; a thousand recollections rent his heart. Here he instructed his daughter in the art of song; there they often wandered together. Nothing is so bitter as the view of places which we inhabited in the time of happiness, when we have lost that which constituted the charm of our life. The citizens of Messenia were touched by the woes of Demodocus. They permitted him to interrupt his sacred functions, which he could never perform but in the midst of tears. His life wasted gradually away; with rapid steps he hastened to the tomb. The letters of his daughter miscarried in the East, and never reached him. The family of Lasthenes could not bestow its care upon the old man: it was persecuted, and the mother of Eudorus had lately died. How many victims did the priest of Homer immolate to the gods who were deaf to his prayers! how many hecatombs did he vow to Neptune, would he but restore Cymodoce to the banks of the Pamisus! The day dawned and closed, and still found Demodocus with his hands imbrued in gore, interrogating the entrails of bulls and heifers. He offered his vows at every shrine; he went to consult the haruspices as far as the summits of Tenarus. Sometimes he clad himself in mourning, and knocked at the brazen portals of the Furies; he made offerings of expiation to the fatal sisters, as if his misfortunes were crimes! Sometimes he crowned himself with flowers; and while his eyes were bathed in tears, affected an air of gaiety, that he might render propitious some divinity who was an enemy to grief. The rites long since abolished; the ceremonies practised in the days of Inachus and Nestor, were revived by Demodocus; he consulted the prophetic books of the Sibyls; he pronounced no other words than those deemed of good omen; he abstained from certain kinds of food; he avoided meeting certain objects; he was attentive to the winds, the birds, and the clouds; there were not oracles enough to satisfy his paternal love! Ah, unhappy old man, listen to the sounds of that trumpet which echoes on the summit of Ithome: they will inform thee of the destiny of thy daughter.

With a numerous attendance, the governor of Messenia traversed the country, proclaiming Galerius as emperor, and publishing the edict of persecution. Demodocus could scarcely believe what he heard; he hastened to Messenia; everything confirmed his misfortunes. A vessel that had just arrived from the East at the port of Corone brought an account that the daughter of Homer had been carried away from Jerusalem and conveyed to Hierocles. What should Demodocus do? The excess of his adversity gave him strength: he determined to fly to Rome, to throw himself at the feet of Galerius, and to reclaim Cymodoce. Before quitting the temple of the demigod, he consecrated at the shrine of Homer's statue, a small ivory figure of a ship, and a vase to contain tears—an offering and symbol of his anxiety and his grief! He then sold his penates, the purple ornaments of his couch, and the nuptial veil of Epicharis which had been destined for Cymodoce; he carried with him his whole fortune to redeem the child of his love. Useless cares! Heaven would not yield up its conquest, and all the treasures of the earth would not have purchased the crown of the new Christian.

Cymodoce belonged no longer to the world. In receiving the waters of baptism, she was about to take her rank among the celestial spirits. She had already quitted the grotto of Bethlehem with Doretheus. At the first dawn of day they began their journey over these rugged and barren tracts. Jerome, arrayed like St. John in the desert, pointed out the path to the catechumen. They soon reached the last range of the mountains of Judæa, which stretch along the banks of the Dead Sea and the valley of the Jordan. Two high chains of mountains, extending from north to south, without breaks and undulations, burst on the view of the three travellers. On the side of Judæa, these mountains are heaps of chalk and sand, resembling in form piles of arms, waving standards, or the tents of a camp ranged on the borders of a plain. On the Arabian side they are black perpendicular rocks, which pour into the Dead Sea torrents of sulphur. Amidst this barren scene, not the smallest bird of heaven would find a blade of grass for its sustenance; everything announces the country of a reprobate people; everything seems to breathe the horror of that incest from which sprung Ammon and Moab.

The valley that stretched between these two chains of mountains, displayed a soil resembling the bottom of a sea that has long retired from its bed; beaches, covered with salt, dried mud, and moving sands, that seemed furrowed by the waves. Here and there, a few stunted shrubs vegetated with difficulty on a soil almost deprived of the principle of life: their leaves were covered with the salt that had nourished them, and their bark had the smell and the taste of smoke; instead of villages, nothing was seen but the ruins of a few towers. Through the middle of the valley flowed a discolored river: it crept with reluctance toward the pestilential lake which ingulfed it. Its course could not be distinguished through the midst of the sand, but it was edged with willows and reeds, in which the Arab lay in wait to plunder the traveller and the pilgrim.

"You see," said Jerome to his astonished companions, " places rendered memorable by the benedictions and the curses of heaven: this river is the Jordan; yonder lake is the Dead Sea; it appears brilliant to the eye, but the guilty cities entombed in its bosom have poisoned its waters. Its depths are solitary, and destitute of any living creature; no vessel ever ploughed its waves; its shores are without birds, without trees, without verdure; its waters have a horrible bitterness, and are so heavy, that the fiercest winds can scarcely agitate them. The skies of this region seem inflamed with the fires that consumed Gomorrah. Cymodoce, these are not the banks of the Pamisus, and the valleys of the Taygetus. You are on the way to Hebron, on the spot which resounded with the voice of Joshua, when he arrested the course of the sun. You are treading a land yet reeking with the wrath of Jehovah, but which has since been cheered by the words of the mercy of Jesus Christ. Young catechumen, it is through this sacred solitude that you pass to seek him whom you love; let the recollections of this vast and sorrowful desert be associated with your love, to strengthen it and render it more grave: the view of this scene of desolation is alike fitted to nourish or to extinguish the passions. Innocent virgin, thine are legitimate; thou art not compelled, like Jerome, to stifle them beneath burdens of burning sand !"

As he spoke thus, they descended into the valley of the

Jordan. Tormented with burning thirst, Cymodoce gathered from a shrub a fruit resembling a golden citron; but no sooner had she tasted it, than she found it filled with a bitter and calcined dust.

"It is the image of the pleasures of the world," cried the solitary.

And he pursued his road, shaking off the dust from his feet.

Meanwhile, the pilgrims approached a grove of balm-trees and tamarinds, which grew in the midst of the fine white sand: all at once Jerome stopped, and pointed out to Dorotheus, almost under his feet, something in motion amidst the immobility of the desert: it was a yellow stream, the turbid and sluggish waters of which were deeply sunk below its banks. The anchorite saluted the Jordan, and exclaimed:

"Thrice happy virgin, let us not lose an instant! Come and receive life in the very spot where the Israelites passed the river when they quitted the desert, and where Jesus Christ was pleased to receive baptism from the hand of the precursor. It was from the height of yonder Mount Abarim that Moses discovered for you the promised land; it was on the summit of the opposite mount that Jesus Christ prayed for you during forty days. Let the view of the ruined walls of Jericho break down the barrier of darkness which environs your soul, in order that the living God may enter therein."

Immediately Jerome entered the stream, and Cymodoce descended after him. Dorotheus, the only witness of this scene, threw himself upon his knees on the bank. He served as a spiritual father to Cymodoce, and confirmed to her the name of Esther. The waves divided around the chaste catechumen, as they parted in this same place around the sacred ark. The folds of her virginal robe, drawn along by the current, floated gracefully behind her; she inclined her head before Jerome, and in a voice that charmed the reeds of Jordan, renounced Satan, his pomps and his works. From a shell taken from the stream, the anchorite poured the water of regeneration on the forehead of the daughter of Homer, in the name of the Father, of the Son, and the Holy Ghost. Her loosened locks fell on both sides of her head, beneath the descending wave that moistened and relaxed their ringlets: thus the soft showers of spring bedew the flowery jasmin, and glide adown its odoriferous branches. Oh, how affecting was this baptismal rite, performed by stealth in the waters of the Jordan! How touching was the appearance of this virgin, who, concealed in the depth of a desert, had, as it were, stolen heaven away! Never had sovereign beauty appeared so charming in this spot, except, when the heavens were opened, the Spirit of God descended on Jesus Christ in the form of a dove, and a voice was heard to exclaim:

"This is my beloved Son."

Cymodoce quitted the waves full of faith and fortitude against the evils of life; the new Christian, bearing Jesus Christ in her heart, resembled a woman who, become a mother, finds that strength for her son which she had not for herself.

At this moment a company of Arabs appeared not far from the river. Jerome, at first alarmed, soon discovered that they were a Christian tribe, of which he had been the apostle. This little church, that had adored God under a tent, as in the days of Jacob, had not escaped the persecution. The Roman soldiers had deprived them of their horses and flocks, and left them nothing but their camels. Their chief had fled to the mountains where he ordered them to join him, and they were now hastening to fulfil his command: these faithful servants were carrying a quantity of milk as a tribute to their masters, as if they had divined that these masters had no other nourishment.

Jerome saw the hand of Providence in this meeting.

"These Arabs," said he to Dorotheus, "will conduct you to our brethren at Ptolemais, where you will readily find a vessel to Italy."

"Gazelle, with gentle look and airy step, virgin, more pleasant than the limpid spring, fear nothing," said the chief of the Arabs to Cymodoce; "I will conduct you wherever you desire, if Jerome, our father, command it."

16

The day being too far advanced to commence their journey, they halted on the banks of the stream; a lamb was killed, which they roasted whole, and served upon a platter of aloe wood; each one tore off a part of the victim, and drank a little of the milk which the camel yields in the midst of the burning desert, and which preserves the flavor of the date. Night came on. They lighted a fire, and seated themselves around it. The camels were bound to their stakes, and formed a second circle around the descendants of Ishmael. The father of the tribe recounted the evils that were being inflicted on the Christians. By the light of the fire were seen his expressive gestures, his black beard, his white teeth, and the various forms that his mantle assumed in the varied attitude of his recital. His companions listened with profound attention: bending forward with their faces over the flame, they sometimes burst into expressions of admiration, and sometimes repeated with emphasis the words of their chief; the heads of their camels projected above the group, and were dimly outlined in the obscurity. Cymodoce contemplated in silence this pastoral scene of the East; she admired that religion which humanized the savage, and taught him to succor weakness and innocence, while the false gods were plunging the Romans into barbarity, and stifling in their hearts the cries of justice and compassion.

At the first dawn of day the whole assembled troop offered their prayers to the Eternal on the banks of the Jordan. A carpet spread on the back of a camel was the altar, on which were placed the sacred emblems of this wandering church. Jerome delivered letters to Dorotheus for the leading faithful at Ptolemais. He exhorted Cymodoce to patience and courage, and congratulated himself on sending a Christian spouse to his friend.

"Go," said he, "daughter of Jacob, formerly the daughter of Homer! The queen of the East, thou quittest the desert shining with light. Brave the persecutions of men. Seated beneath the palm-tree, the new Jerusalem weeps not like Judæa when captive under Titus, but, victorious and triumphant, plucks from this same palm-tree the immortal symbol of her glory!"

As he finished these words, Jerome took leave of his guests, and returned to the grotto of Bethlehem.

The company of Arabs conducted the two fugitives over inaccessible mountains to the gates of Ptolemais. The sovereign of the angels, who ceased not to watch over Cymodoce, had sustained her miraculously amidst these fatigues. In order to screen her from the eyes of the pagans, she enveloped her, as well as Dorotheus, in a cloud. Both entered Ptolemais under this veil. The Church, which as yet had escaped destruction, announced to them the abode of the pastor. In these days of tribulation, every persecuted Christian was received with the tenderness and respect due to a brother; the faithful concealed him at the risk of their own lives, and exercised toward him every kind office that charity could suggest. The pastor was informed that two strangers had presented themselves at his gate; he hastened to greet them. Dorotheus, without uttering a word, made himself known by the sign of salvation.

"Martyrs!" exclaimed the pastor, "happy the day that brings you to my dwelling! Angels of the Lord, enter under the roof of Gideon; here you will find the harvest hidden from the Moabites."

Dorotheus delivered to the pastor the letters of Jerome, and at the same time recounted the misfortunes of Cymodoce.

"What," cried the priest, "is this the spouse of our defender? Is this the virgin whose history is proclaimed throughout Syria? I am Pamphilus of Cæsarea, and formerly knew Eudorus in Egypt. Daughter of Jerusalem, how great is your glory! Alas! your former protectress, the pious Helena, can no longer render you any assistance; she is herself arrested. The ministers of Hierocles are everywhere in pursuit of you; you must quit this city with all speed; but there are still resources left: where do you wish to go?"

Dorotheus, whose faith was less ardent than that of Jerome, and who had not, like him, penetrated the counsels of heaven; Dorotheus, who still mingled human affections with his religion, did not believe that Cymodoce would have sufficient resolution to join her spouse.

"It is to deliver yourself to Hierocles," said he, "without hope of saving or even of seeing Eudorus. Permit me to conduct you to your father. Your presence will restore him to life. We will conceal you in some unknown retreat, and I will go to Rome to seek the son of Lasthenes."

"I am young," replied Cymodoce, "and without experience; guide me, O thou best of men! thy Christian daughter will obey thy counsels."

They found but one vessel in the port of Ptolemais, which was bound for Thessalonica: the new Christian and her generous conductor were obliged to avail themselves of it. They assumed fictitious names, and quitted that port, which, the great St. Louis, rescued from the hands of the infidels, was, so many centuries afterward, to render illustrious by his virtues. Alas! Cymodoce was hastening to seek her father on the banks of the Pamisus, while the old man himself was vainly demanding her of the waves of the Tiber. A stranger in Rome, without protection and support, he had counted upon Eudorus; but the confessor, separated from men, could neither hear nor succor him.

At the foot of Mount Aventinus, and immediately under the walls of the Capitol, stands an ancient prison of the state, which was built as far back as the age of Romulus. From these dungeons the accomplices of Catiline once heard the voice of Cicero, when he pronounced their accusation in the temple of Concord. The captivity of St. Peter and St. Paul afterward purified this asylum of criminals. Here Eudorus awaited in daily expectation the orders that were to deliver him over to the judges; here, too, he received the news of his mother's death, the commencement of his sacrifice. He had often written letters full of piety and tenderness to the daughter of Homer: some had been intercepted by his enemies, the rest had been lost at sea; but even in prison he tasted some of those consolations and those mournful joys which are known only to the Christians. Each day added to the number of his companions in misfortune and glory.

When a rich husbandman gathers in his new harvests, he heaps in a spacious barn the grain which is to be trodden out by the oxen, that which is to yield up its treasure to the stroke of the flail, and that which is to be separated from the light straw by a heavy cylinder; the village resounds with the shouts of the master and the servants, the voices of the women preparing the feast, the noise of the children at play around the sheaves, and the bellowing of the oxen drawing or going for the yellow ears: thus Galerius collected together in the prison of St. Peter, the most illustrious Christians from every part of the world; the wheat of the elect, the divine harvest is to enrich the good Shepherd! Every day Eudorus beheld the arrival of some of the friends whom he had left in Gaul, Egypt, Greece, or Italy: he embraces Victor, Sebastian, Rogatian, Gervasius, Protasius, Lactantius, Arnobius, the hermit of Vesuvius, and the descendant of Perseus, who prepared to die more royally for the throne of Jesus Christ, than his ancestor had done for the crown of Alexander. Cyril, the bishop of Lacedæmon, came also to augment the joy of the dungeon. Every fresh confessor was hailed with transports of joy, with the kiss of peace, and with hymns of thanksgiving to Divine Providence. These confessors had transformed the prison into a church, in which were heard, day and night, the praises of the Lord. The Christians who were not yet imprisoned, envied the lot of these victims. The soldiers who guarded the martyrs were often converted by their discourse; and the jailers, delivering the keys into other hands, ranged themselves in the number of the prisoners. Perfect order was established among these companions in suffering. Instead of a crowd of men marching to execution, they had the appearance of a peaceful and well-regulated family. Pious frauds were practised in order to procure the faithful all the consolations of humanity and religion. Ten persecutions had rendered the Church adroit. Priests and deacons, under the disguise of soldiers, merchants, and slaves; women and children even, by ingenious and pious impostures, penetrated into the dungeons and mines, and even to the stake. From the concealment of an unknown retreat, the pontiff of Rome guided the zeal of the faithful. An inviolable fidelity, that of religion and misfortune, was the bond of all the brethren. Not only did the Church succor her own children, she still continued to watch over the unfortunate of a religion that was hostile to her; she gathered them into her bosom, and charity made her forget her own woes, to attend to their necessities.

The faithful confined in prison, were witnesses of a thousand marvellous adventures. How was Eudorus one day surprised, to behold in the disguise of a servant of the prison, the gay and beautiful Aglaia!

"Eudorus," said she, "Sebastian has been pierced with arrows at the entrance of the catacombs; Pacomius has retired to the deserts of the Thebais; Boniface has kept his word: he ordered his relics to be conveyed to me under the name of a martyr; Boniface has confessed Jesus Christ! Entreat heaven to accord the same honor to a sinful woman!"

On another occasion, a great tumult was heard without, and Genesius, the famous actor, was led into the prison.

"Fear me no more," cried he, as he entered, "I am your brother! Just now I blasphemed your holy mysteries for the amusement of the crowd about me; in impious jest, I demanded baptism and martyrdom. No sooner was I touched by the holy water, than I beheld a number of radiant angels encircling my head, and a hand that descended from heaven, and effaced my sins from the book of life. On a sudden I felt myself changed, and exclaimed in a tone of serious conviction: 'I am a Christian!' The spectators laughed, and refused to believe me. I then told them what I had seen. I was beaten with rods, and am now come to die with you."

As he uttered these words, Genesius embraced Eudorus. Surrounded by confessors, the son of Lasthenes attracted the notice of all present. The hermit of Vesuvius reminded him of their meeting at the tomb of Scipio, and of the hopes he had then conceived of his virtues. The confessors of Gaul said to him:

"Do you remember that we wished to find ourselves again united at Rome, as we now are? You were then very far from the glory that crowns you at present."

During this conversation, the prisoners beheld a man enter, who wore the helmet of a veteran, and was bent beneath the weight of years; they had never before observed him in the number of those Christians who attended the prison. He brought the martyrs the holy viaticum which Marcellinus had sent to the bishop of Lacedæmon. The old man's features were not distinguishable amidst the gloom of the prison; he inquired for Eudorus, who was pointed out to him at prayer; he approached him, clasped him in his aged arms, and pressed him to his heart with tears of tenderness. At length he exclaimed in broken accents:

"I am Zacharias."

"Zacharias!" repeated Eudorus, overcome with joy and emotion. "You, my father! You, Zacharias!"

He fell at the knees of the venerable man.

"O my son," said the apostle of the Franks, "arise! It is I that should prostrate myself. Compared with you, what am I but a useless and unknown old man!"

All the confessors crowded around the two friends; they were anxious to learn their history, and while the tears streamed in abundance from their eyes, Eudorus satisfied their curiosity. He then inquired what good providence had conducted Zacharias from the banks of the Elbe to the shores of the Tiber.

"My son," replied the descendant of Cassius, "Constantius has entirely subdued the Franks. Pharamond had given me to a petty tribe, which, completely subjugated, was transported into the neighborhood of the colony of Agrippina. This persecution broke out unexpectedly; as it has not yet extended into Gaul, where Cæsar protects the Christians, the bishops of Lutetia and Lugdunum have appointed a certain number of priests to serve the faithful throughout the other parts of the empire. I thought it my duty to present myself in preference to those whose more vigorous years would be of greater service to the Church. They condescended to accept my offer, and I was sent to Rome."

Zacharius afterward informed Eudorus of the safe arrival of Constantine at his father's camp, of the ill health of Constantius, and of the unanimous determination of the army under his command to reserve the purple for his son. This news reanimated the courage of the Christians, and sustained them in these moments of trial. Though the Christians had been deprived of their most powerful protectors, yet Eudorus had never given up all hopes: Prisca had accompanied her spouse to Salona, and Valeria had been exiled into Asia by Galerius. In his very dungeon, Eudorus had been concerting a plan for the safety of the Church and the world; he wished to engage Diocletian to resume the reins of empire, and dispatched a messenger to him in the name of the faithful.

Whilst the whole Church was relying on the courage, the counsels, and the foresight of Eudorus, Cymodoce was claiming in vain the protection of her spouse. She was advancing toward the coast of Macedonia. A band of ruffians surrounded her. She was perpetually exposed to the insults of soldiers and mariners who were plunged from morning till night in drunkenness and debauchery. They soon discovered that Dorotheus and the daughter of Demodocus were Christians There is a virtue in the cross which attracts the notice of vice. This discovery augmented the insolence of these barbarians. Sometimes they threatened to deliver up their unfortunate passengers into the hands of the executioner at the moment of landing; sometimes they swore that they would cast them into the sea to appease the fury of Neptune; they shocked the ears of Cymodoce with abominable songs; and so far had her beauty inflamed their brutal desires, that there was reason to fear that they might proceed to greater outrages. Dorotheus defended her innocence with the prudence of a father and the courage of a hero. But what could one man do against a band of furious tigers?

The son of the Eternal, accompanied by the celestial choirs, was returning at this moment from the most distant bounds of creation. He had quitted the incorruptible abodes to restore life and youth to superannuated worlds. From globe to globe, from sun to sun, his majestic steps had passed over all those spheres inhabited by the divine intelligences, and perhaps by races unknown to man. Returned to the impenetrable sanctuary, he seated himself at the right hand of God; his pacific glances soon fell upon the earth. Of all the works of the Almighty, there is none more pleasing in his eyes than man. The Saviour perceived the vessel of Cymodoce; he saw the perils of this innocent victim, who was to draw down upon the Gentiles the benediction of the God of Israel. If heaven permitted the new Christian to experience this trial, it was but to give her strength to surmount those last afflictions which were to crown her with immortal glory. But the time of her probation was deemed sufficient. Cymodoce was not to wander further from the theatre of her victory. The day of her triumph had come, and the decrees of the Eternal summoned the predestined virgin to the scene of combat.

By a sign from the midst of the cloud, Emmanuel made known to the angel of the seas the will of the Most High. Directly the wind, which till then had been favorable, fell: a calm reigned in the air; the uncertain breezes that veered to the different quarters of the heavens, scarcely ruffled the glassy surface of the deep, and just moved the languid sail, which it had not power to fill. The sun grew pale in the midst of its course, and the azure of the sky, streaked with greenish bands, seemed transformed into masses of uncertain and troubled light. Leaden clouds stretched illimitably over the dead and heavy sea; the pilot raised his hands toward heaven and exclaimed:

"O Neptune! what presage is this? If experience does not deceive me, never did a more horrible tempest threaten the deep."

At the same moment he ordered the sails to be lowered, and bade each one to prepare for the danger.

16*

The clouds collected in the south and in the east; their formidable battalions appeared in the horizon like an army in dark array, or like distant rocks. The sun, descending behind these clouds, pierced them with a livid ray, and discovered a threatening depth in the piles of vapor. Night came on: a darkness enveloped the vessel; and the mariner was unable to distinguish his comrade, who stood trembling by his side.

Suddenly a sign from the regions of the morning announced that God was preparing to open the treasure of his storms. The barrier which restrained the whirlwind was broken, and the four winds were let loose. The vessel drove before the gale, and presented her laboring stern to the impetuous blast of the east; all night she furrowed the sparkling billows. Day dawned, giving only light enough to show the tempest; the waves rolled in regular succession. No sound was heard on the ocean but that of the wind, which howled through the masts, and beat against the sides of the vessel. Nothing could be more terrible than this silence in tumult, this order in disorder. But how escape a tempest which seemed not fortuitous, but raised for some destined purpose?

For nine successive days the vessel was driven toward the west with irresistible violence. When the tenth night had passed, they perceived, by the glare of the lightning, a gloomy coast which appeared of an immeasurable height. Shipwreck seemed inevitable. The captain ordered each man to his station, and commanded the passengers to retire to the bottom of the vessel; they obeyed, and heard the fatal plank closed upon them.

It is in such moments that the characters of men are discoverd. A slave sung aloud; a mother wept over the child that she suckled at her breast, which should shortly need no longer her maternal care; while a disciple of Zeno bewailed the loss of life. As for Cymodoce, she wept for her father and spouse; and, together with Dorotheus, offered up her prayers to Him who can rescue us, even when swallowed up by the monsters of the deep.

The vessel now dashed against a shoal and sprung a leak;

a torrent of water burst into the cabin which held the passengers, and all was outcry and confusion.

By a sudden shock of the vessel, Dorotheus and Cymodoce were thrown at the foot of the ladder which led to the deck. They mounted it, half suffocated. What a spectacle! The vessel had struck upon a bank of sand, and a rock at a few paces distant from the prow elevated its summit above the waves, and seemed to threaten their immediate destruction. Some of the seamen, carried away by the waves, were swimming in the vast gulf; others clung firmly to the anchors and the cordage. The pilot was endeavoring to cut away the mast of the vessel; while the helm, abandoned, was beating furiously from side to side.

A feeble hope remained: the waves, as they rushed into the strait, might raise the vessel, and throw her on the other side of the sand-bank. But who would dare guide the helm in so critical a moment? One false movement of the pilot might be the destruction of two hundred souls. Humbled by a sense of their danger, the mariners no longer insulted the two Christians; on the contrary, they recognized the power of their God, and entreated them to obtain from him their deliverance. Cymodoce, forgetting their insults and her own danger, threw herself on her knees, and besought the protection of the mother of the Saviour. Dorotheus seized the deserted rudder; breathless with fear, and with eyes turned toward the stern, he waited the returning sea which was to give the vessel either to life or death. The billow rolled on, and broke against the vessel: the rudder was heard to turn with difficulty on its grating hinges; the shoal seemed to glide from beneath the prow; and with mingled joy and fearful apprehension, they felt the vessel heaved from the bank, and carried rapidly along. A moment of the most awful silence ensued. Suddenly a voice called for the lead: the line was thrown; they were in deep water. A cry of joy resounded to heaven! Star of the seas, patroness of mariners, the safety of these unfortunates was a miracle of thy divine goodness! No imaginary god was seen to raise his head above the waves and command their silence; but the clouds were half-unclosed by a supernatural light: in the midst of a halo of glory appeared a celestial woman, bearing an infant in her arms, and calming the waves by a smile. The mariners threw themselves at the knees of Cymodoce, and confessed Jesus Christ; such was the first recompense granted by the Eternal to the virtues of a persecuted virgin!

The vessel gently approached the shore, on which stood an abandoned Christian chapel. The sailors cast into the sea sacks of stones attached to a Tyrian cable, and the sacred anchor, the last resource of the shipwrecked mariner. They then disembarked for the shore, and Cymodoce was borne to land on the shoulders of the seamen, like a queen surrounded by a band of captives, whom she has just delivered from slavery. That very instant she accomplished her vow. She proceeded to the ruined chapel. The sailors followed her in pairs, half naked, and covered with the foam of the waves. Whether from chance, or the decree of heaven, there was left in this deserted asylum a half-destroyed image of Mary. Upon this, the spouse of Eudorus suspended her veil, wet with the waters of the sea. Cymodoce took possession of the land that was to witness her glory, and entered triumphant into Italy.

BOOK TWENTIETH.

SUMMARY.

Cymodoce, arrested by the Satellites of Hierocles, is conducted to Rome. Public Outbreak. Cymodoce, freed from the Hands of Hierocles, is thrown into Prison as a Christian. Disgrace of Hierocles. He receives an Order to depart for Alexandria. Letter of Eudorus to Cymodoce.

The dawn had recalled mortals to labor and sorrow; each one resumed his painful toil: the husbandman followed the plough while the toil-drops fell from his brow, and bedewed the furrow which the oxen had traced; the forge resounded with the blows of the hammer which fell in cadence on the burning iron; and each city again resounded with the voice of industry. The sky was serene, and the east radiant. Cymodoce no longer beheld a vessel adorned with flowers, or a chariot drawn by snow-white steeds awaiting her arrival on shore. The honors that Italy had in store for her were those which she conferred on the Christians—persecution and death.

The decrees of heaven had conducted the daughter of Homer to a part of the coast not far from Tarentum, under a projecting promontory which concealed the country of Archytas from the eyes of the shipwrecked crew. The pilot ascended a rock, and casting his eyes around the shore, suddenly exclaimed:

"Italy! Italy!"

At this name Cymodoce felt her knees falter beneath her; her bosom heaved like the billow swelled by the wind. Dorotheus was obliged to support her in his arms, so great was her joy at treading the same earth with her spouse. Since God had separated her from her father, whom she believed to be still in Messenia, she could at least fly to Rome.

"I am now a Christian," said she; "Eudorus can no longer prevent me from sharing his sorrows."

As Cymodoce pronounced these words, a vessel doubled the neighboring promontory. It was hauled along by a bark crowded with soldiers. At length the sailors ceased to row. The soldiers cut the cord which fastened it to their vessel: immediately it stopped, sunk by degrees, and disappeared beneath the waves.

It was one of those galleys filled with the poor and unfortunate, whom Galerius had ordered to be drowned on these solitary shores. A few of the victims, freed from their prison by the waves, swam toward the soldiers' bark; the latter drove them back with their spears, and, joining insult to barbarity, ordered them to go to sleep with Neptune. At this spectacle, the sailors of Cymodoce's vessel fled in terror along the sands; but Dorotheus and his companion could not conquer in their hearts that charity which is the unmistakable sign of the Christian. They called these unfortunates, who still struggled for life; they stretched out their hands to them, and succeeded in saving them. At this moment the ministers of Galerius reached the shore, and surrounded Dorotheus and the daughter of Demodocus.

"Who are you," cried the centurion, with a menacing voice, "that presume to save from death the enemies of the emperor?"

"I am Dorotheus," replied the Christian, whose indignation betrayed his prudence; "I have only fulfilled the common duty of humanity. Alas, Tarentum must have preserved her angry divinities, to be thus lost to every sentiment of pity and of justice!"

At the name of Dorotheus, a name known throughout the empire, the centurion durst not lift his hand against a man of such exalted dignity; but he demanded who that woman was, whose imprudent pity had rendered her guilty of a violation of the edicts.

"She is certainly a Christian," cried he, struck with her humanity and modesty. "Whither are you going? whence do you come ? what design has brought you hither ? Are you ignorant that no one can enter Italy without the special orders of Hierocles ?"

Dorotheus gave him an account of their shipwreck, and endeavored to conceal the name of his companion. The centurion repaired to the stranded vessel. When, threatened by the seamen, Cymodoce had apprehended that her life was in danger, she had written to her spouse and her father two farewell letters, filled with sorrow and tenderness. These letters, which she had left on board, betrayed her name to the soldiers, and a cross, found on her couch, discovered her religion: thus the amorous lays of Philomela betray her to the fowler; thus the spouses of kings are known by the sceptre which they bear.

The centurion said to Dorotheus:

"I am compelled to detain you in custody together with this young Messenian. The orders against the Christians are executed with the utmost rigor; and by liberating you, I should expose my own life to danger. I will instantly dispatch a messenger to the minister of the emperor, for he is the person to decide upon your fate."

Hierocles was now exercising absolute power over the Roman world; but deep anxieties still tormented his breast. Publius, the prefect of Rome, began to gain an ascendency over him in the favor of Galerius. The rival of Hierocles opopposed him in every project. Weary of awaiting the arrival of Cymodoce, did the persecutor wish to consign Eudorus to torments, Publius discovered some means of delaying the sacrifice. Did Hierocles, faithful to his former designs, suspend the trial of the son of Lasthenes, Publius said to the emperor:

"Why does not the minister of your Eternity give up to justice this dangerous chief of the rebels ?"

The silence which was observed in the East concerning the daughter of Homer, alarmed the guilty love of her persecutor. In his impatience, he had stationed sentinels at every port of Italy and Sicily. Numerous couriers were employed day and night to convey any tidings that might be received. It was in the midst of these perplexities that the messenger from Tarentum arrived. At the name of Cymodoce, he uttered a cry of joy, and started from his couch: thus the bard of Troy represents the monarch of Tartarus as darting from his throne, with trembling lips, and eyes wild with love and joy.

"Let my Messenian slave be brought into my presence!" cried he. "My good fortune has again delivered her into my hands."

At the same time, he gave orders that the officer of the palace of Diocletian should be restored to liberty.

Dorotheus still possessed at Rome many partisans and zealous protectors, even among the pagans. This just man had never employed his wealth or his power but to prevent violence, or to protect the innocent. In this moment he reaped the fruits of his virtues, and public opinion served to defend him against a perverse minister. The meeting of this powerful Christian and of Cymodoce appeared to Hierocles the effect of chance, and he wished not to raise against himself new enemies when he had already Publius to combat. The apostate felt in his heart that public hatred was gathering about his head, and in fear of arousing the people in favor of an aged priest of the gods, he had permitted Demodocus to wander in obscurity about the city of Rome. God now began to blind the sinner. Instead of accomplishing the ends he had in view, his foresight served only to involve him in perplexity; his arts of deceit, and his ingenious policy, led him into the very snare which he thought to avoid. In the eyes of the multitude, Hierocles still appeared omnipotent; but a penetrating eye could discover in him the symptoms of weakness and decay: such is the appearance of an oak whose head seems to touch the skies, and whose roots reach even to the abyss; it seems to brave the winter, the tempest, and the lightnings; the traveller seated at its feet, beholds with astonishment its mighty branches, which have seen so many mortal generations pass away; but the shepherd who contemplates this monarch of the forest from the brow of the hill, discovers a withered crown spreading over its verdant foliage.

Upon a hill which commanded a view of the amphitheatre of Vespasian, Titus had erected a palace, on the ruins of the magnificent abode of Nero. Here were collected all the masterpieces of Greece. Vast peristyles, halls incrusted with the marble of the East, and paved with costly mosaics, presented to the eye the wonders of ancient sculpture: the *Mercury* of Zenodorus, which had been brought from the city of Arverni in Gaul, astonished the beholder by its colossal dimensions, which detracted nothing from its lightness; the *Fluteplayer* of Lysippus seemed to reel, while laughing, under the influence of Bacchus; the bronze *Venus* of Praxiteles, vied in beauty with the marble *Venus* of the same divine artist: his *Matrona in Tears*, and his *Phryne in Joy*, displayed the versatility of his art: the passion of the sculptor was conspicuous in the features of the courtesan, who seemed to promise to genius the recompense of love. Next to *the Phryne* stood the *Lioness without a tongue*, the ingenious symbol of that other courtesan who chose rather to die in tortures than to betray Harmodius and Aristogiton. The statue of *Desire*, which raised the same feelings it was designed to represent, that of *Mars asleep*, and of *Vesta* in a seated posture, immortalized in these places the talents of Scopas. To these invaluable monuments of art, Galerius had added the brazen bull, which Perillus invented for Phalaris.

The new emperor inhabited this beautiful palace. Hierocles, his worthy minister, inhabited one of the porticos of the residence of this master of the world. The apartments of the stoic philosopher surpassed in magnificence even those of Galerius. Upon the polished walls were represented charming landscapes, vast forests, and cooling cascades. Pictures of the most renowned masters adorned his enchanting baths and voluptuous chambers: here appeared the *Juno Lacinia;* to serve as models for this masterpiece of art, the Agrigentines had formerly exposed their daughters to the eyes of Zeuxis: there was the *Venus* of Apelles issuing from the wave, worthy to reign over the gods, or to be beloved by Alexander. Here, too, you beheld the *Satyr* of Protogenes dying of love: the inhabitant of the forests was breathing his last upon a bed of moss, at the entrance of a grotto tapestried with vines : his pipe was falling from his hand, his thyrsus was broken, and his bowl overturned ; and such was the skill of the painter that he had succeeded in uniting those attributes of Venus which are most material in the brute and most celestial in the man. Woe to him who removed the fine arts from the temples of the gods to adorn the dwellings of mortals! Then it was that the most sublime works of silence, meditation, and genius became the causes, the elements, and the witnesses of the greatest crimes, or of the most shameful passions.

Hierocles awaited the daughter of Homer in the most magnificent hall of his palace. At one of the extremities of this hall breathed the *Apollo* destroying the serpent that attacked Latona; at the opposite end appeared the group of *Laocoön and his sons*, as if the sage, in the midst of his pleasures, could not dispense with the image of suffering humanity ! Purple, gold, and crystal glittered on every side. Here was constantly heard the soft murmur of fountains, and of distant music. The rarest flowers of Asia embalmed the air, and exquisite perfumes were burning in vases of alabaster.

The satellites of Hierocles at length brought him the prey which he had so long pursued. Through obscure windings and secret doors which were carefully closed behind her, Cymodoce was conducted to the feet of the persecutor. The slaves retired, and the daughter of Demodocus remained alone with this monster, who feared neither gods nor men.

She concealed her grief beneath the folds of her veil. No sound escaped her but the murmur of her sobs; such is the sound of a rill that is heard in the forest, but the source of which remains concealed. Her breast, agitated with fear, heaved against her snowy robe. She filled the hall with a sort of light, resembling the brightness that emanates from the bodies of angels and blessed spirits.

Hierocles remained for a moment abashed before the authority of innocence, weakness, and misfortune. He was struck by the charms he beheld; he contemplated with a fearful ardor her whom he had never before beheld so near to him, her whose hand or whose veil he had never touched, her whose voice he had never heard but among the choirs of virgins; and who, nevertheless, had disposed of the days, the nights, the thoughts, the dreams, and the crimes of the apostate. The passion of this man devoted to hell, soon surmounted the first moment of trouble and confusion. At first he affected a moderation which soon gave way to the solicitations of love, jealousy, vengeance, and pride. He addressed Cymodoce in these words:

"Cymodoce, whence this dread and these tears? You know that I love you. Submissive to your slightest wishes, you shall see me obey you as a slave, if you will but listen to me."

The insolent favorite of fortune raised the veil of Cymodoce He remained fixed in astonishment at the charms he beheld The virgin blushed, and hiding in her bosom her countenance bathed in tears, exclaimed:

"I desire nothing of you; my only request is to be restored to my father. The groves of Pamisus are more agreeable to my heart than all your palaces."

"Well," replied Hierocles, "I will restore you to your father; I will load the old man with glory and with riches; but consider that a vain resistance might destroy forever the author of your days."

"Will you give me back my spouse, too?" cried Cymodoce, joining her suppliant hands.

At this name, Hierocles turned pale, and was scarcely able to repress his rage.

"What!" cried he, "that wretch who has gained possession of your heart by philters and enchantments? Listen: he is about to lose his life in torture. Judge of my love for you: I will snatch from death this odious rival."

Deceived by this language, Cymodoce uttered a cry of joy, fell at the feet of Hierocles, and embraced his knees.

"Illustrious sir," cried she, "you are placed at the head of the sages. Demodocus, my father, has often told me that philosophy raises mortals above those whom we call our gods. Protect, then, O mighty ruler! protect innocence, and reunite two spouses unjustly persecuted."

"Celestial nymph," cried Hierocles, transported with love, "arise! Do you not see that your charms destroy the effect of your prayers? Who could ever yield you to a rival? True wisdom, lovely child, consists in following the dictates of your heart. Do not believe a savage religion which seeks to command your senses. Precepts of purity, modesty and innocence are, without doubt, useful to the crowd; but the philosopher enjoys in secret the bounties of nature. The gods either do not exist at all, or never meddle with things here below. Come, then, ingenuous virgin, let us abandon ourselves without remorse to the delights of love and the favors of fortune."

At these words Hierocles threw his arms around Cymodoce, as a serpent entwines itself around a young palm-tree, or an altar consecrated to Modesty. The daughter of Demodocus tore herself with indignation from the embraces of the monster.

"What!" she exclaimed, "is this the language of wisdom? Enemy of heaven, darest thou speak of virtue? Hast thou not promised to save Eudorus?"

"You have mistaken me," cried Hierocles, while his heart palpitated with jealousy and with anger. "You speak too much of that man more horrible to my eyes than that hell with which the Christians threaten me. The love which you bear toward him, is the decree of his death. For the last time, learn the conditions upon which Eudorus may be saved: he dies unless thou art mine."

Reprobation appeared marked on the countenance of Hierocles. A smile contracted his lips, and his eyes seemed suffused with blood. The Christian virgin, who hitherto had been struck with terror, felt herself suddenly reanimated by the blow which was intended to overcome her. Sorrow is terrible only in its commencement; in the height of adversity, in proportion as we recede from the world, we discover regions of tranquillity and delight: thus when the traveller stands in a valley by the fall of a furious torrent, the roar of the waters fills him with dread; but as he ascends the mountain the waters diminish, the sound gradually dies away, and he at length reposes in the regions of silence and in the vicinity of the skies.

Cymodoce cast a look of contempt on Hierocles:

"I understand you now," cried she; "I now discover the reason why my spouse has not yet received his crown; but know, that I would not purchase by dishonor this life of the warrior, whom I love more than the light of heaven. There is no punishment that Eudorus would not rather suffer than to see me thine; feeble as he is, my spouse laughs at your power: you can but give him the palm, and I hope to share it with him."

"No," cried Hierocles, transported with rage, "I will not lose the fruit of so many schemes, sufferings, and humiliations: I will obtain by force that which you deny me; and you shall behold the traitor, whom you will not save, perish before your eyes."

He spoke, and pursued Cymodoce, who fled through the vast hall. She threw herself at the feet of the *Laocoön;* she threatened the persecutor to dash her head against the marble; she embraced the statue, and seemed a third child expiring with grief at the feet of an unfortunate father.

"My father," cried she, "wilt thou not come to my assistance? Holy virgin, have pity on me!"

Scarcely had she pronounced this prayer, when the palace resounded with a thousand tumultuous voices. Redoubled blows shook the brazen portals.

Hierocles, astonished, suspended his pursuit. God, by a sudden dread, fixed him motionless to the spot, and congealed the blood around his heart.

"'Tis the holy virgin," cried Cymodoce; "she comes! Wretch, you will now be punished!"

The noise increased. Hierocles opened the door of a gallery which commanded the courts of the palace; he beheld an immense concourse of people, in the midst of which was a venerable old man, who held in his hand the emblems of a supplicant, and wore the robe and fillets of a priest of the gods. Shouts were heard on every side:

"Restore his daughter to him! Deliver up the traitor to the supplicant of the Roman people!"

These words reached the ears of Cymodoce; she darted forth into the gallery, and recognized her father. . . . Demodocus at Rome! . . . Cymodoce, from the heights of the palace, bent forward and stretched forth her arms toward Demodocus. A cry arose:

"Behold her! She is a priestess of the Muses! she is the daughter of this aged priest of the gods."

Demodocus recognized his daughter; he called her by her name; he shed torrents of tears; he rent his garments, and stretched out his supplicating hands to the people. Hierocles called his slaves, and would have seized upon Cymodoce, but the crowd exclaimed:

"Hierocles, thy life is at stake; we will tear thee to pieces with our own hands, if thou offerest the least violence to this virgin of the Muses."

The soldiers that were scattered among the people drew their swords, and threatened the persecutor. Cymodoce clung to the columns of the gallery; the queen of the angels held her there by invisible bonds: nothing could tear her from her hold.

At this moment, Galerius, alarmed at the tumult which he heard in the palace, made his appearance on an opposite balcony, surrounded by his courtiers and his guards. The people exclaimed:

"Justice, Cæsar, justice!"

The emperor, by a gesture, commanded silence; and the Roman people, with the good sense that characterized them, were all silence and attention.

The prefect of Rome, who secretly favored this scene, in order to overthrow Hierocles, was at the side of Galerius; he thus interrogated the people:

"What do you demand of the justice of Augustus?"

"Old man, answer," cried the multitude.

Demodocus then spoke:

"Divine emperor! son of Jupiter and of Hercules, have pity on a father who comes to reclaim his daughter. Hierocles has confined her in your palace: in yonder portico you behold her with hair dishevelled, in the presence of her ravisher; he wishes to offer violence to a priestess of the Muses; I am myself a priest of the gods; protect innocence, old age, and their altars."

Hierocles answered from the top of the portico:

"Divine Augustus, and you, Roman people, you are deceived; this Greek is a Christian slave, whom they wish unjustly to take from me."

"She is not a Christian," replied Demodocus; "my daughter is not a slave: I am a Roman citizen. People, do not listen to our enemy."

"Is thy daughter a Christian?" cried the people, with one voice.

"No," answered Demodocus; "she is a priestess of the Muses: it is true that in order to espouse a Christian she wished " . . .

"Is she a Christian?" interrupted the people. "Let her speak for herself."

Cymodoce, raising her eyes to heaven, replied:

"I am a Christian."

"No, thou art not!" cried Demodocus, with sobs. "Canst thou be so cruel as to wish to be eternally separated from thy father! Augustus, and you, Roman people, my daughter has not been marked with the seal of the new religion."

At this moment the daughter of Homer discovered Dorotheus in the midst of the crowd.

"Father," cried the virgin, in tears, "I behold Dorotheus near you; it was he, no doubt, who conducted you hither in order to rescue me from Hierocles: he knows that I am a Christian, and that I have been marked with the seal of my religion: he was an eye-witness of my happiness. I cannot deny my faith: I wish to become the spouse of Eudorus."

The people addressed themselves to Dorotheus:

" Is she a Christian ?"

Dorotheus bent his head, and made no reply.

" You see," cried Hierocles, " she is a Christian. I reclaim my slave."

The people, astonished, remained in suspense between their fury against the Christians, their hatred to Hierocles, and their pity for Cymodoce; at length, satisfying at once both justice and their rage, they exclaimed:

" Cymodoce is a Christian ; let us deliver her up to the prefect of Rome, and let her undergo the fate of the Christians ; but let us free her from the hands of Hierocles, whose slave she cannot be : Demodocus is a Roman citizen."

Augustus confirmed this species of sentence by a motion of his head, and Publius hastened to put it in execution.

Galerius retired into his palace, a prey to shame and indignation : he could not pardon Hierocles for having been the author of a seditious tumult, which had dared to violate even the abode of the prince.

The prefect of Rome returned to Galerius.

" Augustus," said he, " the tumult is quelled : this Christian virgin of Messenia is cast into prison. Prince, I cannot conceal from you, that your minister has compromised the safety of the empire. He pretends to be an enemy to the Christians, yet how long has he spared the life of the most dangerous of the rebels. Cymodoce was the spouse destined for Eudorus : it is unfortunate that your prime minister should have been so absurd as to have had jealous quarrels with the chief of your enemies."

Publius perceived the effect of this discourse, and thus continued :

" But, prince, these are not the only crimes of Hierocles : if we may believe him, it was he that bestowed on you the title of Augustus ; this Greek, who is indebted to your bounty for everything he possesses, pretends that you are indebted to him for the purple."

Publius broke off his discourse at these words, as if he kept back something still more injurious to the majesty of the prince. Galerius blushed, and the skilful courtier saw that he had touched a secret wound.

Publius had not been ignorant of the arrival of Dorotheus in Rome, of his interview with Demodocus, and of the measures he pursued in order to assemble the multitude and conduct them to the palace: it would have been easy for Publius to have prevented this popular commotion, but he took care not to oppose a project that might overthrow Hierocles; he even favored the designs of Demodocus, by means of his secret agents: master of all the springs that moved this vast machine, his insidious discourses struck alarm into the breast of Galerius.

"Let me be delivered from this Christian and his accomplices," cried the emperor. "I see with regret that Hierocles can no longer remain about my person; but in recompense for his past services, I nominate him governor of Egypt."

Publius was transported with joy.

"May it please your divine majesty," said he, "to intrust me with all these cares. Eudorus merits death a thousand times, but as he has not been publicly convicted of treason, let it suffice that he be tried as a Christian. As to Cymodoce, she will be condemned in her turn with the rest of the unbelievers. The orders of your Eternity shall be immediately conveyed to Hierocles."

Thus spoke Publius, and hastened without delay, to make known to Hierocles the destiny that awaited him.

The perverse minister read over several times the imperial letter that banished him from court. His pallid cheeks, his wandering eyes and half-opened mouth, betrayed the grief of the criminal courtier, who beheld all his expectations and projects perish in an instant.

"God of the Christians," cried he, "it is thou who dost thus pursue me! To obtain Cymodoce I have spared the life of Eudorus, and now Cymodoce has escaped from my power, and my rival will perish by the hand of another! I despised an obscure old man wandering about Rome; I thought it my duty to liberate a powerful Christian, and Demodocus and

Dorotheus have been the very cause of my ruin! O blind human foresight! O vain and deluding wisdom, which can no longer preserve my power, or afford me any consolation!"

Such was the avowal that grief forced from Hierocles. Tears of indignation moistened his eyelids. He bewailed his fate with the weakness of a woman of little sense and of less fortitude; he still wished to save the life of Cymodoce, but the coward had not sufficient courage to risk his own life.

Whilst he was hesitating between a thousand projects, and could neither resolve to brave the storm nor consent to depart, Dorotheus had informed Eudorus of the arrival of Cymodoce, and of the events that had taken place at the palace. The confessors assembled around the son of Lasthenes, and congratulated him upon his choice of so courageous and so faithful a spouse. The joy of Eudorus was great, although he was troubled by the fresh dangers to which the young Christian was exposed.

"She is, then, the first who has confessed Jesus Christ!" cried he in holy transport. "This honor was reserved to her innocence!"

The thought that his well-beloved had received baptism in the waters of the Jordan, by the hands of Jerome, drew from his eyes tears of emotion.

"She is then a Christian!" he continually repeated. "She has confessed Jesus Christ before the Roman people; I can die in peace: she will soon be restored to me!"

A ray of hope began to shine through the gloom of the prison. The disgrace of Hierocles might cause a change in the empire. Constantine threatened Galerius from the extremities of the West; the messenger that Eudorus had dispatched to Diocletian might bring back happy tidings. Thus when a vessel has been wrecked during a tempestuous night, the helpless mariners drink the briny flood, and scarcely struggle against the billows; if a deceitful ray of light pierces the gloom for a moment, and discovers to their eyes some neighboring shore, joy enters their breasts, and they swim vigorously toward the land; but soon the light is extinguished, the rage of the tempest is renewed, and the mariners are buried in the abyss: such was the short-lived hope, such the fate of the Christians.

The martyrs were still chanting a hymn of praise to the Most High, when they beheld Zacharius enter the prison. The apostle of the Franks already knew the destiny of his friend :

" Sing on, fellow-sufferers," cried he, " sing on ! You have just cause for joy ; to-morrow, perhaps, a great saint will augment the number of your intercessors before God !"

All the confessors were mute. Silence reigned for a moment in the prison. Each one sought to divine who was the happy victim; each one wished that the lot might fall upon himself; each one weighed within his own breast the titles he had to this honor. Eudorus had instantly understood Zacharius; but he banished the hopes of martyrdom, as a proud thought and a temptation of hell. He feared to sin through pride by designating himself; he considered himself unworthy to die in preference to these venerable confessors who had so long combated for Jesus Christ. Zacharius soon put an end to this sublime uncertainty, and this celestial emulation; he approached Eudorus :

" My son," said he, " I saved your life; you are indebted to me for your glory: do not forget me when you are in heaven."

Instantly all the bishops, the priests, and the prisoners, fell at the knees of the martyr, kissed the hem of his garment, and recommended themselves to his prayers. Eudorus, standing erect in the midst of these prostrate old men, resembled a young cedar of Lebanon, the only remaining scion of an aged forest that has fallen at its feet.

A lictor, preceded by two slaves bearing torches of cypress in their hands, entered the prison. Surprised at the prostration of the prisoners, who remained in the same attitude, he could scarcely believe his eyes.

" King of the Christians," said he to the spouse of Cymodoce, " which among thy people is the tribune who is called Eudorus ?"

" I am he," replied the son of Lasthenes.

"Well," replied the lictor, still more astonished, "it is you, then, who are to die!"

"You perceive this by the honors that are paid me," answered Eudorus.

A slave unrolled the fatal edict, and read with a loud voice the orders of Publius:

"Eudorus, son of Lasthenes, native of Megalopolis, in Arcadia, formerly tribune of the Britannic legion, master of the cavalry, prefect of the Gauls, is commanded to appear to-morrow at the tribunal of Festus, the judge of the Christians, to sacrifice to the gods, or to die."

Eudorus bowed, and the lictor retired.

As in the feasts of the city of Thesca a young Canephoros conceals herself from the eyes of the multitude who extol her modesty and her graces; thus Eudorus, who already bore the palm of martyrdom, retired to a recess of the prison, in order to avoid the praises of his companions in glory. He demanded the mysterious liquor which the Christians made use of in the times of persecution, and traced his adieus to Cymodoce.

Angel of holy love, thou who faithfully guardest the history of virtuous passions, deign to confide to me the page from the book of memory, whereon thou hast engraven the tender and pious sentiments of a martyr!

"Eudorus, servant of God, in chains for the love of Jesus Christ, to our sister Cymodoce, designed for the spouse and the companion of our sufferings, peace, grace, and love.

"My dove, my well-beloved, we have learnt with a joy worthy of the love which we bear for you in our heart, that you have been baptized in the waters of the Jordan by our friend Jerome the anchorite. You have just confessed Jesus Christ before the judges and the princes of the earth. O servant of the true God, how resplendent must be your beauty now! Can we, who are too justly punished, complain, whilst you, an Eve yet unfallen, suffer all the persecutions of men? It is a dangerous temptation to us to think that those arms so feeble and so delicate are loaded with heavy chains; that that head, adorned with all the graces of a virgin, and worthy to be supported by the hands of angels, reclines upon a stony pillow, amidst the gloom of a prison. Ah! were it permitted us to be happy with you! . . . But far from us be the thought! Daughter of Homer, Eudorus is about to precede you to the regions of everlasting bliss; he must cut short the thread of his days, as the weaver cuts the thread of his half-woven warp. We write to you from the prison of St. Peter, in the first year of the persecution. To-morrow we shall appear before the judges, at the hour when Jesus Christ expired upon the cross. My well-beloved, could our love for you be greater, if we wrote to you from the house of kings, and during the year of happiness?

"We must quit thee, O thou most beautiful among the daughters of men! With tears we entreat heaven to permit us to see you again here below, if but for a moment. Will this favor be granted to us? Let us wait with resignation the decrees of Providence. If our loves have, alas! been short, they have at least been pure! Like the queen of heaven, you preserve the sweet name of spouse, without having lost the beautiful name of virgin. This thought, which would cause despair to human tenderness, makes the consolation of divine affection. What happiness is ours! O Cymodoce, we were destined to style you either the mother of our children, or the chaste companion of our eternal felicity!

"Adieu, then, O my sister! Adieu, my dove, my well-beloved! entreat your father to pardon us for his tears. He must indeed be unhappy! Alas, he will, perhaps, lose you, and he is not a Christian!

"Remember this salutation which I, Eudorus, add to the end of my letter:

"Remember my bonds, O Cymodoce.

"May the consolation of Jesus Christ be with you."

BOOK TWENTY-FIRST.

SUMMARY.

Eudorus is released from his Penitence. Complaints of Demodocus. Prison of Cymodoce. Cymodoce receives the Letter of Eudorus. Acts of the Martyrdom of Eudorus. Purgatory.

It was the hour when the courtiers of Galerius, stretched on purple couches around a table furnished with every expensive luxury, prolonged the delights of the banquet into the shades of night. With hands filled with branches of dill, and brow crowned with chaplets of roses and violets, each guest abandoned himself to transports of joy. Fluteplayers, skilled in the art of Terpsichore, inflamed the passions by effeminate dances and voluptuous songs. A bowl of rare beauty, and deep as that of Nestor, animated the joyous assembly. The god who bears the quiver and the bow, and who laughs at the mischiefs he has caused, was, as at the banquet of Alcibiades, the subject of conversation amidst these happy men. Marble, crystal, silver, gold, and precious stones, reflected and multiplied the blaze of torches, while the odors of the perfumes of Arabia mingled with those of the wines of Greece.

At this hour, the Christian confessors, abandoned by the world, and condemned to death, were also preparing a feast and a banquet within the dungeons of St. Peter. Eudorus was to appear the following day before the tribunal of the judge; he might expire in the midst of torments; it was time therefore to release him from his penitence.

A lamp was lighted in the prison. Cyril, to whom the bishop of Rome had delegated his powers, was to celebrate the mass of reconciliation. Gervasius and Protasius were chosen to assist at the sacrifice: they arrayed themselves in white tunics that the brethren had brought; their fair locks fell in curls upon their shoulders; their whole air breathed a virginal purity. Such was the modesty, such the animation painted upon the countenance of these two youths, that one would have thought they were preparing to go forth to martyrdom.

The prisoners threw themselves on their knees around Cyril, who commenced in a low voice a mass without a chalice and without an altar. The alarmed confessors knew not where the spotless victim was to be consecrated. O sublime invention of charity! O affecting ceremony! the aged bishop placed the host upon his heart, which thus became the altar of the sacrifice. Jesus Christ, a martyr, was offered a holocaust upon the heart of a martyr! A God arose from this heart; a God descended into this heart!

. And now Eudorus threw off his penitential habit, and received in exchange a robe of the purest white. Persius and Zacharius arose to perform the office of deacon and archdeacon, and in the name of the Christians they addressed themselves to Cyril:

"Beloved of God, now is the moment of mercy; this penitent wishes to be reconciled to the Church; the Church itself demands his reconciliation; he has successively passed through the degrees of penitence; let him now be admitted to the rank of the elect."

"Penitent," said Cyril, "do you promise a change of life? Raise your hands to heaven in token of this promise."

Eudorus raised toward heaven his arms laden with chains: he seemed adorned with his bonds, as a youthful bride with her bracelets and the golden fringes of her robe. Cyril pronounced over him these words:

"Believer, I absolve thee through the mercy of Jesus Christ, who looses in heaven whatever his apostles loosen upon earth."

At these words, Eudorus fell at the feet of the bishop, and

received the sacred viaticum from the hands of the deacon—that bread of the Christian traveller, which is to be his support on his pilgrimage to eternity. The confessors admired this chosen martyr in their midst, who, like a Roman consul chosen by the people, was soon to display the marks of his power. The world would have seen nothing in this assembly of outlaws, but a crowd of obscure men, condemned to perish beneath the hand of the executioner; and yet here were met the chiefs of a numerous race that was destined to cover the earth; here stood those victims whose blood was to extinguish the flames of persecution, and to spread the reign of the cross throughout the world. But how many tears were to be shed before this persecution should bring the day of triumph!

Demodocus arrived at Rome, but it was only to experience fresh afflictions. Informed of the first evils that threatened the priestess of the Muses, he had assembled the people, and conducted them to the palace of Galerius; but scarcely had he rescued Cymodoce from the grasp of Hierocles, before she was torn from his arms as a Christian. The old man was forbidden the sight of his daughter; all pity had vanished since the young Messenian had declared herself of the proscribed sect. The keeper of St. Peter's prison was humane, compassionate and accessible to gold, and it was easy to visit the martyrs confined there; but Sævus, the jailer of the prison of Cymodoce, was a furious enemy of the Christians, because his wife Blanche, who was a Christian, abhorred his debaucheries. He would allow no one to speak to Cymodoce, even in his presence, and he repulsed Demodocus with menaces and insult.

Not far from the asylum of grief, in which moaned the spouse of Eudorus, arose a temple consecrated by the Romans to Mercy: the frieze was adorned with basso-relievos of the marble of Carrara, and represented subjects consecrated by history or sung by the muse: there was seen that pious daughter who nourished her father in prison, and became the mother of him from whom she derived her existence; beyond this was Manlius, returning victorious from the Capitol, after having immolated his son; before him marched the hoary fathers of Rome, but the youth avoided meeting the victor. Here a beauteous vestal had launched on the Tiber the vessel that bore the image of Cybele, and was drawing by her girdle the destinies of Rome and of Carthage; there Virgil, as yet a shepherd, was forced to abandon his paternal fields; beyond, Ovid, on the fatal night of his exile, was receiving the last farewell of his spouse.

The stars had finished and again commenced their course, yet they still found Demodocus seated in the dust under the portico of this temple. His torn and dirty cloak, his neglected beard, his dishevelled locks sprinkled with ashes, announced the anguish of the venerable suppliant. Now he would embrace the feet of the statue of Mercy, and bedew it with his tears; then he would entreat the compassion of the people; at other times, to attract the notice of the passing crowd, he sung to the music of his lyre, to attract by accents of pleasure that attention which men feared to give to tears.

"O age of brass," cried he, "ye men whom Jupiter hates for your obduracy, can you remain insensible to the grief of a father! Romans, your ancestors erected temples to Filial Piety, and my hoary locks cannot move you to pity! Am I then a parricide, abhorred by cities and peoples? Do I deserve to be devoted to the Furies? Alas, I am a priest of the gods; I have been nurtured on the knees of Homer, in the midst of the sacred choir of the Muses! I have passed my life in imploring heaven for men, and they show themselves inexorable to my prayers! What is it that I demand? What, but that I may be permitted to see my daughter, to share her bonds, and to die in her arms before she is ravished from me? Romans, think of the tender age of my Cymodoce! Ah! I was the happiest mortal that the sun illumined in its course. Now, what slave would exchange his lot with mine? Jupiter had given me a hospitable heart: of all the guests that I received at my hearth, or who have drained with me the cup of joy, is there not a single one who will come to share in my sorrows ? How insensate is that mortal who believes prosperity lasting ! Fortune reposes nowhere !"

At these words Demodocus, striking his hands together in despair, threw himself prostrate on the earth. His cries could not penetrate the walls of his daughter's prison. The faithful who had preceded the new Christian in these gloomy dungeons, had all given their lives for Jesus Christ. Cymodoce remained the sole inmate of the prison. Wearied with the cares that he was obliged to render his orphan charge, Sævus often insulted her anguish: thus, when brutal villagers have borne a young eagle from the mountain, they shut up the sovereign of the airy regions in unworthy confinement; with inhuman sports they insult his fallen majesty; they strike that crowned head; they extinguish those eyes that would have contemplated the sun; they torment, in a thousand ways, the royal bird, who has no wings to fly, or talons to defend himself from outrage.

Nurtured in the smiling ideas of mythology, and surrounded, hitherto, by images of gracefulness and beauty, Cymodoce had scarcely known the name of sorrow and adversity. She had not been formed in that school of Christianity, where man learns from his cradle that he is born to suffer. Some time since, submissive to the trials of Providence, the daughter of Homer had changed her religion in changing her fortune, and Christianity came to offer her that assistance against the afflictions of life the worship of the false gods did not offer her. She studied with ardor the sacred books which she found in the prison, and which had belonged to some martyr; but unceasingly beset by the recollections of her infancy and youth, she could not yet perfectly relish those high consolations of religion that lift us above regrets and human miseries. Often, in the midst of her reading, her head would fall upon the sacred page, and overpowered with grief, the new Christian would sink for a moment into the priestess of the Muses. She beheld in imagination the brilliant skies of Messenia; she wandered in the groves of Amphissa; she revisited those beautiful festivities of Greece, those chariots rolling through the woods of Nemea, those religious processions winding by the sound of the flute over the summits of Ira, or the plains of Stenyclerus. She thought of the happiness that she once enjoyed with her father, and of the anguish that her aged sire must now feel. "Where is he? what is he doing? who cares for his age and tears?" she exclaimed. "How light are the sorrows of Cymodoce compared with those that overwhelm my father and my spouse!"

Whilst the daughter of Demodocus was indulging in these bitter reflections, she suddenly heard the sound of footsteps at the extremity of the prison. Blanche, the keeper's wife, appeared, and put in the hands of Cymodoce the letter from Eudorus, instructing her, at the same time, in the secret means of discovering its contents. This timid Christian, who durst not openly brave her husband and the tortures, hastened to retire and close the doors of the prison.

Cymodoce, left alone, prepared the liquid that, to be poured on the blank page, would bring out the mysterious characters that religion and love had traced thereon. At the first attempt she recognized the hand-writing of Eudorus; ere long, she succeeded in reading the first expressions of his love; the expressions of the martyr became more tender; she caught a glimpse of some fatal announcement; Cymodoce durst not further decipher the fatal writing. She stopped; resumed the letter; stopped again; and again commenced; at length she read the following words:

"Daughter of Homer, Eudorus is about to precede you to the regions of everlasting bliss. He must cut short the thread of his days, as the weaver cuts the thread of his warp that is but half woven."

Suddenly the eyes of the young Christian grew dim, and she fell in a swoon upon the floor of the prison.

But, O celestial Muse! whence arise those transports of joy that resound through the celestial domes? Why do those melodious sounds burst from the harps of gold? Why does the prophet king pour forth the sweetest of his canticles? What joy among the angels! The first of martyrs, the glorious Stephen, enters the Holy of Holies, and brings thence a brilliant palm, which he carries toward the earth with a look of mingled joy and veneration. Ye heavens, recount the triumph of the just! The afflictions of a life that endures but for a moment, are about to be exchanged for a happiness that shall never end: Eudorus has appeared before his judge!

He has bid adieu to his friends; he has recommended to their charity his spouse and Demodocus. The soldiers have conducted the martyr to the temple of justice, built by Augustus near the theatre of Marcellus. On an elevation, at the extremity of an immense hall, stood a chair of ivory, surmounted by a statue of Themis, the mother of Equity, of Law, and of Peace. The judge takes his seat: on his left are the sacrificers, an altar, and the victim; on his right stand the soldiers and centurions; and before him are placed fetters, a rack, a stake, and a chair of iron, with a thousand other instruments of torture, and a numerous band of executioners: the body of the hall is filled with a promiscuous crowd. Eudorus, in chains, is stationed at the foot of the tribunal. The heralds, the ministers of Jupiter and of men, proclaim silence. The judge begins his examination; the scribe indites upon his tablets the acts of the martyr.

Following the usual forms, Festus began:

"What is your name?"

"I am called Eudorus, the son of Lasthenes," replied the martyr.

"Are you ignorant," resumed the judge, "of the edicts that have been published against the Christians?"

"I know them," replied Eudorus.

"Sacrifice, therefore, to the gods," said the judge.

Eudorus answered: "I sacrifice but to one only God, who is the creator of heaven and earth."

Festus ordered them to strip Eudorus, to stretch him on the rack, and fasten the weights to his feet. He then addressed him:

"Eudorus, I see that you grow pale, that you suffer. Have pity upon yourself; recollect the glory and the honors that have been heaped upon you. Cast your eyes upon your family, whose name will expire with you; see the tears of your father; listen to the complaints of your ancestors. Do you not fear to heap anguish and despair upon the grey hairs of those who have given you life?"

"My glory, my honors, and my relatives are in heaven," replied Eudorus.

"Are you, then, insensible to the charms and promises of a chaste marriage?"

Eudorus was silent.

"You are beginning to relent," continued the judge; "own yourself vanquished; sacrifice, or tremble for the miseries that await you."

Eudorus replied: "What would it avail me to tremble before an earthly judge, who like myself must die?"

Festus gave orders that Eudorus should be torn with iron hooks. The blood covered the body of the confessor as the Tyrian purple dies the ivory of India, or the spotless wool of Miletus.

"Are you vanquished?" cried the judge. "Will you sacrifice to the gods? Think, if you persist in your obstinacy, that you will involve in your destruction your father, your sisters, and her who was destined for your spouse."

"Whence comes this happiness of being three times sacrificed for my God?" exclaimed Eudorus.

They now proceeded to fetter the feet of the confessor; they heated the chair of iron, and prepared the boiling pitch and the burning pincers to tear his flesh. Eudorus did not appear to suffer. Joy, mingled with a gentle gravity, illumined his countenance, and his whole air breathed majesty and grace. The chair of iron was prepared. The doctor of the Christians, from the burning seat, preached the Gospel still more eloquently. Seraphim shed around Eudorus a heavenly dew, while his guardian angel overshadowed him with his wings. He appeared in the flame like a delicious viand that was being made ready for the eternal tables. The most intrepid of the pagans turned away their heads; they could not support the effulgence of the martyr. The wearied executioners relieved each other; the judge gazed on the Christian with a secret terror, for he thought he beheld a divinity in the burning chair. The confessor cried aloud to him:

"Mark my countenance well, that you may recognize it again on that terrible day when all mankind shall be summoned to judgment."

At these words, Festus, disturbed, oade them suspend the torture. He retired hastily from the tribunal, passed behind a curtain, and dictated the following sentence to his trembling scribe:

"The invincible Augustus ordains, in his clemency, that whoever shall refuse to obey the sacred edicts, and sacrifice to the gods, shall on the day of the sacred birth of our Eternal Emperor, be exposed to wild beasts in the amphitheatre."

Eudorus was now carried back by the soldiers to prison. Already had the confessors been informed of his triumph. As soon as the gates of the prison were unclosed, and discovered to the bishops the pale and mutilated martyr, they advanced to meet him, with Cyril at their head, singing the following hymn in chorus:

"He has triumphed over hell, he has plucked the palm of triumph! O illustrious priest of Jesus Christ, enter into the tabernacle of the Saviour.

"What effulgence beams from his wounds! He has been tried in the fire like silver seven times refined.

"He has triumphed over hell, he has plucked the palm of triumph! O illustrious priest of Jesus Christ, enter into the tabernacle of thy Saviour."

The angels repeated this hymn in heaven, and a new subject of joy charmed the beatified spirits.

Eudorus, in the course of his glorious acts, had secretly offered up his sacrifice for the salvation of his mother. For some time past, he had been admonished in a dream of the situation of Sephora, and had besought the Most High to grant this virtuous woman a place among the elect. At her departure from this world, she had fallen into that place where the souls complete the expiation of their errors, because she had loved her children too weakly, and had thus become the first cause of the wanderings of her son. Eudorus, by the voluntary offering of his own blood, had obtained a remission of Sephora's trials. The three prophets, who read in the presence of the Eternal the book of life, Isaiah, Moses and Elias, announced the name of the liberated spirit. Mary rose from her throne: the angels who present to her the prayers of mothers, the tears of infants, and the sorrows of the poor and unfortunate, suspended for a moment their offerings. She ascended to her Son; she entered the place where the Lamb reigns amidst twenty-four elders; she advanced to the feet of Emmanuel, and bowing before the second uncreated essence, exclaimed:

"O my Son! since, being still but a weak mortal, I have borne in my bosom the weight of thy Eternity; since thou hast deigned to confide to my love the care of thy suffering humanity, deign to listen to my prayer. Thy prophets have announced the deliverance of the mother of the new martyr. Are the faithful then at last about to enjoy the peace of the Lord? Thou hast permitted me, the daughter of men, to present to thee their tears. I see a confessor whom a tiger is about to rend; will not the blood he has already shed suffice to ransom this Christian, and suffer him to enter into thy glory? Must he finish his sacrifice, and can the voice of Mary make no change in the rigor of thy counsels?"

Thus spoke the Mother of the seven sorrows. The Messiah, in a pitying tone, replied:

"O my mother, thou knowest that I have compassion on the tears of men; for them I have taken upon myself the burden of all the miseries of the world. But the decrees of my Father must be accomplished. If my confessors are persecuted for a moment upon earth, they will enjoy in heaven a glory without end. Nevertheless, O Mary, the moment of their triumph approaches: grace even has begun. Descend to those abodes where errors are effaced by penitence; bring back with thee to heaven the woman whose beatitude has been declared by the prophets, and let the felicity of the martyr for whom thou implorest me commence with the happiness of his mother."

A smile accompanied the pacific words of the Saviour of the world. The twenty-four elders bowed on their thrones; the cherubim veiled themselves with their wings; the celestial spheres paused to listen to the eternal Word; and the depths of chaos leaped up and were illumined, as though some new creation were about to emerge from nothingness.

Immediately Mary descended to the place of the purification of souls. She proceeded thither by a road studded with suns, in the midst of incorruptible perfumes and celestial flowers, which the angels strewed under her feet. The choir of virgins preceded her, singing hymns. By her side appeared the most illustrious of women—Elizabeth, whose infant leaped at the approach of Mary; Magdalen, who poured the precious ointment over the feet of her master, and wiped them with her hair; Salome, who followed Jesus to mount Calvary; the mother of the Maccabees, with her seven martyred children: Leah and Rachel; and Esther, still a queen; Deborah, from whose tomb grew the oak of tears; and the spouse of Elimelech, whom angels call the Beautiful, and men Naomi.

Between heaven and hell stretches a vast abode, consecrated to the expiation of the dead. Its base touches the regions of everlasting woe, and its summit the empire of inexhaustible joys. Mary carried consolation to those parts at the greatest distance from the heavenly abodes. There, the sufferers, panting and covered with sweat, toss in the midst of profound night. Their dark eyelids are only illumined by the neighboring flames of hell. The souls that are here suffering the rigors of expiation, do not partake of eternal tortures, but they live in perpetual dread of them. They hear the shrieks of the sufferers, the sound of the scourge, and the clank of chains. A burning flood, formed from the tears of reprobates, is the only barrier that separates them from the abyss, in which they would fear to be buried, were they not reassured by a hope, continually dying out, then reviving again.

The apparition of the Queen of angels, in the midst of these unfortunates, suspended for a moment the horror of their fears. A divine light illumined these prisons of expiation, which penetrated even to hell; and hell, astonished at the unusual sight, thought Hope had entered these abodes of despair. Moved with a heaven-born pity, Mary proceeded with her angelic pomp to regions less obscure and unhappy. In proportion as she ascended into these places of purgation, they became more beautiful, and the torments of the unhappy criminals began to diminish. Angels compassionate, although severe, watched over the penitence of these victims of expiation. Instead of insulting their pangs, as do the reprobate spirits the tears of the damned, they offered them consolation, and invited them to repentence; they depicted to them the beauty of God, and the happiness of an eternity passed in the contemplation of the supreme Being.

An extraordinary spectacle struck the view of the holy women who accompanied the Queen of virgins: some of the souls assumed a sudden and unusual splendor in the midst of those that surrounded them; a halo of glory encircled their brow; transfigured by degrees, they ascended to regions more elevated, where they could hear the music of the celestial choirs. These were the spirits, whose pains were abridged by the prayers of friends and relatives still on earth. Celestial prerogative of friendship, religion, and misfortune! The poorer, more unfortunate, infirm and despised the supplicant is here below, the more efficacious are his prayers in giving eternal happiness to some liberated soul!

The happy Sephora shone with extraordinary splendor in the midst of these ransomed souls. The mother of the Maccabees immediately took the mother of Eudorus by the hand, and presented her to Mary. The retinue then slowly ascended toward the everlasting tabernacles. The different worlds, those which meet our gaze at night, those which escape our sight in the profundity of space, the suns, the whole creation, the choruses of powers that presided at this creation, chanted this hymn to the mother of the Saviour:

" Open, eternal gates, admit the Sovereign of the skies!

"I salute thee, Mary, full of grace, model of virgins and of wives! Bear on your wings, ye ardent cherubim, the daughter of men and the mother of God. How tranquil are her glances! how calm and modest is her smile! Her features still preserve the beauty of the sorrow she felt on earth, as if to temper the eternal joys. The worlds tremble with love when she passes; she effaces the lustre of the increated light in which she walks and breathes. All hail, thou blessed among women! refuge of sinners, comforter of the afflicted!

"Open, eternal gates, admit the Sovereign of the skies!"

BOOK TWENTY-SECOND.

SUMMARY.

The Destroying Angel smites Galerius and Hierocles. Hierocles goes to find the Judge of the Christians. Return of the Messenger sent to Diocletian. Sadness of Eudorus, Demodocus and Cymodoce. The Repast of Freedom. Temptation.

WHAT are the pains of the body when contrasted with the torments of the soul? What fire can be compared to the fire of remorse? The just is tormented in his body; but his soul, like an impregnable fortress, remains tranquil when all is ravaged without: the wicked, on the contrary, reposes among flowers on his purple couch; and he seems to enjoy peace; but the enemy lurks within, and a thousand appearances betray the secret anguish of the man who seems so happy: thus, in the midst of a smiling plain, the eye discovers the funereal drapery that floats upon the towers of a city of which pestilence and death are disputing the empire.

Hierocles denied heaven: heaven abandoned him to hell. Publius, anxious to complete the ruin of his rival, discovered to the emperor the perfidy of his minister: the sophist had embezzled a part of the treasures of the prince. Every one sought a new crime for Hierocles; for men became as cowardly in accusing the fallen wretch as they were cowardly in excusing him when triumphant! What should this enemy of God do? Should he set out for Alexandria without attempting to rescue her whom he had destroyed? Should he remain at Rome to witness the bloody massacre of Cymodoce? The public hatred pursued him; a terrible prince menaced his ruin; his heart was a prey to a fearful love. In this perplexity, the eyes of this reprobate were suffused with blood, his gaze became fixed, his lips half unclosed, and his livid cheeks, with his whole frame, were convulsed: thus, when a serpent has poisoned himself with the deadly juices from which he extracts his venom, stretched in the public way, the reptile writhes in the dust, and foams with agony; he still inspires the spectator with terror, but it is a terror no longer ennobled by the idea of his power. Oh, how different is the Christian, whose almost exhausted veins have still retained blood enough to animate a noble heart!

But these pangs, both of body and mind, were but precursors to the punishments reserved for the persecutor of the Christians. God made a sign to the destroying angel, and pointed with his finger at two victims. The minister of vengeance instantly fastened to his shoulders his wings of fire, the rustling of which was like unto thunder. In one hand he took one of the seven golden vials filled with the wrath of God; with the other he seized the sword that struck the first-born of Egypt, and made the sun recoil before the camp of Sennacherib. Whole nations, condemned for their crimes, have vanished before the presence of this inexorable spirit, and the place of their monuments is forgotten. It was he, who, at Belshazzar's feast, traced the fearful handwriting on the wall; it was he who cast on the earth the sickle of the vintage, and the sickle of the harvest, when John, amidst the solitudes of Patmos, beheld the terrors of futurity prefigured to his view.

Wrapped in lightnings, the destroying angel descended, like one of those meteors that fall from the skies, and fill the heart of the mariner with dread. Enveloped in a cloud, he entered the palace of the Cæsars, at the moment when Galerius, seated at the festive board, was celebrating his prosperity. Immediately the lamps grew pale; the sound as of a multitude of chariots of war was heard without; the hair of the guests rose on their heads; involuntary tears trickled from their eyes; the shades of the ancient Romans were seen gliding along the halls, and Galerius felt a confused presentiment of the destruction of the empire. Unseen, the angel approached the master of the world, and poured into his cup some drops of the wine of the celestial wrath. Urged on by his evil destiny, the emperor raised the devouring liquor to his lips; but scarcely had he drank to the fortune of the Cæsars, when he felt himself instantly intoxicated: a disorder as sudden as it was uncommon, stretched him at the feet of his slaves: God, in a moment, had humbled the giant to the dust.

A beam cut on the summit of Gargarus has grown old in a palace, the abode of an ancient race; suddenly the flames darting from the hearth of the king mounts to the dry oak, the beam takes fire, and falls noisily in the echoing halls: so fell Galerius. The angel abandoned him to the effect of the eternal poison, and flew to the residence of the groaning Hierocles. With one blow of the sword of the Lord, he struck the side of the impious minister. A hideous disorder, the seeds of which Hierocles had brought from the East, at once declared itself. The unfortunate beheld a thick leprosy overspread his whole body; his garments clove to his flesh, like the robe of Dejanira, or the tunic of Medea. His reason wandered; he blasphemed against heaven and earth, and at the same instant implored the Christians to deliver him from the spirits of darkness with which he felt himself possessed. It was midnight. Hierocles called his slaves, and ordered them to prepare a litter; he arose from his couch, wrapped himself in his mantle, and half delirious, ordered himself to be carried before the judge of the Christians.

"Festus," said he, "you have in your power a Christian woman, who is the torment of my life: save her from destruction, and yield up this slave to my love; do not condemn her to the wild beasts; the edict allows you to give her up to infamy. . . . You understand me."

At these words, the wretch threw a purse of gold at the feet of the judge, and retired, groaning with anguish.

At this moment the last remaining hope of the Christians was frustrated: the messenger that Eudorus had dispatched to Diocletian, to engage him to resume the empire, returned from Saloua. Zacharius introduced him into the prison. The confessors had all received their sentence: they were condemned to perish in the amphitheatre with Eudorus. Surrounded by bishops who were dressing his wounds, the son of Lasthenes lay stretched on the ground upon the robes of the martyrs: thus the wounded hero, encircled by his brother-warriors, lies reclined on the drapery of the standards that he has won. The messenger melted into tears, and remained lost in silent anguish, his eyes fixed upon the spouse of Cymodoce.

"Speak, my brother," said Eudorus, "the flesh is somewhat weak, but the spirit still preserves all its vigor. Congratulate me on being assisted by those hands, that have so often touched the consecrated body of Jesus Christ."

The messenger, wiping away his tears, gave an account of his interview with Diocletian, as follows:

"According to your instructions, Eudorus, I embarked on the Adriatic, and landed on the shores of Salona. I inquired for Diocles, formerly Diocletian the emperor, and was informed that he resided at his gardens, four miles from the city. I repaired thither on foot. I arrived at the residence of Diocles; I traversed the courts, in which I found neither guards nor attendants. A few slaves were employed in various parts of the garden. I knew not to whom to address myself. At length I observed a man advanced in years who was laboring near me; I approached him, and inquired where I might find the prince, whom I was seeking.

"'I am Diocles,' replied the old man, still continuing his work; 'if you have anything to tell me, speak out.'

"I remained mute with astonishment.

"'Well,' said Diocletian, 'what business brings you hither? Have you any rare seeds that you wish to give, or exchange with me?'

"I delivered your letter to the aged emperor; I described the miseries of the Roman people, and the desire that the Christians felt to see him once more at the head of the State. At these words Diocletian suspended his labors, and exclaimed:

"'Would to the gods, that those who sent you could behold

like yourself the gardens that I am cultivating with my own hands here at Salona; they would not invite me to resume the empire!'

"I made the observation, that another gardener had once consented to wear the crown

"'Ah,' said he, 'the gardener of Sidonia had never, like me, descended from a throne, and he was tempted to mount it: Alexander would not have succeeded with me.'

"I could obtain no other answer. In vain I attempted to insist upon it.

"'Do me a favor,' he said to me abruptly; 'you are young, I am old; draw me some water, my plants need it.'

"At these words Diocletian turned his back on me, and Diocles took up his watering-pot."

The messenger was silent. Cyril thus addressed him:

"Brother, you could have brought us no better news. After your departure, Eudorus acquainted us with the object of your journey: the bishops feared lest you should succeed. Martyrdom has enlightened the son of Lasthenes; he now knows his duty; Galerius is our lawful sovereign."

"Yes," said Eudorus, repentant and humiliated; "I feel that I am justly punished for a criminal design."

Thus spoke these martys, broken by the irons and the rack of Galerius: thus the courageous animal, that arouses the bear and wild boar in the forests of Achelous, incurs the huntsman's unmerited displeasure; pierced by the weapon destined for the savage beast, the lime-hound falls and purples the moss with his blood; yet, even in expiring, he casts a look of submission toward his master, and seems to reproach him with having deprived himself of a faithful servant.

Though in hourly expectation of quitting the earth, Eudorus was tormented with a tender solicitude. Despite the fervor of his faith and the exaltation of his soul, the martyr could not think without a shudder on the destiny of the daughter of Homer. What would become of this victim? Would she fall again into the hands of Hierocles? If interrogated by the judge, could she stand the terrible trial? Was she condemned to death upon her first avowal, with the confessors of the prison of St. Peter? Eudorus pictured to himself Cymodoce torn by lions, and vainly imploring the aid of her spouse, for whom she was giving her life. To this picture he opposed that of the happiness he might have tasted with so fair and pure a woman. But the voice of conscience suddenly exclaimed:

"Martyr, are these the thoughts that should occupy thy soul? Eternity! Eternity!"

The bishops, skilled in the knowledge of the heart, beheld the internal conflicts of the warrior. They divined his thoughts, and sought to reanimate his courage.

"Friend," said Cyril, "let us exult together, for we shall soon be companions in glory. See in this prison, as in a smiling field, this produce ripe for the harvest, which shall fill the granaries of the good shepherd. Cymodoce will be, perhaps, of our number: she is a flower in the midst of the wheat, which sheds a sweet perfume around. If God ordains it thus, may his will be done! But rather let us supplicate heaven to leave your spouse behind, that she may offer in our behalf to the Eternal the acceptable sacrifice of her innocent prayers."

As the seaman, whose vessel during the sultry summer night has languished on the motionless deep, salutes the Zephyr, the child of Aurora, which breathes freshness on his senses, and wafts him on his way, thus the words of Cyril reanimated the martyr, and urged him on in the way of heaven. Still, he could not entirely divest himself of the man: for some time since he had solicited the most intrepid of the Christians to save Cymodoce, and to spare neither pains nor expense for that purpose; above all, he relied upon the courage of Dorotheus, who had already twice vainly endeavored at night to scale the prison of the daughter of Homer.

More successful in respect to Demodocus, Dorotheus had succeeded in rescuing him from prison, and had conducted him to a place of safety.

"Unfortunate old man," would he say, "why will you thus seek to shorten your days? Do you fear that they will not fly away with sufficient speed? Reserve your grey hairs for your daughter. If God should again restore her to your embraces, she will need consolation more than yourself, for she will have lost her spouse."

"What!" answered the aged priest, "do you wish me to cease to reclaim my daughter? It was upon her that I turned my eyes from the brink of the tomb. The last inheritor of the lyre of Homer, the Muses had lavished precious gifts upon her. She governed my household; in her presence none would have dared to insult my old age. Children, reflecting the image of their mother, would have prattled upon my knees! O Cymodoce, whose words had so many charms, what have become of thy promises? Thou wouldst say to me: 'O dearest father, what would be my grief, if the inexorable Fates should ever tear you from my love! I would cut off my tresses, and place them on thy funeral pyre; I would pass my days in bewailing thy loss with my companions!' Alas, my child, it is I that am left to weep for thee! It is I, who, in a strange land, without home, without children, bowed down by the burden of years, will three times invoke thy name around thy funeral pyre!"

As a bull that is deprived of the honors of the pasture, to separate him from the heifer about to be sacrificed to the gods; thus Dorotheus had forced Demodocus from the prison of Cymodoce.

The new Christian had reopened her eyes to the light, or rather to the darkness of the prison. Twenty times she perused the letter of Eudorus, and twenty times did she bedew it with her tears.

"Beloved spouse!" she exclaimed in the confused language of her two religions, "my lord and master, thou hero so like a divinity, art thou then to be dragged before the judge? . . . Methinks I see the fatal weapon! . . . And I am not there to dress thy wounds! O my father, why have you abandoned me? Hasten, conduct me to the fairest among mortals! Give way, ye pitiless walls, and let me bear my life to the sovereign master of my heart."

Thus Cymodoce complained in the silence of her prison, whilst noise and tumult surrounded the dungeons of the martyrs. They heard a confused murmur without, like the dashing of mighty waters, the blast that howls among the mountains, or the roaring of a fire kindled by the imprudence of a shepherd in a forest of pines: it was the people.

There was a custom at Rome of ancient usage; on the evening before the execution of criminals condemned to the wild beasts, a public meal, called the free repast, was given them at the gates of the prison. In this repast every species of delicacy was served up in the most sumptuous profusion. This was either the barbarous refinement of the law, or the brutal clemency of the religion; the former wished to inspire with a regret for life those who were about to lose it; the latter, considering pleasure as man's supreme felicity, wished that at least he should enjoy it in the last hours of his existence.

This repast was served up on an immense table in the vestibule of the prison. The people, prompted at once by curiosity and by cruelty, crowded in a circle round the front of the prison, while soldiers were stationed to preserve order. The martyrs soon came forth from their dungeons, and took their seats at this funereal banquet: they were all fettered, with their hands only at liberty. Those who were unable to walk by reason of their wounds, were carried by brethren. Leaning on the shoulders of two bishops, Eudorus dragged himself slowly along, while the rest of the confessors, out of pity and respect, spread their garments under his feet. When he appeared at the gate, the crowd burst into an involuntary cry of compassion, and the soldiers gave their old commander a military salute. The prisoners ranged themselves on couches in front of the spectators; Eudorus and Cyril occupied the centre of the table. Everything that was captivating in youth, and venerable in age, was united on the countenances of these two chiefs of the martyrs: one might have fancied that he saw Joseph and Jacob, seated at the banquet of Pharaoh. Cyril proposed to his brethren, that they should distribute this sumptuous feast among the people, and substitute in its place a simple repast, composed of a little bread and some pure wine : the astonished multitude kept silence, and listened eagerly to the words of the confessors.

"This repast," said Cyril, "is justly styled the free repast, since it delivers us from the fetters of the world and the miseries of humanity. God did not create death; man was the cause of it. To-morrow man will give us his handiwork, but God, who is the author of life, will give us life eternal. My brethren, let us pray for this people: to-day they seem touched by our destiny; to-morrow they will clap their hands at our death ! Let us pray for them, and for our emperor, Galerius."

And the martyrs prayed for the people and for Galerius, their emperor.

The pagans, accustomed to behold the criminals at these funeral orgies either abandoning themselves to insane mirth, or lamenting the loss of life, could not recover from their astonishment. The better instructed said:

"What is this assembly of Catos, discoursing tranquilly of death on the eve of their sacrifice ? Are not these men philosophers, who have been represented to us as the enemies of the gods ? What majesty on their brow ! what simplicity in their actions and their language !"

The multitude cried out:

"Who is that old man who speaks with so much authority, and whose instructions are so harmless and so gentle ? The Christians pray for us and for the emperor; they pity us; they give us their repast; they are covered with wounds, and they say nothing against us or against their judges. Is their God the true God ?"

Such was the discourse of the multitude. Among so many unhappy idolaters, some withdrew, filled with terror, others wept, and exclaimed:

"Great is the God of the Christians ! Great is the God of the martyrs !"

These remained to ask instruction, and believed in Jesus Christ.

What a spectacle for pagan Rome! What a lesson might it not learn from this communion of the martyrs! These men, who were soon to abandon life, continued to discourse in language full of unction and of charity: thus, when the swallows prepare to quit our regions, they assemble on the banks of a solitary pool, or on the towers of a village church: every place resounds with the sweet song of their departure; at last the northern breeze springs up, they wing their flight toward heaven, and go to seek another spring and a more hospitable clime.

In the midst of this affecting spectacle, a slave was seen approaching in haste: he forced his way through the crowd, inquired for Eudorus, and placed in his hands a letter from the judge. Eudorus unrolled the missive; it was couched in these words:

"Festus the Judge, to Eudorus the Christian, greeting.

"Cymodoce is condemned to the abodes of infamy. Hierocles is there awaiting her. I entreat you, by the esteem with which you have inspired me, to sacrifice to the gods: come and reclaim your spouse: I swear to deliver her to you pure, and worthy of you."

Eudorus swooned; all crowded around him; the soldiers near him seized the letter; the people demanded it; a tribune read it in a loud voice; the bishops stood mute in consternation; the whole assembly was tumult and disorder. Eudorus recovered his senses, and the soldiers were already at his knees, saying to him:

"Companion, sacrifice to the gods! Here are our eagles in default of an altar."

And they presented him a cup full of wine for the libation. A horrible temptation seized the soul of Eudorus. Cymodoce in a place of infamy! Cymodoce in the arms of Hierocles! The bosom of the martyr heaved with emotion; the bandages burst from his wounds, and his blood flowed in streams from his body. The people, seized with pity, fell themselves at his knees, and repeated with the soldiers:

"Sacrifice! Sacrifice!"

"Where are the eagles?" said Eudorus, in a hollow voice.

The soldiers struck their bucklers together in token of triumph, and hastened to bring the banners. Eudorus arose; the centurions supported him; he advanced to the foot of the eagles; silence reigned in the crowd. Eudorus took the cup; the bishops veiled their faces in their robes, and the confessors uttered a cry: at this cry, the cup fell from the hands of Eudorus, he overthrew the eagles, and turning toward the martyrs, exclaimed:

"I am a Christian!"

BOOK TWENTY-THIRD.

SUMMARY.

Satan reanimates the Fanaticism of the People. Feast of Bacchus. Explanation of the Letter of Festus. Death of Hierocles. The Angel of Hope descends to Cymodoce. Cymodoce receives the Robe of Martyrdom. Dorotheus takes Cymodoce away from the Prison. Joy of Eudorus and the Confessors. Cymodoce finds her Father. The Angel of Sleep.

THE prince of darkness trembled with rage as he beheld the pity of the people and the victory of the confessors.

"What!" cried he, "shall a martyr insult my power, when I have made him whom angel-slaves call Almighty tremble on his throne, when a few moments have been enough for me to deface the work of six days, and when I am about to triumph over Christ! Ah, let us reanimate against the Christians the fury of an insane people, and let Rome intoxicate herself to-day with the incense of idols and the blood of martyrs!"

He spoke, and directly assumed the figure, the gait, and the voice of Tages, the chief of the haruspices. He divested his immortal head of the remnant of his brilliant locks, scorched by the fires of the abyss; the scars that despair and the thunder of omnipotent wrath had traced upon his brow, were changed into venerable wrinkles; he concealed his folded wings beneath an ample linen robe, and leaning upon an augural staff, he advanced to meet the crowd who were returning from the banquet of the martyrs.

"People of Rome," cried he, "whence springs this sacrilegious compassion? What! your emperor is preparing to entertain you with spectacles, and you are weeping over wretches, the vile outcasts of the nation? Soldiers, they overturn your eagles, and you suffer yourselves to pity them! What would the Scipios and Camilluses say, if they were again to behold the light? Banish this criminal compassion, and instead of pitying here the enemies both of gods and men, go and pray in your temples for the safety of the emperor, and celebrate the feast of the gods."

As he pronounced these words, the rebel angel breathed on the fickle crowd a spirit of giddiness and fury. A thirst for blood and for pleasure was kindled in every breast, and extinguished their short-lived compassion. At this moment, one of the priests exclaimed:

"O heavens! what prodigy strikes my sight! This instant I left Tages in the Capitol, and yet I behold him here! Romans, it is incontestable; this is some divinity concealed under the figure of the chief of the haruspices, who comes to reproach you for your criminal compassion, and to announce to you the will of Jupiter."

At these words, the prince of darkness disappeared from the midst of the crowd, and the people, seized with terror, ran to the altars of the idols to atone for this moment of humanity.

Galerius celebrated at the same time the day of his birth, and that of his triumph over the Persæ. This day fell on the festival of Flora. In order to secure the favor of the people and the soldiers, the emperor reëstablished the festivities of Bacchus, which had long since been suppressed by the senate. This scene of horrors was to be crowned by the games of the amphitheatre, where the Christian prisoners were condemned to die.

Extravagant largesses, which had their source in the ruin of the citizens, and above all in the spoils of the faithful, had turned the minds of the crowd. Every kind of license was permitted and even commanded. A party of the populace assembled by the light of torches in the Patrician Way, and abandoned themselves to every species of lewdness in honor of that Flora who left the gains of her dishonor to a people who had not then lost all regard to decency. Galerius advanced to the Capitol in a car drawn by elephants; before him marched the captive family of Narses, king of the Persæ. The dances and vociferations of the votaries of Bacchus varied and multiplied the disorder. Innumerable wine skins and amphoræ were placed near the fountains and in the public places of the city. The people besmeared their countenance with the lees, while the very drains of the city flowed with wine. Bacchus appeared elevated upon a trestle, surrounded by a throng of Bacchantes. His priestesses waved lighted torches about him, and the thyrsus wreathed with branches of the vine, and bounded along to the sound of drums, clarions, and cymbals; their locks floated in disorder; they were clothed in the skins of stags, which were bound to their shoulders by adders that curled around their necks. Some bore tender fawns in their arms; others presented their breasts to the whelps of a wolf; all of them were crowned with branches of oak and fir; men disguised like satyrs accompanied them, dragging along a he-goat adorned with garlands. Pan appeared with his flute; not far from him advanced Silenus; his head, heavy with wine, rolled from one shoulder to the other; he was mounted on an ass, and supported by a troop of Fauns and sylvan divinities. A Mœnad carried his crown of ivy, an Ægipan half-filled his cup with wine; the noisy cortege stumbled at every step, and drank to Bacchus, to Venus, and to Mischief. Three choirs chanted alternately this strain:

"Let us sing Evoe; let us repeat without ceasing, Evoe, Evoe!

"Son of Semele, honor of Thebes, of the golden buckler, come, dance with Flora, the spouse of Zephyrus, and the queen of flowers! Descend among us, O consoler of Ariadne, thou who traversest the summits of Ismarus, of Rhodope and Cithæron! God of delight, child of the daughter of Cadmus, the nymphs of Nysa brought thee up, assisted by the Muses, in a grotto of perfumes. Scarcely delivered from the thigh of Jupiter, thou subduedst the mortals who rebelled against thy worship. Thou laughedst at the Tyrrhenian pirates, who carried thee off as the child of a mortal. At thy command a flood of delicious wine flowed over the deck of the sable vessel; branches of the vine, covered with fruit, fell from the sails; an ivy, laden with berries, twined around the verdant mast; garlands covered the benches of the oarsmen; a lion appeared at the stern; and the mariners, changed into dolphins, darted into the deep waves. Thou laughedst, O king Evoe!

"Let us sing Evoe; let us repeat without ceasing, Evoe, Evoe!

"Nursling of the Hyades and the Hours, pupil of Silenus and the Muses, thou who hast the dark eyes of the Graces, the golden locks of Apollo, and his immortal youth, O Bacchus, quit the shores of conquered India, come, and reign over Italy. The wines of Cæcubus and Falernus foam in our presses; twice in the year the ripened fruit hangs from the tree, and the lamb to the teat of its mother. Steeds eager for the course bound over our plains, and the banks of the Clitumnus are grazed by the oxen without stain, which are led to the Capitol before the triumphant Roman. Two seas waft to our shores the treasures of a world. Brass, silver, and gold are flowing in torrents in the bowels of this sacred land. It has given birth to famous nations, and to heroes still more famous. Hail, fruitful earth, land of Saturn, and mother of illustrious men! May you long bear the treasures of Ceres, and reëcho to the joyful cry of Evoe!

"Let us sing Evoe; let us repeat without ceasing, Evoe, Evoe!"

Alas! men inhabit the same earth; but how great is the difference between them. Could we take for brothers and inhabitants of the same city, those people, some part of whom pass their days in joys, and others in tears; the happy who are chanting the nuptial song, and the unfortunate who are celebrating the funeral rites? How touching, in the delirium of pagan Rome, to see the Christians humbly offering their prayers to God, deploring these criminal excesses, and giving every example of modesty and reason in the midst of drunkenness and debauchery! The persecuted faithful assembled round their secret altars, in the dungeons, in the depths of the catacombs, and upon the tombs of the martyrs. They fasted, they watched, and offered themselves as voluntary victims to expiate the crimes of the world; and whilst the names of Flora and of Bacchus resounded in abominable hymns amidst blood and wine, the names of Jesus Christ and of Mary were secretly repeated in the chaste hymns of the Christians, in the midst of tears.

All the Christians remained shut up in their houses, at once to avoid the fury of the people, and the spectacle of their idolatry. None were seen abroad, except the priests who attended the hospitals and the prisons, the deacons that were commissioned to rescue the poor condemned to death by Galerius, and the women who went in search of slaves abandoned by their masters, and infants deserted by their mothers. Oh, the charity of the early Christians! Their death formed the principal ornament of the pagan festivities; yet they felt the same concern for the fate of the idolaters, as though these idolaters had been to them brethren full of tenderness and compassion.

Meanwhile, after having repelled the assaults of the prince of darkness, the martyrs had returned to their prisons; thus of yore, a band of heroes sallied from the gates of Ilion, and attacked the enemy who besieged the town: the outworks are destroyed, the trenches are filled, the palisades are torn down, and the sons of Laomedon return triumphant within their sacred ramparts. But Eudorus, overcome by the last combat, was unable to raise his drooping head: in vain the bishops spoke to him, consoled him, and extolled his courage to the skies; he remained mute and insensible to their exhortations. Nothing could divert his mind from the thought of the fresh perils of Cymodoce. What must have been the torments of this martyr! Already almost seated upon the clouds, he has hesitated, and is perhaps still hesitating, between the shame of apostasy, an eternity of the sorrows of hell, and the evils which at this moment he endures.

The son of Lasthenes knew not that he had been purposely deceived by the judge. Festus was the friend of the prefect of Rome, and this alone would have hindered him from delivering Cymodoce to Hierocles. But Festus had been struck with the answers and the magnanimity of Eudorus. No sooner had he quitted his tribunal, than he repaired to the palace of Galerius and entreated him to appoint another judge over the Christians.

"There is no longer any need of judges," cried the angry tyrant. "These wretches glory in their sufferings, and the obstinacy with which they persevere in their errors corrupts the people and the soldiers. With what insolence has the chief of this impious sect presumed to suffer! I wish no more time to be lost in torturing them. I condemn all the Christians in prison to be exposed to the wild beasts on the day of my birth, without distinction of age or sex. Go, and publish this decree."

Festus knew the violence of Galerius' disposition: he made no reply. He went out, and declared the orders of his prince, but at the same time exclaimed, like Pilate:

"I am innocent of the blood of these just men."

When Hierocles came to seek him at midnight, he felt himself moved with fresh compassion toward Eudorus. A man naturally cruel, as was the judge of the Christians, may at the same time be an enemy to baseness: he was indignant at the cowardly designs of the fallen minister; the thought occurred to him to profit by the proposals of this wretch, to save the son of Lasthenes, by engaging him to sacrifice to the gods. With this intent, he wrote the letter which Eudorus received during the funeral repast.

God, who willed the triumph of his Church, turned to the glory of the martyrs, all that might have ravished away their crown. Thus the fortitude of Eudorus in tortures, did but hasten the death of his companions, and the letter of Festus aggravated the evils that it was designed to prevent. Galerius, informed of the prisoners' banquet, broke the centurions who had testified any respect for their old general; the foreign legions were, under various pretexts, sent to a distance from Rome; and the prætorian bands, gorged with wine and gold, were the only guard of the city. The names of Cymodoce, Eudorus and Hierocles, again meeting the ears of the emperor, plunged him into a violent rage: Galerius particularly marked out the spouse of Eudorus for the next day's massacre; he commanded that the son of Lasthenes should appear the first and alone in the amphitheatre, thus depriving him of the happiness of dying with his brethren; lastly, he commanded Hierocles to be sent on board a vessel, and to be conveyed to the place of his exile.

This sentence, suddenly announced to Hierocles, brought with it the stroke of death. The mercy and the patience of God had now reached their limit, and his justice was about to begin. Scarcely had Hierocles quitted the house of Festus, when he felt himself struck anew by the sword of the destroying angel. In an instant the malady with which he had before been afflicted, left the physicians no further hope. The pagans, who regarded leprosy as a malediction of heaven, fled from the apostate; his very slaves abandoned him. Deserted by the whole world, he found no succor but from those men whom he had so cruelly persecuted. The Christians, whose charity alone dared brave all human miseries, opened their hospitals to their persecutor. There, stretched by the side of a mutilated confessor, Hierocles felt his pangs assuaged by the same hand that had just dressed the wounds of a martyr. But so many virtues only served to irritate this man rejected of God; sometimes with loud shrieks he called Cymodoce; sometimes he fancied that he beheld Eudorus, with a flaming sword in his hand, menacing him from the heights of heaven. It was in the midst of these transports, that messengers came to announce the last order of Galerius. Raising himself like a spectre from his pestiferous couch, the false sage muttered these words in a trembling and terrified voice:

"I am going to repose forever."

He expired. Awful and fallacious hope! This soul, which had thought to perish with the body, suddenly beheld, instead of a profound and tranquil night, a portentous light in the depths of the grave. A voice issued from the midst of this light, which distinctly pronounced these words : "I am that I am."

At that moment living eternity was revealed to the soul of the atheist. Three truths at the same instant struck this confounded spirit: its own existence, that of God, and the certainty of recompense and punishment without end. Oh, that it were buried beneath the ruins of the universe, to hide it from the face of the sovereign Judge! An irresistible force impelled it, in the twinkling of an eye, naked and trembling before the tribunal of God. It beheld, for a single moment, him whom it denied in time, and whom it shall see no more in eternity. The Omnipotent appeared on the clouds; his Son was seated at his right hand; the army of his saints encompassed him; hell darted forward to claim its prey. The guardian angel of Hierocles, confused, and moved even to tears, still kept his station by the side of the unfortunate.

"Angel," said the Sovereign Arbiter, "why have you not defended this soul?"

"Lord," answered the angel, veiling his face with his wings, "thou art a God of mercies."

"Creature," said the same voice, "has not the angel given thee salutary warnings?"

Trembling with terror, the soul stood self-condemned, and returned no answer.

"He is ours," exclaimed the rebel angels; "this soul has deceived the world with false wisdom; it has persecuted innocence, outraged modesty, violated the votaries of chastity, shed innocent blood; it has never repented."

"Open the book of life," said the Ancient of Days.

A prophet opened the volume: the name of Hierocles was effaced.

"Go, accursed, into everlasting fire!" said the incorruptible Judge.

Instantly the soul of the atheist began to hate God with the hatred of the reprobate, and fell into burning abysses. Hell opened to receive it, then closed again, pronouncing the word:

"Eternity!"

The echo of the abyss repeated:

"Eternity!"

The Father of mortals, who had just punished crime, thought now of crowning innocence.

There is in heaven a divine power, the assiduous companion of religion and virtue; she aids us in supporting life, embarks with us to show us the port in a tempest, alike gentle and helpful to obscure passengers and to travellers of renown. Though her eyes are covered with a bandage, her looks penetrate the future; sometimes she holds budding flowers in her hand, sometimes a cup full of an enchanting liquor; nothing approaches the charm of her voice, and the magic of her smile; the nearer the Christian advances toward the tomb, the more lovely and brilliant is the form she assumes. Faith and Charity call her sister, and her name is Hope. The Eternal ordered this beautiful seraph to descend to Cymodoce, and to show her from afar celestial joys, in order to sustain her amid the tribulations of earth.

A false rumor had for a few moments interrupted the sorrows of the young Christian. The rumor had been spread through Rome, that Eudorus had just received his pardon: the letter of Festus, and a false interpretation of the scene of the banquet, had given rise to this popular report. Blanche had hastened to communicate this false intelligence to the daughter of Demodocus, as if it had been a certain fact; but how she repented of her indiscreet kindness, when she learned the real destiny of Eudorus, and the sentence that condemned to death indiscriminately all the Christians in the prisons! Filled with a brutal joy, Sævus ordered her to carry to Cymodoce the dress destined for those women who were to suffer martyrdom. It consisted of a blue tunic, a black girdle, buskins and a mantle of the same color, and a white veil. The feeble and afflicted woman weepingly executed her mournful office. She had not the courage to undeceive the orphan, and acquaint her with her fate.

"Here is a new dress, my sister," said she. "May the peace of the Lord be with you!"

"What dress is this?" cried Cymodoce. "Is it my nuptial robe? Does it come from my spouse?"

"It is for him that you must wear it," replied Blanche.

"Oh!" exclaimed Cymodoce, full of joy, "my spouse has received his pardon, we shall yet be united."

The heart of Blanche was ready to break; she could only utter:

"Pray, my sister, for yourself and for me!"

She retired. Left alone with the raiment of glory, Cymodoce gazed at it, and took it in her beauteous hands.

"They order me," said she, "to adorn myself for my spouse; I must obey."

She immediately arrayed herself in the tunic, which she bound with the girdle about her waist, and fitted the buskins to her feet that surpassed the marble of Paros in whiteness; she threw the veil over her head, and suspended the mantle from her shoulders: thus the Muse of Fable depicts Night, the mother of Love, enveloped in her azure veil and sombre drapery; thus Marcia, though less young, less beautiful, less virtuous, appeared to the eyes of the last of the Catos, when she claimed him for her spouse amidst the calamities of Rome, and appeared at the altar of Hymen in the dress of a mourning widow. Cymodoce knew not that she was wearing the robe of death. She viewed herself in this sorrowful attire, which rendered her beauty a thousand times more striking; she recalled the day when she adorned herself with the ornaments of the Muses, to go with her father to thank the family of Lasthenes.

"My nuptial robe," said she, "is not so splendid as the one I then wore; but perhaps it will be more pleasing to my spouse, since it is the robe of the Christians."

The recollections of her former happiness and of the sweet country of Greece, inspired the daughter of Homer. She seated herself before the window of her prison, and resting her head, adorned with the veil of the martyrs, upon her hand, sighed forth these harmonious strains:

"Swift vessels of Ausonia, cleave the calm and brilliant surface of the deep! Slaves of Neptune, spread the canvas to the amorous breath of the breeze! Ply the vigorous oar! Waft me back to the happy banks of the Pamisus, under the keeping of my father and my spouse.

"Fly, birds of Libya, whose flexible necks bend with such grace, fly to the summit of Ithome, and say that the daughter of Homer is coming to revisit the laurels of Messenia!

"When shall I again behold my couch of ivory, the cheering radiance of my native skies, the meadows enamelled with flowers which limpid rivulets water, which Modesty embellishes with her smile!

"I was like unto the tender roe departing from her grotto, wandering upon the mountains, and led forth to pasture by the music of the rustic pipe. Now, in a solitary prison, upon the wretched couch of Ceres! . . . .

"But whence comes it, that while wishing to sing like the linnet, I sigh like the flute consecrated to the dead? I am, however, clothed in the nuptial robe; my heart will feel maternal joys and inquietudes; I shall behold my son clinging to my robe, like the timid bird that seeks refuge under the wing of its mother. Ah! am I not myself a tender bird that has been torn from the parent nest?

"O my father and my spouse, whence this delay? Ah, if it were permitted me still to implore the Graces and the Muses! If I could interrogate heaven in the entrails of the victim! But now I should offend a God whom I scarcely know! I will repose on the cross."

Night already enveloped intoxicated Rome. Suddenly the gates of the prison opened, and the centurion, commissioned to read to the Christians the sentence of the emperor, appeared before Cymodoce. He was accompanied by several soldiers; some remaining in the outward courts, detained the keeper and lavished on him the wine of the idols.

As the dove, which the fowler has surprised in the crevice of a rock, remains motionless with dread, and dares not dart into the plains of heaven, thus the daughter of Demodocus remained struck with fear and astonishment upon the half-broken seat where she reclined. The soldiers lighted a flambeau. O prodigy! The spouse of Eudorus recognized Dorotheus under the habit of a centurion! Dorotheus, unable to speak, contemplated in turn this woman clothed in the garb of a martyr! Never had he seen her so beautiful: the blue tunic and the black mantle heightened the fairness of her complexion; and her eyes, fatigued by weeping, had an angelic softness: she resembled a tender narcissus that droops its languishing head on the banks of a solitary stream. Dorotheus, and the Christians who attended him in the guise of soldiers, raised their hands to heaven and burst into tears.

"Is it you, the companion of my wanderings far from my country!" cried the young Messenian, as she threw herself on her knees, and stretched out her hand toward Dorotheus. "Do you come at last to visit your Esther? Generous mortal, have you come to conduct me to my father and my spouse? How long the night would have been without you!"

"Cymodoce," replied Dorotheus in a voice broken by sobs, "are you then acquainted with your destiny? This robe" . . . . .

"It is my nuptial robe," said the unsuspecting virgin. "But if all is over, if my spouse is saved, if I am free, whence these tears and this mystery?"

"Let us fly," resumed Dorotheus; "wrap yourself in this cloak: we have not a moment to lose. Accompanied by these brave friends, I have stolen into your prison under cover of this disguise. I showed a copy of the emperor's decree: Sævus mistook me for the centurion commissioned to announce the fatal sentence."

"What sentence?" resumed the daughter of Homer.

"Do you not know, then," replied Dorotheus, "that all the Christians in the prisons are condemned to suffer death to-morrow in the amphitheatre?"

"Is my spouse included in the number?" cried the new Christian, with an air of firmness which she had not hitherto displayed; "speak, do not deceive me. I do not know the inviolable oath of the Christians; formerly I should have sworn by Erebus, and by the genius of my father. Here is your sacred book ; it is written in this book : 'Thou shalt not swear falsely ;' swear, then, upon the Gospel, that Eudorus is saved."

Dorotheus turned pale ; with eyes bathed in tears, he exclaimed :

"Woman, do you wish me, then, to tell you of the glory which your spouse has already gained, and of that which still awaits him ?"

Cymodoce trembled like the palm-tree struck by lightning.

"Your words," said she, "have pierced my heart like a sword. I understand you. And you wish me to fly ! I do not recognize in this the maxims of a Christian. Eudorus is covered with wounds for his God ; to-morrow he is to combat with wild beasts ; and I am counselled to escape my fate and abandon him to suffer alone ! I feel at my side a hope which I cannot describe, which gives me a glimpse of happiness and celestial glories. If at one time feeble and discouraged, I cast a longing look on life, all these fears are dissipated. No, the waters of Jordan shall not have been poured on my head in vain ! I salute thee, sacred robe, of whose value I was ignorant ! I see now that thou art the robe of a martyr ! The purple with which thou shalt to-morrow be tinged, shall be immortal, and shall render me more worthy to appear before my spouse !"

As she pronounced these words, Cymodoce, seized with a divine enthusiasm, raised her robe to her lips, and kissed it with respect.

"Well," cried Dorotheus, "if you will not follow us, we will all perish with you ; we will remain here, we will declare ourselves Christians, and to-morrow you shall conduct us to the amphitheatre. But, what ! does religion exact from you such barbarity as this ? You wish to die without receiving the benediction of your father ; without embracing that old man who is awaiting you, and whom your resolution will bring to the tomb. Ah, Cymodoce, had you but seen him defiling his silvery locks with hot ashes, tearing his robes, and rolling himself in the dust before the walls of your prison, you would suffer yourself to be softened."

As the ice which is formed in a single night in the early spring melts at the first beams of the sun; as the flower which is ready to blossom, bursts from the slight envelope of the bud that confines it; thus the resolution of Cymodoce vanished at these words; thus filial affection re-blossomed in her heart. She could not resolve to compromise the generous men who had exposed themselves to save her; she could not die without endeavoring to console Demodocus: for a moment she remained in silence; she listened to the inspirations of the angel of celestial hope, who whispered to her soul; then, meditating within herself a sublime design, she suddenly exclaimed:

"Let us hasten to see my father."

The Christians, transported with joy, covered the tresses of the young virgin with a helmet; they wrapped Cymodoce in one of those white robes embroidered with purple, which the Roman youths assume when they arrive at the age of manhood: she might have been mistaken for the fleet Camilla, the beautiful Ascanius, or the unfortunate Marcellus. The Christians placed the daughter of Homer in the midst of them; they extinguished the lights, quitted the dungeon together, and left the keeper, overcome with drunkenness, to close with caution the gates of the empty prison.

The holy company separated in the night, and Zacharius went to convey to Eudorus the tidings of the deliverance of Cymodoce.

The generous falsehood of the letter of Festus was already known in the prison of St. Peter, and the son of Lasthenes was relieved from insupportable grief. But when Zacharius came to inform him that the lamb had escaped from the den of the lions, he burst into exclamations of joy, which were repeated by all the martyrs. The confessors, while admiring the faithful who combated for the faith, had no desire to witness the effusion of the blood of their brethren. The victims, saddened by the grief of the son of Lasthenes, recovered their serenity: nothing now remained but to prepare to die. They began by returning thanks to that God who saved Joash from the hands of Athaliah. Then their serious discourses and pious exhortations were resumed: Cyril spoke with majesty, Victor with energy, Genesius with joy, Gervasius and Protatius with brotherly unction: Perseus, the descendant of Alexander, offered lessons drawn from history; Thraseas, the hermit of Vesuvius, conveyed his maxims in pleasing images.

"Since the whole period of our life," said he to Perseus, "is reduced to a few days, what would all the grandeur of your birth have availed you? What matters it to you now whether you have performed your voyage in a skiff or a galley? Nay, the skiff is preferable, for it can float in the river along the shore, which affords a thousand shelters from the storm; while the galley sails on a tempestuous ocean, where ports are few, where shoals abound, and where often the sailor cannot cast his anchor, by reason of the depths of the abyss."

Such was the freedom of mind, the cheerfulness and the repose of these men, who were passing their last night upon earth. Equally animated by the Holy Spirit, both the young and aged martyrs opened all the treasures of their virtues, and presented, united and confounded, the most agreeable fruits of wisdom: such is the scene amidst the fertile plains of Campania; the young wheat is sown under the shadow of the aged poplar which supports the vine; soon the yellow grain mounts to seek the blushing grape, which in its turn descends to the golden ears; the zephyr breathing over the smiling scene, waves the poplars, the grain and the clusters of the vine, and mingles the sweet odors of the harvest, the gardens and the groves.

Meanwhile Dorotheus, like a courageous shepherd, forced his way through the idolatrous crowd. On one of the declivities of the Esquiline Mount stood a retreat which Virgil had once inhabited; a laurel that still grew at the gate offered itself to the veneration of the people. In the days of his prosperity, Dorotheus had purchased this mansion with an intent to adorn it for his place of residence. To this he conducted the daughter of Homer. This secret asylum was already filled with the cries of Demodocus. The old man was seated in the dust under one of the porticoes: he thought he beheld two warriors advancing through the gloom.

"Who are you?" cried he in a voice of terror. "Phantoms, sent by the inexorable Furies, are ye come to drag me into the night of Tartarus? Are ye Christian spirits, come to announce the death of my daughter? Perish Christ and his temples, perish the God who attaches his worshippers to the cross?"

"They are the votaries of this God, however, who restore to you your daughter," cried Cymodoce, throwing herself upon the neck of her father.

The helmet of the young martyr fell to the earth, her locks flowed upon her shoulders: the warrior became a charming virgin. Demodocus fell senseless; they hastened to restore him to life; they explained to him mysteries which in his joy he could scarcely comprehend. Cymodoce soothed him with words and caresses.

"O my father, I find thee again after a cruel separation! Behold me again at thy feet! It is I, it is thy Cymodoce, for whom thy lips learned to pronounce the tender name of daughter. Thou didst take me in thy arms at my birth, and loaded me with caresses and benedictions. How often have I hung upon thy neck, and promised to render thee the happiest of mortals! And shall I now be the cause of this anguish! O my father, is it thou that I press to my heart? Let us prize these moments of unexpected happiness. Thou knowest but too well, that heaven is prompt in taking back the gifts that it has bestowed!"

"Glory of my ancestors," replied Demodocus, "daughter more precious to my heart than the light which illumines the blest shades in Elysium, how can I recount my griefs to thee! How have I sought thee in those places where I had seen thee, and round those prisons that held thee captive from my love! 'Ah!' said I to myself, 'I shall never prepare her nuptial couch, nor light the torch of Hymen for her; I shall remain alone upon that earth, from which the gods have taken my consolation, and my joy. When I embraced my daughter on the shores of Attica, did I embrace her then for the last time? How sweet was the last look she cast on me! With what tenderness she smiled on me! Was that her last smile?' O cherished features that I have found again! O brow on which candor and innocence are painted, ye seem made for happiness! What pleasure to feel a heart so young and full of life, palpitate against this heart so aged and so exhausted by grief!"

In this manner did Demodocus and Cymodoce intermingle their sorrows: thus Alcyone, who builds her nest upon the wave, is heard with her brood to utter plaintive cries from the floating cradle which the vast sea is soon to ingulf. Dorotheus ordered torches to be brought, and conducted the father and his daughter to an apartment where two couches were prepared; he then withdrew, and left them to indulge their tenderness. The whole night would have passed in mutual details and in tender caresses, had not the priest of Homer thrown himself at the feet of Cymodoce, and exclaimed:

"O my daughter, put an end to my fears and calamities! Abjure those altars that expose thee without ceasing to fresh persecution; return to the religion of thy father. We have nothing now to apprehend from Hierocles. He who was to have been thy spouse . . ."

Cymodoce threw herself in turn at the knees of her sire.

"My father at my feet!" cried she, as she raised up Demodocus. "Ah! I have not the strength to support this trial. O my father, spare thy daughter's weakness; seek not to seduce her; leave her the God of her spouse If you knew how much this God has augmented my respect and love toward you!"

"This God," replied Demodocus, "has sought to ravish my daughter from me; he robs you of your spouse."

"No," replied Cymodoce, "I shall not lose Eudorus: he shall live forever, and his glory shall redound to me."

"What!" replied the priest of Homer, "will you not lose Eudorus when he descends into the tomb?"

"There is no tomb for him," answered the inspired virgin; "we weep not for Christians who die for their God, as we do for other men."

Cymodoce, however, whose heart meditated some great design, invited her father to repose. She prevailed upon him by her prayers to retire to his couch. The old man could not reconcile himself to be deprived for a moment of the presence of his daughter, who had been just restored to his arms; he feared constantly lest she should escape from him: thus when a man awakes from a frightful dream that has for a long time troubled his repose, he still beholds the terrific image, and the rising day does not remove the impression from his mind. Cymodoce complained of fatigue, and reclining on the second couch at the other extremity of the hall, she addressed, in a low voice, this prayer to the Eternal:

"Thou unknown God, who canst penetrate the secrets of my heart; thou God, who hast beheld the death of thy only son; if my design is agreeable in thy sight, send down to my father one of those spirits that are called thy angels; close his eyes, that are weary with weeping, and watch over his helpless age, when I shall have quitted him for thee."

She spoke, and her prayer, borne on wings of flame, ascended to the ear of the Eternal. The Eternal accepted it in his loving kindness, and the angel of sleep immediately quitted his ethereal abode. He held in his hand the sceptre of gold, with which he assuages the pangs of the just. He passed the region of the suns, and descended toward the earth, to which he was conducted by a prolonged cry of sorrow. On reaching this globe, he paused for a moment on the highest summit of the mountains of Armenia; he turned his eyes toward the desert where once smiled the plains of Eden; the scene reminded him of that first sleep that came upon man, when God took from the side of Adam that beautiful companion of his days, who was destined to destroy and to save the human race. He next directed his flight to Mount Lebanon, and beheld the deep valleys, the foaming torrents, and the towering cedars of the vast landscape that stretched beneath his view. He rested a moment at those scenes of pastoral innocence, where the patriarchs enjoyed their blessings under the palm-trees. He then glided over the seas of Tyre and Sidon, and leaving far behind him the land that witnessed the exile of Teucer, the tomb of Aristomenes, Crete cherished by kings, and Sicily beloved by shepherds, he discovered the shores of Italy. He cleft the air with noiseless flight, and without moving a pinion; he diffused in his passage coolness and dew. He appeared; the waves subsided; the flowers drooped upon their stems; the dove nestled her head beneath her wing; the lion stretched himself along his den to repose. The seven hills of the eternal city at length met the view of the angel of consolation. With horror he beheld a million of idolaters disturbing the tranquillity of night; he abandoned them to their guilty vigils; he was deaf to the voice of Galerius, but he closed, in passing, the eyes of the martyrs, and thence fled to the solitary retreat of Demodocus. This unfortunate father was tossing on his couch in feverish restlessness; the divine messenger extended his peaceful sceptre and touched the old man's eyelids. Demodocus fell instantly into a placid and profound repose. Heretofore he had known only that sleep which was called the brother of death; that inhabitant of the infernal regions; the child of those demons called gods among men. He was a stranger to that sleep of life which descends from heaven; that powerful charm composed of peace and innocence, which is untroubled by dreams, which does not sit heavy on the soul, but seems like a sweet vapor of virtue. The angel of rest durst not approach Cymodoce: he bent with respect before the praying virgin, and leaving her upon earth, returned to await her arrival in heaven.

BOOK TWENTY-FOURTH.

SUMMARY.

Adieus to the Muse. Illness of Galerius. The Amphitheatre of Vespasian. Eudorus is led to Martyrdom. Michael plunges Satan into the Abyss. Cymodoce escapes from her Father, and goes to the Amphitheatre to find Eudorus. Galerius learns that Constantine has been proclaimed Cæsar. Martyrdom of the two spouses. Triumph of the Christian Religion.

O MUSE, who didst deign to sustain me in a career as long as perilous, return now to the celestial abodes! I am in sight of the goal; I am about to descend from the chariot, and to chant the hymn of the dead I have no need of thy aid. Where is the inhabitant of France, that has not heard in our days the funeral song? Who among us has not mourned at some tomb or raised the funeral lament over some grave? It is finished, O Muse! a moment more, and I abandon thy altars forever! I shall no longer recount the loves and the alluring dreams of men: I must quit the lyre with youth. Adieu, consoler of my life, thou who hast shared my pleasures, and much oftener my sorrows! Can I separate myself from thee without shedding tears? Scarcely had I quitted infancy when thou didst mount my swift vessel and sing the tempest that rent my sail; thou didst follow me into the savage's cabin of bark, and teach me to find amidst the solitudes of America the groves of Pindus. To what shore hast thou not conducted my reveries or misfortunes? Borne on thy wing, I have visited the cloud-capped heights of the solitary Morven; I have penetrated the forests of Erminsul; I have beheld the waves of the Tiber; I have hailed the olive groves of the Cephissus, and the laurels of the Eurotas. Thou hast shown me the towering cypress of the Bosphorus, and the desolate sepulchres of the Simois. With thee I have traversed the Hermus, the rival of the Pactolus;

with thee I have adored the waters of the Jordan, and have prayed upon the mountain of Sion. Memphis and Carthage have witnessed my musing among their ruins; and amidst the ruins of the palaces of Granada I have invoked with thee the memories of honor and of love. Then wouldst thou whisper:

"Appreciate this glory, the scene of which an obscure and feeble traveller can traverse in a few days."

O Muse, thy lessons shall never be forgotten! My mind shall never descend from those sublime regions whither it has soared with thee! The intellectual gifts which thou impartest become enfeebled by age, the voice loses its sweetness, the fingers grow benumbed upon the lyre; but the noble sentiments which thou inspirest shall remain when the rest of thy gifts have yielded to the effects of time. Faithful companion of my life, in remounting to the skies, leave me independence and virtue. Henceforward let the volume of Poesy be closed, and open to me the pages of History. I have consecrated the age of illusions to the smiling pictures of imagination; I will employ the age of regrets in the severe portraiture of truth.

But what do I say! have I not already quitted the fairy regions of imagination? Alas, the woes which Galerius inflicted on the Christians are not vain fictions!

The time had now arrived for heaven to avenge the cause of oppressed innocence. A prey to the rage of the destroying angel, sleep fled the eyes of Galerius. The wine of the wrath of God, in penetrating the bowels of the persecutor of the faithful, had caused a latent malady, the fruit of intemperance and debauchery, to break forth. From the head to the waist, Galerius was nothing but a skeleton covered with a livid skin, that clung to his bones; the lower part of his body was inflated like a wine skin, and his feet were deformed. When on the borders of a rushy pool, a serpent has twined around the grazing steer, the animal writhes beneath the folds of the reptile, and beats the air with his horns, till, overpowered by the venom, he falls to the earth and fills the air with roaring: thus tossed and roared Galerius. The gangrene devoured his intestines. The nauseous remedies that were applied served but to augment his disease, while the worms continually preyed upon the vitals of this master of the world. Apollo, Æsculapius, and Hygiea were invoked: vain idols, unable to free themselves from those worms which eternally gnawed their own breasts! Galerius felt his disorder increasing; he condemned the physicians who could find no remedy for his sufferings to be beheaded.

"Prince," said one of them, who had been secretly brought up in the Christian religion, "this distemper is above our art: you must have recourse to higher powers. Reflect on what you have done to the servants of God; and learn whither to fly for assistance. I am ready to die like my brethren; but medicines cannot cure you."

This ingenuous declaration plunged Galerius into transports of rage. He could not resolve to acknowledge the impiety of the title of Eternal, which he had given to the life of a moment. His fury against the Christians redoubled: far from suspending their punishments, he confirmed his former sentence; and only waited for daylight to show at the amphitheatre the spectacle of a dying prince come to witness the death of his subjects.

His impatience was soon gratified: already the rising beams of Aurora trembled on the yellow floods of the Tiber, and gilded with a blaze of light the hills of Alba, and the forests of Tibur and Lucretilis. The dew-drops hung like manna from every flower; the surrounding country breathed the freshness of the morn, and appeared to rejoice at the new birth of light. The distant mountains of Italy were enveloped in a veil of dewy light, which appeared of the color of the plum, when its soft purple hue is just whitening with down. The smoke was beginning to ascend from the hamlets; the tops of the trees were just bursting from the mists, which were flying along the sides of the verdant hills; never did a more delightful morn arise from the orient sky to witness the abominations of men. O king of day, who from thy lofty throne dost survey all the children of men, what dost thou care for our tears and our sorrows? Thy rising and thy setting are uninterrupted by all our miseries: thou shinest alike on the good and the evil; generations pass away, and thou pursuest thy course.

The people in the meantime were assembled at the amphitheatre of Vespasian: all Rome flocked hither to drink the blood of the martyrs. A hundred thousand spectators, dressed in robes worn on such occasions, were collected round the gates. The multitude, rushing through the portico, ascended by the exterior staircases, and took their stations on the marble seats. Grates of gold guarded the seat of the senators from the attacks of the ferocious beasts. To refresh the air, fountains threw up floods of wine and saffron water, which fell back in showers of fragrant dew. Three thousand statues of bronze, an infinite variety of pictures, columns of jasper and porphyry, pilasters of crystal, vases of immense value, decorated the interior of this magnificent edifice. A hippopotamus and several crocodiles floated on the surface of a canal which surrounded the arena; five hundred lions, forty elephants, tigers, panthers, bulls, and bears, trained to rend men in pieces, shook with their terrific roar the dens of the amphitheatre. A body of gladiators, not less ferocious than the beasts, were preparing themselves for the sports of blood. Near these caves of death were the places of public prostitution: a number of courtesans, and Roman ladies of the first rank, augmented, as in the days of Nero, the horror of the spectacle, and came, the rivals of death, to dispute with each other the favor of an expiring prince. Add to this the last groans of the Bacchanals, who lay in the streets, expiring under the influence of their god, and you will know all the pomp and the dishonor of slavery.

The prætorians, commissioned to conduct the confessors to martyrdom, already surrounded the prison of Saint Peter. Eudorus, by the order of Galerius, had been separated from his brethren, and chosen to suffer the first: thus the hero who commands a gallant troop, is always the first object marked out for destruction. The keeper advanced to the door of the prison and called the son of Lasthenes.

"I am here," said Eudorus; "what do you wish?"

"Come forth to die," cried the keeper.

"To live," replied Eudorus.

And he arose from the stony couch on which he lay. Cyril, Gervasius, Protasius, Rogatian and his brother, Victor, Genesius, Perseus, and the hermit of Vesuvius, could not restrain their tears.

"Friends," said Eudorus, "we soon shall embrace each other again. Separated a moment on earth, and we shall meet to part no more in heaven."

Eudorus had reserved for this last moment a white tunic which had been prepared for his nuptials: to this he added a robe embroidered by his mother; he appeared more beautiful than a shepherd of Arcadia, who is disputing the prize of the bow or the lyre in the plains of Mantinea.

The people and the prætors grew impatient, and called aloud for the son of Lasthenes.

"Let us go," cried the martyr.

And overcoming the pains of his body by the vigor of his soul, he passed the threshold of the prison. Cyril exclaimed:

"Son of woman, a brow of adamant has been given you: fear nothing, and stand unmoved before them."

The bishops raised the hymn of praise, lately composed at Carthage by Augustine, the friend of Eudorus:

"We praise thee, O God, we bless thee, O Lord! The heavens, the angels, the thrones, and the cherubim, proclaim thee thrice holy, Lord, God of Sabaoth!"

The bishops were still singing this hymn of victory, when Eudorus, already anticipating his triumph, advanced from the prison: he was immediately delivered over to outrage. The centurion of the guards pushed him rudely along, saying:

"You have kept us waiting a long time."

"Friend," said Eudorus with a smile, "I marched as quick as you against the enemy; but now, as you see, I am wounded."

They fastened on his breast a leaf of papyrus, inscribed with these words:

"EUDORUS THE CHRISTIAN."

"Where is his God now?" cried the people, in an insulting tone. "What has it profited him to prefer his worship to life? We shall see if he will rise again with his Christ, or if his God has sufficient power to free him from our hands."

The blood-thirsty rabble gave a thousand praises to their gods, and congratulated themselves on the vengeance which they took on the enemies of their altars.

The prince of darkness and his angels believed themselves ready to triumph over the cross—that cross which was soon to hurl them into the abyss. They excited the fury of the pagans against the new apostle: stones were hurled at him; flints and fragments of broken vessels were strewed under his feet; he was treated as if he had been the Christ for whom these wretches had so much horror. He advanced slowly along the sacred way, from the foot of the Capitol to the amphitheatre. At the arch of Titus, at the temple of Jupiter Stator, at the Rostra, in fine, at every place where an image of the gods appeared, the shouts of the multitude redoubled: they wished to force the martyr to bend before these idols.

"Does it become a conqueror to salute the vanquished?" cried Eudorus. "A few moments more, and you shall judge of my triumph. O Rome, I behold a prince, who shall cast his diadem at the feet of Jesus Christ. The temple of the spirits of darkness is shut, its gates shall be closed forever, and bolts of brass shall guard the entrance from generations that are to come!"

"He denounces evil against us," cried the people: "let us crush the wretch, and tear him in pieces."

The prætorians with difficulty protected the inspired martyr from the rage of these idolaters.

"Let them alone," cried Eudorus. "It is thus they have

often treated their emperors; but you need not employ the points of your swords to force me to raise my head."

All the triumphal statues of Eudorus, save one, were demolished: this stood in the very road by which the martyr passed; a soldier, moved at this singular event, drew his helmet before his face in order to conceal the emotion visible in his countenance. Eudorus perceived him, and thus addressed him:

"Friend, why dost thou weep at my glory? It is to-day that I triumph! Merit the same honors!"

These words made a deep impression on the soldier; and a few days afterward he embraced the Christian religion.

Eudorus arrived at the amphitheatre, like a generous steed which has been pierced with a javelin on the field of battle, and which advances to the combat without seeming to feel the mortal wound that he has received.

But of those who pressed upon the confessor all were not his enemies: a great number consisted of the faithful who sought to touch the garment of the martyr, of old men who treasured up his words, of priests who gave him absolution in the midst of the crowd, of young people, and of women who exclaimed:

"Let us die with him!"

The confessor hushed with a word, with a motion, with a look, these ejaculations of virtue, and appeared to feel no other concern than for the danger of his brethren. Hell waited at the gate of the arena in order to endeavor to shake his faith by a last assault. The gladiators, according to custom, wished to clothe the Christian in a robe of the priests of Saturn.

"I will not die," cried Eudorus, "in the disguise of a base deserter, and under the colors of idolatry; I will rather tear off with my own hands the bandage from my wounds. I belong to the Roman people and to Cæsar: if you deprive them by my death of the combat which I owe them, you must answer for it, on your heads."

Intimidated by this threat, the gladiators opened the gates

of the amphitheatre, and the martyr entered alone and triumphant into the arena.

Immediately a maddening shout of universal applause burst from the multitude, which shook the walls of the amphitheatre, and echoed through its deepest recesses. The lions, and the other beasts inclosed in the dens, answered these bursts of savage joy with a roar not less savage; the people themselves trembled with dread, the martyr alone was not afraid. Suddenly the presentiment which he formerly had in this very place rushed on his mind. He blushed at his past errors; he thanked God who had received him into his mercy, and had conducted him by mysterious counsels to so glorious an end. He thought with emotion on his father, his sisters, and his country; he recommended Demodocus and Cymodoce to the Eternal: these were his last thoughts of earth; he turned his heart and his soul toward heaven.

The emperor had not yet arrived, and the superintendent of the games had not, therefore, given the signal. The wounded martyr asked permission to sit down upon the arena, the better to recruit his strength: the people consented, in hopes of seeing a longer combat. The young confessor covered himself with his robe, and bent upon the sand which was shortly to drink his blood, as a shepherd seats himself upon a mossy bank in the midst of a solitary forest.

But in the depths of eternity, a more resplendent light burst from the Holy of Holies. The angels, the Thrones, and the powers, transported with joy, fell prostrate before the Eternal, and heard a voice which said:

"Peace to the Church! Peace to mankind!"

The victim was accepted: the last drop of the blood of the just was about to cause that religion to triumph, which was to change the face of the earth. The cohort of martyrs arose: the celestial warriors assembled together at the blast of a trumpet sounded by the angel of the armies of the Lord. There appeared Stephen, the first of confessors, amidst a blaze of glory; there, too, was seen the intrepid Laurence, the eloquent Cyprian, and you, the honor of that pious and faithful city, which the Rhone ravages and the Saone caresses. Borne on a resplendent cloud, they descended toward the earth to receive the soul of the happy soldier, for whom this great victory was reserved. The heavens bowed down and opened. The choirs of patriarchs, of prophets, of apostles, and of angels, came forth to admire the combat of the just. The holy women, the widows and the virgins, surrounded and congratulated the mother of Eudorus, who alone turned away her eyes from the earth, and kept them fixed on the throne of the Eternal.

Then Michael armed his right hand with the sword that precedes the Lord and which strikes unlooked-for blows; he took in his left hand a chain forged in the fire of the lightnings, in the arsenals of celestial wrath. A hundred archangels formed its indestructible links under the direction of an ardent cherub; with admirable art the iron with the silver and gold was moulded beneath their ponderous hammers; to these they added three rays of the eternal vengeance, despair, terror, and malediction, a bolt of thunder, and some of that living matter that composed the wheels of the chariot of Ezekiel. At a sign of the Mighty God, Michael darted from the heavens like a comet. The stars were terrified and thought the end of their course was at hand. The archangel fixed one foot upon the sea and the other upon the land. He spoke in a terrible voice, and the seven thunders joined their voice to his:

"The reign of Christ is established; idolatry is passed away; death shall no longer triumph. Perverse race, free the earth from your presence; and thou, Satan, shalt be cast into the abyss, where thou shalt be chained for a thousand years."

At these formidable accents, the rebel angels were seized with terror. The prince of hell wished still to resist, and to combat the messenger of the Most High; he called Astarte and the demons of False Wisdom and Homicide; but already precipitated into the abode of sorrows, they were punished by **new torments for the ills that they had just wrought on earth.**

Satan, left alone, attempted in vain to resist the celestial warrior: his power was suddenly taken from him; he felt that his sceptre was broken and his power destroyed. Preceded by his bewildered legions, he plunged with a fearful roar into the gulf of the abyss. The living chains fell with him, encircled him and bound him to a burning rock in the centre of hell. The son of Lasthenes heard in the air concerts of ineffable sweetness, and the distant swell of a thousand golden harps, mingled with voices of celestial melody. He raised his head and saw the army of martyrs overturning in Rome the altars of the false gods, and sapping the foundations of its temples amidst whirlwinds of dust. A marvellous ladder descended from a cloud to the feet of Eudorus. This ladder was of jasper, hyacinth, sapphire and emerald, like the foundations of the heavenly Jerusalem. The martyr contemplated the vision of splendor, and sighed for the moment when he should join the celestial company.

But this was not all the glory which the God of Jacob had in store for his people. He inspired the heart of a feeble virgin with the most exalted, and the most generous designs. When seated upon the new-ploughed furrow the lark awaits the return of light, as soon as the new-born day has silvered the edges of the clouds, she quits the earth, and mounting in the air, pours forth the song that cheers the traveller; thus the watchful Cymodoce awaited with impatience the rising dawn, to sing in heaven the hymns that ravish Israel with delight. A ray of Aurora darted into the apartment of the young Christian, through the laurel of Virgil. Immediately she arose in silence, and resumed the robe of martyrdom which she had been careful to preserve. The priest of Homer was still wrapped in the slumber with which the angel had sealed his eyes. Cymodoce approached him softly, and threw herself on her knees by the side of the bed of Demodocus. She gazed on her sleeping father, whilst a silent flood of tears stole down her cheeks; she listened to the tranquil breathing of the old man; she thought upon his terrible awakening, and could scarcely restrain the sobs of filial affection. Suddenly she recovered her former courage, or rather her love and her faith, and privately withdrew, as the new bride of Sparta retired from the presence of her mother to enjoy the caresses of her spouse.

Dorotheus had not passed the night in the house of Virgil; the Christians did not thus sleep on the eve of the death of their brethren. Accompanied by his servants and Zacharias, he had repaired to the amphitheatre. Disguised, amidst the multitude, they waited for the combat of the martyr, in order to bear away his glorious body, and give it burial: thus a flight of doves alight near a farm where the new corn is threshed, and wait till the swains have retired, in order to collect the scattered grain.

Cymodoce meets no obstacles, therefore, to oppose her flight. Who could have guessed her intentions? She descended under the portico, and opening the outward gate, entered into that Rome to which she was an entire stranger.

She wandered at first through deserted streets: all the people had flocked to the amphitheatre. She knew not which way to direct her steps; she stopped, and listened with attentive ear, like a sentinel who is endeavoring to catch the sounds of an approaching enemy. She thought she heard a distant murmur, and immediately hastened to the quarter whence it proceeded: as she advanced, the noise grew louder. She soon perceived a long train of soldiers, slaves, women, children and old men, all of whom were pursuing the same path; she beheld litters passing along, and chariots, and horsemen flying in the same direction. In the midst of a thousand voices, and a thousand confused shouts, Cymodoce could distinguish this cry, which resounded from every quarter:

"The Christians to the beasts!"

"Here am I," cried she, even before her voice could be heard.

And she then ascended a hill which overlooked the multitude that surrounded the amphitheatre. Cymodoce, descending from this hill at the break of dawn, appeared like that star of the morning which night lends a moment to the day. Prostrate Greece would have taken her for the lover of Zephyrus, or of Cephalus; Rome immediately recognized her as a Christian: her azure robe, her white veil, and her black mantle, betrayed her less than did her modesty.

"This is a Christian escaped from prison," cried the multitude: "stop her!"

"Yes," replied Cymodoce, blushing and confused before this multitude, "I am a Christian, but I have not escaped, I have only lost my way. I who am young, and was born far from here on the shores of Greece, my sweet country, might easily mistake the way. Powerful sons of Romulus, will you conduct me to the amphitheatre?"

This language, which would have disarmed tigers, drew down nothing but insults and outrages upon Cymodoce. She had fallen into the hands of an infuriate multitude, who were reeling under the effects of intoxication. A voice whispered that perhaps this Greek was not condemned to the beasts.

"I am," replied the young Christian with timidity, "they are awaiting me at the amphitheatre."

The rabble directly conducted her thither amidst shouts of joy. The gladiator who was appointed to receive the martyrs, had no orders for the introduction of this victim, and refused to admit her into the place of sacrifice. But just at this instant one of the gates of the amphitheatre flew open, and Cymodoce discovered Eudorus, who was seated in the middle of the arena; immediately she darted forward, swift as an arrow, and fell into the arms of the Christian.

"She is his spouse," exclaimed the multitude; "she is a Christian who is sentenced to death: she wears the robe of the condemned."

Some cried: "She is the slave of Hierocles; we know her again; she is the Grecian who declared herself an enemy to the gods, when we wished to save her."

Others whispered in a tone of timid compassion:

"But she is so young and so beautiful!"

The multitude interrupted them, and exclaimed:

"Well, let her be delivered to the beasts, before multiplying this impious race throughout the empire!"

Horror, transport, grief, and joy intermingled with anxiety, deprived the martyr of the power of utterance: he pressed Cymodoce to his heart; then again he wished to repel her from his embraces; he saw that every moment hastened the end of a life for which he would a thousand times have devoted his own. At length he found words, while tears streamed from his eyes.

"O Cymodoce!" he exclaimed, "what has brought you hither? O God! is it in this moment that I am destined to behold you! What charm or what misfortune has conducted you to this field of carnage? Why do you come now to shake my faith? How can I see you die?"

"My lord," said Cymodoce, in a voice interrupted by sobs, "pardon your servant. I have read in your sacred books, 'That a woman shall quit her father and her mother to follow her spouse.' I have quitted my father, I have torn myself from his love whilst he was buried in sleep; I come to obtain your pardon from Galerius, or to share your fate."

Cymodoce perceived the pallid countenance of Eudorus, and his wounds covered with a mockery of apparel: she uttered a cry, and, in a holy transport of love, kissed the feet of the martyr, and the sacred wounds of his arms and his breast. Who can express the sentiments of Eudorus, when he felt her pure lips press his disfigured form? Who can tell the inexpressible charm of these first caresses of a beloved woman, felt upon the wounds of a martyr? On a sudden, heaven inspired the confessor; his head appeared radiant with light, and his countenance resplendent with the glory of God: he took a ring from his finger, and bathing it in the blood of his wounds, addressed Cymodoce:

"I can no longer oppose your designs; I can no longer deprive you of the crown which you seek with so much courage. If I may believe the secret voice that whispers to my heart, your mission on this earth is completed: your father has no further need of your assistance; God has taken upon himself the charge of this old man; the light of the true faith shall soon dawn upon him, and ere long he will rejoin his children in those abodes where nothing shall ever ravish them from his arms. O Cymodoce, as I foretold you, we shall be united; it is decreed that we shall die as spouses! Here is the altar, the church, and the nuptial couch. Behold this pomp which encircles us; these perfumes which are showered upon our heads. Lift up your head, and contemplate in heaven, with the eyes of faith, a pomp far more resplendent. Let us render legitimate those everlasting embraces that shall follow our martyrdom: receive this ring and become my spouse."

The angelic pair fell on their knees in the midst of the arena; Eudorus placed the ring, bathed in blood, on the finger of Cymodoce.

"Servant of Jesus Christ," cried he, "receive my faith. Thou art amiable as Rachel, wise as Rebecca, and faithful as Sarah, though not so mature in years. Let us increase; let us multiply for eternity; let us fill heaven with our virtues!"

At the same instant the heavens opened and celebrated these sublime nuptials: the angels chanted the canticle of the spouse; the mother of Eudorus presented to God her united children, who were soon to appear before the throne of his Eternity; the virgin-martyrs wove the nuptial crown for Cymodoce; Jesus Christ blessed the happy pair, and the Holy Ghost bestowed on them the gift of an everlasting love.

The multitude, who beheld the two Christians on their knees, thought they were begging for life. Immediately making a motion with their hands, as in the combats of the gladiators, they rejected their prayer by this sign, and condemned them to death! The Roman people, who, in consideration of their great privileges, had been styled a royal people, had long since lost their independence: at present they remained absolute masters only in the direction of their pleasures; and as these same pleasures served to enchain and corrupt them, they possessed, in fact, nothing but the sovereign disposal of their own slavery. The gladiator who attended the arena came at this moment, to receive the orders of the people with regard to Cymodoce.

"Free and powerful people," said he, "this Christian has entered the arena out of her turn; she was condemned to die with the rest of the impious, after the combat of their chief, but she escaped from prison. Wandering about Rome, her evil genius, or rather the genius of the empire, has conducted her to the amphitheatre."

The people cried out with one voice:

"It is the will of the gods: let her remain, and suffer death!"

A small number, secretly touched by the God of mercies, appeared moved by the tender age of Cymodoce, and expressed a wish that this Christian should be pardoned; but the multitude repeated:

"Let her remain and suffer death! The more beautiful the victim, the more acceptable is she to the gods."

They were no longer the sons of Brutus, who called down curses on Pompey for having incited peaceful elephants to combat; they were men brutalized by slavery, blinded by idolatry, and in whose breasts all humanity was extinguished with the feeling of liberty.

A voice was heard from the midst of the spectators:

"Lo, another victim! Dorotheus renounces life."

"Romans," cried he, "it is I who am the cause of all this; it was I who this very night rescued this angel of heaven, who comes to throw herself into your hands. I am a Christian; I demand martyrdom. May the infamous Jupiter soon fall with his temple to earth. May it crush in its fall his abominable idolaters! May heaven launch forth its vindictive lightnings, to destroy the barbarians who can remain insensible to all the charms of misfortune, of youth, and of virtue!"

As he pronounced these words, Dorotheus overthrew the statue of Mercury. Immediately the attention and indignation of the populace was directed toward that quarter.

"A Christian in the amphitheatre! Let him be seized and delivered over to the gladiators!"

Dorotheus was dragged out of the edifice, and condemned to perish amidst the promiscuous crowd of the confessors.

Suddenly the clash of arms was heard: the bridge which led from the palace of the emperor to the amphitheatre was let down, and a few paces conducted Galerius from his bed of torture to the scene of carnage: he had surmounted his disease to appear once again in the presence of the people. He saw himself at the same moment on the point of losing both his empire and his life: a messenger had just arrived from Gaul to inform him of the death of Constantius. Constantine, proclaimed Cæsar by the legions, had, at the same time, declared himself a Christian, and was preparing to march toward Rome. This news, by disquieting the soul of Galerius, had rendered the hideous wounds that covered his body more intolerable; but concealing his anguish within his own breast, whether to deceive himself or those around him, this spectre came to seat himself in the imperial balcony, like Death with his crown. What a contrast to that beauty, that vigor, and that youth, which was exposed on the arena to the fury of the leopards!

When the emperor appeared, the spectators arose, and greeted him with the usual salutations. Eudorus bowed respectfully before Cæsar. Cymodoce advanced under the balcony to supplicate the emperor to pardon Eudorus, for whom she offered herself a voluntary victim. The crowd delivered Galerius from the embarrassment of appearing either cruel or compassionate: for a long time they had been awaiting the combat, and the sight of the victims had redoubled their thirst for blood. A universal cry arose:

"The beasts! Let loose the beasts! The Christians to the wild beasts!"

Eudorus wished to address the people in favor of Cymodoce; but his words were drowned amidst a thousand voices that shouted:

"Let the signal be given! The beasts! The Christians to the wild beasts!"

The trumpet sounded: it was the signal for the wild beasts to appear. The chief of those gladiators, who combated with the net, crossed the arena and opened the den of a tiger that was remarkable for its ferocity.

Then arose a contest between Eudorus and Cymodoce that can never be forgotten: each contended for the happiness of dying last.

"Eudorus," said Cymodoce, "if you were not wounded, I should entreat permission to combat the first; but now I have more strength than you, and shall be able to support the sight of your death."

"Cymodoce," replied Eudorus, "I have been a Christian longer than you: I can better support the grief; let me be the last to quit the earth."

As the martyr pronounced these words, he stripped himself of his mantle, and threw it over Cymodoce to conceal her charms from the vulgar gaze, when the tiger should drag her along the arena. Eudorus feared lest a death so chaste should be sullied by the least shadow of an impure idea, even though in others: perhaps this was a last instinct of nature, a sudden impulse of that jealousy which accompanies true love even to the tomb.

The trumpet sounded a second time.

The iron door of the tiger's den grated upon its hinges: the gladiator who had opened it was filled with terror and fled. Eudorus placed Cymodoce behind him. He was seen standing erect, his soul rapt in prayer, his arms extended in the form of a cross, and his eyes raised toward heaven.

A third time the trumpet sounded.

The chains of the tiger fell, and he darted with a dreadful roar into the midst of the arena. The spectators started upon their seats with an involuntary impulse of terror. Cymodoce was seized with dread, and exclaimed:

"O save me! save me!"

Eudorus turned himself toward her, and she flew into his arms. He pressed her to his bosom, and would fain have concealed her in his heart. The tiger darted at the two martyrs, and raising itself erect, struck its claws into the sides of the son of Lasthenes, and lacerated the shoulders of the intrepid confessor. When Cymodoce, who still remained locked in the embraces of her spouse, opened her eyes, which were strongly expressive of love and of fear, she perceived the blood-stained jaws of the tiger near the head of Eudorus. Immediately the vital warmth left the limbs of the victorious virgin; her eyelids closed, and she remained suspended in the arms of her spouse, like a flake of snow on the branch of a pine in the groves of Menalia or Lycæus. The holy martyrs, Eulalia, Felicitas and Perpetua, descended from heaven to receive their companion: the tiger had dislocated the ivory neck of the daughter of Homer. The angel of death smiled as he cut the thread of her life. She breathed forth her last sigh without the least effort, and without pain; she gave back to heaven that divine breath which seemed without a struggle to quit a frame so delicate, that it seemed to have been formed by the fingers of the Graces; she sunk like a flower that is severed by the scythe of the reaper, and droops its languid head upon the verdant turf. Eudorus followed her, a moment after, to the mansions of everlasting bliss: this scene recalled to mind one of the peace-offerings of ancient days, when the sons of Aaron sacrificed to the God of Israel a dove and a young bullock.

These martyred spouses had scarcely received the palm of victory, when a cross of resplendent light appeared in the air, like that hallowed banner which led the victorious Constantine to the scene of triumph; the thunder broke over the Vatican, a hill then lonely and deserted, but frequently visited by an unknown spirit: the amphitheatre was shaken to its foundations; all the statues of the idols fell to the earth, and a voice, like that which was formerly heard in Jerusalem, exclaimed:

"The gods are departing!"

The dismayed crowd left the games. Galerius, having returned to his palace, gave himself up to black rage; he gave orders that the illustrious companions of Eudorus should be put to the sword. Constantine appears at the gates of Rome. Galerius succumbs under the weight of his ills; he expires blaspheming the Eternal. In vain a new tyrant possesses himself of the supreme power: God thunders from the height of heaven; the standard of the cross is borne aloft; Constantine strikes; Maxentius is thrown into the Tiber. The conqueror enters the queen city of the world: the enemies of the Christians are dispersed. The prince, friend of Eudorus, then hastens to receive the last sighs of Demodocus, whom grief bows to the earth, who demands baptism, in order to go and rejoin his well-beloved daughter. Constantine flies to the places heaped with the bodies of victims: the two spouses preserved all their beauty in death. By a miracle of heaven, their wounds were found effaced, and an expression of peace and happiness was stamped upon their brows. A grave was dug for them in that very cemetery where the son of Lasthenes was once cut off from the number of the faithful. The legions of Gaul, formerly led to victory by Eudorus, surrounded the funeral monument of their old general. The warlike eagle of Romulus is decorated with the pacific cross. On the tomb of the young martyrs, Constantine receives the crown of Augustus, and on this same tomb he proclaims the Christian religion the religion of the empire.

www.ingramcontent.com/pod-product-compliance
Lightning Source LLC
Chambersburg PA
CBHW032130010526
44111CB00034B/570